INTERNATIONAL ECONOMIC ASSOCIATION
CONFERENCE VOLUMES, Numbers 1–50

NUMBER 38

Methods of Long-Term Planning and Forecasting

Methods of Long-term Planning and Forecasting

Proceedings of a Conference held by the International Economic Association at Moscow

EDITED BY
T. S. KHACHATUROV

M
STOCKTON PRESS

First published 1976

This 50–volume set reprinted 1986 jointly by
THE MACMILLAN PRESS LTD
Houndmills, Basingstoke, Hampshire RG21 2XS
and London
Companies and representatives
throughout the world
and
YUSHODO CO. LTD
29 Saneicho, Shinjuku-ku
Tokyo 160 Japan. Tel: 03(357)1411
Distributed exclusively in Japan
through Publishers International Corporation (P.I.C.)

Published in the United States and Canada by
STOCKTON PRESS
15 East 26th Street, New York, N.Y. 10010

Printed in Great Britain by
Antony Rowe Ltd
Chippenham

50–volume set ISBN 0–333–40626–5

This volume ISBN 0–333–18518–8

Contents

Acknowledgements

The International Economic Association wishes to express its great gratitude to the U.S.S.R. Academy of Sciences, whose generous grant paid all the local expenses of the conference here recorded as well as part or all of the costs of transportation of many of the participants from East European countries. For the transportation of the participants from the rest of the world the Association depended on the general grant provided to it for these and other purposes by the Ford Foundation, and to that Foundation it wishes, as so often in the past, to express its gratitude.

Apart from the help of those two great institutions, the Association has special reasons for gratitude to a number of individual persons in the U.S.S.R. who did more than we had any possible right to expect to make the conference a success. We would especially mention Academician Nikolay P. Fedorenko, Director of the Central Economic Mathematical Institute; Professor V. A. Vinogradov, Director of the Institute of Scientific Information on Social Sciences; Dr E. E. Filippovski, Scientific Secretary of the Association of Soviet Economic Scientific Institutions and his band of friendly and efficient helpers. But above all, we wish to thank Professor Tigran S. Khachaturov, who was architect of the conference and chairman of its programme committee, and whose indefatigable personal attention throughout assured its smooth running and very friendly atmosphere.

PROGRAMME COMMITTEE

T. S. Khachaturov (U.S.S.R.)
J. Pajestka (Poland)
J. Bénard (France)
H. B. Chenery (U.S.A.)
E. Jantsch (Federal Republic of Germany)

List of Participants

Professor A. G. Aganbegyan (U.S.S.R.), Prospect of Science

Professor D. A. Allahverdian (U.S.S.R.), Institute of Economics, U.S.S.R. Academy of Sciences

Professor A. I. Anchiskin (U.S.S.R.), Central Economic Mathematical Institute, U.S.S.R. Academy of Sciences

Professor A. V. Anikin (U.S.S.R.), Institute of World Economy and International Relations, Moscow

Professor Augustinovics (Hungary), Planning Committee of the People's Republic of Hungary

Mr Henri Aujac (France), Bureau d'Information et de Prévisious Économiques, Neuilly sur Seine

Professor I. A. Bazshenov (U.S.S.R.), Urals Centre, U.S.S.R. Academy of Sciences

Professor Jean Bénard (France), CEPREMAP, Paris

Professor Eva Berković (Yugoslavia), Union of Economists of Yugoslavia

Professor D. Bradistilov (Bulgaria), Union of Economists of Bulgaria

Professor Bruno (Israel), Hebrew University, Jerusalem

Professor H. B. Chenery (U.S.A.), International Bank for Reconstruction and Development, Washington, D.C.

Mr N. Ciulei (Roumania), Economic Planning Committee of Socialist Republic of Roumania

Mr Angus Deaton (U.K.), Department of Applied Economics, Cambridge

Professor E. Denison (U.S.A.), The Brookings Institution, Washington, D.C.

Professor M. Drăgan (Roumania), Economic Planning Committee of Socialist Republic of Roumania

Gordana Draghichevitch (Yugoslavia), Beograd

Professor Entov (U.S.S.R.), Institute of World Economy and International Relations, U.S.S.R. Academy of Sciences

Professor N. P. Fedorenko (U.S.S.R.), Director, Central Economic Mathematical Institute, U.S.S.R. Academy of Sciences

Dr Gerhard Fels (F.R.G.), Institüt für Weltwirtschaft, Universität Kiel

Dr E. E. Filippovski (U.S.S.R.), Scientific Secretary, Association of Soviet Economic Scientific Institutions, Moscow

Professor B. Fritsch (Switzerland), Centre of Economic Research, Zürich

Professor E. I. Gromov (U.S.S.R.), Institute of World Economy and International Relations, U.S.S.R. Academy of Sciences

Dr David Grove (U.S.A.), Economist and Vice-President, International Business Machines Corporation, Armonk, N.Y.

Professor F. G. Gurvitch (U.S.S.R.), *Economic Mathematical Methods*. Moscow

Professor I. Hetényi (Hungary), National Planning Office, Budapest

Mr Reino Hjerppe (Finland), Central Statistical Office of Finland

Mr M. Horimoto (Japan), Economic and Business Survey Department, Sumitomo Chemical Company, Osaka

Professor N. V. Hristova (U.S.S.R.), International Institute of Economic Problems of the World Socialist System, Council for Economic Assistance, Moscow

Mr E. John (Hungary), Economic Planning Committee of the People's Republic of Hungary

Professor L. V. Kantorovitch (U.S.S.R.), Institute of Management, U.S.S.R. Academy of Sciences

Professor T. S. Khachaturov (U.S.S.R.), Chairman of the Presidium, Association of
   Soviet Economic Scientific Institutions
Professor G. A. Kozlov (U.S.S.R.), Academy of Social Sciences, Moscow
Professor V. P. Krasovski (U.S.S.R.), Institute of Economics, U.S.S.R. Academy of
   Sciences
Professor U. R. Leibkind (U.S.S.R.), Central Economic Mathematical Institute,
   U.S.S.R. Academy of Sciences
Professor H. Lindner (G.D.R.), Institute of Scientific Research, Ministry of Science
   and Technology, Berlin
Professor F. Machlup (U.S.A.), President, International Economic Association,
   Princeton University, Princeton, New Jersey
Professor H. Maier (G.D.R.), Central Economic Institute, Academy of Sciences
Professor V. F. Maier (U.S.S.R.), Economic Institute of Scientific Research, Economic
   Planning Committee, Moscow
Professor E. Z. Majminas (U.S.S.R.), Central Economic Mathematical Institute,
   U.S.S.R. Academy of Sciences
Professor V. L. Makarov (U.S.S.R.), Siberian Department of the U.S.S.R. Academy
   of Sciences, Novosibirsk
Professor E. Malinvaud (France), Direction de la Prevision, Ministère de l'Economie
   et des Finances, Paris
Professor E. Mansfield (U.S.A.), Wharton School of Finance and Commerce,
   University of Pennsylvania, Philadelphia, Pennsylvania
Professor J. Marczewski (France), The University of Sorbonne, Paris
Professor V. A. Martinov (U.S.S.R.), Institute of World Economy and International
   Relations, U.S.S.R. Academy of Sciences
Professor F. M. Metelski (U.S.S.R.), International Institute for the Economic
   Problems of the World Socialist System, Council for Economic Assistance,
   Moscow
Professor N. K. Moiseev (U.S.S.R.), U.S.S.R. Academy of Sciences
Professor H. Nick (G.D.R.), Institute of Social Sciences, Central Committee of the
   G.D.R.
Professor Fred Oelssner (G.D.R.), Academy of Sciences
Professor K. Porwit (Poland), Institut Planowania, Warsaw
Professor A. A. Rivkin (U.S.S.R.), Institute of World Economy and International
   Relations, U.S.S.R. Academy of Sciences
Professor D. V. Rjabushkin (U.S.S.R.), Central Economic Mathematical Institute,
   U.S.S.R. Academy of Sciences
Professor E. A. G. Robinson (U.K.), General Editor of I.E.A. publications, University
   of Cambridge
Professor A. M. Rumjantsev (U.S.S.R.), Presidium of the U.S.S.R. Academy of Sciences
Professor V. I. Sedov (U.S.S.R.), Institute of World Economics and International
   Relations, U.S.S.R. Academy of Sciences
Professor S. S. Shatalin (U.S.S.R.), Central Economic Mathematical Institute, U.S.S.R.
   Academy of Sciences
Professor D. Shimon (U.S.S.R.), International Institute of Economic Problems of
   the World Socialist System, Council for Economic Assistance, Moscow
Professor G. M. Sorokin (U.S.S.R.), Institute of Economics, U.S.S.R. Academy of
   Sciences
Professor Radmila Stojanović (Yugoslavia), Union of Economists of Yugoslavia
Mr M. Stuparu (Roumania), Scientific Research Institute, Economic Planning
   Committee, Roumania
Mr G. Szepesi (Hungary), Planning Committee of Hungary

Professor A. S. Tolkachev (U.S.S.R.), Economic Institute of Scientific Research, Economic Planning Committee, Moscow

Mr E. V. Topala (Roumania), Scientific Research Institute, Economic Planning Committee of Roumania

Mr G. Vangrevelinghe (France), Institut National de la Statistique et de les Études Economiques, Paris

Dr N. Velikov (Bulgaria), Union of Economists of Bulgaria

Professor V. A. Vinogradov (U.S.S.R.), Director, Institute of Scientific Information on Social Sciences, U.S.S.R. Academy of Sciences

Professor V. A. Volkonski (U.S.S.R.), Central Economic Scientific Mathematical Institute, U.S.S.R. Academy of Sciences

Professor C. C. von Weizsäcker (F.R.G.), Institute of Mathematical Economics, Universität Bielefeld

Professor Yershov (U.S.S.R.), Central Economic Mathematical Institute, U.S.S.R. Academy of Sciences

Secretariat

Miss Mary Crook, Administrative Secretary, I.E.A., Paris

Miss Tanya Dyomina, Administrative Secretary, Association of Soviet Economic Scientific Institutions

Professor L. Fauvel, General Secretary, I.E.A., Paris

Dr E. E. Filippovski, Scientific Secretary, Association of Soviet Economic Scientific Institutions

Mrs Galina Modina, Central Economic Mathematical Institute, U.S.S.R. Academy of Sciences

Introductory Note

E. A. G. Robinson

EDITOR OF INTERNATIONAL ECONOMIC ASSOCIATION PUBLICATIONS

This was the first time that a conference of the International Economic Association had been held in the Soviet Union, and the I.E.A. owes a special debt of gratitude to Professor Tigran S. Khachaturov, whose name as the architect of the conference and chairman of the programme committee rightly stands on the title page. He was helped in the preparation of the scientific programme of the meeting by a committee consisting of Professor Jean Bénard, Professor Hollis Chenery, Professor Erick Jantsch and Professor Josef Pajestka.

For many of us who took part in the conference, one of the most interesting features of it was the vigorous exchange of ideas and the discussions and criticisms of each others' procedures among the participants from the different socialist countries, and at the same time the friendly good temper which thoughout animated all our discussions, formal and informal, in the huge Hotel Ukrania in which we lived, conferred, ate and argued in warmth and comfort that contrasted with the outside conditions of a Moscow December.

The conference worked in two languages, English and Russian. For the papers by non-socialist authors an original English text was, of course, available. For the papers by socialist authors the English text had in all cases been prepared by translators in the countries of the authors concerned. Some of these translations were lucid and are published almost as they stood. A few of the translations were, on the other hand, somewhat obscure and involved a certain amount of guess-work before the author's meaning could be surmised. It has been my task as editor of all the publications of the International Economic Association to produce texts which a reader can understand without a similar effort of his own and which reach the standards of readable English very reasonably required by our publishers. I have confined my tasks as editor to that sole objective, excluding nothing. I have not abbreviated, because I did not want to alter the balance of the author's presentation. If I have anywhere failed to discover and bring out the author's own intended meaning, I apologise in advance.

Hardly any of us who came from the non-socialist countries knew more than a few words of Russian. Thus the conference was more than ordinarily dependent on the simultaneous translation in one direction or the other, and in our case particularly on that from Russian to English. The fact that Russian was extensively used, and that the summary of the discussion had to be compiled from an English translation of the Russian shorthand record, has made the task of editing this volume somewhat more arduous than usual.

Now that I am able to read the revised summaries of what was said in the discussions, I realise that on a number of occasions we may have failed to take in fully some of the more sophisticated arguments of our socialist colleagues and that we may have sometimes seemed to them to have failed to pick up and to reply to their points. For that I think we owe them some apology. This has emphasised again – in spite of the excellent performance of the interpreters in Moscow – the extent to which an effective international meeting of minds depends not only on the skill and technical knowledge of those who are responsible for these very difficult and onerous tasks of interpretation but also on the opportunity given to participants to reflect on the arguments put forward in the sessions. I trust that the summary of the discussions in the present volume will contribute to this better understanding which was our aim.

Part One

General Problems of Long-term Planning

1 Methodological Problems of Socio-economic and Scientific-technological Forecasting in the U.S.S.R.

N. Fedorenko

I. INTRODUCTION

Speaking to the 15th Trade Unions Congress, the General Secretary of the Central Committee of the Communist Party of the Soviet Union, L. I. Brezhnev, emphasised the necessity for starting work on a long-term plan for the national economic development of the U.S.S.R. covering the period 1976–90. This work is now in progress with increasing intensity.

The earlier experience with the working out of the first long-term plan in the Soviet Union (Lenin's GOERLO Plan), the work on the preparation of the general long-run perspective down till 1980, conducted during 1959–60, the party and government decisions concerning the long-run prospects (plans for intensive introduction of chemical processes and materials, for agricultural development, for soil reclamation, urban construction, and the like), as well as the activities of a number of administrative agencies and research and development organisations and institutions in the field of forecasting during the past four or five years – have all served to show that work in drawing up a long-term plan necessarily breaks down into three stages, each with its own particular set of participants, methods and time scales.

The first stage is that of preparing a forecast, that is to say alternative probabilistic long-range estimates in science and technology, social developments, demographic trends, economic factors, natural resources, and so on.

The second stage is that of elaboration of a concept of the long-term development (long-range policies) that is in keeping both with the directives of policy and the results of these forecasts.

The third stage is that of building up the long-term plan, including the working out of the main targets (assignments) for the long-run development and the detailed goal-oriented programmes required to meet the targets proposed.

Thus, the forecasting of the nation's socio-economic and scientific and technological progress is one component of the general system of forecasting, and it has to be tied in with the other operations of forecasting. None the less, the socio-economic and scientific and technological forecasts are the core of this system. They are all intrinsically interconnected with each other, and this determines the guidelines of the concept of the nation's long-run development and the main outlines of the long-term plan.

The socio-economic forecasts for the most part have a goal-oriented, normative character. They assess the feasibility of achieving this or that 'assigned' goal for the standard of living, for the educational system, for the pattern of incomes, or whatever it may be.

The scientific and technological forecasts mostly have a resource-oriented, genetic, character. They indicate the possible lines of scientific and technological progress and, on that basis, the probable alternatives for the development of resources, economical potential, and other purposes.

The methodological principles of overall forecasting are a combination and reconciliation of the two types of forecast. Socio-economic forecasts provide the goal orientation for the scientific and technological forecasts, while the latter make it possible to judge the attainability of the targets of the socio-economic development set in the corresponding forecast.

The scientific and technological forecasts should serve as a basis for recommendations for the support of particular trends of scientific and technological progress, for the time scales of developments, for recommendations on the allocation of resources between individual lines of research and development and their timing. Scientific and technological forecasts thus make it possible to work out the major elements of the scientific and technological background and policy as a part of the general background of the long-range development.

Finally, all these data can serve as a basis for preparing detailed and specific target programmes for inclusion in the long-term plan. In this case it is not forecasts but long-term plan decisions that are made, specifying the distribution of the relevant investments, labour resources, R & D and engineering staff, time periods of construction, planned industrial outputs, and the rest.

We are thus faced with a task of an enormous national importance and practical difficulty – the working out of a long-term socio-economic and scientific-technological policy for the Soviet state for the coming fifteen or twenty years. This task is formulated in accordance with the well known injunctions of V. I. Lenin on the necessity for a consistent technological policy, embodying the guidelines and decisions of the 24th Congress of the C.P.S.U. and aimed at utilising the achievements of the scientific and technological revolution to promote the building of communism.

II. THE PRINCIPLES AND MAJOR TRENDS OF SOCIO-ECONOMIC FORECASTING

A comprehensive socio-economic forecast must comprise an overall analysis of the trends of social development and estimate these trends in terms of such development alternatives as will ensure:

(i) consistent and harmonious solution of the key social problems of the development of Soviet society on the basis of the expected growth of the economic and scientific-technological potentials;

(ii) the greatest practicable achievement of the material and non-material needs of the Soviet people, as representing the main and ultimate goal of the development of the socialist economy, together with an increasing effect of the rising standard of living upon the growth of social production;

(iii) stable and balanced progress of the socialist economy and of all its units, avoiding maladjustments and shortages of industrial resources and products;

(iv) that rapidly increasing efficiency of productive resources shall become the chief source of the economic growth, with unconditional prevalence of the intensive over extensive forms of the economy;

(v) improvement of the system of national economic planning and management, the working out and creation of a system for the optimum functioning of the economy, so as to ensure an efficacious solution of all socio-economic problems.

The complete elaboration of a socio-economic forecast is impossible unless it covers both the regional aspect and the foreign trade aspect.

Thus a comprehensive socio-economic forecast must include:

(1) the general aspects of social development, including forecasts of the social composition and the dynamics of social structure, the implications for distribution, the changes in the composition of the labour force, and so on;

(2) issues of national welfare, and in particular predictions of consumption, incomes and the pattern of demand, trends in nutrition, clothing, housing, communication facilities, health services, social provisions, and the like;

(3) social aspects of the national economic growth;

(4) problems of the expansion of production and the efficient balancing of the national economy, taking account of the latest achievements of science and engineering; this is a large and complex section of any socio-economic forecast, which must take into account alternative economic growth rates,

macro-economic and inter-industry balances, and the growth
of the main national economic sectors, in particular fuel and
power, raw materials, metals and construction materials,
building, transport, and so on, which must incorporate the
scientific and technological progress in industrial production
(we shall expand on this matter in the next section);

(5) population movement problems and demographic policy;
(6) regional socio-economic policy and the geographic distri-
     bution of the productive forces;
(7) socio-economic aspects of exploitation of the natural en-
     vironment;
(8) problems of the development of foreign trade relations;
(9) improvement of the national economic planning system;
(10) organisational structure and the management mechanism of
      the national economy.

A forecast of a nation's socio-economic development over a long
period makes it possible to identify and deal with the key problems
whose solutions will determine the guidelines for development and
the items requiring priority in the concentration of resources. These
problems will determine the goal orientation for the whole process
of long-term planning. Above all they will establish the socio-
economic requirements for scientific and technological progress and
make it possible to gear the advances of science and engineering
to the interests of the community. I shall dwell on these issues in
the fourth section of this paper.

Uncertainties and the complexities of the processes that are being
forecasted constitute the central methodological problem of the
system of long-term forecasting. The high rates of scientific and
technological progress and the qualitative shifts in the socio-political
picture of the world set strict bounds to the possibilities of direct
extrapolation of trends and call for identifying the likely inflexions
in the qualitative changes of the processes being predicted, since
these will determine future trends in the latter's development. On
the other hand, the complex interplay of influences between these
processes necessitates a comprehensive prediction of their consequences in respect of all the ramifications of their interconnections.

The essential approach to compilation of long-term forecasts is a
clearcut organisation of the efforts of highly skilled experts and the
integration of the different forecasting techniques, and first and fore-
most a combination of genetic and normative forecasts.

Depending on the object under consideration, different forecasting methods need to be employed, including duplication and reci-
procal verification of results, obtained by different methods in respect
of the same object. A great part of these methods are informal, and

based on heuristic procedures facilitating and consolidating the work of experts. Some methods are of a more rigorous nature, and they make use of a mathematical apparatus (mostly, mathematical statistics and computers), though they place rather rigid requirements on the input data and the postulates of the object being forecasted.

In elaborating forecasts for industries and sectors, one needs to treat as 'consultative' the models of development and location of the major special complexes of the sector or industry (optimisation sectoral models). These make it possible to tie in the individual elements of a sectoral forecast – the variants of the sector's structure, new engineering processes, the raw material base – taking into account its spatial distribution, outputs, production capacities, labour requirements, and requirements of the related sectors. In forecasting, various criteria and constraint systems can be used to calculate these models.

Regional forecasts use, for inter-co-ordination of the individual aspects, a system of regional inter-industry models of various types (dynamic, in physical and value terms, and so on). The most important thing in this case is to secure a uniform modelling method for all the regions.

The 'consultative' models of the individual processes to be used in preparing comprehensive forecasts are forms of mathematical modelling, population models, macro-economic models (e.g. growth models), methods of scientific and technological forecasting and various simulation models (e.g. models of political situations).

In preparing comprehensive forecasts of achievement of plan targets one can apply heuristic methods, including the brainstorm method, the Delphi technique of expert panel estimation, case studies, and 'business games'.

The complex of inter-industry and inter-product balances can be used as the balancing tool for co-ordinating the indices of the forecast of development of the national economic complexes.

Uniformity of the input data base, and especially of the dynamic series that serves as the base of calculations, is a *sine qua non* of reliable quality and compatibility of forecasts.

Every forecast must be subjected to external expertise, to establish a detailed characterisation of its overall quality and especially of the feasibility and time scales of the particular events predicted.

Based on the results of this expert examination, adequate predictions are selected at every step of forecasting for incorporation in the general plan and, naturally, this reduces the total number of alternatives.

The quality and reliability of the calculations of both particular and overall general forecasts necessarily depend on the availability and quality of the input data used for the respective sections of the forecasts.

III. THE PRINCIPLES AND MAJOR TRENDS OF SCIENTIFIC AND TECHNOLOGICAL FORECASTING

In embarking on a long-term scientific or technological forecast, it is necessary to define clearly what is to be expected of the forecast: that is to visualise the requirements for the future forecast and identify the basic predictions, or the problem areas and directions of research and engineering, for which the predictions concerned need to be prepared.

Every large-scale scientific or technological forecast must identify and evaluate the long-range trends in the given field of science and technology, so as to foresee any major scientific discoveries and engineering improvements that are likely to imply substantial changes in the overall scientific–technical and production potential of the nation, or in social relations and world politics.

The specific content of the processes under investigation determines the peculiar features of each particular line of scientific and technological forecasting. At the same time, within each line, the following chief ranges of the scientific and technological progress can be distinguished, determining the corresponding sequence of analysis and forecasting:

(a) analysis of the basic scientific and technological changes in the field under study during the past twenty to twenty-five years,[1] making it possible to determine the real trends, and the likely continuity of future developments in relation to past and present, to detect the qualitative break-points, to compare past expectations with the actual course of scientific and technological advancement;

(b) identification of the scientific and technical problems that have already been solved in technological terms before the period under forecast but have not yet been actually introduced on a wide scale (e.g., atomic power stations using uranium fuel, magnetic hydro-generators, lasers and their

---

[1] For instance, according to certain authors, the main technological innovations in the past sixty to seventy years were: aluminium, synthetic resins (plastics), synthetic fibre and leather, motor and air transport, electron valves, television, programme-controlled machines, semi-conductors, printed circuits, electronic computers, titanium, vitamins, antibiotics, nuclear energy, freezing and dehydration of foodstuffs.

    engineering applications, synthetic diamonds, continuous steel teeming, new methods of metal hardening, and the like);

(c) identification of problems solved by science in the pre-forecast period but not yet technologically developed (e.g., fourth-generation computers, fast neutron breeder reactors, super-conductivity applications, chemical moulding of construction materials;

(d) competent estimates on the possible results of R & D presently under way and to be expected either during the forecast period or at some later time, but which are likely to require heavy expenditures in the very near future (e.g. thermonuclear power engineering, deciphering of the genetic code, utilisation in engineering of the principles of regulation of system functions in the living organism, biological principles of computer design, artificial foods);

(e) evaluation of new trends of development in the basic sciences likely to emerge in the forecast period, but whose results will be very uncertain in the foreseeable future, though requiring considerable immediate outlays.

In short, a complete forecast of scientific and technological progress can be divided into three parts:

(i) a forecast of the dissemination of the scientific and techno-logical innovations already introduced;

(ii) a forecast of the introduction of the scientific and techno-logical results which are at present, so to speak, midway between the laboratory and industry;

(iii) a forecast of the basic trends of science requiring considerable expenditures despite great or complete unpredictability of future practical results.

Naturally, both the panel of experts and the method of forecasting must vary according to the proportions of the applied and theoretical elements in the forecast. The dissemination forecasts should be mostly compiled on the basis of the judgements of industrial engineers, technological specialists, economists, and applied scientists; exact quantitative prediction methods should be predominant here. Theoretical scientists should also be involved and have their say in the forecasts of the applications of scientific and techno-logical discoveries; quantitative methods of forecasting will largely be replaced in this case by expert judgements and qualitative estimates. In the forecast of the basic lines of development of science, this should unquestionably be done by theoretical scientists, though even here the participation of practical experts, technical specialists and economists is desirable; the forecasting methods in this case cannot be other than subjective and represent expert judgements, so that their reliability will wholly depend on the personal competence of the experts.

The decision of the list of specific scientific and technological forecasts to be made is directly connected with the tasks and general content of forecasting.

The main lines of applied scientific and technological forecasting should preferably be chosen with regard to specific types of *social need* or to *major types of national economic problems.* Here is a list of examples of these:

(1) Energy (all sources)
(2) Construction materials (all types)
(3) Textiles (all types)
(4) Nontextile materials for light industries, telecommunications, paper
(5) The production system of manufacturing industry
(6) Engineering processes
(7) Construction
(8) Foodstuffs (the entire cycle from the production of crude foodstuffs to the storage and transportation of finished foodstuffs)
(9) Agriculture (agro-technical and biological problems, development of the whole range of agricultural machinery and technological processes).
(10) Transport (all types)
(11) Production, processing, transmission and storage of all kinds of information (development of information systems, computers, communications, control and measurement systems, printing and reproduction facilities)
(12) Management and planning
(13) Personnel training and R & D potential
(14) Health services
(15) Restoration and reproduction of the ecological environment
(16) World oceans
(17) Fresh water
(18) Outer space

In general, all lines of scientific and technological forecasting can be reduced to four major directions:

(i) satisfaction of the personal and social needs;
(ii) increase of the production potential of the nation, science and education;
(iii) development of the infrastructure, including management and planning;
(iv) utilisation and reproduction of the natural environment.

For all the conventional character of the above classification, its basic principle appears to be well grounded: the trends of scientific and technological progress which have already an obvious 'applied' importance should be forecasted not as such but in terms of their ultimate contributions to the fuller and more efficient meeting of particular types of social need (e.g., to the food or to the housing problem) or to the solution of a major national economic problem (e.g., all-round motorisation).

It is much more difficult to group into specific trends the forecasts for basic research work and their likely results. By way of example the following lines can be named:

Physics: use of superconductivity in power engineering and other fields of technology, creation of superconductive materials;
solid state physics and the development of superhard materials;

Chemistry: artificial foodstuffs; organic semiconductors; physical methods of stimulation of chemical processes;

Biology: genetics and development biology; brain and higher nervous activity problems; bionics, physics and chemistry of motoric functions.

The main purpose of forecasting the basic lines of scientific advance is to make it possible to predict the qualitative leaps, which are sometimes termed 'scientific break-throughs'. Some of these break-throughs can herald a revolution in existing fields of science and technology, others the emergence of new forms and methods of production, new engineering processes, new products and services. In the former case the basic R & D forecast should not be separated from that relating to the corresponding 'applied' forecast, but rather conceived as the latter's 'upper storey'; in the latter case, new specific scientific or technological trends may emerge.

IV. FORECAST OF THE SOCIAL AND ECONOMIC RESULTS OF SCIENTIFIC AND TECHNOLOGICAL PROGRESS

Scientific and technological progress, particularly its perspective evaluation in terms and concepts of a given field of science and technology is unquestionably the key element in scientific and technological forecasting. But a scientific and technological forecast cannot be regarded as complete if it fails to comprise, as an organic component, an appraisal of the social and economic preconditions to and implications of the scientific and technological progress involved. This is an indispensable condition for comparing individual scientific and technological development trends, for establishing priorities in an allocation of social resources, and for reduction of the various individual lines and problem areas to a uniform scientific and technological framework. Otherwise we shall have a lengthy list of sound individual forecasts, but no forecast of scientific and technological progress as a whole.

One must therefore strive from the outset towards an organic unity of the scientific and technological forecasting on the one hand, and the socio-economic forecasting on the other.

Two types of socio-economic requirements for scientific and technological forecasts can be formulated. The first group of requirements are relevant to the forecasts concerned with individual trends of the scientific and technological progress; the second type are general requirements for scientific and technological forecasting conceived as a total of particular forecasts.

The general principle in the economic evaluation of individual lines of scientific and technological progress should be comparison of the various expenditures with their economic effects (the input–effect principle), with an attempt to secure the best possible approximation to the total national economic input and effect (for instance, it often happens that an innovation produces indirect effects through a long series of related production sectors). The implementation of this principle comprises the evaluation of:

(i) the consequences of the innovations concerned and their large-scale introduction measured by indices of specific capital expenditures, labour productivity, raw material per unit of output, power input per unit of output or in terms of useful effect; in each case it is necessary to establish the dependence of the efficiency level on the scale of the introduction of the innovation;

(ii) the possibilities of expanding the scale of the innovation and the sequence of its introduction in individual sectors and industries; the constraints on this expansion should be estimated (the time required to get production of this kind of equipment running, the preparedness of consumers to absorb the new product or technology, and so on);

(iii) the total expenditure on the introduction and implementation of the relevant lines of R & D, including investment, personnel training, the requirements of raw materials and power supplies;

(iv) requirements for the development of the allied fields of science and engineering.

Moreover, the non-economic implications of a given line of

scientific and technological development (the social, ecological, and other effects) have to be taken into account; this may be the most important consideration for some lines of science and technology; special importance attaches in this context to the social aspects of scientific and technological forecasting, where it is necessary to establish the implications for such issues as the character of the work and life of the nation, for education and training, for health and social psychology, and similar considerations. For example, progress in the field of transport cannot be viewed in separation from such problems as growth of national mobility, traffic over-saturation in large cities and the damaging effects of commuting on human health, the elimination of the hard physical work of loading and unloading operations. The revolution in communications media and information transmission and storage facilities has led to changes in methods of planning and management, has given rise to shifts in the occupational composition of employees and in methods of education, and has enhanced the capacities for collective and individual utilisation of various kinds of information, and the intensity of the latter's impact on social and individual thought. We have made an attempt to classify the various social problems related to scientific and technological problems. It has turned out that these social problems often have an equal or even greater importance in the evaluation of individual scientific and technological trends and their technical and economic results. Thus it is absolutely necessary to enlist in the scientific and technological forecasting not only economists, but also sociologists, medical scientists, biologists and educationalists.

The socio-economic requirements for individual scientific and technological forecasts are different depending on whether the dominant aspects are 'applied' or 'basic'. The complete range of requirements listed above, and if possible in quantified form, relates to the applied aspects of scientific and technological progress. As regards basic research, both the outlays and the effects can be determined only with great uncertainty, and especially the latter. Nevertheless, the essential requirements in this case must be the same as in the other.

The economic requirements for the whole system of scientific and technological forecasts are determined by the fact that it must serve as a basis for elaborating a policy of long-range scientific and technological development, regarded as a component of an overall long-term programme of socio-economic growth. At the stage of the compilation of a global scientific and technological forecast and the definition of the key points of the scientific and technological policy, the main task is to choose and establish priorities between the various individual lines of applied and basic R & D. What are the general economic requirements for this final stage of scientific and technological forecasting?

First, while aggregating and co-ordinating the individual forecasts, it is necessary to make a global estimate of the probable overall productivity of scientific and technological progress in comparison with the national economic expenditure on its implementation. It is commonly known that scientific and technological progress has been becoming a more and more important and even the main factor in the economic growth of the developed countries. In the not far distant future, it will become the main source of economic growth in the Soviet Union. It has been emphasised at the 24th Congress of the C.P.S.U. that the effects of the extensive factors of production growth have been declining—the effects of manpower growth, of the physical volume of productive resources, of new lands and of mineral resources contributing to production—and that, as a result, the key resource for the expansion of production will be the raising of productive efficiency; for this, scientific and technological advances form the material basis. Hence, forecasting the progress of science and technology must provide the answer to the fundamental question—what can science and engineering contribute to the growth of the Soviet economy.

Since scientific and technological progress requires tremendous expenditure, this must be estimated in as full detail as is required. It is necessary to include expenditures on personnel training, design and development of new technological systems, and on introduction of new techniques and equipment, including losses of production due to stoppages or for dismantling of outdated machinery.

Second, a general requirement for an overall scientific and technological forecast is that the choice and selection of individual scientific and technological lines shall be based on clearly stated economic and social criteria. No nation, big as it may be, can possibly promote simultaneously all existing and likely R & D lines with equal success. A choice has to be made. Otherwise, attempts at 'embracing the unfathomable' are fraught with lags and risks of stagnation. What criteria can be adopted for this selection? One must take cognisance of the existing trends, traditions, engineering and personnel capabilities, of comparative advantages and the potentialities of international division of labour, and of the situation in the world scientific and technological markets.

Selection and scheduling of individual lines of the scientific and technological progress presupposes also their inter-co-ordination, that is they must be balanced both in time and space.

One must probably attack this problem by drawing up a comprehensive picture of the existing distribution of resources between particular scientific and technological lines of work and by comparing this distribution with the necessary outlays for the completion of the R & D projects already under way in order to reach the required final stage.

Third, there are the separate problems of the distribution of resources between basic research, applied research, and experimental development and of the choice of lines for promotion within the total of basic research; these two problems should be formulated and solved independently. The distribution of resources within the domain of basic research is the more involved and important, since it is in this domain that the future trends of R & D and D & D (which need to be co-ordinated for each particular field) take shape. In this context the problem of the 'leader' science emerges. The common opinion that research into living nature and the science of man are likely to take a leading place in the coming decades seems justifiable (biology, genetics, medicine, psychology, as against the physical sciences). Even today one can predict that in the coming decades we are to witness a drastic redistribution of R & D resources between the individual lines of basic science. We must begin to prepare for these shifts even today, since the shifts must begin in the spheres of education and personnel training and take years to complete.

In conclusion, it must be stressed that the synthesis of socio-economic and scientific–technological forecasting determines both the goal and resource aspects of a comprehensive long-term forecast and serves as a basis for working out in detail a long-term plan of the overall economic development of the nation.

Discussion of the Paper by Academician N. Fedorenko

(*Chairman, Professor T. Khachaturov*)

After Academician Fedorenko and Professor Machlup had welcomed the participants and had formally opened the Conference, *Professor J. Bénard* (France), in opening the discussion of Academician Fedorenko's paper, said that long-term planning could be divided into three stages which differed in the periods covered, in their methodologies of preparation and in the persons responsible for them. The first stage was a forecast, that is to say a probabilistic study of alternative estimates of the socio-economic, demographic, scientific and technological changes over the period involved. The second stage was the working out of the corresponding development policies. The third stage was the detailed preparation of the long-term plan. Academician Fedorenko had been concerned almost entirely with the first of these three stages, and had emphasised that the socio-economic and scientifico-technological forecasts represented the core of the prognosis, the socio-economic forecasts being normative in character, the scientifico-technological forecasts representing constraints and determining the attainability of the objectives established by the former.

Four fields of prognosis could be identified: social progress and welfare, ranging from social structures to public and private consumption; the possible increase of production and better distribution of resources in the light of the latest achievements of science and engineering and of knowledge of natural resources; the probable changes of population, regional development, and foreign trade; the potential improvements in national economic planning, in the system of planning and in business administration. All of these covered not only the forecasting of objectives but also of means of achieving them. The phenomena being forecasted were uncertain and complex, and the forecasting required sophisticated techniques and a combination of various methods, ranging from simple inquiries to formalised mathematical models. Academician Fedorenko had said that the latter could be used only as 'consultative instruments'. He would like to hear more about these instruments, since in his view it was mathematical models which could best answer questions without dictating decisions.

After dealing with the methods of forecasting socio-economic trends, Academician Fedorenko had gone on to discuss the methodology of scientifico-technological forecasting. Here he had distinguished three separate problems: the forecasting of the diffusion of already existing innovations; the forecasting of the introduction of developments that had already been achieved in the research institutes; the forecasting of important trends in the underlying sciences which justify large expenditures but involve great uncertainties. The principal objectives were: the better satisfaction of personal and social needs; the increase of the productivity of education and science; the improvement of the national infrastructure, including that of management and planning; the use and conservation of natural resources and environment. All these objectives seemed to M. Bénard to be target variables that might be incorporated in an optimal growth model.

Professor Marczewski (France) found himself in general agreement with Academician Fedorenko's paper. He had two questions that he wished to ask. Academician Fedorenko had discussed the applications of cost–benefit analysis to long-term planning. Such analysis assumed a certain system of prices. How was one to establish a long-term price system if changing the structure of the economy – which was the objective – presupposed changing the system of relative prices? The problem became even more difficult if – as the author had stressed and he himself agreed – one wished to take into account all the effects other than economic. But how could this be done except in terms of a system of values?

Secondly, Academician Fedorenko had emphasised the necessity of establishing the priorities for different lines of scientific and technical research. He himself was afraid that to do this involved grave danger of excluding and eliminating research which in twenty years time might prove immensely fruitful but the results of which were at the moment very uncertain. Was there not a danger of excluding promising lines of long-term research which were not of top priority on a short-term basis and which, by such criteria, might never achieve inclusion?

Professor Austin Robinson (U.K.) thought that some of the interesting questions for the conference would be the similarities and the differences between what was being done in the way of forecasting in different countries in the world. He wondered whether the similarities were not much greater than the differences. Countries which did not have formal plans, none the less required and used forecasts of differing degrees of formality and authority to guide both public and private investment. Such forecasts had been made for many of the countries of Europe, including his own, and also for the United States.

In the western countries the final decision-making regarding investment was, of course, in many cases the decision of a private company. But such a company had to go through many of the processes described by Academician Fedorenko, to make its own forecasts of future trends, and its own plans for future developments. But the plan for the individual manufacturing unit was in many respects more difficult than the plan for the industry as a whole, and raised certain problems he would like to be allowed to put to Academician Fedorenko.

He hoped the conference would forgive him if he illustrated these problems from the case of a book printing and publishing company with which he had himself been concerned. They were faced by the need to build and equip a new printing works. This involved not only building a new plant but also the types of facilities and equipment they should instal in it. In order to guide their decisions they had begun by attempting to estimate the long-term growth of the total book demand of the country. They had examined the history of their own past share of the national market and made an estimate of their future share. They had begun, that is to say, in much the same way as did a socialist country from the trends of the whole market.

But at the next stage they had necessarily become involved in problems that Academician Fedorenko had not discussed, but which he himself thought must at some stage enter into the planning of a socialist country. Any publishing company in a western country, and the printing works associated with it, was in some degree specialised within the whole framework of its industry. The company with which he was concerned was specialised in publishing academic, scientific and educational books and journals. They had to go on to forecast the trends for such publishing within the total for the industry as a whole, to examine the economies of different types of printing equipment for the sorts of printing orders relevant to such publication. In a competitive world, they had to consider the extent of the competition in this particular field and the chances that they could increase their share in the total.

All these questions that they had to consider made him wonder how similar problems were decided in a socialist country. The literature of socialist planning available in Western countries was mostly concerned, as Academician Fedorenko's paper had been, with, so to speak, macro-economic planning. But clearly their planning could not stop there. How did they deal with the problems of planning at the much more micro-economic level? The problems at this level were much more complex. Not only were firms specialised within an industry, gaining much of their efficiency from such specialisation. At the same time for most products (books as it happened were exceptions to this) the national market is in fact a composite of many smaller regional markets, whose size depended on transport costs for the product concerned. Professor Robinson thought that, even if one started by forecasting the national market, one had to end by forecasting the various regional markets. It was only when one had done that that one could see where additions to productive capacity could most advantageously be made.

He would very much like to know more about the ways in which demands were estimated for the specialised products of sub-industries and about the ways in which regional demands were forecast. Was there elaborate calculation and forecasting of the comparative advantages of regions and of balances of trade between them?

Academician Fedorenko had examined the interrelation between the socio-economic and the scientifico-technological forecasting, emphasising the importance of forecasting the effects of the latter upon the former, the importance of analysing the economic consequences of expenditures on scientifico-technological development (the input–output effects), and the necessity of taking into account not only all the benefits and costs internally but also the implications for comparative advantages and international division of labour in the light of the world markets in the scientific and technological fields.

Professor Bénard had one factual and two methodological questions he wished to put to Academician Fedorenko. First, did his long-term forecast take account of such things as the shift away from rural areas and into cities, the possibilities of exhausting natural resources as the result of increases of population, production and environmental pollution? If so, how did they establish what he had called 'normative views' regarding them?

His two methodological questions were these. Academician Fedorenko had not only stressed the interrelations between the socio-economic forecast and the scientifico-technological forecast but also what he would venture to call the dialectical character of this linkage as a result of the many feedbacks between the two forecasts. He had mentioned the 'nodes' which affected the trends of the subsequent growth path. It was very important to predict these turning points. He would like to know more about the methods used to predict them.

Finally, at the end of his paper Academician Fedorenko had seemed to advocate the use of some macro-economic cost–benefit analysis to classify and select possible development paths for science and technology. M. Bénard agreed about the desirability of doing this but thought it would be very difficult to do in practice. One needed some criteria by which to classify and determine priorities. Academician Fedorenko seemed to adopt three different criteria: economic, social and even international. The questions he wished to put were these. First, how did they establish the priorities as between various alternative forms of public and private consumption – for instance, between housing, public transportation, private transportation, national defence, education? Second, how in a system of long-term planning did they propose to take account of comparative advantages and opportunities for international division of labour and of the situation in the world markets for equipment of advanced technology? Third, how did they reconcile the three criteria – the economic, the social and the international? Had the Soviet scientists and economists evolved a methodology for solving their possible conflicts?

Professor Sorokin (U.S.S.R.) emphasised the need for a broad socio-economic approach to planning. Without it there was danger of planning becoming a mere system of calculations. One had to think of planning as a science which provided the necessary knowledge to establish objectives capable of achievement and to choose specific ways of achieving them. The long-term plan for the U.S.S.R. aimed to make the transition from the socialist state to the communist state, and this general aim determined the specific tasks for industry and construction and the priorities within those tasks. The chief problem was to establish the rates and scales and timings of the basic social changes on which the more specific parameters depended, and which shaped the demands and the possibilities of meeting them. Even the period to be covered by the plan depended on these general aims. A period of fifteen years was usually adopted, as not too short to permit substantial change and not too long to maintain the interest of those now living in its fulfilment.

A long-term plan was concerned with the implementation of the programme of the Communist Party. It was necessarily the party that was responsible for it. But no planning was possible without material and financial resources. Only socialist ownership of the means of production could ensure the availability of resources and the necessary accumulation and redistribution.

It was obvious that the compiling of specific elements of the plan had only subordinate place in the general concept of planning. Quantitative parameters taken out of their socio-economic context were no more than a cemetery of calculations. Professor Sorokin reminded the conference that Kant had described the making of plans as an easy task of vanity in which one appeared as a creative genius demanding the impossible, perfecting what cannot be improved and revealing what cannot be found.

Model-making had its proper place in general planning methodology. Already the views about its place were visible in the conference. Professor

Malinvaud believed that Western econometricians had adopted various simplifying hypotheses, while in the socialist countries ambitious models with multitudes of parameters were adopted, which required much closer testing of their validity. Professor Aganbegyan, on the other hand, held that models and methods which had been used successfully in medium-term planning should be applied only with great caution to long-term planning because, beyond a certain planning horizon, their behaviour became improbable. For example they indicated very rapid increase or decrease of rates of growth. Professor Leontiev had recently commented that in no other branch of empirical research had such sophisticated statistical apparatus ever produced such uncertain results.

Academician Fedorenko had rightly emphasised the limits to the use of simple extrapolation of existing trends. The State Planning Committee of the U.S.S.R. (Gosplan) had the experience of preparing nine five-year plans. Not once, even for such an aggregation as total industrial output, had the development of a basic parameter been planned simply by extrapolation. None the less, the limitations of existing models should not overshadow the great improvements in model-making and in the application of mathematical techniques.

Dr Grove (U.S.A.) thought that the essence of planning was forecasting. Planning consisted in making decisions and taking action in the present to produce desired or expected results in the future. It implied also an understanding of the relationship between present actions and future results. The advantage of the use of a model was that it forced one to be precise about this relationship and precluded vagueness. If you designed a model you had to be specific about the variables and relationships involved.

Model-making led on to testing to see whether a model performed well or ill and whether the relationships implied could or could not be confidently expected. The performance by the model demonstrated the accuracy of your forecast and indicated whether or not one really understood the underlying relationships.

In any planning, whether for a country or a firm, the model provided the essential discipline. Without it one could delude oneself into thinking that one understood the relationship better than one really did, because without a model one had little opportunity to test one's understanding of the relationships.

Professor Kantorovitch (U.S.S.R.) said that the success of long-term planning depended on two factors: width of vision and flexibility. As regards the first of these, it might on the one hand be a very simple linear-programming model presented as a list of targets, or alternatively it might take fully into consideration all the real constraints, such as natural resources, available manpower, and take account of the technological matrices and forecast the methods of production, the methods of management and so on. The second factor, that of flexibility, involved taking account of the magnitudes of the inevitable discrepancies between forecasts and actualities and the need for a built-in capacity to correct mistakes. This was provided both by the plan itself and by the capacities of managements and also by the economic and technical solutions adopted, which should provide for reserves and some measure of flexibility to make adjustments to these inevitable deviations from forecasts.

As regards the narrowing of the gap between planning methods in socialist and private-property countries to which Professor Robinson had referred, there were some obvious explanations for it, such as increasing mutual awareness of methods used and their applications. But with the development of the two systems it would be reasonable to expect widening differences to emerge between methods used in socialist and in capitalist countries. Planners in socialist countries were still not fully aware of all the possibilities and advantages presented by a socialist economy and further developments were to be expected, for example with such difficult problems as the scientific evaluation of the needs of a society measured in economic terms. The amount of research on these problems in the U.S.S.R. was still very inadequate while the problems themselves were inherent to and very important to socialist planning.

Another point to be mentioned was the necessity for a complex approach to planning problems. From a theoretical standpoint the methodology had not yet been adequately developed. There was a growing use of the principle of 'national-economy-interest' as against the still prevalent 'sector-interest' in solving practical problems. But this required better methods of measuring productivity, from the point of view of the national economy, than mere profitability or other sector indices for purposes of a complex approach to planning. What was required was not only the establishment of overall economic indicators for planning purposes but also the development and use for forecasting purposes of prices which might represent true parameters of the national economy.

Academician Fedorenko (U.S.S.R.) in replying to the discussion commented that most of the remarks and questions had been concerned with the relationships between socio-economic and scientifico-technological forecasting. The Communist Party of the Soviet Union and the Soviet government had made the raising of the standards of life of the people of the U.S.S.R. a major objective. This was not just an objective for the current five-year period, but a long-term goal for the development of the Soviet economy. The principal means of achieving this was to increase the productivity of the socialist economy, and that in turn depended on scientific and technological progress. But everything could not be measured in roubles or dollars. Sometimes steps towards a social objective imply a reduction of economic productivity, for instance an improvement of working conditions would obviously imply economic expenditures. The same was true of conservation of the environment. When such a policy involved an increase of production costs it was the more important to offset them by technological advances. It was equally necessary to direct scientific and technological advances towards the solution of the most urgent problems, such as those of water supply or environmental conservation. It was in this way that the problem of 'nodes' mentioned by Professor Bénard emerged. To take one example, if a problem of food supply had to be solved it created problems for genetics, problems of increasing soil fertility while protecting the environment. Thus it both made use of existing technological advances and created new problems to solve. This involved the difficult problem of establishing priorities for objectives that they could not yet achieve. They were forced to measure their available resources and lower their targets somewhat if resources were inadequate.

Naturally they were using econometric models, though they did not give priority to extrapolation. This was useful if one needed to check how present trends might develop 'if' present policies were unchanged. Forecasting could answer this question of 'if'. But a long-term plan, being essentially a directive, showed what needed to be done to achieve certain socio-economic objectives. For this not only general socio-economic policies but also regional policies to achieve specific economic and technical objectives had to be worked out.

The whole process was essentially dynamic. In establishing and executing a long-term plan it was likely that some changes would be foreseen while others would not. The so-called 'sliding' method of compiling plans was being used in the U.S.S.R. This method permitted plans to be modified in the light of advances in science or technology or in the light of important international developments. But there were still no reliable models to allow for foreseen changes in long-term plans.

Consultative models were being developed and used as auxiliary models in designing the strategy of development. The paper had also mentioned more limited sector models. They did not start when building up a plan from limited sector requirements or problems. These emerged as derivatives from the global plan and its objectives. They did use such models, but as derivative from the plan and subordinate to it. In the last five-year plan, such models were employed for optimisation of the planning of eighty sectors of the economy, with up to 10–15 per cent saving both in capital and operating costs.

Much the same might be said about the economic balance models, including that for dynamic inter-sectoral balance. These models included, so far as was thought practicable, cost–benefit relationships. For example, in the light of the planned scientific and technical developments, the planners could be given the required energy balance, the required capacities of power plants and the corresponding cost–benefit relationships. Naturally there were uncertainties involved. But in many sectors the relationships were fairly stable. Natural resources might become more difficult to extract, more remote or of lower quality. All this was taken into account in the long-term development programmes.

No country in these days, however rich and well-provided with resources, could solve all the problems of scientific and technical progress. For this reason a realistic policy to take advantage of international division of labour was desirable, not only with socialist but also with western countries, and thus increase the efficiency of the national economy. This necessarily made assumptions about the extent of international co-operation.

To go back to the establishment of priorities, a given objective for one sector might produce sub-objectives for a number of other sectors. This involved looking for potential scientific break-throughs. Here again the general socio-economic objective became the decisive criterion in identifying the most important economic problems and thus predetermining the distribution of research funds to the various sectors of science and the balance between fundamental science, applied research, and the development and diffusion of innovations. Of course there were risks involved (this in answer to Professor Marzcewski's question) but in establishing the priorities they started from the general socio-economic objective, and the dynamic, flexible character of the plan made it possible to minimise the dangers. The plan was not a dogma. It was a programme for action. By controlling the research funds they could stimulate research and development in a desired direction.

It had been asked how they used the price system. Down to 1990 they were using throughout the existing constant prices. Of course they could not know the prices of 1990. But they used these constant relative prices to compare alternative costs, to measure the labour resources needed, to discover how to minimise labour inputs and how to increase productivity.

Professor Robinson had asked how they planned the future production capacities of industrial enterprises. This was regarded as a secondary problem. If a general policy had been determined for a given sector the production capacity of a particular plant could be determined on the basis of available inputs and the sales parameters. His institute, for example, had calculated something like a thousand alternative locations for an automobile plant which was finally built in the city of Logliatty, which did not represent any of the forty locations proposed by different organisations anxious to build it. When working out a plan they took account of the regional dimension. This was necessary because of the individual development of the different national republics of the U.S.S.R., because of local availability of natural resources, power supplies, and labour resources, and because of the size of the country. It was not only regional economic policy which had to be considered, but also regional technological policy. They had special machinery and equipment designed for the north, for the south, for the far east.

2 Thoughts on Planning in Western Economies

E. Malinvaud

I. INTRODUCTION

Future economic growth raises for the developed nations of the world many questions, some of which have recently been the subject of heated debate [13].[1] The theory of long-term planning seeks to clarify these questions in such a way that irreversible decisions about the future are taken in the best possible conditions. Hence it is a very important activity for those countries which are most advanced on the road of material progress.

But we must recognise that scientific research about it is full of gaps. It is true that the various sciences bring a better knowledge of the conditions of human progress; it is true also that many detailed research projects deal with particular problems of economic development. The whole operation of planning is, however, little studied, either as a complete process or in some of its most essential parts.

This paper presents some personal thoughts on what planning is, or should be, in a complex society in which individuals and organisations each act with some degree of autonomy. It attempts to appraise the present situation and to suggest areas in which systematic research ought to be encouraged. Deliberately it is neither technical nor specific, which seems desirable at this exploratory stage of the inquiry. It deals occasionally with problems equally concerning short- or medium-term and long-term planning. It refers to 'the market', but would apply as well, on many points, to the institutions of eastern countries. Its three parts are devoted respectively to the purpose of planning, to the organisation of the information system and to the relation between planning and decision-making.

II. THE PURPOSE OF PLANNING

Common sense is enough to show the great difficulty of conscious control of future economic and social development. None the less a great deal of what is written and some widely held views fail to

---

[1] References in square brackets are to the list of bibliographical references on pp. 37–8 below.

consider important aspects of this difficulty. It is thus not out of place here to recall what the problem really is, even though most of my comments cover familiar ground.

i. A misleading stereotype

Let us first avoid the hackneyed distinction between a 'centrally planned economy' and a 'market economy'. The picture suggested by this distinction may be convenient for argument, but it gives a false idea of the real situation.

It is too easy to think of two distinct methods for the control of development. With the first, a central agency would know both the objectives of the community and the constraints to which it is subject; thanks to a proper computing algorithm it would find the 'optimal programme' and secure its implementation. With the second, 'the market' would ensure that decisions individually taken by the various responsible bodies would automatically be consistent with one another and would result in an 'optimal' development.

Everyone can see that the various regimes that exist throughout the world correspond to neither of these two simple images. Decision processes are actually much more complex. They everywhere combine decentralised actions with decisions taken by the highest national authorities; in many cases they have to solve conflicts between contradictory objectives.

If this is the case the reason does not lie in the failures of the institutions that have been set up in the various countries, and have in many cases been more or less drastically revised during this century. It is to be found rather in basic logical reasons which I am anxious to make quite explicit in order to deal better with them.

ii. Multiplicity of agents

The literature on planning has rightly stressed the fact that economic activity presupposes the participation of a large number of individuals, firms and other organisations, none of which knows, or could know, all the physical and technological constraints limiting production and consumption. One must not forget that information is very decentralised: any attempt to work out a plan at the central level must necessarily lead to a very crude result since it is based on a very partial and imperfect knowledge of the conditions of the activity involved.

From this fact two conclusions must be, and frequently have been, drawn. In the first place, one must, so far as possible, associate in the preparation of the plan those who possess the basic information. The preparation of the plan should provide opportunity for the communication of whatever information is most relevant for future policy. No matter how well this is taken into account, this principle cannot be applied to the point where the difficulty will have disappeared: the number of persons possessing relevant information and the complexity of what each of them knows are such that what is available centrally necessarily represents only a fraction of the detailed basic knowledge shared by all the responsible agents.

In the second place the plan prepared at the central level will seldom serve to provide a direct answer to problems of choice in economic and social policy. Designed to show the possibilities for development, it will rather serve as a reference when some particular decision becomes the matter of more thorough study. This is particularly true of long-term planning; it is less obvious when the text of a 'plan' combines the results of central calculations with the presentation of certain decisions simultaneously adopted by political authorities.

For purposes of analysis it is convenient, however, to distinguish between planning and decision-taking, and thus also between planners and political authorities. Planning and decision-taking are often conducted simultaneously and in close relation to one another, for reasons that I shall discuss in the third section. But if we wish to consider how to improve the preparation of plans, we must avoid confusing the technical work of planning with the process of political decision.

iii. *Multiplicity of beneficiaries*

Economic activity not only represents the result of many decentralised actions. It also benefits very many individuals whose needs are partly interdependent, partly conflicting. By their very nature economic phenomena imply conscious or implicit sharing among 'consumers', who are both numerous and differently situated.

But, except for a point that will be mentioned in the third section (choice between generations), the literature on planning is conspicuously silent on this subject. Written by economists who do not feel confident when touching equity problems, it frequently forgets to face the difficulty: it deals with the aggregate consumption of the various goods without considering its distribution among individuals.

Practical planning is less guilty in this respect. Indeed, under very clear public pressure, it often indicates how the incomes of various social groups will vary. It may thus provide basic material for political debate about various measures designed to improve income distribution. It is here that one can see one of the essential functions of a plan prepared by a technical staff: to provide an objective basis for political discussion by showing the true alternatives.

The same function occurs in the planning of collective consumption. Since the various public services usually benefit different groups, a plan covering them provides the necessary basis for the discussion which should precede final policy decision.

iv. Plan and market

Even in western countries, decisions of public authorities play a major role in economic development: they are concerned with the legal rules for contracts between agents, the management of a large public sector, the system of transfers that affects the distribution of incomes. Nevertheless decisions on many industrial and other projects are taken by private undertakings acting with almost complete autonomy. What role does the plan play in securing their mutual consistency and their right direction?

According to a rather widely held view, private decisions taken with the guidance of the 'market' will naturally become consistent among themselves and consistent with the main intentions of the 'plan'. This view does not seem to have been examined with the care that it deserves, considering that its purpose is really fundamental to a clear understanding of economic organisation. One may trace its origin as follows.

Known theoretical results establish that, when a development programme for an economy has been worked out in such a way that it uses the national resources efficiently, one may associate with it a system of discounted prices such that, using these prices, each individual undertaking may ensure that its activity in accordance with the programme is that which is most profitable to it (for a lucid and rigorous exposition, see [5]). The institutions actually determining the trade terms between participants are considered to be roughly approximating the price system in question, and individual decisions as being then consistent with one another and as leading to the levels of production and consumption that are implied by the programme fixed in the plan.

Naturally, I do not want to throw doubt either on the correctness of the theoretical results that one is here invoking, or on their relevance to the actual organisation of production and consumption. On the contrary others have shown better than I can do here the extent to which a clear understanding of these factors is necessary if one wishes to avoid wasteful loss of resources, and how prices, correctly and objectively determined, may be utilised for the most varied economic purposes. It will suffice here to quote [4]. My own purpose is rather to define, as clearly as I can, the respective roles of the plan and the market. For this one must study precisely what functions the one and the other can really perform.

The formal assumptions introduced for the proof of the theoretical results mentioned above are notorioulsy unrealistic in some respects. They assume in particular the divisibility of productive operations and rule out external effects as well as collective consumption. A first justification for public intervention, and thus for planning, has its origin here. Decisions about prices, taxes and public projects must be designed to correct the detrimental consequences of whatever differences may emerge between the assumptions and the real world. We shall see in the third part of this paper that it is not a simple job.

Even when the difficulty just mentioned does not arise, the theoretical results cannot be considered as providing the justification for an exclusively market regime. The statement of them indeed makes it clear that the prices are to be regarded only as appropriate for sustaining a programme the selection of which must take account in particular of the requirements of equity. This is a second reason for public intervention in economic development, and thus also for planning it. When such problems are not tackled deliberately, the free play of markets and individual decisions, even if they may promote an efficient use of resources, are likely to benefit inequitably the various social classes, and even various individuals within these classes.

Finally the price system assumed in the theory far exceeds in its complexity any that can be actually observed. It assumes the existence of a discounted price for every commodity, for every date and even, when uncertainty matters, for every possible situation of the environment. This price ought to be known to everybody and to apply immediately to contracts for future delivery.

The price system that a statistician can construct by observing actual price schedules and transactions is a very poor thing in comparison with these theoretical requirements. One may describe it analytically by saying that it contains only one price for the immediate delivery of each good and one interest rate for each period. In their profitability calculations firms must forecast the prices, the tax rates and the wage rates that will apply in the future. If there existed no collective public determination of the pattern of growth, the consistency of individual decisions would be very doubtful. This third reason for public planning has seldom been stressed in the literature until quite recently (see [12]).

v. Plans in western societies

To make a plan is to make explicit a lucid framework for decision-taking about the future. The maker of a plan performs the function of discovering the future prospects, of indicating the main options and of presenting the consequences of the decisions that have already been taken. In western countries, and in eastern countries as well, it is now common to prepare plans with three lengths of horizon: short-term (one or two years), medium-term (about five years), long-term (fifteen to twenty years).

I have not attempted to survey systematically all the plans made in western countries, nor even all the long-term plans. International organisations are better equipped for that than the individual research worker. One may, however, draw on other studies of this subject [14]. I shall merely draw attention here to three features which seem to me to deserve serious thought.

Firstly, it is clear from a very cursory look at the present arrangements that the bodies responsible for long-term planning have a very varied administrative status, belonging sometimes to the governmental administration, sometimes to public or private universities or institutions. This situation seems to be due partly to the fact that long-term planning, like any new activity, has not yet found its proper place; partly also to the fact that it is essentially an intermediary function as distinguished from decision-taking but involved with the study of issues very intimately associated with political policies; partly again to differences in national institutional practices, the extent of the collaboration between government and universities varying a good deal from one country to another.

In the second place long-term planning is very macro-economic. Prepared on the basis of population forecasts and of projections of the main economic equilibria, it does not consider in detail the development of each of the various industries. Admittedly it is often followed by specific prospective studies of particular sectors: fuel and power, transport and the like. But full internal consistency between the various industrial studies is not systematically attempted.

Finally, one may add that, more and more frequently, long-term plans provide sets of variants, which start from different assumptions either regarding certain basic growth factors (technical progress, the international environment, and so on) or regarding the political objectives that may be chosen (see [1] for instance). I shall argue later that such a procedure seems actually to be required by the very function of a long-term plan.

III. THE INFORMATION SYSTEM

In order to examine more closely the various operations involved in constructing a plan, it is convenient, even if slightly artificial, to look in turn at each of the two roles of planning: that of providing a framework of forecasts to assist those responsible to make their decisions without complete central control; that of helping to achieve a greater rationality in decisions reached at the central level. This I shall do in Sections ii and iii, respectively.

In order to succeed in providing to the national community the relevant information about future growth, the plan-makers must first gather together the very widely dispersed knowledge that is possessed by all the various persons concerned; they must then make a synthesis of this knowledge and show the future prospects that result from it. These two points will now be considered.

i. Provision of relevant information

Those to whom the plan forecasts are addressed have very varied needs, the complete list of which would be tedious. In developed western economies it will be sufficient to consider the needs of individuals and of firms.

Now perhaps more than at any other time, men are conscious that long-term economic development raises important political issues: the balance between individual and collective satisfaction of human wants, aid to countries that are less advanced in their development, the efficient management of resources that may one day be exhausted – these are some of the main questions to which a reasoned answer must be given. Governments, preoccupied with immediate business, are ill-placed to do this. Individual members of the public must examine the issues and choose between various programmes stressing different priorities.

Long-term plans must, therefore, enlighten the 'collective con-science'. To meet this need they must look far ahead, present a wide range of alternatives and show how, with each one of them, the results of growth will be used. They must look far ahead because only with a rather long horizon do the true choices appear. They must present the clear alternatives because the economic technician is not entitled to narrow or circumscribe the range of choice. They must show the results because it is the examination of these that is needed to enlighten the political debate.

From this point of view one may doubt whether existing practices really meet the need. A plan that consists of a single projection without any variants and is computed only for a single target year, fifteen years ahead, is wholly inadequate, even if it is accompanied by a medium-term five-year plan. Whatever doubts one may have about some of the theories advanced by the disciples of J. W. Forrester [13], one must give them credit for the way in which they present their results: several clearly distinct alternatives and, for each one of them, a path computed at regular intervals and extending far into the future. This method of presentation has certainly something to do with the impact that their report has had on public opinion.

The needs of firms concern a less distant future. They are interested, however, in long-term planning because many industrial projects involve equipment that will last far beyond the horizon of any medium-term plan.

A hasty look at the problem might suggest that these needs are contrary to the needs of a properly informed collective conscience. Firms expect the plan to 'reduce uncertainty about the future'. Thus they want it to give them a single and precise picture of future growth. But one can quickly see the inherent contradiction of this wish. In fact it is this concept, which is now predominant, that must be held responsible for some serious gaps, with respect to the needs of firms, that are to be found in the plans prepared in western countries.

Indeed, it is too often thought that a plan will reveal a definitive choice by the government of a clearly described development path. One thus expects the plan to make fully explicit what policy has been adopted. But no government can commit itself to being completely bound by its own earlier decisions; it must keep some freedom of action to deal with unforeseen events and to correct mistakes. It is thus inevitable that the plan will often remain silent or obscure on some essential elements of economic policy: regarding changes of tax rates or of various transfers, the allocation of public expenditures, and so on. Such a practice will not, of course, reduce the uncertainty that firms are facing. But if one considers the real problems one must reach the conclusion that the needs of the firms would be better served if the plan were presented as a tree with several variants between which no choice had yet been made, but with each variant clearly described.

Private firms take their decisions by considering the profits they may derive from them, public sector enterprises by considering the results of some economic value calculations. Plans should, therefore, not be limited to quantitative estimates of how the demand for various goods will change. They should provide also, to a much greater extent than at present, estimates of the parameters affecting such calculations of economic returns: actual or shadow prices, discount rates for a range of future dates, labour costs, tax rates and the like.

ii. Collection of relevant information

To make such projections and their variants, the planning agency must collect and synthesise data some of which are known only to individual firms or other bodies. In practice the collection of data is initiated either directly by those in charge of the technical planning work, or more formally to meet specific needs of commissions, committees or working groups organised sometimes to study particular industries, sometimes to deal with particular important constraints on growth.

The collection of this information from representatives of various types of bodies remains for the moment limited in scope, rather unsystematic, but yet a very laborious task. Thus it does not receive much attention in long-term planning. But it will have to be improved if progress is to be made in methods of controlling economic growth.

The theory of planning had, of course, devoted attention to the analysis of procedures to promote efficient information collection. The work of F. M. Taylor [15] and O. Lange [8] deserves special mention. Our conference cannot neglect this aspect of our work. I should like, therefore, to attempt to bring out the results hitherto achieved by the theoretical work on this question.[1]

Being theoretical, these various writings had naturally to make certain assumptions which I do not propose to discuss here. It must be mentioned, however, that they have not hitherto taken into account the time dimension; they have been concerned with the determination of a programme involving inputs and outputs as if these were to be achieved once and for all, with no implications for the future. This very serious limitation must be kept in mind. On the other hand a rather extensive range of situations has been considered; some recent work goes beyond the traditional model of resource allocation and deals in particular with collective consumption, the study of which is difficult to conceive except in terms of a planning perspective.

The techniques that have been studied consist of a simultaneous search for a programme and for prices that are equal to marginal rates of substitution with respect to this particular programme (or more generally for 'objectively determined values'). Thus they correspond to what is done in practice when one attempts to find, after balancing demands and supplies, the discount rate, the shadow price of labour, or that of a foreign currency. They should progressively become more and more relevant to the extent that planning places more and more emphasis on the determination of prices.

Two alternative approaches have been suggested. With the first the central planning agency announces prices, then asks firms and others responsible to estimate, on some agreed basis of rules, the quantities of the various commodities that they would demand or supply at these prices (for collective consumption the prices are individualised, as is well known). The answers are collected and analysed by the central agency; in general they will reveal some

[1] An incomplete list of references to work on this subject includes [2], [7], [9], [11], [16].

cases of excess demand and some of excess supply. The initial prices are then revised and submitted again; a new set of answers come back. Interchanges continue in this way until the answers are found to be sufficiently consistent with the requirement of zero excess demand for each commodity (theoretical research has shown that, with such procedures, a balance must eventually be reached).

With the second approach the central agency announces a programme of quantities to be produced or consumed by the various bodies. The latter must answer by indicating the marginal rates of substitution that apply to them. Comparison of these rates by the central agency reveals inconsistencies and suggests how the original programme must be changed. A revised programme is circulated. With this approach also, iterative interchanges are continued until a satisfactory consistency is reached.

Study of these two approaches, each one of which may be applied in various ways, seems to me to show that they are not as different as one might suppose. It has sometimes been argued that the first emphasises a form of social organisation that gives the major role to the market and the second a form in which quantitative controls over the activity of firms and consumers are emphasised. Such an interpretation seems to me exaggerated or at least premature.

Certain properties of the procedures studied lead me to give preference to a mixed system in which the central agency is responsible for estimating certain output targets, the prices for privately consumed goods, and the volumes for collective consumption. Such a scheme of planning seems to be broadly compatible with what is increasingly happening both in eastern countries and in western countries.

Research on the efficient collection of decentralised data emphasises two important facts. I shall come back in the last section of this paper to one of them – that one cannot plan without considering distribution between individual consumers. The second is that, when relevant information is widely scattered, one cannot be certain that those possessing it will report accurately. When he gives his answer each person may have interest in distorting to some extent the result of his calculations.

The various procedures suggested are not equally subject to this risk. But it cannot be wholly removed, for it obviously exists in any system of planning in which those concerned have an interest in the decisions that the planning is designed to affect. Economists should give very serious consideration to this difficulty and try to discover incentives that would reduce the risk of biased reporting without being damaging in some other way. But sociologists should also have something to contribute; for participation in the collective operation of planning may, in some circumstances, appeal to the individual as being something that involves his duty as a good citizen and even as justifying certain sacrifices.

iii. *Use of inductive research on 'economic laws'*

Even if the collection of information becomes better organised, long-term planning will still impose heavy technical obligations on the central agency. This will involve construction of one or more models to be used to calculate the main projections.

For this purpose the role of models is well recognised. It is illustrated by many examples in [14]. If I do not stress this here, it is because I do not believe I have anything to contribute to this question on this occasion. On the other hand I would like to express my sincere belief that the progress of inductive econometric research is essential to the progress of planning in general, and more particularly to that of long-term planning.

Models and projections made at the central level can only be macro-economic. Intended to provide an aggregative picture of a real situation that is immensely complex at the micro-economic level, they are inevitably remote from the detailed activities of firms or consumers and their decisions. The information collected from these activities must therefore be interpreted and combined in terms of inductive investigations conducted at precisely the same macro-economic level as the projections contained in the plan.

Looking at the same question from a different angle, one can see that, under the various regimes existing today, most persons have a fair or even a large degree of autonomy within the constraints imposed by nature and by the social organisation under which they work. Consumers choose what they buy, taking the prices and their resources into account. Firms produce, invest, recruit, with a freedom that is more or less limited by targets and constraints imposed by administrative authorities. To make good projections, planners must have acquired the habit of asking themselves how far various macro-economic laws derive from such decisions at the micro-economic level.

The establishment of such laws is not, of course, simple. Observed trends provide a factual basis that is too narrow to reveal them clearly. Thus examination of macro-economic data is not enough. It must be supplemented by the study of systematic differences that appear between the behaviour of various agents. These differences, observed in samples of individual data, must then be correctly transposed to the macro-economic level. Moreover, for the study of the two kinds of data (aggregate time series or cross-sections of individuals), thorough preliminary conceptual and theoretical analysis is required because phenomena are far too complex to be revealed by a purely empirical examination.

Applied econometrics devotes great effort to deriving macro-economic laws. In the past thirty years or so it has made very substantial progress, not only in establishing a number of permanent regularities or associations but also in estimating important parameters. It has been learning, progressively and after many failures, how efficiently to combine preliminary theoretical analysis with the use of the numerical procedures indicated by statistical methodology.

The importance of this progress is probably not recognised by everybody in western countries. But those preparing long-term plans are well aware of it because they make great use for their projections of the laws derived from econometric research. Not being fully informed of the most recent developments in the methods adopted in eastern countries, I may be wrong. It seems to me, however, that planning in these countries is too little supported by inductive research. Very ambitious models are being built, each containing a large number of parameters. Will it be possible to use with confidence the results of these models without having to examine very closely the exact meaning of these parameters and how they can be estimated?

IV. PLANNING AND THE DECISION PROCESS

Given the complexity of social organisation and of the problems to be settled, one should not be surprised to see how unconsidered and hasty are many important public decisions. Such occurrences nevertheless testify that planning is still underdeveloped and not fully adapted to actual administrative and political procedures. Without waiting for the solution of all the institutional problems raised by a more rational organisation of public decision-making, academics have much that they can do to demonstrate clearly how the main choices in economic development ought to be made.

i. An over-simplified scheme

According to a formulation that naturally comes to mind, a best set of decisions could be satisfactorily computed as the solution of a somewhat elaborate mathematical programme. Using perhaps the information collected from the various sources, the planner would build a model representing the constraints of the real situation; this model would show how the instruments of economic policy affect the values obtained for certain important variables representing the objectives. The decision-maker would disclose his preference system; more precisely he would give the planner a function showing his ranking by order of preference of the various possible sets of values that might be achieved by the objective variables. The planner would then include this function in his model and discover what set of values for the instrument variables would yield the highest feasible value of the function. The decision-maker would then merely have to adopt these values for the instruments without having to go back to the specifications of the model and his preference function and without even knowing the values implied for the objective variables.

No doubt to work out such a concept is of considerable theoretical interest. People too often forget the constraints that limit their activities. To bring to the surface the factors that condition future growth and to require a quantitative statement of preferences and priorities can only help to clarify thinking as to where the major problems lie.

Such a concept is none the less misleading. It does not provide even a crude representation of the actual decision processes that apply today or that one can imagine in the future.

This is partly because it suggests that one can hope to build a universal model representing the conditions of economic development and quite independent of what may be the priorities of the decision-maker. Reality is far too complex for this ever to be the case. Planning models must always reflect certain main preoccupations. A dialogue between decision-makers and planners is therefore essential.

The lack of realism of the idea under discussion is partly due also to the fact that one cannot hope to impose the intellectual discipline required for actual specification of a social preference function. Economists themselves do not yet have a sufficient experience with such functions to identify immediately the choices they imply, save in very simple cases. The theoretical literature on optimal growth has clearly demonstrated this (it may indeed be its most significant result).

Last but not least, to regard the decision process as the solution of a mathematical programme assumes a single decision-maker. But that is never the case. Actual processes involve many participants whose interests inevitably conflict. To theorise about planning with a single decision-maker, when political organisation is wholly different, implies missing the actual problems and providing inadequate answers.

I cannot claim to build a precise theory of political organisation in western societies and of the place that planning should have in them. My ideas are much too confused. Such a task requires close collaboration between economists and specialists in political science. I shall be content to suggest finally one or two tentative ideas. But before doing so, I should again like to call to mind the results of some recent research in theoretical and applied economics.

ii. Clarification of the main options

Whatever may be the institutional links between planners and decision-making bodies, one must always look to the former to clarify the main options facing national development policy. The main function of planners is not to determine the values of the instruments but rather to describe correctly and precisely this 'tree' that is composed of several distinct variants and has been mentioned already twice in my paper. In other words planners should be asked to show, both at the national level and for the various sectors, the probable consequences of the alternative decisions contemplated.

But to identify correctly the main options, the planners must make a first selection. The number of conceivable policies is so vast that to consider them all is out of the question. Attention must be concentrated on just a few, chosen in such a way as to give a good representation of the full range of the alternatives actually open. Even though they know that they will not have the last word, planners must therefore put themselves in the place of decision-makers in order to identify a few development policies, each one of which is not only feasible but also the best among those representing that particular option.

This is why planning must often involve difficult decision problems. By the study of these problems, economic science may contribute significantly to their solution. Let me take two important examples.

Long-term planning has to pay particular attention to the choice of the rate of capital accumulation. On the one hand, this choice particularly affects the future. On the other hand, its determination is a prerequisite to establishing the appropriate rules to be applied in project appraisal and in particular in fixing the value of the discount rate.

Economic science has recently attacked this problem in two complementary lines of research work. In the first place the theoretical analysis has been greatly developed; the subject of 'optimal growth' has even become highly fashionable. Even though many of the published articles do not deserve close study, significant progress has been achieved towards a better understanding of the problem. I shall not try to summarise them here but rather refer to a thoughtful survey made by T. Koopmans [6].

In the second place, numerous econometric studies, based either on time series or on cross-sections of individual data, have attempted to measure the extent to which increased capital accumulation will benefit labour productivity. The results hitherto obtained are valuable, but one must recognise that their precision does not yet reach the level that would be required for a complete application of the theoretical research just mentioned. One of the most interesting findings is that the discount rate to be applied in economic planning calculations is appreciably higher than one used to think.

One of the difficulties in the technical work of planning arises from the indivisibility of certain large projects which absorb a considerable part of national resources and have a very long life. This indivisibility upsets the rules of appraisal that are usually adopted for purposes of economic estimating, all the more so because it is often combined with external effects that are particularly difficult to calculate: technological fall-out, stimulus to regional development and so on. In practice, however, one cannot avoid using prices when considering such projects; one cannot determine in physical terms all the consequences that may follow from the adoption or non-adoption of each project.

Recent theoretical research has shown all the complexities involved in selection of indivisible projects. Even if they are viewed as collective consumption, the fixed costs involved are not easily incorporated into satisfactory calculations (see [10] on this for instance). But even though theory does not provide here a general and practicable rule, it serves nevertheless as a guide; it shows the kind of mistakes into which one may fall through using either recorded prices or prices that are extrapolated on the basis of macro-economic planning. To my mind, the practical conclusion is that, in such cases, estimates made in terms of money values should be supplemented by a critical direct examination of the possible causes of error. Such an examination is necessarily very crude, with common sense playing a major role but guided by theoretical analysis to suggest where the error may arise.

iii. Relation to a political system

It is clear that, even in the most liberal western countries, public authorities are taking more and more economic decisions, either because the control of growth becomes more and more conscious or because the conditions of modern production requires more and more frequent public intervention.

From this point of view the existing political organisation seems no longer to be wholly appropriate. On the one hand it does not explicitly recognise the function, and hence define the powers, of the technicians and 'planners' who are preparing for decisions. On the other hand, following principles that date from the eighteenth century, it basically consists of a central government and of institutions with local authority. In practice a major role is also played by trade unions representing groups based on professional activities; but the function of trade unions is not constitutionally defined and remains ambiguous. Moreover, territorial and professional structures are not enough to cover all the various needs and demands of an increasingly complex society. Thus reforms of the politico-administrative structures of western countries are needed.

The place to be given to the offices responsible for planning (or of Planned Program Budgeting Systems) must, therefore, be seriously considered. Thus it is fortunate that persons like C. Gruson [3] have raised to the institutional level the discussion on the role of planning. Even if one does not agree with his specific proposals, one must share his concern for greater efficiency in our planning.

For my own part, I should recommend that planning offices should be decentralised but articulated with each other: decentralised in such a way as to be placed alongside the various decision-makers for which they must collect their information, study the problems and pose the main options; articulated with one another in such a way that information collected at one level is accessible at other levels. One cannot but deplore that so many studies needed for administrations are today commissioned from private groups that have neither the professional standards, nor the continuity, nor the liaison required for a fully effective study.

iv. A final comment

The comments with which I have ended this paper may seem, perhaps, to lead away from the subject of long-term planning. One must, however, remember that it is the problems with a horizon ten years or more distant that increasingly require the intervention of 'planners' working closely with public undertakings and various administrative bodies. And does not the long-term perspective afford the appropriate occasion for raising these wider institutional problems?

REFERENCES

[1] E. Andréani and A. Gauron, 'Cinq esquisses de croissance pour 1985', *Economie et Statistique* (Sep 1970).
[2] J. Drèze and D. de la Vallée Poussin, 'A tâtonnement process goods', *Review of Economic Studies* (Apr 1971).
[3] C. Gruson, *Renaissance du plan* (Paris: Editions du Seuil, 1971).

[4] L. V. Kantorovitch, *Calcul economique et utilisation des ressources* (Paris: Dunod, 1963).

[5] T. Koopmans, *Three Essays on the State of Economic Science* (New York: McGraw–Hill, 1957) chap. 1.

[6] T. Koopmans, 'Objectives, Constraints and Outcomes in Optimal Growth Models', *Econometrica* (Jan 1967).

[7] J. Kornai and T. Liptak, 'Two-level Planning', *Econometrica* (Jan 1963).

[8] O. Lange, 'On the economic theory of socialism', *Review of Economic Studies* (1936) pp. 53–71, 123–42.

[9] E. Malinvaud, 'Decentralized Procedures for Planning', in E. Malinvaud and M. O. L. Bacharach (eds), *Activity Analysis in the Theory of Growth and Planning* (London: Macmillan, 1967).

[10] E. Malinvaud, *Lectures on Microeconomic Theory* (Amsterdam: North Holland, 1972).

[11] E. Malinvaud, 'Prices for individual consumption, quantity indicators for collective consumption', *Review of Economic Studies* (Oct 1972).

[12] P. Massé, *le Plan et l'anti-hasard* (Paris: N.R.F., 1965).

[13] D. Meadows *et al.*, 'Rapport sur les limites de la croissance', in Meadows, *Halte à la croissance?* (Paris: Fayard, 1972).

[14] United Nations, *Planification à long terme* (New York, 1971).

[15] F. M. Taylor, 'The guidance of production in a socialist state', *American Economic Review* (Mar 1929).

[16] M. Weitzman, 'Iterative Multilevel Planning with Production Targets', *Econometrica* (Jan 1970).

Discussion of the Paper by Professor Malinvaud

Professor Shatalin (U.S.S.R.), opening the discussion, said that Professor Malinvaud's paper went far beyond economic planning, narrowly defined. He touched on the role and place of planning in the general economic and political structure of western countries. He rightly described his topic as what planning was, or what it should be, in a western country. These two issues were often confused, so that 'what planning is' became substituted for 'what planning should be'. It was not always clear where Professor Malinvaud himself drew the line, and he would like him to clarify his ideas about this.

Professor Malinvaud's paper was concerned with three issues. First he discussed the character of planning, principally in western countries, though he remarks that many of the problems of methodology and techniques of planning are relevant to socialist countries also. Second, he was concerned with the organisation of the information system and its application to the techniques of planning. Third, he was concerned with the relationship between the framing of a plan and the decision-making progress in terms of specific administrative and political actions.

Professor Malinvaud did not regard the normal distinction between centrally planned and market economies as very constructive, since in any country planning represented a combination of centrally made and locally made decisions. The differences between centrally planned and market economies could not be reduced just to a principle of socio-economic decision-making. It was also to some extent a matter of the political and economic structures of societies, so that the market economy or the centrally planned economy prevailed.

It was quite clear that the market economy and purely economic forces could not establish the right interrelations between specific partial decisions. The need for planning derived from the need to take account of social factors and of the distribution of incomes and wealth in a society. Professor Malinvaud seemed to regard this as an inevitable part of the economic decision-making system, just as a number of production and other economic processes, and especially long-term and large-scale investments, are inseparable.

Another important issue was the relationship between a plan and a market. It was far from clear how one can distinguish between the methodologies and problems of short-, medium, and long-term planning, and what the plan–market relationship should be in each case. A general planning system should provide for each question. But in each of such plans there must be certain specific ways of co-ordinating centralised and decentralised decisions. After studying the various familiar principles for co-ordinating centralised and decentralised decisions, and without questioning their theoretical validity or the concept of co-ordination, Professor Malinvaud had reached the conclusion that an overall planning of the general objectives of development and the planning by appropriate bodies of the total output of private sectors represented the most constructive and rational solution and ensured an optimal use of resources.

Professor Shatalin believed that many of the western models of optimal planning had attempted technological and economic optimisation without taking account of the distribution of incomes or of public or private consumption. Economists in the U.S.S.R. had realised the inadequacy of such an approach and were now trying to include the distribution of incomes and wealth in their models. This was a very sophisticated problem and one could not assume an easy solution. They in the U.S.S.R. felt that the distribution of incomes and wealth was not always satisfactorily solved by the formal processes of models. A new methodology was needed, and particularly because the distribution of incomes and wealth had important feedback effects and represented a major factor in determining economic growth.

He was partly at least in agreement with Professor Malinvaud's argument that, even if some models yielded an optimal use of resources, there still remained a need for planning and social control, since without it the problems of the distribution of wealth could not be solved. This was quite correct. But the assumption that market forces would result in an optimal distribution of resources at least needed further clarification. It was not clear what criteria were being adopted. For Professor Malinvaud himself pointed out the limitations of the economic criteria determining the optimal use of resources.

Professor Malinvaud thought that a number of problems regarding long-term planning faced both the western and what he called the 'eastern' countries. The first problem was the place of long-term planning in the existing planning organisations which were numerous in western countries. The place occupied by long-term planning reflected the absence of an adequate methodology for it and the fact that mere extrapolation was inadequate for this purpose. It was his personal view that long- and short-term planning should form a single complex to examine possible alternatives in socio-economic development and the implications of alternative policies. He believed that current research in the U.S.S.R. met this need.

Professor Malinvaud had discussed the use of inductive methods for the study of economic phenomena. Since they had to make use of macro-economic analysis in long-term planning, it was very important to discover how far micro-economic events corresponded to certain general laws that had been propounded at the macro-economic level and which were applied to long-term planning. It was in practice a problem of partial econometric studies and the estimation of certain parameters and their applicability to certain policies of socio-economic development.

Professor Malinvaud had suggested that the use of such inductive methods in eastern countries had not been pushed far enough, while the characteristics of many of the parameters used in large 'ambitious' models were far from clear. Without agreeing that these models were ambitious, he found himself in partial agreement with Professor Malinvaud's criticism of some of the very detailed Soviet models which attempted to produce a theoretical account of the whole economy and included a number of parameters whose relevance was far from obvious and which could not be adequately estimated statistically. This was partly because econometric methods had only recently been developed, but also because such studies were designed to test some theoretical hypothesis rather than just engage in econometric experimentation.

Professor Machlup (U.S.A.) said that when Professor Malinvaud spoke of development plans in western countries, his use of the term development was misleading. Development to an American meant the change in social and political institutions that were thought to be necessary before an 'undeveloped' country could start industrialisation. Thus to speak of a 'development plan' for an already industrialised country was somewhat confusing. Such countries had policies – fiscal policies, monetary policies and so on. But did they have a plan for the economy as a whole? Professor Malinvaud had suggested that their plans were principally macro-economic. But he wondered whether such a plan was anything more than a medium-term fiscal, or monetary, or growth policy. He thought that one should distinguish between, firstly, the sort of plan that is made for a firm, or an industry; secondly a sort of macro-economic growth plan for an economy, concerned with savings, taxation and the like; and thirdly a comprehensive plan, which has to solve all the allocation problems 'and the problems of balances between different sectors in the terms of a general equilibrium model. He thought that this third type was fundamentally different from the other types.

Professor Bradistilov (Bulgaria) suggested that there were two other distinctions: firstly, how far the overall planning was related to a regional planning; secondly, how far one introduced social considerations and indicators into one's planning.

Professor Robinson (U.K.) said that Professor Machlup was no doubt formally right in saying that western countries did not have plans, but it would be very misleading to suggest that they did not have long-term forecasts, sometimes official, more often unofficial but prepared by competent and professional institutes, which were used in shaping policies not only of private enterprises but also of public bodies. Such forecasts existed for the United States, for the United Kingdom, for the Netherlands, for France, for Italy and a number of other western countries and were readily available. Though there were few cases of formal plans, there were many cases of very serious attempts in the western countries to look forward. There was a great deal of common interest between those in the west and in the socialist countries in perfecting the techniques of forecasting and in exchanging information and experience to that end.

Professor Porwit (Poland) thought that it was misleading to speak about the planning of a market economy. There were two contrasting ways of planning. If central planning was regarded as an attempt to solve everything starting from the top and going down to the bottom on the basis of one model, that was a one-sided conception. In most centrally planned economies it had become recognised that it had to be a two-way process. The first process, working from the top downwards, established the general scheme of the whole economy, and defined the social objectives and the strategy for attaining them. It was, however, very important to supplement this with the second process, working from the bottom and concerned with the best use of resources and providing the optimum solution of the various micro-economic problems. Professor Shatalin had been right in stressing that the chief difference between the market economy and the centrally planned economy was in the social and political aims for which the economic structure was designed. He would himself add a difference in attitude to the problems of developing the economy and of improving its functioning. The improvement in the functioning of the economy was an important factor in growth. It was not simply a matter of increase of measurable resources. Better management of the economic infrastructure was an important difference between the two types of economy.

Professor Porwit's second point was concerned with the fundamental importance of qualitative changes over long periods. In planning in Poland they had two methods of approach. The first was concerned with quantifiable data and made use of various models and calculations. But there always remained the second group of problems as to how the more qualitative interrelations between these quantifiable variables would change and what forces would cause them to change. It was very difficult to discover formalised procedures for producing reasonably accurate predictions of these changes.

His third point, related to what Professor Malinvaud had said about the need to provide variants, very much depended on how these variants were to be used. One way was to work with variants during the process of making the plan, on the assumption that the planning process would itself select one particular variant. A second way (he wondered whether this was what Professor Malinvaud had in mind) was to leave some given strategy for the future undecided, with variant policies between which choice would be made in the light of factors which would become known later. In this sense the variants might be used to make it possible to start action immediately, with later choice between the variants when certain factors were known.

His final point was concerned with the problems of combining the work at the aggregate level with that at the micro-economic level, which in practice implied fixing the prices of particular constituents in the micro-economic calculations. Two points needed to be clarified. The first was that, when working at more than one level, one had to take account of the motivations of particular participants. One had to consider how they could best be induced to work in a way that would lead towards an optimal solution. The second was the need to leave some elasticity for future adaptation to changing circumstances. Any delegation procedure that was static in its assumptions and assumed that everything had been fixed, left problems to be solved in the future.

Professor Majminas (U.S.S.R.) said that Professor Malinvaud had very rightly stated that econometric models, and the whole approach by way of overall balance in particular, were not practicable instruments for the purposes of long-term planning. This view was widely held by Soviet experts in this field. There was considerable disappointment with econometric models, especially when applied to long-term planning. But he wondered whether there was not a danger of tipping out the baby with the bath water. Professor Malinvaud had been right in saying that long-term planning had failed to develop its own models, mathematical apparatus and methodology. The question he wished to ask was what prospects Professor Malinvaud saw of the development of such a system. How could they take more fully into account the uncertainties of technical progress and of changing objectives while still retaining some techniques of optimisation and some models, if only for consultative and not for decision-making purposes?

If one read the literature, one got the impression that the people working on long-term planning, both in the west and in the U.S.S.R., were in some sense isolated from those working on econometric models for short- and medium-term planning. Long-term planning had developed methods to determine national objectives and to work out long-term programmes, such as the Planned Program Budgeting System (P.P.B.S.) in the U.S.A. But these methods were being developed somehow independently of econometrics and of those working in traditional fields. He wanted to suggest that further development required more critical evaluation of the experience with programmed-target planning, such as the Planned Program Budgeting methods, the Delphi methods, pattern and other methods, and with attempts to construct linkages between these methods and those used for problems of a medium-term character. What were Professor Malinvaud's views about this?

His third question was concerned with the problems of information. Planners and forecasters had to collect information from a variety of separate and independent sources. It had been suggested both in the West and in the U.S.S.R. that large national data banks should be created. He wanted to ask whether Professor Malinvaud could visualise greater use of such data banks in France or in the U.S.A. and their development with the needs of medium- and long-term planning very much in mind. The essential issue was how they could bring together all the information that was now scattered and take advantage of all the experience of the past.

Professor Marczewski (France) thought that Professor Machlup might have given the impression that there were wide differences between socialist and capitalist countries in respect of long-term planning. He himself thought that the differences were small or non-existent. Neither in socialist nor in capitalist countries was there long-term planning in its true sense. This was true of both groups of countries despite certain long-term elements in the programmes of the Communist Party of the U.S.S.R. for 1960–80 and in the long-term plans of Poland and other countries. These were not plans in the same sense that were their medium-term plans. They were simply outlines of possible lines of development and very broad indications of appropriate policies. Exactly the same could be said of the French long-term plan. The differences here were very small indeed.

There was, moreover, a strong tendency not only in socialist but also in capitalist countries to construct long-term plans, and all countries were busy asking themselves about their future technologies and patterns of life. This trend of thought was even more common in capitalist than in socialist countries. Everyone was trying to foresee the future and to control some of the damaging consequences of progress such as pollution. No country, he thought, had real long-term planning, but all countries were concerned with it.

Professor Khachaturov (U.S.S.R.) argued that the issue was not whether a long-term plan could be constructed but whether, if it was, it represented a plan and not merely a forecast. A twenty-year forecast had recently been completed in the U.S.A. and similar forecasts were being made in other countries. The essential distinction was that a plan not only provides an outline of future development but also measures that will be taken to implement it.

If one compared the two systems, the socialist state had the ability not only to plan but also to manage the economy. In a western economy, there were some sectors, such as the U.S. Apollo space programme, or within a single corporation, where both planning and management were possible. Indeed, no corporation could survive without such planning. In the Second World War in all the countries concerned there had been created special authorities which could not only plan various sectors of the economy but also manage them. The question he wanted to ask was what powers a western country really possessed to implement an overall plan, except in the cases he had mentioned. He thought that their means of implementation were limited to such instruments as taxation, tariffs, price control, wages policies and financial controls. Thus he believed that, though a long-term plan might in practice be constructed by a capitalist country as well as by a socialist country, it could by the nature of things only be an indicative plan.

Professor Machlup (U.S.A.) was again anxious for greater precision in the use of words. There were three different concepts that needed to be distinguished, but were constantly being confused: long-term planning, long-term forecasting, long-term guessing. Operations such as the Apollo space project or sewage disposal were plans. The latter had been both planned and executed for centuries. If one spoke of economic plans one should mean the solution of the problems of allocating resources and products.

Professor Stojanović (Yugoslavia) wanted to return to something that Professor Sorokin had said in the previous session. The establishment of socio-economic objectives had to precede any planning and those objectives had to be determined by the political authority. On the technical side – the construction of the actual plan – it seemed to him obvious that purely econometric techniques could not possibly take into account all the many different factors involved, ranging from the international situation to the rate of scientific and technical progress. In the U.S.A. it was believed that not more than 25 per cent of the relevant factors could be estimated. In the U.S.S.R. they suggested a figure of 25–30 per cent. If not more than 25–30 per cent of all the factors involved were capable of estimation it seemed clear that one must adopt not only econometric methods, but also any other available, including inductive and heuristic methods.

Professor Augustinovics (Hungary) wanted to come back to the problem of selection between alternatives. Professor Malinvaud had spoken of the astronomic number of possible alternatives and of the need to do some preliminary pruning of the tree before going on to actual planning or forecasting or even guesswork. Were his comments based on theoretical presumptions or on actual practice – in France for example? In Hungary they had started with the same presumption. In their early work they had been obsessed by the problem of selecting the appropriate branches of the tree. It turned out that the real difficulty was a different one. The difficulty was to persuade the planners to admit that there was more than one alternative. They insisted that they were confident within plus or minus 10 per cent of this alternative solution. Very often they had good reasons. But common sense argued that there must in the long period be more alternatives.

One explanation might be the difficulty of ridding oneself of today's pressures and problems and inability to visualise a more distant future.

Another explanation was that too much preliminary pruning had already been done. Planners were supposedly unbiased professionals. They were in fact human beings who identified themselves with certain groups, professions or interests. Was there a country where the planners were not like this? Or was the assumption of an infinite number of alternative possibilities just a theoretical presumption? Did long-term planning really face quite different problems?

Professor Denison (U.S.A.) wanted to return to the problems of long-term projections. In the U.S.A. they had long-term projections, but nothing that could be called either a medium-term or short-term plan, still less a long-term plan. When the Bureau of Labour made a projection for 1980 or 1985, he himself was certain that it was going to be revised. It was not that they had estimated wrong or that something had gone wrong with the economy, or that some policy had not been followed. It seemed to him there was no possible sense in which a projection of what might conceivably happen could be, or ought to be, called a plan. Reading Professor Malinvaud's paper, he got the impression, perhaps wrongly, that what he was calling plans were no more than projections. He did not think that the French experience had much relevance to the U.S.A., or even most other European countries.

Professor Malinvaud (France) replying to the discussion said that in his paper he had been aiming rather at raising questions of theory and methodology, and not at describing the present state of the field either in the West or in the East. Apart from that, a survey of long-term planning in a western country would have been beyond his capabilities, not to speak of his intentions. He thought he had been misunderstood at some points, and in particular regarding the aim of examining what economic science could do to improve planning.

One of such misunderstandings was the distinction between a centrally planned and a market economy. He never intended to say that there was no distinction between the two types of economy: such distinctions were obvious, and it was not his purpose to minimise them. He merely wanted to say that a model of a centrally planned economy, in which all decisions would be taken by one decision-maker at the centre was not a correct representation of what has been happening in eastern countries, just as a model of a market economy, such as the Walrasian model, was not a correct reflection of a western economy. To be precise at this point, he would speak only of France, but he was sure that exactly the same thing was happening in the United States. As an example, development of the atomic energy industry in France was decided by the state and not by the market. The question of where to locate a steel plant was also decided by the state. Perhaps France was more state-oriented than the United States but he was sure that an American political scientist describing his own country would have no difficulty in identifying production decisions that had been taken by central authority.

Thus what he meant was simply that our theoretical model of a market economy was inadequate for describing a western economy, and he did not think that participants from the eastern countries would claim that they had a model in which everything was decided from the centre.

A second point at which there seemed to have been some misunderstanding was the question of distribution, which was not adequately discussed in theoretical planning. He had not meant to say that planners did not take into account distribution considerations. On the contrary, it would be impossible to avoid doing so. But in their thinking about planning they very often minimised the importance of this question. They very often presented an objective function which was not very precise on how consumption, for instance, would be allocated among various people, or how the consumption would be directed towards collective satisfaction of needs as against their private satisfaction.

In respect to the place of long-term planning in the West, he did think that there was some place for planning for growth in the West. He did not think the market did that for us. He did not think, for instance, that we had prices for the goods of the future, for the market could not decide on a price for some product in twenty years from the present. This was information that the market did not give. Theoreticians could build models of an ideal market economy in which the market would give this information – he had done it himself – but these models were not realistic models of the operation of a western economy. Thus we had to supplement the market as it is with some-thing that was certainly in the nature of planning, because it involved trans-ferring information between decentralised units and individuals and some centralised body. In the same way, the market did not tell us how much should be allocated to collective consumption or to public goods, and here again we needed something else than the pure market economy model.

Thus he thought we did need a good deal of planning for growth, but perhaps we did not analyse it adequately. He was sure that in the U.S., for instance, people working in big corporations were trying to find out what would be the oil price in twenty years' time from today, and they were trying to do so not by looking at markets where supplies and demands are recorded, but by comparing different pieces of information and examining their consistency. They did some planning even if the state did not take it into account.

In respect to planning for development what he had said was that we in the West needed further development, and that our presently achieved stage was by no means final. Our colleagues from the East also did not go that far and did not claim that they had reached the stage of communism. So we faced some further development, and for this, in the West at least, we needed some conscious device to focus the main issues, and he was prepared to call this device 'planning'. That meant that he favoured a rather wide definition of planning and not its excessive limitation.

To his surprise, he had been quoted as one who had serious doubts about mathematical methods in planning. On the contrary he believed that economic science would progress mainly by using the type of rigorous method that the physical sciences had been using, and everybody knew how much mathematics was used in the physical science. He thought that mathematical methods were useful for planning, though they might not be enough in themselves because some of the main issues that societies face were not to be solved automatically by mathematics, and also because the present stage of mathematical methods might be inadequate.

Speaking of inductive methods, he might not have been fair to his colleagues from eastern Europe who, as he now understood, had large projects for estimating parameters that were being used in long-term planning. What he would guess was that in implementing these projects they would run into many difficulties.

Some doubts had been raised as to the extent of the use of inductive methods in long-term planning. On this question he would agree with Professor Augustinovics. He did not think one needed to rely on econometric models for everything. Some long-term models would include information from other sources than econometrics; nevertheless one could draw the best information from the past by systematic inductive methods.

In discussing an algorithm of decentralised planning, the distinction he made was not between the public and private sectors in respect of ownership of means of production, but between goods that were collectively consumed, whether they were produced privately or publicly, and goods that were privately consumed, again whether they were produced privately or publicly. It seemed to him that the role of prices as indicators was predominant for private goods, whereas the role of quantity indicators was predominant, or should be predominant, for public goods.

Professor Shatalin had suggested that econometric methods might not be adequate for long-range planning when it was desired to change, for instance, the structure of a society in some direction. That might be true, but one did not have to extrapolate the whole growth of the society. What one would do in most cases would be, first, to analyse the problem and distinguish certain specific questions, such as how much would people save in the future under such and such conditions, and whether the people were to decide for themselves whether they were going to consume or to save; if one was planning for a period when one was not intending to change this institution, one might try to find the best information as to how much they were likely to save. Thus even if it was an extrapolation, it was an extrapolation of specific behaviour, and such extrapolations could be combined and used in any appropriate way.

He agreed with most of what had been said by Professor Porwit, and in particular about the use of variants in decision strategy – when the political authority did not propose to make a decision for the whole period but only for the immediate future, and to indicate what was the range of decisions that was still open. One of the limitations of western planning was that people who took planning seriously did not want to commit themselves too deeply, and therefore, instead of saying which decisions were still open, they merely tried to hide the fact that they had not yet made their decision by making the plan imprecise on specific points.

Finally, with regard to preliminary pruning of alternatives, he knew many researchers who were prepared to provide a number of variants and alternatives. Whether one called them planners was a question of terminology.

Part Two

Methods of Planning and Forecasting in the U.S.S.R.

C

3 Growth Models and their Application to Long-term Planning and Forecasting

L. V. Kantorovitch and V. L. Makarov

I. INTRODUCTION

A general picture of growth models, their basic types and features, is given in the paper. Possibilities of their implementation at the stage of preliminary long-term planning are discussed, as well as their application to calculations of a highly aggregated long-term plan, i.e. for a period of about ten years. In the last part of the paper a specific class of models based on input–output information is examined. Results of experimental calculations are given, together with discussion of ways and means of utilisation of such models in the practical work of Gosplan.

II. A GENERAL DESCRIPTION OF GROWTH MODELS

From the very outset growth models were aimed at the elucidation of possibilities of an economic system's growth through time, and in particular at clarifying the dependence of the growth rate on different external and internal conditions and factors influencing economic development. Historically, two directions have emerged and developed independently, models of growth proper and models of optimal economic growth. A well-known example of the first is the Harrod–Domar one-good model, while von Neumann's model is typical of the second.

The basic issue of the one-good model is the elucidation of the dependence of the growth path on the production function parameters, the growth rate of the labour supply and other exogenous factors of production. Von Neumann's problem was to determine the maximum possible rate of growth of an economic system constrained only by its 'technological' or productive capabilities. Much interesting research was done in each of these directions. Thus, the one-good model was extended to cover a number of sectors, and personal consumption and exogenous factors, for example, independent increase in labour resources, were introduced into the von Neumann model. Gradually adequate methods of mathematical description of production and consumption of labour utilisation and of other factors were developed. The two directions have finally merged in recent years, thus allowing discussion of growth models in general.

III. DESCRIPTION OF PRODUCTION

Productive possibilities of an economic system at a certain point of time are mathematically given by a set Z of 'industrial' or 'technological' productive activities. Let (X, V, Y) be a random element of the set Z, in which X and $Y \in R_t^n$ and $V \in R^m$. The vector X may be interpreted as quantities of the factors of production used per unit of time; vector Y – as quantities of the same factors which remain within the system at the end of a time unit; and the vector V indicates input or output, depending on the sign of the corresponding component, of products, services and labour time. It may be said, in a somewhat different terminology, that X and Y are quantitative measures of long-term or capital inputs (goods, services, labour and other resources), while V indicates quantity of current inputs (products, types of labour, services). For mathematical analysis of models it is generally assumed that Z is a convex closed set, sometimes in addition it is assumed to be a cone. We shall not dwell here upon the economic nature of these and other constraints imposed upon the model, for most of them are traditional and have been extensively discussed in the literature.

The generally accepted term of 'productive activity' for vector $(X, V, Y) \in Z$ does not fully reflect the essence of the matter, that is why the word 'productive' is put in inverted commas. In fact, the activities may include transport activities, the reproduction of labour, worker retraining, consumption activities, etc. It will be demonstrated later how these can be included into dynamic input–output models.

The set of productive activities may sometimes be given somewhat differently, in the form of families of point-set mappings:

$$a_v : x \longrightarrow a_v(x)$$

where $x \in R_t^n, v \in R^m$.

$$a_v(x) = \{y | (x, v, y) \in Z\}$$

In particular models of growth the set Z is usually given specifically, that is constructively.

We shall describe here how Z is given in a classic one-good model and in a dynamic input–output system, to the extent that this is essential for the discussion to follow.

In a classic single product model Z is given as:

$$Z = \{Z \in R^6 | Z = (K, \omega, a - K', -W, K', \omega \cdot \rho), 0 \leqslant a \leqslant F(K, W)$$

$$0 \leqslant K' \leqslant a, 0 \leqslant W \leqslant \omega, K, \omega, \rho \geqslant 0\}$$

Here K is the quantity of capital at the beginning of a unit time interval, ω is the corresponding volume of labour resources so that $X = (K, \omega)$. The production function $F(K, W)$ indicates the volume of output depending on the quantity of capital K, and use of labour W, so that $V = (a - K', -W)$. K' is the quantity of capital at the end of the period, $\omega\rho$ the amount of labour at the end of the period, and ρ the exogenous growth rate of the labour force, so that $y = (K', \omega\rho)$.

The simplest dynamic input–output model is determined by the following initial information: square $(n \times n)$ matrices A, B, P, n-dimensional vectors $F(o)$ and W and scalars ω and α, where A is an input–output matrix for current expenditures, B is a matrix of physical depreciation rates per unit of capital, P is a matrix of necessary capital–output ratios, $F(o)$ is a vector of opening capital stocks in industries, W is the vector of labour per unit of growth, ω is the initial labour resources, and α is the rate of growth of the labour force.

The set Z of productive activities of the dynamic input–output system is a convex polyhedral cone generated by the rows of the matrix.

0	P	$I - A$	$-W$	0	P
0	0	$-B$	0	0	I
ω			ω	$\omega\alpha$	

As a rule, negative elements, indicating non-utilisation of some factors are added to the rows of this matrix.

The production sector of this simple model can easily be extended to include the case when there are several methods of production, capital formation, depreciation rates, several types of labour, etc.

IV. DESCRIPTION OF CONSUMPTION

Mathematically, consumption is given by a vector $c = (c_1, \ldots c_m)$ of quantities of personal consumption. The function U which is usually called the utility or preference function is defined over the vectors C.

This function varies greatly between different models. The simplest form of the U-function is

$$U(c) = \max_{\lambda} \{\lambda | \lambda \bar{c} \leqslant c\}$$

where $\bar{c}$ is some basic or standard bundle of consumption.

V. DESCRIPTION OF TECHNOLOGICAL PROGRESS

Technological progress can be taken account of in growth models in various ways.

(1) *Exogenously.* In this case it is assumed that technological change occurs independently of actual production and decisions. More precisely, the set of production possibilities Z is given as a function of time (t) so that in the model, technology is given by a sequence of sets $(Z_t)_{t=0}^{\infty}$. The simplest way of introducing technological progress into a one good model is by multiplying the production function by an exponential function of time, that is $F_t(K,W) = \beta^t F(K,W)$ where $\beta > 1$. Similarly, it may be assumed in the dynamic input–output model that the vector of labour per unit of output ratios, W, is dependent on time, i.e. $W_t = W/\beta^t$ where $\beta > 1$ is the rate of labour productivity growth.

(2) *Endogenous introduction of technological progress* assumes that the evolution of the set of productive possibilities, Z, depends on the output of a certain sector of the economic system, that is, of 'the technological progress industry', which manufactures new 'production' techniques.

It should be noted here that this way of taking account of technical progress reflects reality more adequately and, in particular, allows the resolution of the question of the allocation needed for research and development. However, it is significantly more difficult both for mathematical analysis and for estimation on the basis of existing economic information.

Mathematically the 'technological progress industry' is given as a family of point-set mappings $S = \{s\}$ in which mapping s is given for all possible sets of productive possibilities Z and maps each Z into a set of sets $s(Z)$. From an economic point of view s can be interpreted as a vector $s \in R_t^m$ of quantities of products going to the development of the 'technological progress industry'. If the national economy has productive possibilities Z and s in allocations for science, etc., then the possibilities Z may be enlarged into the set $Z' \in s(Z)$. The mapping s is not one-to-one because, allocated resources can be utilised in different ways which naturally lead to different results.

VI. THE GROWTH OR DEVELOPMENT PATH OF AN ECONOMY

A sequence $(X_t, V_t)_{t=0}^{\infty}$ is called a feasible or (technologically) possible growth path if the following relationships hold for all t

$$(X_t, V_t, X_{t+1}) \in Z_t, \quad V_t \geqslant 0 \tag{1}$$

Condition (1) means that transition from the state X_t into X_{t+1} is 'technologically' possible, while the inequality $V_t \geqslant 0$ is a condition for closedness of the model, that is, it is assumed that no ingredients are introduced into the system from outside.

In the case of the endogenous method of allowing for technological progress, the feasible growth path is a sequence $(X_t V_t S_t)_{t=0}^{\infty}$ which for all t satisfies the following conditions:

$$(X_t, V_t - S_t, X_{t+1}) \in Z_t \tag{2}$$

$$V_t - S_t \geqslant 0, S_t \geqslant 0$$

$$Z_{t+1} \in S_t(Z_t) \tag{3}$$

S_t has a double meaning here. It is a vector of R_t^m in (2) and a one-to-many mapping in (3), where it is defined on convex sets and transforms each such set Z into a set of sets $S_t(Z)$.

Even in the simplest model there are many feasible paths starting from the given initial state X_0. Yet if sequence $(V_t)_{t=0}^{\infty}$ is fixed then both in a one good model and in a dynamic input–output model the growth path $(X_t)_{t=0}^{\infty}$ is uniquely determined because in these models mapping a_v (see above) is one-to-one. This means that production is uniquely given. All variations come from different possible divisions of output between consumption and accumulation (or consumption, accumulation and development of the 'technological progress industries').

In more complex models, e.g. in generalisations of dynamic input–output models to the case of several productive techniques within each industry, the mapping is one-to-many, and variations emerge within the production sector proper. One of the basic problems of the theory of growth models is to distinguish from the set of feasible paths those which reflect reality most adequately. There are several approaches to the solution of this problem. The first rests on absence of variations in the production sector of the model. That is, $a_v(x)$ is a vector and not a set of vectors. To apply this approach to a more general model it is necessary first to specify more closely the mapping a_v. It can be done in different ways, e.g. by directly giving a_v a functional form, as is done in the one-good model and in dynamic input–output models, or by imposing additional constraints upon the range of possible paths, for example, by assuming that the rate of return in all industries should be the same.

So, if there are no variations in the production sector, then, having been given exogenously the trajectory of labour and consumption $(V_t)_{t=0}^\infty, (X_t)_{t=0}^\infty$ is determined uniquely. Several alternative sequences $(V_t)_{t=0}^\infty$ can be examined to find different sequences $(X_t)_{t=0}^\infty$. Thus this approach does include an element of optimisation, though this examination of variants is more characteristic of the methodology of growth models than it is of true optimal models. An example of such an approach for the one-good model can be found in [5] and in subsequent papers by one of the authors.

The second approach is based on formulation and solution of some extremal problem. This approach assumes that some global criteria of optimality is given. Models utilising such criteria are usually called optimal growth models of an economy.

It is easy to see that any model aimed at maximisation of some criterion over the set of feasible trajectories can be reduced to maximisation over a set of trajectories $(V_t)_{t=0}^\infty$ only, without considering trajectories $(X_t)_{t=0}^\infty$. In most models studied in the literature the objective function P defined over trajectories $V = (V_t)_{t=0}^\infty$ takes on the specific form $P(V) = \sum_{t=0}^\infty U_t(V_t)$ where U_t is a function which depends on time and is defined on R^m. Function P is thus given by a sequence of functions $(U_t)_{t=0}^\infty$.

A trajectory $(\bar{X}_t, \bar{V}_t)_{t=0}^\infty$ is called optimal if, of all feasible trajectories starting from the same initial state $\bar{X}_0$, it is on that trajectory that function P reaches its maximum.

It may unfortunately happen that sequence (U_t) will produce $\sum_{t=0}^\infty U_t(V_t) = \infty$, for some paths. In this case optimality is defined in a more complex way. More precisely let $\gamma_t(V) = \sum_{r=0}^t U_r(V_r)$. Trajectory $(\bar{X}_t, \bar{V}_t)_{t=0}^\infty$ is optimal if there is no feasible trajectory $(X_t, V_t)_{t=0}^\infty$, $X_0 = \bar{X}_0$, such that $\gamma_t(V) > \gamma_t(\bar{V})$ starting from some moment in time, t_0. This is a very general definition and trajectories optimal in this sense exist for a broad class of models. The more precise definition of optimality, that is 'trajectory' $(\bar{X}_t, \bar{V}_t)_{t=0}^\infty$ is optimal if for any feasible $(X_t, V_t)_{t=0}^\infty$ there is a moment t_v starting from which $\gamma_t(\bar{V}) \geqslant \gamma_t(V)$ would be unsuitable because trajectories optimal in this sense are very scarce.

There is also the concept of an efficient trajectory which is very useful. Trajectory $(X_t V_t)_{t=0}^\infty$ is efficient if there is no feasible trajectory $(X_t V_t)_{t=0}^\infty X_0 = \bar{X}_0$ and time t_0 so that $(\bar{X}_{t_0} \cdot \gamma_{t_0}(\bar{V})) = \lambda(X_{t_0} \gamma_{t_0}(V))$ with $\lambda < 1$. It can be easily seen that every optimal trajectory is an efficient trajectory. Efficient trajectories have been investigated most. For them there exists a theorem about necessary and sufficient conditions, which is similar to the duality theorem in linear programming (see [6] for details).

The concept of an optimal trajectory based upon an objective function is a constructive approach to the description of an economic system. The term 'welfare economics' is frequently used in the West to refer to models studying optimal states or sequences of optimal states. Models of optimal growth study optimal trajectories of economic development proper, without considering the socio-economic conditions of their realisation.

The clearest conception of optimal growth is to be found in the von Neumann model. The von Neumann problem is to determine the maximum rate of growth which the economic system can support indefinitely on the assumption that the set of productive possibilities Z does not alter over time. As von Neumann initially put it, it was even assumed that all the factors of production, labour and natural resources included, were reproduced within the model, that is, it considered only the technological constraints upon the rate of growth. Later the von Neumann model was generalised in the sense that constraints on the reproduction of labour, the level of consumption, etc., and not only technological constraints, were included in the analysis (see [3]). Yet the main idea remained, and the answer was sought to the question of the maximum possible rate of economic growth under a certain set of constraints. Models of optimal growth as they are now provide an answer to that question in respect of production and technological possibilities, conditions of reproduction, labour resources, limitations of natural resources, and different hypotheses on the development of final consumption allowing for possible changes in tastes. Yet the existing theory takes no account in principle of conditions of socio-economic development, specifically of human motivation, social organisation, etc. That is why, generally speaking, models of optimal growth cannot be classified as models describing some specific – say, the socialist – socio-economic system. Yet it seems obvious that the problem of long-term optimal growth is of greater interest under the socialist mode of production.

In the following sections of this paper it will be shown how models of growth theory can be applied to long-term planning and forecasting under our system of economic management.

VII. CALCULATION OF TURNPIKES ON THE BASIS OF INPUT–OUTPUT DATA

The technique of planning and forecasting provided by growth models can become an essential part of practical planning only if the growth model itself is made consistent with other plans at both industry and aggregate level. This paper will concentrate on growth models proper and these problems will not be discussed further. Models of growth can provide substantial information at the pre-planning stage of calculations when the basic aggregate outlines of a would-be plan are being sought. In this section we discuss in more detail the calculation of a specific type of optimal trajectory, the so-called turnpike.

i. *The concept of the turnpike*

The concept of a turnpike was originally introduced by von Neumann. The essence of it is that a trajectory of economy growth is sought which is dependent only on technological and other 'natural' constraints and is not dependent on constraints caused by the initial state and existing structure of the economy. The turnpike is not just an optimal path. It is doubly optimal for it is derived from a state which is already optimal. More precisely it can be put as follows. An arbitrary optimal trajectory $X(x_0)$ is dependent on the initial state x_0 and is characterised by a certain scalar which is called the growth rate of the path. The turnpike is the optimal trajectory with the highest growth rate.

It has two remarkable features:

(i) For an extremely broad class of models of growth an arbitrary optimal trajectory tends to the turnpike in the course of time independently of the initial conditions (the turnpike theorem).

(ii) It is much easier to calculate the turnpike than an arbitrary optimal trajectory. The concept of the turnpike gives precise meaning to such terms as 'optimal structure of the economy' and 'optimal balance between consumption and accumulation'.

It should be noted that the concept of the turnpike to an important extent depends on the criteria of optimality used, for it rests on the concept of an optimal trajectory. It is sometimes incorrectly thought that the turnpike theorem eliminates the problem of choosing an objective function because the turnpike is the same for a rather broad class of criteria. Yet there are some other no less reasonable criteria which lead to different turnpikes.

Let us consider the simple dynamic input–output model discussed above. It is based on the data of the input–output table:

$$\{A, B, P, W, F(o), \bar{\omega}, \bar{c}\}$$

where A, B, P, W have already been defined. $F(o)$ is a vector of capital stocks in industries at the beginning of the period considered,

$\bar{\omega}$ is the initial labour resources employed in the national economy, and $\bar{c}$ is a vector of final consumption in the base year.

Let X_t be the volume of output and K_t capital investment in industries in year t; let C be volume of final consumption and ω labour resources in year t.

Then the feasible trajectory of the economy's growth, given by $(X_t, K_t, C_t)_{t=0}^{\infty}$ is determined by the relations:

$$X_t \geqslant X_t A + K_t B + C_t \tag{1}$$

$$X_0 P \leqslant F(o) \tag{2}$$

$$X_{t+1} P \leqslant X_t P + K_t \tag{3}$$

$$W X^t \leqslant \omega_t \tag{4}$$

$$C_t \geqslant 0 \quad X_t, K_t \geqslant 0. \tag{5}$$

The optimal trajectory $(\bar{X}_t, \bar{K}_t, \bar{C}_t)_{t=0}^{\infty}$ is the one in which function $\sum_{t=0}^{\infty} \omega_t U(C_t/\omega_t) \mu^{-t}$ reaches its maximum over all the possible trajectories. Here $U(c) = \max \lambda, \; \lambda \in \{\Lambda | \lambda \bar{c} \leqslant C\}$ that is $U(c)$ is the maximum number of baskets of final consumption c which is contained in vector C. The scalar $\mu > 1$ is the discount factor or rate of time preference. The quantity $\sum$ (as above) is the total utility arising from the consumption of a sequence of baskets $(c_t)_{t=0}^{\infty}$ during period $[0, \infty]$ all discounted at the rate μ. In this it is assumed that the total utility derived by consuming the basket C_t is determined by summing individual utilities over the population.

The turnpike which is calculated for this model is an optimal path $(\bar{X}_t \bar{K}_t \bar{C}_t)_{t=0}^{\infty}$ of the type $(\bar{X}_t, \bar{K}_t, \bar{C}_t) = \rho^t(\bar{X}, \bar{K}, \bar{C})$ for all t; consequently, $\bar{X} P$ is taken as $F(o)$ for this trajectory. The scalar ρ is called the rate of growth of the economy for the given turnpike.

Assumptions concerning the sequence of labour resources $(\omega_t)_{t=0}^{\infty}$ and the vector of unit labour requirements $W = (W^{(1)}, \ldots, W^{(n)})$ should be mentioned now. Since the industrial structure remains constant along the turnpike the rate of economic growth ρ is fully determined by the rate of growth of labour (α) and the rate of growth of productivity β.

Precisely, $\rho = \alpha \cdot \beta$. Thus the conditions $\omega_t = \omega_0 a^t$, $W_t = W/\beta^t$ hold along the turnpike formulated above. Because the 'technology' given by the matrices A, B and P does not alter over time all of the growth of the productivity of labour can be expressed as a decrease in unit labour requirements, which is what was done in the last formula.

Thus, in the model discussed technological progress is considered in the simplest exogenous form (as a constant rate of decrease of unit labour requirements irrespective of the actual growth path). Consumption per capita increases at a rate of $\rho/\alpha = \beta$ along the turnpike, that is at the rate of growth of labour productivity. Because the turnpike $(\bar{X}_t, \bar{K}_t, \bar{C}_t)_{t=0}^{\infty}$ is fully determined by the vectors $\bar{X}, \bar{K}, \bar{C}$ and the scalars α and β, the turnpike will subsequently be denoted $[(\bar{X}, \bar{K}, \bar{C}), \alpha, \beta]$.

ii. Calculation of the turnpike

Calculation of the turnpike for the model discussed, as well as for more complex models, is a problem of finding an eigenvector of some point-set mapping, the latter being determined by the solution of a convex programming problem. Let us define the necessary point-set mapping Γ for the model considered. Mapping Γ is defined on non-negative n-dimensional vectors, and its values lie in a subspace R_+^n, $X \in R_+^n$, $\Gamma(X) \in R_+^n$. So, let $\tilde{X} \in R_+^n$. Let us formulate for the given $\tilde{X}$ the following linear programming problem. Maximise λ subject to

$$X \geqslant XA + KB + \lambda\bar{C}$$
$$X(\lambda - \rho.\mu)P + K \geqslant \tilde{X}(\rho - \rho.\mu)P \qquad (6)$$
$$XW \geqslant \omega_0$$

Let the solution be $[X(\tilde{X}), K(\tilde{K}), \lambda(\tilde{X})]$. Then $\Gamma(\tilde{X})$ is the set of all solutions $X(\tilde{X})$ of the problem. In this case, of course, the set $\Gamma(\tilde{X})$ will as a rule consist of a single point.

The turnpike is determined by a fixed point of the mapping Γ. That is, let $\bar{X}$ be such that $\bar{X} \in \Gamma(\bar{X})$ and the solution of the problem (1) with a given $\bar{X}$ be $(\bar{X}, \bar{K}, \bar{\lambda}\,\bar{C})$. This solution is the turnpike corresponding to the particular value assumed for ρ(6). The proof that $(\bar{X}, \bar{K}, \bar{\lambda}\,\bar{C}, \rho)$ is the turnpike is not given here; on this see [7]. Thus, if ρ and μ are given, it becomes possible to determine the turnpike which would correspond to the given rate of economic growth ρ and the given rate of interest μ by the procedure described. Then the question arises what values of ρ and μ lead to a turnpike satisfying reasonable requirements, and how such a path is influenced by alterations in the values of ρ and μ.

Let us consider first dependence of the turnpike on the values of ρ. Let the turnpike corresponding to the given value of ρ be $[X(\rho), K(\rho), \lambda(\rho)\bar{C}]$. It can be shown, first, that $\lambda(\rho)$ decreases as ρ increases. Secondly, there exists some ρ, say ρ max, such that if $\rho > \rho$ max, the problem (6) no longer has a solution. The value ρ max, is the maximum rate of economic growth possible provided that labour resources and final consumption impose no constraints, i.e. there is sufficient labour even when consumption is zero. In other words ρ max is a purely productive (or technological, after Neumann) rate of growth which is inherent in the technology of the model. When $\rho = 1$, i.e. when the rate of growth is zero, the problem of finding the turnpike becomes the problem of maximising consumption in a static input–output system. It is extremely difficult to derive analytically the relationship between ρ and industrial outputs X and investment K, yet it can be shown by a series of simulations.

VIII. CALCULATIONS AND RESULTS

Calculations were carried out on the basis of the 1965 input–output table both at the 18×18 and 5×5 levels of disaggregation. Since the turnpike $[X(\rho), K(\rho), \lambda(\rho)]$ determines only the structure of economy, the results of calculations can be more clearly and conveniently presented as the ratios $X(\rho)/X_0, K(\rho)/K_0, \lambda(\rho)/\lambda_0$, where $X_0, K_0, \lambda_0 = 1$, based on 1965. These results are given in the tables on pages 62–3.

It can easily be seen from Table 3.1 that the relative outputs on the turnpike are closest to the existing state of economy at $\rho - 1 = 0.093$; correspondingly, shadow prices are closest to actual prices at $\mu = 1.1$. It is also noticeable that the value $\rho - 1 = 0.093$ is the solution of equation $\lambda(\rho) = 1$. Because the function, $\lambda(\rho)$ falls as ρ increases the value $\rho - 1 = 0.093$, is the maximum rate of economic growth along the turnpike for which final consumption at the starting point is no less than its actual level. For larger values of ρ, final consumption will eventually exceed consumption on the turnpike with $\rho = 1.093$, yet initial consumption will be lower. The value $\rho = 1.093$ is remarkable in yet another respect. If instead of a model with labour given exogenously, we analyse a closed model in which labour is reproduced similarly to materials by means of inputs of products equal to final consumption, then the maximum technologically possible growth rate (i.e. von Neumann's) will be just $\rho = 1.093$. Calculations demonstrate also that each component of the vectors $X(\rho)$ and $K(\rho)$ either increases or decreases monotonically with ρ. Industries can be classified on this basis, and this can be thought of as a more precise classification of the standard A and B type (group A – producer goods industries; group B – consumer goods industries).

The systematic tendency of the investment ratios on the turnpike to fall below 1 is due to the assumption that the period of capital gestation is the same for all industries and is equal to one year.

Thus the turnpike indicates the best structure of economy, the optimal balance of outputs between different industries for the system to grow at the given rate ρ. Solving the inverse problem, i.e. finding values for ρ and μ which bring the existing structure of the

TABLE 3.1

Industries	Relative Outputs for Different ρ's						
	$\rho = 1.08$	$\rho = 1.09$	$\rho = 1.093$	$\rho = 1.095$	$\rho = 1.10$	$\rho = 1.11$	$\rho = 1.12$
1. Electricity	99·33	98·86	100·01	100·12	100·39	100·93	101·50
2. Ferrous metals	95·30	98·86	99·92	100·65	102·47	106·04	109·90
3. Non-ferrous metals	95·30	99·06	100·19	100·96	102·88	106·71	110·74
4. Other forms of energy	98·38	99·58	99·94	100·18	100·79	101·98	103·29
5. Capital goods assembly	96·08	99·11	100·02	100·64	102·18	105·24	108·50
6. Finished machines and equipment	92·73	98·67	100·84	102·12	105·30	111·76	118·35
7. Chemicals	98·25	99·63	100·04	100·32	101·02	102·42	103·90
8. Timber products	98·09	99·33	99·70	99·95	100·58	101·77	103·15
9. Building materials	94·84	98·09	99·08	99·75	101·40	104·53	108·21
10. Glass and porcelain	98·03	99·32	99·71	99·97	100·62	101·87	103·32
11. Clothing and footwear	102·36	100·66	100·14	99·79	98·93	97·24	95·37
12. Food manufacturing	102·97	100·84	100·19	99·76	98·67	96·56	94·22
13. Other manufactures	102·52	100·71	100·16	99·79	98·87	97·07	95·08
14. Construction	94·67	98·01	99·02	99·69	101·40	104·58	108·37
15. Agriculture	102·88	100·81	100·18	99·77	98·71	96·66	94·39
16. Transport and communication	97·95	99·42	99·86	100·16	100·91	102·36	103·98
17. Distribution	100·05	100·00	99·99	99·98	99·96	99·91	99·86
18. Other industries n.e.s.	101·02	100·31	100·09	99·95	99·59	98·89	98·11
19. Final consumption	101·02	100·88	100·20	99·75	98·62	96·40	93·95
20. Labour	100·00	100·00	100·00	100·00	100·00	100·00	100·00

TABLE 3.2

Industries	Relative Volumes of Capital Investment for Different ρ's						
	$\rho = 1.08$	$\rho = 1.09$	$\rho = 1.093$	$\rho = 1.095$	$\rho = 1.10$	$\rho = 1.11$	$\rho = 1.12$
1. Electricity	70·19	79·38	82·16	84·02	88·68	98·07	107·58
2. Ferrous metals	54·63	63·76	66·60	68·53	73·43	83·60	94·51
3. Non-ferrous metals	67·37	78·78	82·33	84·75	90·90	103·71	117·41
4. Other forms of energy	65·04	74·06	76·81	78·65	83·30	92·71	102·43
5. Capital goods assembly	85·35	99·04	103·28	106·15	113·45	128·53	144·57
6. Finished machinery and equipment	82·68	99·28	104·52	108·13	117·16	137·03	158·30
7. Chemicals	49·11	56·03	58·13	59·55	63·12	70·40	77·90
8. Timber products	91·09	103·77	107·63	110·22	116·75	129·95	143·69
9. Building materials	79·62	92·65	96·70	99·44	106·42	120·66	136·28
10. Glass and porcelain	81·59	92·99	96·47	98·80	104·69	116·58	129·99
11. Clothing and footwear	110·48	122·22	125·65	127·90	133·46	144·30	154·39
12. Food manufacturing	138·72	152·83	156·91	159·59	166·16	178·86	190·39
13. Other manufactures	120·51	133·18	136·88	139·30	145·28	156·90	167·66
14. Construction	87·94	102·40	106·92	109·97	117·73	133·58	150·99
15. Agriculture	97·73	107·73	110·64	112·54	117·21	126·25	134·49
16. Transport and communication	95·24	108·74	112·87	115·64	122·64	136·85	151·65
17. Distribution	156·81	176·32	182·16	186·10	195·82	215·28	234·75
18. Other industries n.e.s.	138·73	154·98	159·80	163·00	170·96	186·74	202·11

TABLE 3.3

Industries	Shadow Prices of Output for Different ρ's						
	$\rho = 1.08$	$\rho = 1.09$	$\rho = 1.093$	$\rho = 1.095$	$\rho = 1.10$	$\rho = 1.11$	$\rho = 1.12$
1. Electricity	98·43	100·50	101·73	102·56	104·64	107·62	113·13
2. Ferrous metals	114·94	117·46	118·22	118·73	120·02	122·24	125·29
3. Non-ferrous metals	95·16	97·36	98·02	98·47	99·59	101·42	104·18
4. Other forms of energy	92·76	94·88	95·52	95·95	97·03	98·81	101·46
5. Capital goods assembly	103·06	104·33	104·71	104·98	105·62	106·90	108·27
6. Finished machinery and equipment	103·08	104·35	104·73	104·99	105·64	106·93	108·29
7. Chemicals	97·24	99·28	99·90	100·32	101·36	103·15	105·63
8. Timber products	116·06	117·14	117·47	117·69	118·24	119·48	120·50
9. Building materials	128·94	131·16	131·84	132·29	133·43	135·51	138·09
10. Glass and porcelain	98·72	99·61	99·88	100·06	100·51	101·52	102·37
11. Clothing and footwear	69·88	69·69	69·64	69·60	69·50	69·63	69·11
12. Food manufacturing	90·43	90·36	90·34	90·33	90·29	90·81	90·14
13. Other manufactures	69·76	69·84	69·87	69·89	69·93	70·22	70·11
14. Construction	109·21	109·87	110·07	110·21	110·54	107·60	111·93
15. Agriculture	167·49	166·56	166·28	166·09	166·61	165·56	163·66
16. Transport and communication	149·41	152·48	153·41	154·03	155·60	158·67	162·05
17. Distribution	196·63	192·99	191·89	191·15	189·29	187·45	181·69
18. Other industries n.e.s.	81·70	81·59	81·56	81·53	81·48	81·64	81·23
19. Final consumption	100·00	100·00	100·00	100·00	100·00	100·00	100·00
20. Labour	177·99	174·15	172·99	172·20	170·24	168·18	162·19

TABLE 3.4

Industries	Shadow Prices of Output for $\rho = 1.093$ and Different Values of μ (1965 = 100)		
	$\mu = 1.10$	$\mu = 1.11$	$\mu = 1.14$
1. Electricity	148·99	156·74	171·11
2. Ferrous metals	148·14	152·56	163·47
3. Non-ferrous metals	123·82	127·81	137·23
4. Other forms of energy	120·46	124·29	133·39
5. Capital goods assembly	119·90	121·99	127·46
6. Finished machinery and equipment	199·04	122·03	127·51
7. Chemicals	124·11	127·72	136·54
8. Timber products	130·59	132·23	136·93
9. Building materials	158·42	161·44	171·88
10. Glass and porcelain	110·62	111·97	115·82
11. Clothing and footwear	67·66	67·08	66·25
12. Food manufacturing	89·87	89·42	89·11
13. Other manufactures	71·01	70·99	71·31
14. Construction	114·19	118·98	122·03
15. Agriculture	155·85	153·56	149·46
16. Transport and communication	190·86	195·85	209·49
17. Distribution	149·89	142·38	126·55
18. Other industries n.e.s.	80·83	79·92	79·35
19. Final consumption	100·00	100·00	100·00
20. Labour	128·47	120·59	103·85

economy closest to a turnpike, it can be deduced from the calculations that the structure of economy as it existed in 1965 corresponded most closely to the 9·3 per cent rate of growth.

As it is clear from the formulation of the problem (1), the turnpike depends on all the information in the input–output matrix as well as on the utility function U and on the values of α, β and $\mu(\rho = \alpha . \beta)$. A series of alternative calculations can be easily carried out for changes in these structural parameters. Specifically, variants of the input–output matrix can be considered. The utility function U can also be made more sophisticated, e.g. if several weighted vectors of consumption are introduced instead of the one basic consumption vector $\bar{C}$.

A principal limitation of the problem as formulated is the exogenous nature of technical progress. Alterations in input–output coefficients are either given exogenously or result from alterations in the relative utilisation of different techniques. In the latter case the aggregate coefficients are variables; however, the techniques themselves are given irrespective of resources devoted to fostering technical progress. At present the Institute of Mathematics of the Siberian Branch of the Academy of Sciences is working on this problem with technical progress being regarded as endogenous.

Our general conclusions are as follows:

At present there are theoretical models, algorithms and computer programmes available for practical calculations of turnpikes on the basis of input–output data allowing for variations in coefficients and for future technical change. Knowledge of the turnpike can be used as a means of planning orientation, for it indicates the optimal structure of economy under certain assumptions. A turnpike also determines the criteria of optimality in highly aggregated models for optimal planning, which are the top level of a general system of models of optimal planning. For example, either costs necessary for the transition from the existing state of economy to the turnpike, or the time necessary to reach it, may be used as such criteria. Such criteria of optimality guarantee the optimal plan from unwanted effects at the end of planning horizon or from miscalculations in the period after its end.

IX. THE INVERSE PROBLEM OF GROWTH MODELS

As has already been mentioned, the basic problem of growth models is the finding of a growth path $(X_t C_t)_{t=0}^{\infty}$ given a sequence $(Z_t)_{t=0}^{\infty}$ of production-possibilities sets (technical progress is exogenous). Actually, of course, the set Z_0 is the only one reliably given; as for the rest, only more or less reliable forecasts are available. Besides, many of the parameters determining the sets Z_t are controllable and may be consciously manipulated to achieve desirable goals. Finally, it is essential in practical planning that relationships between the parameters should be known independently of whether they are given or are being sought in a specific problem.

For all these reasons an inverse problem naturally emerges in growth models when the initial set of production methods Z_0 is given as is a desired growth path, and what is wanted is a sequence $(Z_t)_{t=1}^{\infty}$ belonging to some class of possible sequences which can make possible the given trajectory $(X_t C_t)_{t=0}^{\infty}$.

Let us consider the precise formulation of the inverse problem in the growth model taking the example of the dynamic input–output system. Let $\{A_0, B_0, P_0, W_0, F(0)\}$ and the desired growth path $\{X_t K_t C_t W_t\}_{t=0}^{\infty}$ be given. It is required to find a sequence $M = \{A_t, B_t, P_t, W_t\}_{t=1}^{\infty}$ such that the relationships (1)–(5) hold and $M \varepsilon . \mathbin{/\mkern-4mu/}$ where $. \mathbin{/\mkern-4mu/}$ is the set of feasible sequences of input–output coefficients. This set can vary with the specific formulation of the problem. For example, $M \in . \mathbin{/\mkern-4mu/}$ if any coefficient at a moment t differs from a corresponding coefficient at a moment $t + 1$ by not more than some $\varepsilon > 0$. This inverse problem of dynamic input–output analysis can be constructively solved for a very broad class of sets $. \mathbin{/\mkern-4mu/}$. The idea of the solution is that all the input–output coefficients for period t can be found using a system of linear equations and inequalities defined by parameters

$$(A_{t-1}, B_{t-1}, P_{t-1}, W_{t-1}, C_t, X_{t-1} K_{t-1}, X_t, K_t).$$

Thus, the sequence of input–output matrices can be constructed recursively on the basis of a given desired growth path.

This inverse problem of dynamic input–output analysis lends itself to different extremal formulations depending on the specific aims of planning and economic analysis. This is connected with the fact that the unknown input–output coefficients which permit the given growth path are not uniquely determined, hence the possibility of posing extreme problems. In the example given, either a minimal ε determing the set $. \mathbin{/\mkern-4mu/}$ can be found, or some coefficients may be fixed while the extremal problem can be posed for the others, or alternatively the minimum number of coefficients which must change for the realisation of the given path can be found.

REFERENCES

[1] R. Allen, *Matematicheskaya economia* [Mathematical economics] (Moscow, 1963).

[2] D. Gale, 'Zamknutaya lineinaya model proizvodestva' [The closed linear model of production], in *Lineiniye neravenstva i smezhniye voprosi* [Linear inequalities and related questions] (Moscow, 1959).

[3] M. Morishima, *Ravnovesiye, ustoichivost, rost* [Equilibrium stability, growth] (Moscow, 1972).

[4] V. L. Makarov, 'Modeli optimalnogo rosta economiky' [Models of optimal economic growth], in *Ekonomika i matematicheskie metodi*, no. 4 (1969).

[5] L. V. Kantorovitch and L. I. Gorkov, *Doklady akademii nauk SSSR* (1959).

[6] V. L. Makarov and A. M. Rubinov, 'Superlineiniye tochechno-mnozhestvenniye otobrajeniya: modeli ekonomicheskoi dinamiky' [Super-linear point-set mappings: models of economic dynamics], in *Uspekhi matematicheskih nauk*, no. 5 (1970).

[7] V. L. Makarov, 'Suchestvovanie magistrali v modeli s diskontom' [The existence of a turnpike in a model with interest], in *Optimizatsiya*, no. 2 (19) (1971).

Discussion of the Paper by
Professors Kantorovitch and Makarov

Professor Malinvaud (France) in introducing the discussion said that the authors were principally concerned in improving pre-planning calculations, that was to say in the preliminary work for long-term planning, to provide background for more detailed analytical work. They were proposing something that would be better than the present not wholly satisfactory practice. The present practice was that, in order to plan for fifteen to twenty years ahead, one forecasted for a target year, whereas it was useful, and indeed necessary, to know what would happen both before and after the target year. It seemed at first sight that to conduct such an exercise instead of concentrating on a target year was far more difficult. Yet if approached systematically the difficulty could be overcome.

The formulation of the model was very general and could be made to fit any particular case. A supplement to the formulation was a method of integrating into the analysis the activity of generating technical progress. It was a very interesting extension, though in its present form it was not yet specific and apparently had not been applied in practice.

Two methods were then suggested for the selection of a growth path compatible with the existing system of production possibilities. One method was a model of growth permitting just one visible path. It was rightly pointed out that such a model implicitly possessed some kind of selection device, and the optimisation problem was assumed implicitly to be solved. A second method was to build an optimal growth model with explicit criteria of optimality. The use of such a model should be understood as a constructive device to get a better description of the actual economic system.

The authors went on to suggest that in order to achieve the long-term planning task the competitional problem could be simplified without any real loss in understanding. The solution was to consider the 'main trajectory', or turnpike, calculation of which was not very difficult. The calculational algorithm was considered in detail, with experimental results covering eighteen industries ranged in two groups, one group producing the means of production and being important if the rate of growth was high, the other group manufacturing consumer goods and becoming more important if growth rate was low.

Somewhat similar work had been done in Japan by Professor Tsukui who had tried to use the 'main trajectory' idea to make pre-planning calculations, and the authors were concerned very much with the same subject. Professor Malinvaud asked whether Professor Kantorovitch or Professor Makarov would comment on the work of Professor Tsukui?

His second question concerned the assumption that labour productivity would rise at the same rate in all industries. That was a rather unrealistic hypothesis, though to integrate different rates would be very difficult. What would be Professors Kantorovitch and Makarov's solution of this problem?

In regard to calculations of shadow prices, or 'objective evaluation co-efficients', these calculations did not go as far as one would like them to go. In particular they did not provide what in the West were known as discount rates and which were used to compare different projects where the cost of capital depreciation had to be taken into account. The prices presented in the paper were computed to take account of the rate of growth and the rate of discounting future utilities, the latter being defined in a special way by the authors and seeming to provide precisely the rate of discount one would like to have. But that meant that the rate was not calculated but assumed to be given. The reason was simply that, because we were working with a dynamic input–output model, we had just one technique of production in each industry. What would be very interesting for this type of pre-planning calculation would be to determine endogenously the order of magnitude of the rate of discount, on the basis of which evaluation of projects should be made. Had the authors tried to make computational experiments of this kind that would permit an objective evaluation of the discount rate?

Professor Moiseev (U.S.S.R.) said that the Computing Centre of the Academy of Sciences of the U.S.S.R. had for several years been conducting research on the use of a system of models in complex planning. They distinguished three stages in the process of management of the economy: first, a forecast, which represented specially processed information on the possible alternatives in the future aimed at formulation of goals; second, a programme of development which was a set of objectives based on a clear understanding of the possibility of achieving them; third, a plan proper for the allocation of resources and the distribution of responsibilities for the carrying out of the programme. Thus, a forecast, a programme and a plan were three different documents made for three different purposes, and consequently having different degrees of authority and detail.

The whole work was rooted in the assumption of manageability. That is a forecast should start by discovering the extent of the manipulable factors, while the final plan was a synthesis of these factors. If the manipulable factors were managed in one way, the result would be different than if they were managed in another.

In contrast to a plan, a forecast produced not just one single trajectory for a given behaviour, but a cone of possible trajectories, which was to be explained by the existence of multitudes of alternative outcomes owing to the uncertainty of the long-term forecast.

There were at present two possible ways of forecasting. One was expert evaluation, which had been substantially developed in the past decade and seemed likely to maintain its importance, though it was not universally applicable.

The second method was direct modelling and mathematical analysis of models. This method was also not universal, for the analysis of high-dimension optimisation models took astronomical quantities of computation time. They were trying to combine these two classical methods in one synthetic approach which they called an emittance system. What was understood by this term was a system of different models: economic models, models of growth, demographic models, as well as a whole series of special forecasting models. A system might include ecological models if it was to be used for agricultural or fishery forecasts, models of social development, and other such models. Systems of models reproduced the functioning and possible paths of development of any system or organism under consideration. Such modelling included a group of experts operating with every possible facility, as well as a special operation system, special mathematical apparati, and facilities for models managing the system. It was obvious that such a system demanded the close co-operation of economists, sociologists, mathematicians and experts in many other fields. Yet, once established, the system became a kind of permanent tool of research.

Emittance systems implied possibilities of their continuous development. Any forecast was a compromise between different desires to optimise criteria designed to establish an order of possible outcomes corresponding to the structure of actions undertaken. The task of experts was simply to work out the structure of possible actions: the structure of capital investments, the distribution of production, legal norms of economic activities, and so on. Experts might employ their own mathematical models – models of growth or others – to enable them to eliminate clearly unpromising variants of action.

This was an idealised presentation of a new technology of planning. Nevertheless such systems were now being developed for the evaluation of the perspectives for various regions, such as the Western Siberian oil and gas province. This was just a preliminary account of what they were doing; more detailed and specific reports would be presented to the forthcoming Soviet–American seminar on emittance systems. He believed that some work done by Professor Forst at M.I.T. was somewhat analogous to the work done in their center, but there was some difference, particularly in the subject matter and structure of the models used.

Professor Szepesi (Hungary) said that experiment with a dynamic input–output growth model had revealed some interesting features concerning the stability of this model. One of them was that if one changed just one element of the input structure the change in the dynamic path was quite smooth, but once one had left the equilibrium path, the return to the turnpike was very unstable and hardly controllable. This was to be explained by the fact that the growth rate belonging to the turnpike represented the smallest characteristic root of the fundamental matrix related to the differential equation system in their model. Thus, if they started from a non-equilibrium beginning it was very difficult to shift the economy to the main path, which formed a partial solution of the system belonging to the least characteristic route. Thus control could be achieved only with great difficulty.

Professor von Weizsäcker (F.R.G.) pointed out that figures in Table 3.3 seemed to suggest that changes had occurred in the shadow prices in certain industries. For example, transportation and communications (item 16) varied from 149·49 to 162·62, and there were some even bigger changes. If the non-substitution theorem – that the best technique chosen was independent of the structure of demand – held, these shadow prices should not change with the rate of growth. What could be a heuristic explanation of these changes in shadow prices?

Professor Makarov (U.S.S.R.), speaking as one of the two authors of the paper, said that the technique discussed in the paper had been designed to solve just one and only one problem: what could be the maximum possible rates of economic growth if account was taken only of natural or technological constraints but not social constraints. That was why models of the type described could be used only for very preliminary evaluation of desired rates of growth from a technological point of view.

Regarding the work of Professor Tsukui, the difference between his approach and the one presented here was that, as he understood, Professor Tsukui was primarily concerned with finding the maximum rate of growth within the 'main trajectory'. To do this, it was necessary to introduce certain additional, and in his own opinion rather artificial, equations into a model, such as financial balance of demand and supply in monetary terms. As a result the model became closed, and the rates of growth could be determined as a characteristic root of an equation or a matrix.

In their own study they were trying not to introduce additional closing equations but to find relationships between the 'main trajectory', the rate of growth and the rate of discount. Similar research was being done in the U.S.S.R. by Professor Movshovitch at the Central Economic–Mathematical Institute.

The same rate of growth of labour productivity in all industries had been introduced purely for the sake of simpler computation. They had a method of computing a 'main trajectory' for the case of different assumed rates of labour productivity growth in all the industries covered, but that method involved computation of a vast operation with a multitude of dimensions, for each additional coefficient introduced an additional equation. In the same way one could study the dependence of the 'main trajectory' on changes of coefficients of material and of capital available, but that involved a fantastic increase in the number of dimensions of the model. There was a simpler method of endogenous consideration of technological progress when certain relationships between expenditures on technological progress and changes in technological coefficients were introduced.

As regards the rate of effectiveness of capital investment and why it was taken as given, he frankly had no clear idea. He thought there was a kind of functional relationship between a rate of discount and the general criterion of optimality, and by taking the latter as given exogenously they could establish a discount rate. But he did not think that the discount rate could be forecasted by a purely optimal model, because in reality the general criterion of optimality was determined as the result of a conflict of opposing interests. Thus other approaches would need to be tried, including one modelling the conflict of interests.

He did not quite understand Professor von Weizsäcker's question, but formally there was a rather simple answer: that a 1 per cent change in the rate of growth would be followed by a change in final consumption by about 1 per cent or slightly more. The reason for shadow prices changing with the rate of growth, was that the equations which are sources of the evaluation system include 'ρ' as a coefficient, and the price of a product is determined as a sum of prices of materials plus labour price plus capital price multiplied by 'ρ'. Thus shadow prices directly depend on 'ρ'.

Professor Kantorovitch (U.S.S.R.), summing up the discussion, said that the highly sophisticated character of the economic system and the wide diversity of tasks to be solved required a wide variety of methods and models. He was not worried by the fact that so many had been suggested, but all these models needed to be tested and verified before being put to use. More than two centuries of experience in the natural sciences had shown that sometimes one had to reject models which were most complete and precise in their design, in favour of a model which promised practical results even with some loss of perfection. They, in their model, had also permitted some deviations from perfection in order to get practical results. For example, the same rate of progress had been taken for all the industries, though of course it depended on such things as the volume of investment made in the particular industry. They had introduced this factor in some of their other models, however.

When making a short-term plan, more precise methods than to compile a long-term one had often to be used. The methods employed might be inter-sector balances or dynamic or linear models. Yet even for a short period it was very important to keep in mind the state of the system beyond the immediate planning horizon, for how far a system would be able to maintain continuous growth was in part an outcome of the model. It was very difficult and debatable how this characteristic of the final state of the system could best be introduced into the objectives of a plan. More effective was the approach by which the development of the economy or one aspect of it beyond the planned horizon was compared with that during the planned period. The limited accuracy of such a method did not allow it to be used for the plan proper; but it suited conditions beyond the plan, where infor-mation was uncertain and the needs for accuracy were less urgent, since the subsequent plan itself could easily be changed if necessary.

There were different opinions regarding norms of effectiveness or rates of discount. The views of the two authors of the paper were not absolutely identical. Determination of these coefficients on the basis of endogenous evaluation of the model itself was technically possible, and he had done it for a one-product model of the national economy. That was also possible with linear models. These approaches had their own advantages and disad-vantages. In particular, they tended to underestimate some discount rates.

4 An Optimal Approach in Long-range Planning

A. Aganbegyan

I. THE PROBLEMS AND DIFFICULTIES OF LONG-RUN PLANNING AND FORECASTING

In my view the period of long-run planning should be restricted to fifteen to twenty years and that of long-run forecasting to twenty to thirty years. We need to look into such a far-off future for well-grounded decisions for the most important and fundamental problems of scientific-technological and socio-economic development. It usually takes ten years to develop and test in their essentials new systems of technique (e.g. supersonic civil aviation); serial production and introduction require another five years. Besides there exists the necessity to try out the consequences of using this new technique at least in its most general form, and thus the time-horizon to consider the problem should be extended by five to ten years more.

Other examples of large-scale decisions that require a long-range approach are the approval of plans for the development of cities or particular regions (usually they are designed for twenty years), decision-making for the exploitation of major natural resources and for building new territory-production complexes and new large transport systems (e.g. the Baikal–Amur railway main line).

But to make such large-scale decisions wisely (decisions that often involve thousands of million roubles of capital investment, the recruitment of scores and hundreds of thousands of workers, and the essential reconstruction of industry and of territory structure of production) it is necessary to have working estimates of the scientific-technological and economic development of the country over a long period of time, because resources to bring into existence such schemes are limited, while the schemes themselves are closely interconnected. Practical experience has shown that separate decisions for a long-run perspective that are not co-ordinated into one long-run plan often fail because of their general imbalance in material inputs. Thus, the necessity for detailed long-run planning is obvious.

But in drawing up a long-run forecast and plan we come across serious difficulties, specific to this kind of work.

First, the range of freedom in choosing between alternative economic decisions widens greatly with the prolongation of the planning period. This range of freedom may be presented as a cone, the apex of which stands for the present moment. It is difficult to choose the optimal trajectory in a vast range of freedoms and of undefined and vague constraints for future periods.

Secondly, the difficulty is redoubled by the fact that the further we move away from the present the greater the effects of the factor of uncertainty in future periods. For example, fifteen years ago there were no apparent signs of oil and gas in the West Siberian Plain; there was even discussion of the necessity to curtail prospecting there for oil and gas. At that time the deficit of energy in the European part of the country was intended to be made up by building electric transmission lines from the Angara–Yenisey cascade of hydro-electric power stations and from the coal electric power stations of the Kansk–Atchinsk basin in East Siberia. During the past fifteen years extremely rich oil-gas deposits have been discovered in the West Siberian Plain. There has been developed a large-scale output of gas and oil there. Already during the years of the Ninth Five-Year Plan the greater part of the increase of oil output has been derived from West Siberia, and in future, during the Tenth Five-Year Plan, by far the greatest part of natural gas output is likely to be obtained from the West Siberian deposits. For the coming fifteen to twenty years there is a high probability of finding big oil and gas deposits of high yield in the Krasnoyarsk territory and the Irkutsk region. If the predictions of the geologists are confirmed, the economic structure of these regions will be fundamentally changed.

Third, large-scale economic developments such as are considered in long-run plans have, in most cases, a complicated interconnection with other problems and these interrelations have, of course, to be taken into account. Let us take, for example, such a project as the Volzhsky automobile works in the city of Tolyatty that is to produce cars of the 'Zhiguly' ('Lada') type. If we take the value of the construction of this complex as roughly equal to 1 thousand million roubles, then according to calculations 5 thousand million roubles more will have to have been invested in the construction of associated production (metallurgy, rubber industry, glass industry and chemical industry, etc.) in order to provide for the production of 660,000 cars. Moreover, a much bigger sum is necessary to provide service and repair for the increased number of cars, to provide for the building of garages, parking places, the widening of highways, and so on. Each of these developments connected with the building of V.A.S. exerts influence of a very intricate kind upon the development of the corresponding industries and infrastructures, and in a number of cases it has led also to various social and other consequences.

Fourth, a long-run plan, by comparison with a short-run plan or even a medium-run plan, has a wider objective. If the problem of building a new shop at a metallurgy plant or its partial reconstruction (a medium-run plan) is being considered, then calculations of its economic efficiency will be the crucial factor in choosing the best solution. But if we are examining the creation of a completely new metallurgy base – i.e. a complex of metallurgy enterprises – then a merely economic approach is not enough. The creation of a new metallurgical complex will have various long-run consequences.

Experience shows that the building of a new metallurgy works in the perspective of twenty years usually results in creating a new city with a population of 400,000–600,000 people (for example, in Magnitogorsk and Novokuznetsk the building of the metallurgy works was begun in an empty space). The metallurgical works attract like a magnet the machine-building industry, which is metal-consuming; they attract petro-chemical and a number of other industries. The presence of a great number of building workers and a well-developed building industry in the region, arising as a result of the creation of the metallurgical complex, is an additional factor that favours a decision to allocate other new enterprises in this region, and sometimes these enterprises are not connected directly with the metallurgical production. In these conditions the specific expenditures proper to the construction of the metallurgical production are not the final determining factor in deciding the problem where to allocate a new metallurgical base. For instance, in pre-war years, at the time of constructing the Kuznetsk metallurgical works, the costs of building the new metallurgical works in the Ukraine might have been substantially lower. Moreover there was a developed metallurgy in the Ukraine and there were skilled personnel both of building and metallurgy. Yet the strategic decision to build the first metallurgical base in Siberia completely justified itself, as has been shown by historical experience. The Kuznetsk group of enterprises proved to be the advanced post for the industrial development of the vast Kuzbass region. It exerted a great influence upon the development of the rich natural resources of Siberia; it influenced railway building since it produced rails; it influenced the development of machine-building, the chemical and other industries. The existence of the Kuznetsk group of enterprises appeared to be the main factor in determining the allocation of a new giant of metallurgy – the West Siberian plant – in immediate proximity to the Kuznetsk group of enterprises.

At present, the problem of the creation of a second metallurgical base in Siberia is being discussed. From the merely economic standpoint, new metallurgical works are best allocated to Barnaul. Another rival place to allocate the metallurgical works, which is much more expensive, is Taishet in the Irkutsk region of East Siberia. But if we take into account the longer-term consequences, then I believe that the metallurgical works in Taishet should be given preference. The creation of a metallurgical base in the region of the Eastern Siberia will exert a powerful influence upon the development of the immensely rich natural resources of this region and accelerate its economic development.

Thus, in long-run planning it is necessary to take into account social and strategic factors, additional to calculations of the direct measurable economic efficiency, to a greater extent than in short-run and medium-run planning.

Special requirements should also be incorporated in calculations of economic efficiency. It is necessary to take into account and compare the complete results of the undertaking of this or that enterprise with the complete expenditure necessary for this purpose. For instance, if we are considering the exploitation of big new mineral deposits, the calculations of the final result assume a well-based forecast of the prospective outcome of the possible use of these resources in future, a forecast of possible trends of prices in the world market for this kind of resource, and so on. The complete expenditures should embrace the expenditures not only for this industry but also for the co-operating industries as well. This is difficult, especially when one is concerned with attributing all the expenses of creating infrastructure.

The creation of the infrastructure is to a large extent a region-forming factor. The existence of a well-developed infrastructure in a region makes the allocation of new enterprises essentially cheaper in this region, though it is difficult to determine beforehand what kind of enterprises they will be. Thus it is not reasonable to attribute all expenses for the infrastructure or to attribute the overwhelming part of the expenses to those projects which are first to be built in the region. It is a great pity, but this is very often what is done. For instance, to develop the southern coal and iron ore deposits of Yakutia it is necessary to build a railway that will connect south Yakutia with the Trans-Siberia main line. This branch is sure to be the beginning of a long transport route which will be continued up to the Aldan and then up to Yakutsk and further. In the perspective of the future the share of the Yakutsk coal and iron ores is probably comparatively small from the standpoint of justifying the need for this transport route. The existence of this route will bring a new life into these vast territories, rich in deposits of various natural resources. Thus it is scarcely reasonable to attribute the greater part of the cost of this railway line to the coal and iron ore industry of Yakutia, and thus make the economic calculations of exploiting the coal and iron ore deposits markedly less favourable.

The necessity to take into account qualitative, and particularly social and strategic factors in choosing the best solution unquestionably entails serious difficulties for optimisation in long-run planning. The usual optimisation problem assumes the existence of a quantitatively defined objective function (it is usually expressed by economic efficiency indexes). A simple setting of the similar optimisation problems for the long-run perspective is not in itself enough. It is necessary to find new methods and new approaches to the choice of the optimal version in economic decision-making.

Moreover, when we deal with a comparatively short period of time it is possible to separate quite distinctly the objective from the means to attain it; it is possible to take into account complicated dialectic interrelations of the objective and the means to the fullest extent – for instance, interrelations between definite demands and the output of production to meet this demand. In short-run and medium-run planning, with the period of time limited, this or that solution of the system of production does not greatly influence the structure and level of demand that has to be satisfied. But for long-run planning the determination of the objective entirely without respect for the capacity for production is absolutely meaningless. A socio-economic system is a system for the mutual adaptation of the objective and the means to achieve it. A successful achievement of the objective in a long-run perspective requires change of the existing objective and the setting of new objectives. Success in developing production generates new demands and modifies the objective. In normal optimisation problems of such a kind there is ordinarily no interrelation of objectives and means.

That is why it is necessary to be extremely cautious about extension to a long-run period of those economic and mathematical models and methods which are applied and have proved a success in medium-run planning.

There is one further complicating factor. The majority of economico-mathematical models are designed to obtain firmly based results only within a definite period of time-horizon. Beyond this period, models usually begin to behave in a strange way; for example, they show sharply increasing or decreasing rates. This especially refers to various dynamic inter-industry models, to macro-models designed on a regression base, and the like.

Thus, there is a specific setting of the problem of long-run planning and forecasting; serious difficulties that one encounters in identifying the best solutions of long-range development entail the necessity of new approaches to economic decision-making in a long-run perspective.

II. SITUATION ANALYSIS FOR THE CHOICE OF AN OPTIMAL PATH OF ECONOMIC DEVELOPMENT

I am convinced that to overcome the difficulties mentioned above, the alternative solution approach is the best. Direct optimisation with conditions clearly defined – whereby in the course of economico-mathematical calculation non-optimal versions are thrown away and optimal versions must accord with a predetermined criterion – is not an effective approach for long-run planning. It is expedient in this case to estimate economic development paths under different conditions, to draw up various alternatives and to choose the best solutions by means of analysis, comparison and multilateral evalua-tion, not only from the point of view of economics but also from the standpoint of strategic and social criteria.

At the Institute of Economics and Industrial Engineering of the Siberian branch of the U.S.S.R. Academy of Sciences considerable experience of calculating and evaluating future economic develop-ment has accumulated. This experience is primarily applicable to the problems of perspective planning of the economy of Siberia. A brief description of the methods adopted in this work will be given.

First we calculate and analyse a solution that may be regarded as a continuation of the existing trends of economic development. It would be wrong to think that such a solution can be obtained by means of simple extrapolation of growth rates of separate indexes. The difficulty is that, in the very structure of the national economy of the base period and in the trends of economic development that are already visible, an increase or decrease of the growth rates of various indexes is usually implied, a change of structure is implied, and so on. At the Institute various types of dynamic national economy models have been evolved. It is possible to calculate alter-native solutions with their help. First of all, there is a macro-economic model in which the inputs are indexes for the basic starting period of the growth and parameters of change of some of the principal indexes of the development of the economy; these include such ratios as labour cost per unit of product, capital assets per unit of gross product, material input per unit of product, the rate of replacement of capital assets, the growth of occupied manpower, the rate of accumulation of circulating assets, and so on. If we make a change in these parameters as compared with the current trends, it is possible to calculate the resulting trends in the various indexes from year to year with the help of the macro-economic models start-ing from the calculations of a previous year and deriving those for coming years. This trend usually has little in common with a simple extrapolation of rates of economic growth because each year certain balance relations have to be kept, and changes of individual indexes imply a definite structural change in the economy; they have different effects upon the rates of growth of different elements of the economy. It is obvious that in calculating the solution that represents the continuation of existing trends it is necessary to introduce changes into the rate of growth of particular indexes–changes consequent upon the actual limitations, for instance, on the rate of growth of total occupied manpower as a constraint on the increased use of labour resources, which is in its turn related to the demographic indexes.

Another type of dynamic model which can be used to establish the economic results of the continuation of existing development trends is a regressive national economy model.[1] The interdependence of separate indexes of the parameters of this model is expressed with the help of regression equations, which are calculated on the basis of the rates of change of these indexes over a past period (say fifteen to twenty years). In addition to regression equations this model contains balance equations of various types which measure the interrelations between different parameters of the national economy for each year. With the help of regression national economy models, the existing tendencies of economic development are represented in the corresponding regression equations in the full form.

A third type of national economy model commonly used in the work of the Institute is represented by dynamic inter-industry models.[2] The most popular of these is a thirty-industries model. With its help it is possible to calculate possible alternatives of rates and ratios of the development of the national economy for the perspective period. If changes of coefficients of the ratios involved (labour cost per unit of product, capital assets per unit of gross product, material input per unit of product) over the coming period are assumed to change at the rate of existing trends, there will be obtained a solution that reflects the continuation of these trends. The indexes of this version will probably reflect the actual situation in the national economy because they take into account structural shifts in the development of individual industries. With this differentiated industry approach it is possible to follow more precisely the interrelations between changes of the indexes of the various ratios: labour cost per unit of product, capital assets per unit of gross product, material input per unit of product.

A consideration of the probable outcome of a continuation of the

[1] The study of such models is dealt with in S. M. Menshikov (ed.), *On the Problems of Constructing and Using National Economy Models* (Novosibirsk, 1971).

[2] See N. F. Shatilov, 'Computer Simulation of Production on a Large Scale', *Ekonomika* (1967) and *Methodological Comments on the Use of a Dynamic Model of Interindustry Balance in Summary Perspective Planning* (Novosibirsk, 1971).

current trends of actual development in our view represents a very valuable starting point in the analysis. A continuation of the current trends usually results in intensification of existing disproportions in the economy, and enables one to see more clearly both the positive and negative aspects of the current development, and the economic situation into which this or that path of development may bring one.

This general study of the possible alternative policy for the development of the national economy that represents a continuation of existing trends by revealing its strong and weak points, makes it possible to proceed further with the working out of new lines of economic development that imply some change of economic policy. For this one begins by identifying the principal constraints on the solution of which a further growth of national production primarily depends, and one works out a certain set of measures to deal with them. In particular, one can include such things as changes in the policy for modernisation of capital assets (say, a doubling of the rate of retirement of obsolescent equipment), a raising of the rate of productive accumulation and more rapid capital investment in industries that contribute most to technological progress, more attention to the reduction of the ratio of material input per unit of product in the sphere of public production. With this objective one should change the structure of capital investment so as to increase investment in those activities that save resources and materials.

The difficulty here lies in the fact that the resources that are required for the achievement of this or that change of economic policy at any given moment are limited, and a strict balancing of the resources available and their possible uses is necessary. Step by step, solving first one and then another of the main problems of development of the economy with the help of dynamic national economy models, we can obtain various alternative growth rates and proportions for the national economy over a series of coming years.

To study alternative solutions more thoroughly it is necessary to use other types of economico-mathematical models. For instance, the analysis of the economic results of saving resources and material at the expense of special capital investment for these purposes can be carried out in detail by means of multi-industry dynamic models, since arrangements to save resources and materials are specific to each form of production and industry. For this purpose at the Institute a six-hundred-industries optimisation model has been constructed. This model makes it possible to carry out such calculations differentially.[1] As a part of all this, economic measures directed

[1] See K. K. Valtukh 'A Dynamic Model of the National Economy with some Elements of Optimisation', in *On Problems of Constructing and Using Economic Models*, ed. K. K. Valtukh (Novosibirsk, 1970).

towards a serious modification of the structure of national consumption need to be thoroughly analysed by means of models of income formation and consumption for the nation as a whole and especially from the standpoint of the distribution of income and consumption, taking into account the different levels of income and consumption of families with low, average and high incomes and the corresponding shifts in the level of incomes and in the structure of consumption.

As a first stage of such an analysis, it is necessary to calculate and analyse scores of possible alternative lines of development of the national economy under different conditions. The aim of such calculations is not only to evaluate in outline the possible economic results of overcoming some of the main constraints on the development of the national economy, but primarily to evaluate the factors and conditions that are determining the rates of growth and their interrelations in the development of the national economy. For this purpose one of the possible alternatives for the development is taken as a standard and, by changing one or other of the parameters, an attempt is made to measure the extent of the effect of this change upon all the other indexes. Thus these indexes change to different extents: for example, the indexes of the ratios of labour input per unit of product, material input per unit of product, capital assets per unit of gross output, the standards of replacement of capital assets, the standards of productive accumulation, the volume of unfinished construction, the growth of stocks, and so on. Such calculations will only present a true picture if the interrelations of the various indexes and the mutual effects of changing each of them are taken into account.

Finally, these various alternative estimates may be grouped into some essentially different situations of future economic development by means of their concerted analysis. In addition to solutions representing a continuation of existing trends, it may be interesting to analyse solutions with less intensive or more intensive technological progress of different types, designed to save direct human labour, designed to save embodied labour, designed to permit some loss in the growth of productive resources in order to increase human welfare and the necessary reconstruction of the economic structure to permit this, or designed to promote the growth of the contribution of external economic relations and their use to improve the productivity of national development (this implies the existence of the required international conditions). Each of these possible lines of future development in its turn undergoes a complex study from the widest socio-economic and strategic standpoints. The objective of this analysis is to formulate the main projected indexes for a long-range plan.

Up to this point I have been concerned with the problems of policy analysis in the development of the national economy of the country as a whole. In a country so large as the U.S.S.R., with its wide differences of resources, climates and stages of economic development in different regions, the all-union form of analysis inevitably needs to be supplemented by regional analysis and by the study of problems of allocation of productive forces to different regions of the country.

The main problem lies in the integration and co-ordination of indexes of the development of individual regions and individual industries into an integrated whole. It is necessary not merely to co-ordinate but also to ensure that this regional development contributes to the achievement of the fundamental goals of development for the country as a whole. An optimal inter-regional inter-industry model that has been worked out at the Institute can be used to solve this problem. In this model we have both the industries and the regions of the country represented simultaneously (of course, in summarised form).[1] With the help of this model it is possible to develop the outline of a general perspective scheme of allocation of the nation's productive resources, to find the desirable rate of economic development of each region from the standpoint of the national economy, to find the rational structure of production, the necessary capital investments and labour resources, and to find the role of the various separate regions in the all-union regional division of labour.

When one has found the general characteristics of the future development of a separate economic region in relation to the requirements of the whole national economy, it is necessary to proceed to a more detailed study of the problems of the development of the productive resources, taking into account the internal possibilities and conditions for the development of each region. At our Institute such studies have been carried out for certain regions of Siberia. The methodology of such analysis is in principle very similar to that of the national economy study, and it forms a part of the working out of various alternative schemes of economic development and of the examination of different policies. The analysis takes full account of the comparative advantages and disadvantages of individual regions.

For the regional analysis of intra-regional relationships various types of territorial models have been worked out at the Institute. From the standpoint of the long-range plan, there is special interest in models of the development of an inter-regional system of territory-

[1] See A. G. Aganbegyan, K. A. Bagrinovsky and A. G. Granberg, 'System of Models of National Economy Planning', *Misl* (1972).

D

production complexes and in models of the creation of a separate territory-production complex.[1] These two optimisation models have been tested in practice with the development data of a group of energy-industry complexes in East Siberia, such as the Bratsk complex, the Sayan complex, the Low–Angara complex, and others. As a result there has been found the most efficient structure of the development of territory-production complexes, taking account of regional advantages, labour resources, the transport network of the region, the special construction facilities, geographical location, and so on.

III. THE PROGRAMME APPROACH

A policy analysis of perspective development for the purpose of finding the optimal alternative long-run plan needs to be supplemented by a programme approach to solve the main national economy models. In my view, one should distinguish four groups of national economy programmes: the general national programmes (the overall programme of scientific and technological progress, the programme for the increase of welfare, and other similar programmes); inter-industry programmes (fuel and energy, construction, transport, agricultural and industrial, metallurgical, machine-building, etc.); functional programmes directed to solving separately the most pressing problems of the development of the national economy (a programme for economising materials, a programme for the increase of the capital investment efficiency and others of a similar kind), and regional programmes for the overall development of productive resources in the various regions.

An optimal approach to long-run planning assumes the ultimate selection of the alternative that best achieves the long-run objectives of the economic development of the country. Accordingly, there should be constructed an overall programme. For this it is desirable to establish at an early stage a set of objectives fulfilling the requirements of the system analysis so that each programme is directed to achieving this or that basic national economy objective. By this method a long-range perspective plan will emerge as a complete synthesis of interrelated programmes for economic development. The optimisation technique can then be applied to each programme separately.

It is possible to approach optimal computer simulation of the national economy programme either from above – from the stand-

[1] See A. G. Aganbegyan and D. M. Kazakevitch (eds.), 'Optimal Territory-Production Planning', *Nauka* (Siberian Department, 1969).

point of computer simulation of the whole national economy – or from below, by means of the synthesis of models of separate industries included in the various inter-industry programmes. At our Institute both methods have been used. From the national economic standpoint an attempt to dismember the total for the integrated national economy into interrelated systems of inter-industry programmes has been made.[1]

On the other hand, during the past ten years a great deal of experience has been accumulated at the Institute of how to solve the different optimal industry problems of determining perspectives of developing enterprises and the production of separate industries.[2]

We proceed step by step from optimisation of separate industries to solving problems of groups of interrelated industries regarding production. In this connection, multi-stage optimisation models and multi-level models[3] have begun to be developed. With their help we hope to secure optimisation of both inter-industry and programme systems.

At the same time the method of constructing groups of interrelated models has been increasingly developed; these models represent probably the most suitable set of instruments for more detailed optimisation of inter-industry programme systems. Similar studies have been carried out in respect of both industry and the agricultural-industrial complex. The system of models for the optimisation of the national agricultural-industrial complex, for instance, included models to determine the final output of the complex, an inter-industry balance model to determine the requirements for agricultural raw materials to satisfy this final demand, an optimisation model for the regional industrial structure of the agricultural-industrial complex in terms of republics and economic regions of the country, and a group of models of the development and allocation of the separate industries that constitute the agricultural-industrial complex.[4]

Thus, policy analysis, the programme approach, and the process of optimisation that underlies all of them, represent the various ways to improve the rationality and scientific standards of long-range perspective planning.

---

[1] The results of studies in this field carried out by the scientists of the institute are summarised in *A System Approach to Economic Studies* (Novosibirsk, 1971).

[2] This method is summarised in *Methodological Comments on Optimal Industry Planning in Industrial Enterprises* (Novosibirsk, 1972), where detailed references on this subject are given.

[3] See D. M. Kazakevitch, 'Production-transport Models in Long-run Industry Planning', *Ekonomika* (1972).

[4] For details see V. P. Mozhin, 'On Problems of Optimisation of Perspective Development of Agriculture', *Nauka*.

Discussion of the Paper by Professor Aganbegyan

Professor Malinvaud (France), in opening the discussion, said that Professor Aganbegyan's paper consisted of three main parts. The first dealt with specific difficulties of long-term planning and was illustrated by some examples of economic problems of Siberia. These specific difficulties of long-term planning as against, for instance, medium-term planning, were that the range of available alternatives was much wider, the future was more uncertain, various long-term decisions were much more interdependent than medium-term decisions, and the target level was higher than in the case of medium- or short-term planning; when one was engaged in long-term planning one aimed at shaping socio-economic development and thus objectives were much more ambitious. For all these various reasons the methods developed for medium-range planning did not suit the purposes of long-range planning, and this applied in particular to the various mathematical economic models that have been built for short- or medium-term planning and that could not be employed without caution to long-term projections.

The second part of the paper presented the basic methodological approach to long-term planning. This approach was called 'situation analysis' and essentially amounted to a set of variants or 'versions' which were computed for a large number of alternatives and were intended to span the whole range of feasible growth paths. They were then grouped into several essentially different lines of future economic development, this being done by comparative analysis of the variants, and finally the choice was made between these variants.

The situation analysis was thus meant to lead to the choice of the best version, which was described as the optimal variant. The adjective 'optimal' was to be understood not as referring to determination by various criteria, as it would be in the case of solution of a linear programme, but simply described the version that came to be finally chosen.

The third part of the paper insisted on the fact that long-term planning should not be seen as a simple linear operation. It had many facets and should be studied in a great number of aspects: changes in the basic trends, in inter-industry structure, in the composition of capital, in the regional structure, and so on. These various aspects needed to be studied more or less independently from one another and later co-ordinated and combined into a systematic whole. It was in this respect that particular models were being used for studying particular facets of the problem, these models being sometimes systematically integrated by the formal analysis or their results being co-ordinated at a later stage.

Professor Malinvaud thought that one must agree on these general principles. He liked very much the idea that long-term planning was the selection of a small number of versions representing the whole range of available alternatives, and that the choice between various versions could not be done in practice on the basis of an *a priori* given objective function, but only through individual consideration of the many variants that were drawn up. This was because our knowledge about the formulation of appropriate objective functions was, for the time being, too limited.

One thing which was missing from the paper was how the consultations of the decision-makers were organised. At what stage and in what form did they take place? Was the decision-maker consulted right at the end when a number of variants were delivered to him from which to make the best choice, or was he asked to assist at the beginning, or perhaps at some intermediate stages of planning? In other words, how was a long-term plan integrated into the administrative planning machinery?

The paper was very informative on the work of the Institute of Economics of the Siberian Branch of the Academy of Sciences of the U.S.S.R. For instance, one learned about their macro-economic models of the purely deterministic type as well as of the macro-economic regression type, their optimisation and inter-regional models, as well as input–output models for thirty industries, and the like. One also learned about the strategic variables used in long-term planning. Much attention was given to labour input coefficients, to the capital–output ratio, to the degree of replacement of capital, size of the labour force, for example.

The paper also discussed the different types of alternatives that were considered. These variants included more or less rapid application of technological progress in different types of operation, attaching higher or lower priority to productivity increases, the implications of more or less rapid growth of the labour force, the implications of growth of the emphasis on welfare and so on. These variants assumed in other cases more or less development of trade with other economies.

In a paper that was so informative, it was surprising that two points had not been mentioned which he himself would have considered important. Thus, he wanted to ask two questions. First, how were the coefficients used in the various models evaluated? What were the basic data that were used and how were they processed to feed the models? How was the consistency of different estimates checked? Secondly, he was surprised that Professor Aganbegyan said so little about the final consumers of the production. Thus, his second question was what type of society was one aiming to have? What should be the division of consumption between collective and individual?

Professor Denison (U.S.A.) said that he wished to ask about something that had not been much discussed. In any country the major resource was labour and the greatest opportunity to vary the amount of work being done lay with it. Thus, first, what assumptions or what estimates were made as to the effect of changes in working hours upon output? And secondly, what procedures, if any, were used to try to evaluate the desirable ratio between work and leisure or between work and additional output? Rational choice of the second implies some estimate of the first. The answer would be particularly interesting in view of the sharp polarisation of opinion on this subject which existed in the West.

Professor Machlup (U.S.A.) said that on the first day of the conference it had been said that long-term planning did not exist either in non-socialist nor in socialist countries. He believed that this statement could be meant only in the sense that long-term planning in the most comprehensive sense did not exist. That implied the allocation of all productive resources, production of all possible goods, and so on. On the other hand he was sure that everyone agreed that long-term planning in a less comprehensive sense did exist, must exist, and had existed for many years, although previous plans were less scientifically based. What was being done by Professor Aganbegyan was really a large-scale cost-benefit analysis. Professor Aganbegyan spoke of the allocation of cost and regretted that the expenses for infrastructure might be attributed entirely to the initial projects and not to subsequent projects also. That was absolutely correct but Professor Machlup wondered if there were any need to allocate expenses over all the various beneficiaries. It was enough to have all the costs on one side and all the beneficiaries on the other. Of course, neither costs nor benefits could be forecasted without need for any future correction, yet by the best use of our knowledge we could evaluate them somehow, even if with some error.

Professor Marczewski (France) wished first to clarify an earlier statement that he had made regarding long-term planning, which in fact was a strong reaction to the definition of planning proposed by Professor Machlup. That definition could be applied only to short- and medium- but not to long-term planning. Hitherto there had been no long-term plans in the full and precise sense, and even in the U.S.S.R. long-term planning was still at its very beginning, although it had produced some interesting results. The plan of the Communist Party of the U.S.S.R. for the 1980s was not a plan but only a set of general objectives. We had been told that among the models used there is an optimisation model which covers several hundreds of variables. What mathematical devices were used to solve such vast programmes? Were any decomposition methods used – for instance, the decomposition principle of Danzig and Wolfe – and how were they used?

Professor Topala (Roumania) asked what criteria were used in optimising the economy and what methods were used? They in Roumania were constructing such models with the help of linear programming. These models were aimed at the minimisation of overall costs, that was to say capital investment costs plus the costs of production and transportation. They had also attempted to design a model employing dynamic programming. In their case the criteria for optimisation were the maximisation of profits and the allocation of capital investment at different stages so as to take account of the total costs and the impact produced on other industries.

Professor Veinstein (U.S.S.R.) said that in discussing long-term planning, most if not all of the participants of the conference had started from the assumption that the state of the system at any given time could be described in terms of quantitative parameters. In this respect he would like to suggest that economic theory had not as yet reached the level of the theory and methods of measurements of physics or technology generally. While in physics there was international agreement on the fundamentals of substance, space and time, economic theory knew no such agreement. Yet it seemed possible to speak of three basic economic concepts which, either directly or together, served as a foundation for any economic measurement. They were expenditures, time and results. But further analysis of the large systems involved in long-term planning, when approached from the position of Professor Aganbegyan or other participants in the discussion, showed the impossibility of describing the system simply in terms of these three categories. He thought that all participants would agree that the economy shared a difficulty common to that in physics that the larger was the perspective, the greater was the time span and the greater were the desired results, the less was it possible to determine all three categories simultaneously. If time and costs were fixed, the results appeared to be something within a range of stochastic evaluation or within a zone of uncertainties, and hence could be expressed not by some exact quantitative parameter, such as a precise volume of sales, or of the G.N.P. or the national income, but rather by a distribution of probabilities.

The question arose as to which of the three categories – costs, time or results – should be relegated to the zone of uncertainties in the case on long-term planning and forecasting. Traditionally this had often been solved by introducing a range of results. It was said, for example, that sales volume would be within certain limits.

The essence of Professor Aganbegyan's approach was that the results were taken as fixed as a large-scale programme. If by force of the logic of large systems and the many external factors involved there was necessarily some uncertainty, it seemed more sensible to attribute it to the time interval, and this was true of all large-scale programmes, whether it was a space research programme, national education or anything else.

The mention of large-scale programmes immediately raised the question of the criteria of optimality for evaluation of the programme. In Professor Aganbegyan's approach the objective itself was the criterion of optimality, for the programme was such that its fulfilment was required for the achievement of important needs of the whole economy and of society in general.

As regards the establishment of freedom of consumer choice he wondered whether 'free consumer choice' was not really a fiction, a mere combination of three words put together. It had been Professor Galbraith who had voiced the different and rather critical attitude to the creation of 'free choice', and was it not the noble and challenging function of economists and sociologists to shape that demand? Ought we really to be welcoming this freedom – even when it was freedom of choice for pornographic films and drugs?

In his opinion, the economist ought to have a long-range target programme in view. In this sense perhaps Professor Marczewski would agree that although the Communist Party plans were not strictly plans, they nevertheless were plans in a sense of representing a formulated objective which in turn provided a criterion for determining time and costs. When solving tasks of social, national or international magnitude, stochastic evaluation of time was possible, while retaining the objectives.

If one held that only time and expenditures were fixed, then one arrived at the paradox of the fixed time having elapsed, the given expenditures having been made and the final results being within a zone of stochastic evaluation without certain knowledge as to where on the curve it could be expected. That was why he fully agreed with Professor Aganbegyan that as a possible unit of long-term planning one should define not merely and not especially the quantitative parameters but rather the target programme to be achieved.

Professor Robinson (U.K.) wanted to return to the similarities and differences from what was being done in capitalist countries. It seemed to him that one had to distinguish two things: a long-term information system and a long-term decision-making process, which he regarded as fundamentally different. Even if in a capitalist country decision-making was delegated by the central authority, there was still much to be said for the importance of a centralised information system.

Some trends could best be estimated by extrapolating the present trends of an individual decision-making unit. On the other hand, a very large proportion of estimating was in his view much better done by building up of a national total, by looking at the national income-elasticity, estimating the total industry demand for a group of products, and then coming down to the possible demands for the products of the individual decision-making firm. In almost every case, if one were trying to estimate the demand for a firm one had to operate both ways: by trying to extrapolate one's own history and by estimating the general situation on the national market.

It was always fascinating for him to compare the problems which they had in the U.K. with those described by Professor Aganbegyan. In the U.K. they needed a long-term information system because they had a very large public sector, as in many European countries. But quite apart from that they needed such a system for the purposes of private industries. He would argue that at any time one needed to look at least fifteen years ahead. Construction of an electric power station in the U.K. took about ten years, including the designing and negotiating periods, the latter increasing recently because of longer negotiating in respect of the environment and other aspects. One had to consider the location of the station and that in turn depended on the type of fuel used. All of this made necessary considerable preliminary calculation.

They in the West had been basing these calculations on shadow prices for various elements. They did in fact work by making designs suitable for stations in different locations. That meant that they had to work something like ten years ahead of demand. Such a long gestation period applied to a number of industries such as heavy engineering, power, telecommunications, steel, transportation industries, city developments, and other similar investments. For a number of industries this period was much shorter and it was quite unnecessary to start the decision-making process very early. But one needed to ask whether sufficient account had been taken of the lengthening of periods of gestation in designing one's long-term information system.

How accurate did one's estimates have to be? Various factors had to be taken into account here. First of all one had learned to take account of what he would call 'the administrative margin of error'. He thought it was very important, before wasting weeks and months of time trying to determine whether a figure was 155 or 165, to consider whether one would make a different decision if it were 165 rather than 155. If the decision in both cases remained exactly the same, it did not seem necessary to waste time trying to determine the figure very precisely.

The second factor was that the long-term decision-maker needed to be informed not only of what might be the mean figure but also of what, from his point of view, might be the worst figure. If he might come back to his power station example, it was much better to be told in advance that you might need to raise capacity by 75 per cent and not 50 per cent, so that you were well prepared in advance.

The third point in respect to the margins of error was that it was very important for all practical purposes to have a clear idea whether errors in calculations were symmetrical or asymmetrical. If again he might quote from electricity supply, they had calculated the relative damage done by having too much and too little electricity. This damage appeared to be very asymmetrical, with the damage inflicted by shortage of electricity far exceeding that caused by the temporary existence of surplus capacity. How much importance did an error have? Growth naturally did not stop. It was always important to know how quickly growth of demand would eliminate the error.

If one was working with macro-economic forecasts as an information system, it provided a great deal of what one most needed. But it did have extraordinarily serious gaps. One of them was that very few long-term macro-economic estimates included any satisfactory regional breakdown or regional analysis. He himself was increasingly shocked at the incapacity of economic analysis to handle the geographical problems within which all the decision-making had to be done. That would not matter if all manufacturing were on an immense scale and transportation costs were relatively small. There were many cases, however, in which one did need to know where geographically the demand was going to emerge, and this was a form of information with which in the capitalist countries they were very poorly provided.

Professor Khachaturov (U.S.S.R.) said that several speakers had raised the question of objectives in relation to decision-making in long-term planning. He thought it was Professor Aganbegyan's idea that each stage of planning involved its own goals and decisions. The socio-economic goals of a plan were determined by decision-takers already before the plan was compiled. The next stage was the analysis of the existing situation and the level of economic development that was currently being achieved. Analysis of a very large body of statistical information aimed at a generalised appraisal of what was being achieved as well as of the bottlenecks of development.

This was followed by a stage of scientific forecasting and of determining the basic trends of intended development. Here actually was the beginning of the modelling and of the defining of alternatives which had been described in the second part of Professor Aganbegyan's paper. In composing five-year plans they were essentially bound by the processes which had begun in the previous period and would continue in the present. These processes which were taken into account in five-year plans, had to be considered to a much less degree in the case of long-term planning – that is in planning for a fifteen to twenty years period – because of the much greater freedom of possible alternatives.

This second stage began the analysis of the mutual interactions between different target programmes included in the plan. The analysis was based on earlier forecasts and the analysis of the current situation, and involved more precise definition of objectives, which in this stage again were the socio-economic targets set by the decision-makers.

When planning for a long period, they started from a demographic prediction. That prediction firstly made it possible to calculate future total demand

D*

and to compare it with the natural and other production resources available, as well as to estimate the possibilities for further growth. Secondly, it made it possible to estimate the available labour resources in relation to the desired growth.

This, in its turn, raised the question of labour productivity and of the contributions of technological progress and capital investment policy in the sense of indicating the extent to which technological progress and accumulation in the national economy might make it possible to meet the expected demands. Thus, each stage of planning had its own objectives which were further clarified in the course of planning, and each stage involved its own decisions.

After the plan had been more or less co-ordinated, there was a stage of final decision which naturally involved comparisons of costs and benefits and the elaboration of an overall economic policy. He thought, however, that economic policy should be regarded as emerging at each stage of planning, and not just at the final stage as a choice of the most appropriate objectives and priorities for development.

Finally, adjustments were made in the actual course of implementation of a plan and this completed the process of formulation of objectives and of decision-making which went on throughout the whole of planning operation.

He wished to answer affirmatively the question whether there did exist practical long-term planning, at least in the U.S.S.R. It was more than fifty years since the first plan for electrification of the whole of Russia was compiled. That plan was intended to cover a period of ten to fifteen years. Subsequently, long-term plans had been designed for at least the key sectors of the national economy. It was true that the Communist Party programme did not include calculations, but it was backed by detailed calculations made for different republics, sectors and industries. Thus there did exist some experience of long-term planning in his country, which was now being used in making the fifteen-year plan for the future development of the U.S.S.R. economy down to the year 1990. This was being done by various planning committees, by the State Committee on Science and Technology and by the Academy of Sciences of the U.S.S.R.

Professor Kantorovitch (U.S.S.R.) added that Professor Aganbegyan's paper presented a summary of extensive research done by Professor Aganbegyan himself and by the staff of his institute both in economic theory and in the practice of optimisation. He wished to emphasise that in long-term planning the essence of the planning was different from that in short- and medium-term plans, the decisive criterion being the objective of the plan. In making a fifteen- to twenty-year plan they did not adopt the aim of prescribing a certain path of development for the national economy or one of its branches. The aim of such a plan was to create the possibility of visualising the longer-term future while making decisions for the next five or so years. Of course, it was assumed that the plan would be changed with changes in conditions and in the light of later information.

When the economy of a socialist country was discussed, he would still find it possible to call this longer-term perspective a plan in the sense that they did control the long-term development of the economy, and their decisions were more or less final for the shorter period, even if they were subject to modification over longer periods; in both cases they did manage the economy.

He would also like to point out that mathematical modelling was unquestionably useful, though its contribution to long-term planning depended on further development of the methods concerned and on the adoption of more complete and precise models (by complete he did not mean more detailed coverage but more elaborate methodology).

General parameters such as norms of effectiveness of capital investment, estimates of labour supply and of important types of inputs, as well as the use of stochastic techniques, should become elements in specific long-term models which could even suggest possible technical solutions for different alternatives.

Finally, there was the question of how to estimate the final product of a system. In practice, he thought that the fact of misbehaviour of a model beyond the planning horizon mentioned by Professor Aganbegyan, could be attributed at least in part to insufficient consideration of the influence of periods of adjustment to a planned change. He also believed that optimisation models and methods should not be contrasted either with traditional planning for a small number of industries or with long-term programming. The most effective way was somehow to combine all of these methods.

To conclude, he thought that some parameters used by Professor Aganbegyan, such as resource norms or output norms, were rather dependent on circumstances for they very much depended on organisational structure and degree of aggregation. Moreover, the estimates of such parameters were hypothetical in their origin and their rates of change were not known.

Professor Bruno (Israel) agreed with Professor Malinvaud that planning was a systematised idea of what one was going to do in the future. That implied that some aims and objectives were set, but it was difficult to give precise definition to an objective if it embraced many years of activities to come. One of the tasks of the international conference had been to clarify those methods that could be used in economic analysis. In a number of countries mathematical methods formed a major part of the planning mechanism; that is, mathematical models were the basis of a long-term perspective plan. He himself thought models could be useful, but that the value of sophisticated complex models was sometimes overestimated.

There were many different types and degrees of modelling, but he wondered which were actually being used in the process of planning. He might be wrong about this, and he was saying it just to provoke discussion, but he though that the fact that a model was not being used did not always mean that it was useless. He thought that building a model was essentially a teaching device. One might require very different models for analysis of an actual situation or as an integral part of a planning mechanism.

A number of things had been said about the choice of objectives. There were a number of situations, at least in the economy that he was most familiar with, where objectives could not be precisely specified, and where much of the planning was the investigation of conflict between mutually inconsistent objectives. A politician would name such goals as growth, equality, economic independence, better regional distribution, and so on. These objectives could not be reconciled fully, and the task of an economist was to compromise between them. Linear programming with its optimisation did not mean that one could find the real objectives. It might be just a computational device to find the production possibility and the trade off between different objectives. In this sense he found it very valuable to look at the different variants.

Relatively little had been said about the use of the prices that one got from an optimisation model. Were they secured in order to give effect to these prices or not? In particular, if one had in mind the ideal use of these prices for project evaluation or evaluation of opportunity costs, this raised the whole issue of what sort of interpretation was to be attached to prices in conditions in which one did not fully control the resources in the system. The model made one believe one had such control.

Finally, there was the question of various degrees of disaggregation in the models described by Professor Aganbegyan. A model was described in which there were thirty sectors, and another one in which there were 600 industries. What sort of argument lay behind the use of one model or another? In other words, there must be some degree of optimal disaggregation for most working purposes, depending on the purpose of the particular model.

Professor Aganbegyan (U.S.S.R.), replying to the discussion, proposed to begin with the role of long-term projections in the planning mechanism of the U.S.S.R. The most important research in his country was done in relation to the state plan. About five or so years back, the plan had been extended to cover research done by different research groups and institutions in the field of long-term forecasting of the socio-economic development of the U.S.S.R. down to the year 2000. These forecasts covered such complex areas as fuel and power, communications, as well as wide territorial, regional and social problems. As a result of that research a great deal of scientific information had been obtained which made it possible to begin work on the long-term plans for the development of the national economy. The conference was aware from Academician Fedorenko's paper that work was under way in the U.S.S.R. to compile a fifteen-year plan for the years 1975–90. This work was being done in three stages. The first was to construct a complex estimate of scientific and technological progress and of its social and economic consequences. Roughly, this stage could be described as the stage of establishing a general view of potential economic development and of estimating the basic trends of scientific and technological progress. This was a key stage without which no firmly based long-term plans were possible, and it was only natural that the major body of this work was done by scientists. Second came the stage of working out and agreeing the basic concepts of the plan. Medium-term five-year plans were compiled in two stages in the U.S.S.R., with the basic concepts and target figures being worked out first and adopted as directives for a five-year plan; these were subsequently disaggregated into more detailed specific plans. Academic experts participated in all of these stages. The most important stage was the pre-planning stage when certain concepts and data had been accumulated and had to be transformed into quantitative targets and detailed planning. These planning decisions were made at different operational levels and included decisions in respect of structural policy, of target setting, and of the magnitude and practical orientation of a plan.

It should be emphasised that they did not consider the whole of a fifteen-year plan to be incapable of change. This would have been impossible at the present rate of technological progress. A fifteen-year plan was amended and defined in detail in subsequent five-year plans which thus provided for the consistency of long-term and medium-term planning.

A very important question had been raised by Professor Malinvaud regarding the initial body of information and the derivation of the coefficients used in the calculations. These coefficients were obtained in a complicated fashion. In the first place, the dynamics of previous development were analysed. At his institute, for instance, they were using dynamic models covering the period from 1959 down to the present to obtain both the coefficients and an understanding of the factors determining their change. But these coefficients could not be extrapolated without taking full account of scientific and techno- logical progress, which could not possibly be done by planning organisations. For almost a decade they in the U.S.S.R. had organised the co-operation of a large number of specialised research institutions. The Economic Research Institute of the State Planning Committee (Gosplan) of the U.S.S.R. co- ordinated the research done by some 200 specialised institutes which estimated the prospective norms for every individual branch and sector of the economy on the basis of the general trends of technological progress. Their projections were later included into the system of general economic calculations. So that represented the second way in which they obtained information. A third way used was the analysis of foreign experience, which in respect to basic trends and new developments in the advanced capitalist countries was the responsi- bility of the Institute of World Economy and International Relations. They at the Siberian Institute of Economics also had a special division which by means of regressive models interpreted the major changes, especially in the U.S. economy. They enjoyed co-operation and exchange of models and information with a number of U.S. laboratories including the Whitworth laboratory and the University of Maryland.

Thus, these three sources and the initiative of the researcher provided the initial bulk of information from which the coefficients were drawn. The coefficients were usually forecasted in several versions and computations in the 'pessimistic', 'most probable' and 'optimistic' variants of a plan.

Professor Malinvaud had asked a very interesting and pertinent question as to why so little was said in the paper about consumption. The only answer he could give was perhaps that he devoted so much attention to consumption and had exhausted what he had to say on that subject. But he believed that the whole development of the U.S.S.R. economy was consumer-oriented and aimed at fuller satisfaction of consumer's needs; thus perhaps his paper had been unduly brief on this subject.

As regards the very interesting problem of working time and leisure, they in the U.S.S.R. in the past ten years had accumulated a unique experience of transitions: first, from an eight-hour to a seven-hour working day; second, from a seven-hour, six-day working week to an eight-hour, five-day week; and third, in some industries, to a six-hour, five-day week. These transitions and the wide variety of industries involved made it possible for a researcher to study rather deeply the consequences which had emerged.

The research in this field could be subdivided into two categories. The first was concerned with the impact of shorter hours upon the productivity of labour in various industries; this was very different; the impact was quite substantial in the industries with a continuous production cycle, while in the industries with no such cycle it had made possible a more intensive working day and had thus resulted in greater productivity.

Another body of research was concerned with the relationship between working and leisure time. In 1958 a national research project on leisure time use had been undertaken and was later published by the international institute in Vienna in which they were participating. As a result some valuable information on the patterns and amounts of working and leisure time was obtained. His personal view was that within the immediate or perhaps even the foreseeable future it seemed hardly sensible to switch to a four-hour working day because there were vast opportunities for increasing leisure time at the expense of home work, shopping time, transportation, by better services, and so on. Moreover, a certain balance ought to be maintained between the length of the working day and the duration of paid leave. They had twice increased the latter in the past few years, and longer paid vacations appeared to be a valuable form of reducing the overall annual working time.

To turn to Professor Marczewski's question, the optimisation of the 600-industry model was done by a special method of linear programming which made it possible to take account of block structures. They could not use the Danzig–Wolfe method because it required too many iterations for compatibility, although the method in itself was very interesting.

As to the criteria of optimisation, for higher-level dynamic inter-industry models they used the criteria related to the maximisation of welfare. Generally it was maximisation of different consumer sets under various constraints. As regards local problems of optimising an industry in a region, the main criterion used was minimisation of overall costs with account taken of the time factor. That is, all the organisations in the U.S.S.R. treated optimisation problems as dynamic ones. Another somewhat modified criterion was maximisation of integrated results. This criterion was used when optimisation was attempted for industries the products of which could be substituted for the products of other industries, and where it did not seem sensible to fix a ceiling of output long in advance. For example, such an industry in the U.S.S.R. was the fertiliser industry, where at the present level of output the more that was produced the better, with its final effects reflected in agricultural output. They paid special attention to the problem of the interrelations and compatibility of these criteria, and conditions were determined (as a theorem), under which global and local optimalities could be established in accordance with these criteria.

Professor Veinstein had asked what was in fact a rhetorical question, and he thought that the brief answer to it must be in the affirmative. There was a Power Institute in Irkutsk headed by Academician Melentiev. That institute had undertaken a vast research aimed at determining the zone of uncertainty, and they follow that methodology in solving similar problems in large optimisation operations.

He agreed with both Professor Robinson and Professor Kantorovitch that in long-term planning not only output but the dynamics of costs and prices should be considered. He also agreed with Professor Kantorovitch in respect to resource – output norms. These norms should be tackled very cautiously because they really involved both real and fictitious factors and might be misleading. This was true not only for the U.S.S.R. but for other economics as well.

Professor Bruno had said that he could seldom see the value of optimisation models in linear programming models. He wished to emphasise that although those in his country believed that mathematical models were insufficiently used in our planning, and they would like them to be used much more extensively, nevertheless optimal models were in fact much used in their long-term planning. For example, computations have been made for the five-year planning period covering 1976–80, which included eighty industries and sectors and covered more than half of all output and investment of the U.S.S.R. economy. It was in this same way that the location for an automobile plant in Togliatti on the Volga river had been chosen. These optimisation models were based on linear programming methods and were solved by approximation to linear problems. In this sense they believed that it was not nearly so important to set up an optimal plan, which would be changed anyway with changing conditions, as it was to understand its inner logic and the role of its various ingredients, which could not be done apart from mathematical estimates. That was why inverted matrices were treated as a must.

Finally, the criterion used for choosing a particular type of model was the purpose for which the model was constructed. If one wished to obtain a general picture of rates and proportions, one should use an aggregated model, while if what was involved was whether a new metallurgical combine should be built in Eastern Siberia – which implied projections for a fifteen to twenty-year period – nothing could be discovered with a thirty-industry model, and a 600-industry model became necessary. The use of such a model did not imply that the dynamics of every one of the 600 industries was fixed for fifteen years ahead. One should distinguish between information that could be obtained by using the model and a decision based on the model. A model provided a basis for decision but not the decision itself.

Part Three

Methods of Planning and Forecasting in other Centrally Planned Economies

5 The Basic Tasks and Functions of Long-term Planning in Poland

K. Porwit

I. INTRODUCTION

In this paper I shall concentrate on one of the aspects of the broad range of problems in long-term planning, namely, on its place and role in the whole system of the central planning and management of the national economy. I intend thus to discuss these specific tasks and functions of long-term planning which influence, to a considerable extent, the quality of the whole system of central planning which includes also the five-year and annual plans and the system of controlling the functioning of the economy based on these plans. Starting with these premises, I think, one should consider the approaches and solutions, specific to long-term planning, concerning the methods, the procedure and organisation of the process of planning.

It can be seen from the above remarks that I consider the problem of planning under the conditions prevailing in a socialist economy on the basis of experience gained in the management of the economy of the Polish People's Republic.

The subject of planning, i.e. the functioning and development of the national economy, is treated as one great system with a complex structure.[1] The particular elements of this system are interrelated and their functioning is mutually conditioned in various planes. Being aware of these interrelations one must conclude that the management of the functioning and development of the economy has to be based on a system-oriented, complex approach.[2] The point here is not only to take into account the mutual inter-relations and conditions but also to observe the principle of general social rationality and thus to strive for a maximum degree of realisation of the social objectives peculiar to the socialist system, within the means available to the society as a whole.[3] The functioning of the

[1] I have in mind here a socio-economic system characterised by the relatively highest degree of complexity in comparison with other types of systems. Cf. K. E. Boulding, 'General Systems Theory – The Skeleton of Science', *Management Science* (Apr 1956).

[2] Cf. A. Bachurin, 'Usileniye Systemnovo, Komplexnovo podkhoda v Planirovanii', *Planovoye Khoziaystvo*, no. 6 (1972).

[3] Cf. O. Lange, 'Ekonomia Polityczna', *Political Economy* (Warsaw), vol. 1, chap. 5 (1961).

particular links of the whole system must be subordinated to the general social objectives and (as far as the available information permits) to the optimal concept of implementation of these objectives. Central planning and management of the national economy should serve these objectives. However, overall social objectives of the system as a whole can be maximised only when the highest attainable effectiveness in the functioning of the particular links of the system is secured. This means, first, that the effects achieved by the particular links should converge with the requirements of the implementation of the objectives of the whole system, and second that every link of the system must utilise the factors of production on a high level of efficiency.

The achievement of such a high degree of effectiveness depends on directing properly the operations of the particular links, on creating for them the most advantageous conditions for effective functioning and development, and upon the degree of efficiency of operations of every link, of main business units, of their associations, of central management boards, and of all other responsible bodies. Thus, for an efficient functioning and development of a socio-economic system as a whole it is necessary that two conjugate motive powers work in parallel. One of them must operate from above, determining the scope and method of operation of the particular links of the system so as to satisfy the requirement of general social rationality and thus to secure the maximum implementation of the social objectives of the system. The second, operating from below, should ensure the fullest striving for, and implementation of, the possibility of the most effective use of the particular economic processes on the scale appropriate to a given economic unit. The crux of the matter is to make the conditions – legal, institutional, operational – regulating the functioning of the whole socio-economic system conducive to a mutually supporting interaction of these forces and to enhancing their effectiveness.

It has been recognised in Poland that in 'modernising our system of planning and management, efforts should be made to increase the effectiveness of the central planning and management of the national economy and, at the same time, to expand the degree of independence and initiative of associations, combines, production establishments'.[1]

Subordinate to this striving are solutions shaping the management functions at particular levels of the economy, the nature of planning serving the implementation of these functions, and also

---

[1] The resolution by the VIth Congress of the Polish United Workers' Party, *Nowe Drogi*, no. 1 (1972) p. 158.

the specific features of planning concerning the time horizon of various lengths, including long-term perspective planning.

II. THE SCOPE AND MAIN FUNCTIONS OF LONG-TERM PLANNING

The premises of general social rationality provide for the whole national economy the basic criteria of evaluation and choice of development objectives and also of the appraisal of the efficiency of the functioning of the economy as a whole. These premises are determined by the postulate to maximise the satisfaction of the social needs within the resources available to the society. Because of the heterogeneity of these needs it is of essential importance to determine the desirable priorities between various categories of needs from the point of view of their kinds, of the cross-section of the social groups and of the regions of the country, as well as of the rate of growth of satisfaction of the needs in consecutive time-intervals. A distinction should be made between social objectives relating to society as a whole (such as national defence, public order) and the category of needs of individual persons, both for material consumption and for social services. With respect to the objectives pertaining to the satisfaction of individual needs, particular importance is attached to establishing satisfactory ratios between the living conditions of particular social groups on the basis of the principles appropriate to the socialist system.

From the point of view of development planning, particular importance is attached to the following:

(a) setting the social objectives and their internal structure, i.e. determination of preferences and of a specific set of priorities showing in what relative proportions the increased satisfaction of the various needs of the society should take precedence – those of society as a whole, those of particular social groups in different regions of the country, and those of different utility, such as nutrition, clothing, housing, health care, social care, education, and the like;

(b) consideration of the material requirements for the realisation of the social objectives, in respect of the appropriate changes in their size and internal structure, from which there are derived the necessary ideas of the required economic development proportions and their charges; this covers questions relating to the place of our economy in the international division of labour, particularly with reference to integration projects within the framework of the C.M.E.A.;

(c) analysis of the interactions between the problems discussed above, in order to choose such a set of social objectives as will be recognised to be attainable from the point of view of economic conditions and as will be most conducive to the increased efficiency of the economic system and will, at the same time, represent the best way of satisfying the social needs;

(d) determination of the programme for the implementation of the chosen policies, taking account of the functions and roles of the various decision-making bodies at lower levels and methods of controlling their activities;

(e) current and continuous observation of the processes in order to make necessary adjustments, to extend the time-horizon for the implementation programmes, and also, if the need arises, to modify the strategic concepts.

The role and character of central planning appears in different ways in solving the problems mentioned. The functions of central planning may be defined as: first, *determination of strategy*, the object of which is to define an appropriate framework for shaping the socio-economic growth of the economy as a whole and in its particular sectors; second, *development programming*, defining the methods of implementation of strategic decisions; and third, *current control*, or supervision over the actual pattern of the social and economic processes and taking the necessary adjustment steps.

In *long-term planning*[1] the strategy is determined and the basic elements of development programming are defined for the national economy and for its main links. The determination of strategy is based primarily on long-term forecasts and on other development studies covering the more important aspects of the socio-cultural pattern of the socialist society. The assumptions, the various alternatives for social objectives worked out in this way, must be verified, however, by appropriate forecasts and studies of external markets and other aspects of international co-operation, of scientific and technical progress, and of other factors affecting the possibility of better satisfaction of social needs. For these studies, it is very important to make a thorough analysis of the experience of socio-economic growth in the recent past. There are two reasons for this: first, this analysis is one of the most valuable sources of ideas for determining future strategy; second, it provides a basis for determining the more important factors for a 'path' of transition from the present state to that postulated for the future.

---

[1] A more detailed discussion of the nature of long-term planning and of its proper methods can be found, among others, in the following studies by the author of this paper: *The Methods of Long-Term Planning* (Warsaw, 1969); 'On the Problems of Perspective Planning', *Ekonomista*, no. 4 (1969); 'Perspective Planning in Poland: Basic Issues and Experiences', *Journal of Development Planning*, no. 3 (1971).

Within the framework of strategic studies, it is necessary to make a comprehensive approach to social, scientific, technical and international problems, as well as to the relevant economic proportions, in their branch, regional and functional aspects. What we are striving for is to create a solid and realistic foundation for the selected strategic policies, and not merely to outline the general requirements for a better satisfaction of social needs. A comprehensive approach is needed also in order to be able to adjust the development programming so as to take account of particular links of the economy in a broader context of general social rationality. One of the essential objects in setting a strategy is to identify any difficulties and problems to be expected in the future that cannot be solved without taking appropriate action considerably ahead of time. Thus the main task of strategic studies should not be confined to setting targets to show how much to increase satisfaction of social needs. They should also throw light on the factors that, in the specific conditions, may hamper the realisation of these objectives, and should concentrate on overcoming them and on reinforcing the favourable factors. Thus the object of these studies must be the creation of a 'bridge' for development programming.

It follows that the studies leading to strategy setting at the central level should have the following characteristics:

   (i) they should be of an inter-disciplinary nature; being based on a wide range of diagnostic analyses and forecasts pertaining to social problems, they should also comprise similar studies concerning the broadly interpreted (quantitative and qualitative) conditions for implementation of the social objectives;

  (ii) their organisation and procedure should ensure the co-operation of creative minds and centres of scientific and research units, of regional planning centres, and also of basic economic organisations;[1]

 (iii) in the processes of evaluation and choice of desirable economic objectives, it is of great importance to ensure the participation of all representative organisations and bodies, not only to establish the desirable relations between different social objectives, but also to secure a knowledgeable and

---

[1] An essential condition of ensuring appropriate co-operation of economic organisations in shaping the strategy of socio-economic development must be such a formation of the system of functioning of the economy as would create sufficiently strong motivation in economic organisations for searching for the most effective conception of their own development (within the framework of the proportions determined by the social objectives and the conditions of their realisation on a general economic scale).

realistic view of the necessary conditions for achieving these objectives within the given time limits.

Development programming on a central national level thus comprises the following main elements:

(a) preparation of functional programmes covering the main areas of social needs, such as nutrition, clothing, housing, health care, transportation, education, etc., and also the main fields affecting the conditions of achievement of the social objectives, such as infrastructure, the basic policies for development of science and technology, the fuel and power sectors, the construction material sector, and so on, approached from a national viewpoint. Such programmes cover all the factors and operations for achievement of a given development target, regardless of what economic organisation is responsible for them. This includes the preparation of complex inter-regional programmes for socio-economic development; in these programmes, the regional distributions of the social objectives and of the developments of the productive and infrastructure capacities, all from a territorial point of view, need to be taken into account;[1]

(b) the preparation of complex calculations balancing the basic economic development proportions concerning: market equilibrium, foreign exchange resources, macro-economic proportions of investment processes, inter-branch equilibrium of demand and supply in production and basic kinds of non-productive services;

(c) the preparation of complex effectiveness calculations, taking into account the basic economic relations and improved effectiveness of utilisation of the means of production on a national scale, including the policies for changes in the economic relations of the particular branches of the economy and the effects of structural changes in the general economic proportions;

(d) the preparation of programmes relating to social and economic policy and programmes concerning the selected areas of organisation and management, such as information systems, scientific research activities, the organisation of implementation of investment processes, and so on.

---

[1] A more extensive discussion of the regional aspects of planning can be found, among others, in the following studies by the author of this paper: 'Theoretical and Methodological Questions for the Construction of Comprehensive Models in Regional Planning', *Regional Science Association Papers*, Budapest Congress (1968); 'Techniques of Inter-Regional Plan Formulations in Poland', in *Issues in Regional Planning* (The Hague, 1971).

The 'leitmotiv' for shaping the conditions for co-operation, as one of the chief links of the economy in programming growth, should be provision of the best available information concerning future demand and the activation of levers and incentives to encourage a search for the most efficient and effective ways of satisfying this demand, with a strong emphasis on quality and innovation broadly interpreted.

The steering of these various activities toward the implementation of social objectives should be interpreted as requiring that the central development programming shall determine the 'minimum' path for increased satisfaction of the social needs, with an appropriate balance of satisfactions of different needs. The determination of the 'minimum' requirements should be realistic but should also observe strictly the requirement of achieving a conscious improvement in the living conditions of the society. The notion of a minimum requirement for growth should be interpreted as being the creation, through the implementation of the development programmes, of conditions that are conducive to a search for any opportunity for better satisfaction of these needs, in excess of the predetermined lower limit.

III. THE SPECIFIC FEATURES OF LONG-TERM PLANNING

The chief importance of long-term planning in the whole system of planning and management of a national economy stems primarily from the fact that, in a socio-economic system with a hierarchic structure of the centres of management, *the active influence of the higher levels of management should manifest itself in advance*, i.e. sufficiently early to exert a desired effect on the course of the actual process.

In a specific activity and in actual practice, the most important requirement is the knowledge of what should be done, and particularly of what new steps have to be taken in the near future. In this sense it is necessary to make short-term plans, covering the shortest possible period between the moment of making the decision and the moment of the appearance of its effects on what is happening. At the same time, in order to make sure that the decisions are correct it is necessary to consider fully the expected results; moreover, it is necessary to take actions in the near future so as to produce desired effects in the more distant future. For this reason it is necessary to plan for the long run, sufficiently far ahead to give the time necessary for achieving the effects desired. In different social and economic activities the lengths of such time intervals vary, depending upon the characteristics of the particular processes and upon the conditions in which they work. A distinctly long interval – a dozen years or more – is required for only a few processes. Within the time-horizon of five to ten years, however, the number increases considerably, covering more and more forms of socio-economic life as the time-horizon is shortened. But it does not follow that, on the basis of these characteristics, individual plans for particular processes with longer or shorter time horizons will work. The point is that these processes are mutually interrelated and thus the plans for them should take into account, as fully as possible, the mutual relations and interactions between various possible alternative decisions. It is not enough to apply a long time-horizon only to those processes which require long-term planning; it is also necessary to cover, that is to say, the whole field of socio-economic life, by preparing forecasts and initial schemes for the development of those activities also which do not require early decision. This is necessary for two reasons. Firstly, with this approach, a basis is created for making decisions concerning the special fields, with long cycles of project implementation, against a background of known relations between these fields and all other social and economic processes. Secondly, the object is to choose the main strategic development lines for all fields, so that this can provide a basis for more specific decision to be taken later, within relatively shorter time-horizons.

At the same time it should be emphasised that it is essential to ensure a sufficient flexibility in the final shaping of the economic processes. In this respect there are two premises that need to be taken into account:

(a) on the one hand, it is desirable to maintain the arrangements already made for future development objectives;

(b) on the other, one has to take into account an up-to-date appraisal of the current situation, and thus take advantage of conditions more favourable than assumed in the previous state of expectations, or equally to react to less favourable trends than had earlier been assumed.

To combine these features, with longer time-horizons for decisions shaping the basic socio-economic processes and flexibility in practical operations, is very difficult. To do so requires a very clear distinction between particular types of decisions, and especially between strategic ones which establish binding policies for operations, while leaving room for adjustments, and operating ones which require quick and determined action. In various activities the time-horizon and the moment of making each type of decision may be different.

The importance of these problems shows itself more clearly if it is remembered that the assumptions necessary in long-term planning concerning the rate of growth of the economy must be related to an appraisal of the possibilities of raising efficiency, which in turn can be expressed as the attainable improvements in input–output ratios. Let us assume that we are inclined to accept a specific variant of the required minimum rate of growth of national income which will give a real improvement in living conditions to the extent regarded as necessary. This variant will require a specific improvement in economic effectiveness, and appropriate programmes and measures will be prepared to ensure its realisation. In the light of the proportions set in this variant, it is possible to prepare programmes of development for the fuel and raw materials bases, for the infrastructure and so on. At the same time, however, it is necessary to consider other variants with higher rates of growth and primarily the possibilities of speeding up the development of final production through further and more effective utilisation of the power and raw material resources and the adoption of further possibilities offered by increased effectiveness of the use and cost of labour, through further expansion of international division of labour and increased efficiency in the functioning of the economy.

These variants with a higher rate of growth may be treated alternatively as a 'reserve strategy' on the assumption that a final decision on 'switching to a higher rate' (for example, making specific investment decisions) will be taken later; or early efforts may be made to prepare the 'front' (the basis for such an eventual acceleration), particularly if this potential has alternative possible uses for various purposes.

This involves a further question whether it is better to allocate the specific means earlier in order to speed up the subsequent rate of growth and to be able to react more flexibly to future problems with a larger surplus of capacity of certain types, or whether it is better to concentrate the resources in those fields which promise a higher degree of effectiveness within a shorter time-horizon. Furthermore these problems are related to the question whether one should concentrate on selected policies which promise today a higher rate of effectiveness but are more risky if current assumptions concerning the cost and prices are falsified, or whether a different policy should be adopted, with lower expectations of benefits but also with lower risk.

The problems discussed above indicate that in long-term planning it is necessary to make a quite different approach and interpret in a different way the problems of co-ordination, of balancing, and of analysis of effectiveness. In long-term planning we should not confine ourselves to recording and comparing various figures and indicators which are assumed to be strictly determined for future periods. We should instead gear co-ordination ('harmonising' rather than balancing) toward dynamic relationships between particular links in the economy (creation of a potential for adaptation, lowering the degree of rigidity, considering the dangers of some elements being too far ahead of others). This cannot be an 'equilibrium at every moment' but a process of facilitating an equilibrium at a higher level. In this long-term approach to effectiveness, the important point is to take into consideration the scale of probable changes in the main parameters and the degree of probability of benefiting in terms of the given preferences within the limits of acceptable risk.

IV. THE METHODS OF LONG-TERM PLANNING

As a broader framework for the overall methodological consideration of long-term planning we may start from a system with qualitatively different, but mutually interdependent, kinds of activities:

(i) outlining the concepts of the dynamics and structural changes, both quantitative and qualitative, in the satisfaction of the needs of the society concerned;

(ii) identification of the various alternative possibilities of shaping the development patterns of the economy and of its main interconnections, taking into consideration the main factors affecting these possibilities (demographic factors, the development of science and technique, the relations with other countries);

(iii) relative adjustment of the above assumptions (regarding needs and possibilities), and the choice of those alternatives which will best satisfy the needs in the future at the highest attainable level, while securing their most desirable composition.

In identifying the functions mentioned above the reasoning is alternatively based on the general social premises and on the premises under which attention is concentrated on certain selected and more specific problems of strategic importance – that is to say on problems which are crucial to the rest and depend on certain concrete and qualitative projects. Many examples of such detailed problems could be given, particularly for an economy at a higher level of development. The various alternative solutions will form a tremendous number of combinations constituting alternatives for larger groupings of projects, with different networks of relationships from the point of view of subject, place and time of the intended activities, and also with different implications of uncertainty in identifying the best premise for selection. In considering these problems and in forming ideas for their solution, numerous teams of specialists take part, representing different fields of knowledge and using as a basis different types of information and methods of analysis.

Against this background, certain conclusions emerge. The key methodological problem in long-term planning is a search for operationally more effective methods and techniques for the integration of all the elements of long-term planning, so as to make this planning more comprehensive, while maintaining its efficiency in detail. This is the key problem because, as I see it now, there are a variety of different available methods, in the form of forecasting, evaluation of alternatives, programming, for studying macroeconomic proportions and inter-branch structural proportions. And at the same time there are again numerous methods of studying more limited problems in specific fields: the needs of society, the development of science and technique, the trends of development of different branches of the economy. What is insufficiently clear, however, is how to co-ordinate these two approaches more effectively in the process of long-term planning.

It is hardly to be expected that this problem can be solved by formal and algorithmic procedures, or even by some form of simultaneous comprehensive analysis, or by iterative decomposition procedures. I believe that solutions should be sought rather in the forms and ways of the mutual interactions of people guided in their reasoning by different premises, that is by taking advantage of human thought. Thinking can and should be helped by various techniques, making possible a better identification of the problems, a more comprehensive processing and utilisation of all available information. Unquestionably, it is also advisable to take all possible steps towards the systematisation of the planning processes, towards establishing an appropriate sequence of the various stages, efficient channels and terminologies for passing on the information available to all participants in these processes. The procedure should, however, leave room for taking into account subjective appraisals, based to a large extent on premises that are hard to quantify.

On the basis of experience gained hitherto one can infer that it is advisable to use simultaneously some of the following methods of integration and co-ordination of the various particular elements in long-term planning.

Firstly, it is advisable to use macro-economic programming models in order to see the interdependence between the changes of macro-proportions of development and the branch structure of domestic final demand and foreign trade. I have in mind here a fuller use of such models in the sense of getting thereby a better understanding and 'feeling', among the specialist participants in the planning processes, of the relationships and interdependencies which emerge between 'their problems' and the field with which they are mainly dealing and the general economic proportions. There are here at least two procedures which should be used in parallel. One is to make available to all participants the results of the alternative general economic studies; this gives some idea concerning the probable place and role of particular interactions of the economy on the proportions proposed for the future. The second valuable procedure is the identification of the main preconditions for the desired macro-proportions of development, such as the factors upon which may depend the proportions of the distribution of the national income, the efficiency of labour, the productivity of capital resources, the processes of the reproduction of the resources, together with indication of the ways in which these factors depend upon the solutions being sought regarding more detailed interactions of the economy. In contrast with a normal decomposition procedure, the point here is not only and not principally to provide initial information on the constraints on partial programming, but rather to create a better understanding of the problems that have to be solved. An essential aspect here is emphasis on the relationship between success in solving such problems and the expected speed of achievement of any given set of social objectives.

Secondly, an important tool for the integration of the separate elements in a long-term plan is represented by *problem-oriented programmes*, designed from the point of view of an overall approach to all the relevant factors and projects affecting some basic area of social needs such as nutrition, housing, education, health care, or equally for solving other problems of strategic importance to the whole economy, particularly in the fields of scientific and technical progress, international division of labour, management of fuel, power, and raw material resources, main types of construction materials, development of infrastructure, and so on.

The characteristic feature of such programmes is a comprehensive consideration of the groups of projects related to particular branches of the economy, or of various types of projects, such as those for research and development, investment, management, personnel training, those relative to methods of planning and management. The factor binding such different projects together is the attempt to achieve some common objective and the most effective solution of some given problem. The criteria of effectiveness derive from the assumptions of general social rationality. That is, that the desired final decisions affecting a given problem shall be evaluated in terms of the overall considerations of socio-economic growth; that the choice of outlays shall be made by evaluating the benefits attainable with alternative allocations of the resources.

The projects included in the problem-oriented programmes will not cover the whole field of activities of particular elements in the economy, such as branches, organisations, regions, but will refer only to the relevant parts. These parts are of particular importance to changes in the structure and technical and economic level of effectiveness of the economy. These networks of mutually related and deliberately directed projects become in this way an important means of transmission of the general social premises of development regarding the fields of activities that are the subject of direct interest to the responsible planning units, ministries, associations, or regional authorities. This affects indirectly also other processes that are not included in the problem programmes.

Thirdly, one should include the integrating effect of the economic analysis of effectiveness. This is very difficult because of certain features characteristic of long-term planning. The evaluation of benefits and costs should be made in terms of future and not present conditions; one has to take into account, therefore, the interactions between all the consequences of a given alternative decision in one segment and the decisions governing all the related elements in the whole system. In addition, the methods of evaluation should ensure subordination to the criteria of general social rationality. An allowance needs to be made for expected changes in the mutual relations and evaluations of effects and outlays, partly as a consequence of consciously shaped projects and partly through independent factors. And the effects of uncertainty regarding future results and outlays need to be taken into consideration.

In this situation, I think that the influence of the premises of effectiveness should operate on the processes of long-term planning primarily along the following lines:

(1) There is a need for parallel consideration of the expected and desirable dynamics of changes in demand and of the potential conditions of its satisfaction. The point is to concentrate attention on those products for which there is a very high probability of a large growth of demand in the future, both because of priorities in the shaping of the future structure of the social objectives of development and because of the conditions of international division of labour. For such products it is particularly necessary to strive for a greater and more rapid reduction of their unit 'input–output ratios' and to create more favourable conditions for raising the power to satisfy the growing demand. From this angle, the proposals concerning investments, scientific and development studies, specialisation, co-operation, and the like, should be

considered. In parallel, attention should be paid to the types of products which, as the result of the potentialities of the economy, will be available under particularly favourable conditions making possible a rapid increase in the effectiveness of production. With respect to such products we should seek primarily the possibility of stimulating future demand and thus affecting the structure of demand. Particularly worth stressing is the necessity of taking the above premises into account simultaneously. For it is necessary to avoid one-sided domination either of considerations of production effectiveness over the considerations of the desirable structure of demand, or vice versa.

(2) The factor calling especially for a joint examination of the issues mentioned above is, as is well known, the possibility of taking advantage, in various ways, of international division of labour. Under the conditions prevailing in our economy, it is of particular importance to prepare and carry out the programmes of various projects expanding and strengthening different forms of integration of the C.M.E.A. countries. It is necessary, I think, to adopt an approach that would make possible the consideration of such ventures and of their relative effectiveness in relation to the overall policies of development strategy. For it is not enough to act on the basis of the policies determined by partial analysis in a case in which the factors of decisive importance are the current prices and costs and the current profitability of individual enterprises.

(3) The complexity of the problems subject to cost-effectiveness analysis necessitates a corresponding adaptation of the form and character of the calculation techniques. For the crux of the matter is that, in considering alternative solutions for a given sector of the economy, consideration needs to be given to all the essential relations and conditions which will exist in the future, and not those of today, at the point of interaction of this sector with many other sectors. From this point of view proper importance needs to be attached to mathematical programming and electronic data processing.

Discussion of the Paper by Professor Porwit

Mr Hjerppe (Finland) in introducing the discussion said that he thought that the general problems of planning discussed in the paper in relation to Poland had many analogies in other countries as well. The paper was divided into four parts; first, a brief introduction to the problem; second, a definition of the scope and tasks of long-term planning; third, some specific problems of long-term planning; and fourth, the methods of long-term planning. In the introductory section long-term planning was seen as a part of a complex system of the centralised management of a socialist economy. He thought that this functional approach was very interesting and implied several assumptions. The first was that the activities of parts of the system should converge upon the basic activities of the whole system, and the second was that every part of the system should behave efficiently. It was argued that the purpose of planning was to maximise the satisfaction of social needs with the resources available to the society concerned. When considering these needs, one could distinguish public needs and individual needs, and in respect to these needs the problems of planning could be divided into five categories: the setting of social objectives and their mutual relationships; long-term planning concerned with the material conditions required for the achievement of social objectives; the determination of the attainability in existing conditions of the social objectives established; an implementation programme; adjustments needed in the course of implementation.

The various functions of planning were discussed, and these functions were regarded as including, first, the determination of strategy; second, development programming; and third, permanent control of social and economic processes for these purposes. Thus, in this context long-term planning was seen as a procedure to determine the strategy of the system. To create such a strategy it was regarded as practicable to adopt a complex approach to scientific-technological problems and to international economic problems as well as to the economic balances within the country.

In considering the objectives of strategy, Professor Porwit emphasised the aim of identifying future problems that could not be solved in any other way than by special measures that needed to be taken considerably in advance and in anticipation of the emergence of these problems. Such problems were described as usually being interdisciplinary in nature and demanding a constructive approach on the part of individuals and social institutions. The question Mr Hjerppe wanted to put here was what factors had actually been taken into account in their long-term planning in Poland? How did these compare with what should ideally have been done? How was it done?

The preparation of development programmes first included the establishment of a number of functional programmes in the major social fields such as those of nutrition, housing, education, and the like. The second step was to relate these different programmes so as to ensure their feasibility. The next was to ensure the efficiency of the programme. Other special areas of social organisation and management needed to be developed, such as information, the system of scientific research, investment organisation, and so on.

E

Normative strategic and operational planning formed a sort of pyramid, the former representing its apex, and the latter its base. This simple scheme made possible a comparison of different planning systems, though in a market economy norms did not appear as an independent category but were rather built into the system. None the less, there should be some relationship between operational and other forms of planning. Thus he would like to ask how this problem was understood and handled in Poland. In other words, did normative and strategic planning represent different forms of planning work, and if they did then how were they co-ordinated?

The third section of the paper discussed specific features of a long-term plan, and there appeared to be four problem areas. The first was that the normative framework should always be available in operational planning. When making short-term decisions it was essential to realise their general purpose, and this problem was inseparable from the decisions over minor issues which made up the essence of the whole long run. A second distinguishing feature of long-term planning was flexibility, so that a plan could easily be adjusted to unforeseen developments and changes. Third was the problem of the desirable concentration in particular industrial regions, since greater concentration involves greater risk. And finally there was the problem of centralised or de-centralised co-ordination and planning which was a crucial issue for any type of economy.

In regard to methodology it was suggested that it entailed methods of internal integration of operational and long-term planning. That implied, on the one side, that long-term plans needed to be more complex in character while, on the other, they should not lose their special long-term approach. It was also suggested that macro-economic models could be more widely used. In this context he wished to ask what was the current use and role of macro-economic models in Poland?

Another important aspect of long-term planning was the integration of problem-oriented programmes with the tasks of finding the most efficient solution of a given problem. That raised the question whether a series of optimal individual solutions of a number of individual problems did inevitably result in an overall optimum for a system as a whole? That seemed to be the assumption of the author.

To ensure the effectiveness of a programme was regarded as the third tool, both for macro-economic modelling and problem-oriented programmes, requiring integration of these different types of planning into a long-term plan. A question here was that we seemed to be moving from normative to operational planning. Did that imply a change to concentrating on norms, as would seem logical in the light of the triangle that had been described?

Dr Grove (U.S.A.) said there was no reference in the paper to one aspect of long-term planning that received a great deal of attention at least in the company in which he was employed. To his way of thinking the essence of planning was really forecasting. The forecast was in fact both an estimate of desired achievements and of their attainability in terms of necessary actions. Whether these objectives would be achieved depended on the accuracy of the forecast. One thing was certain about forecasts, and in particular about long-term forecasts: they were subject to errors. Thus, in working out an action programme one had to be very much aware of the fact that forecasts would be subject to error. One way to guard against error was to devise tracking or monitoring methods so that it was constantly possible to identify errors in the forecast at the earliest moment possible. But there were other ways, and that led him to his question. The other way was to have one's action programme provide a higher degree of flexibility than would be necessary if one were sure that one's objectives and their priority would not change and that the proposed programme of action could be relied upon to achieve these objectives. One had to be prepared to pay a cost for this, and flexibility for future periods would not necessarily represent an optimum in terms of present circumstances. In state planning in Poland, to what extent was one prepared to pay for extra flexibility, and secondly, how were actions delayed in order to obtain additional knowledge? To what extent were such considerations explicitly and deliberately taken into account in Poland?

Professor Denison (U.S.A.) commented that it was extraordinarily difficult to forecast by any method the developments of new products, new processes and so on. Did the existence of a plan, in Poland or elsewhere, tend to diminish its own value by not introducing new products as quickly as might be done? What mechanism was employed to make sure that it would not have unfavourable effects on technological progress?

Professor Maier (G.D.R.) said that it was not quite clear to him what were the differences between forecasting, social strategy, and long-term planning as they were understood in this paper. He thought that definitions of these should be more precise. He agreed that the basic criterion must be the social rationality of development, which was a qualitative criterion. What quantitative criteria did they regard as necessary from the point of view of long-term planning?

Professor Porwit (Poland) intervening to reply to the discussion thus far, said that he regarded the first two sections of the paper as an introduction to the rest of it. The paper as a whole was not a complete explanation of the practice of planning in Poland but rather a description of certain features of it. Thus in answering the questions put to him he would try also to say something about some of the more general aspects of long-term planning and to provide some more information about Polish planning experience.

Mr Hjerppe's question was concerned with two things: their approach to strategic planning, and the relationship between strategic and normative planning, including interrelations between decision-making at the political level and the strategic planning. His view was that there were two simultaneous and parallel ways of analysing the tasks and functions of planning. The first was to distinguish between strategic, tactical and operational factors; the second was to distinguish between long-term, medium-term and short-term horizons.

These methods could be distinguished only in broad terms, because strategic functions could be performed not only in long-term but also in medium-term and even in short-term horizons while operational and tactical factors were intertwined both in medium and short terms. The explanation of this distinction was that the strategic functions were concerned with problems of crucial importance to the whole economy, problems which were decisive for the existence and welfare of the given society as a whole.

Strategic decisions taken from this point of view did not necessarily have to be very detailed or elaborate, neither was it necessary that they should be fully co-ordinated from the point of view of implementation or attainability. In this sense tactical decisions were concerned with how to implement strategic decisions, while operational decisions were, in his opinion, more concerned with day-by-day production and management processes.

If this were taken as the basis then the difference between normative and strategic planning could be analysed at several levels. At the national level what was absolutely essential – and what was called 'normative' by Mr Hjerppe, though he himself did not use that term – was the definition of some principal criteria for the evaluation of alternative developments which were appropriate to their political and social system. That meant that they approached the problems of working out a strategy with a set order of priorities regarding the achievement of various social objectives, these priorities being of the first, second, third and lower orders.

There were problems that it was difficult to formulate mathematically and thus to insert them into an objective function, so that these problems had to be grouped into priority groupings. That was what, in his view, could be called a normative approach to long-term planning; it was exogenous from the point of view of the criteria of evaluation.

When one came to the lower echelons, then for every accepted set of socio-political priorities there appeared to be corresponding variants of the lower order, concerned with more specifically economic phenomena, such as production, investment, foreign trade, and the like, which were dominant for some sub-systems but which were instruments from the point of view of the overall fundamental criteria. It was in this sense that he had spoken of the necessity to have adequate prior information concerning the bigger issues, to be used within sub-systems for shaping their possible solutions. In this sense the work of the sub-systems could be more quantifiable, though it was always difficult to draw a borderline between planning and making decisions.

Turning to methodological problems, and particularly the overall comprehensive modelling of the economy, he wished to draw attention first to the idea that sometimes what was needed was not so much to have an overall model for finding an optimal solution as to have a consultative model which would form a means of stimulating various possible interconnections and implications, without being so ambitious as to look for one single optimal solution.

The second thing he wanted to say was that if one faced the problem of integrating sub-system approaches and overall approaches, decomposition procedures of even the mixed type suggested by Professor Malinvaud would be very difficult to implement for a long-term time horizon. It might be useful to have a limited number of comprehensive models for sub-systems to see their effects on overall economic balances and the problems requiring solutions in this connection.

In regard to problem-oriented programmes, he thought that these would be more understandable as compared with P.P.B.S. or what was known as an 'economic mission' – that was to give certain fields or groups of products the possibility of complementary substitution, introduction of new products, changing the scope of markets, and so on, rather than the method adopted until a few years earlier which took as its basic organisation structure the individual unit. That form of organisation structure had made the introduction of changes more difficult to handle.

He had never meant to suggest that a summation of optimal solutions for problem-oriented programmes would produce a global optimum. But if they derived some of the problems to be solved from overall considerations, then it was proper to speak of solving these supposedly important problems from the point of view of overall considerations. In practice, they had thirty-two such programmes in operation at present, and these were of widely different types. One related to consumers' needs; another to certain basic needs in the field of resources; a third to the infrastructural network; and so on. These were groups of problems which had been introduced from the top. At the same time there were problem-oriented programmes which had been introduced from below and were dealing with technological and inter-industry problems which might affect a number of different branches of industry.

He had said that he saw the estimation of economic efficiency as one possible tool for integrating the elements of an overall plan. The difficulties were the high degree of uncertainty and the need to use future prices. If one assumed that long-term planning was concerned with qualitative changes then it was very difficult to stimulate them merely by quantitative changes in the structure. In this sense it was important for such ideas of change to be channelled through common interests in discovering the best solutions.

He was advancing ideas that were new, but in his view it was not so much a question of being certain about future prices or the future efficiency of particular products as of looking in dynamic terms at the relative rates of growth of demand for particular commodities and the rates of decrease of costs estimated optimistically, always in relative terms. If greater demand was to be expected, they should look for technological and other means in the relevant field to enable them to be competitive in meeting that demand.

As to other questions, he thought he had answered Professor Maier's question when he emphasised that he wished to see quantitative criteria more closely related to specific problems while overall problems should be handled on a more heuristic basis. In answer to Dr Grove's question he would begin by saying what was the opinion of a number of people in his country, that one of the inadequacies of their past performance had been unwillingness to take decisions that seemed less effective immediately but were more promising for the future. This was becoming more and more recognised as something necessary to have in mind. As for delays in implementation of decisions taken, this was a crucial issue and of vital concern to their whole concept of long-term planning. In the case of, for example, ten to fifteen-year plans no figures included in such plans were considered as obligatory targets. They were regarded as obligatory only as a framework for shorter-term, say, five-year decisions. In regard to the latter, it was not yet agreed whether, for example, it would be useful to have some revision of investment allocations as between different ministries, made within the five-year period, if new assessments of the importance of some particular field should emerge. Would it be enough to have the possibility of introducing additional investment when more information showed this to be desirable?

Professor Denison's question required different answers for different time-horizons, with the long-term horizon leaving some room for adaptation. Of course, there was always the question of risk and uncertainty involved. As for the short period, he thought the problem was more one of the current functioning and management of the economy than one of planning, a question of how far the existing structure could be adapted to changes in demand or other changes. In this respect there was a tendency in Poland to restrict the number of fixed planning indicators and to encourage adaptability and freedom of choice in individual enterprises.

Professor Khachaturov (U.S.S.R.) continued the discussion, saying that the problem of needs was of immense significance for long-term planning in all the socialist countries and had been comparatively little studied. The problem covered the definition of needs, their classification, stratification and comparison. Their classification could first be approached by distinguishing personal and public needs. The material components of the former were nutrition, clothing, housing, personal needs, and the like, while the socio-cultural needs included education, psychological needs, and the like. Public needs covered material needs – for power, resources, information, technology, and the like, and social needs – for science, medical care, social security, and the like. Such a classification could be rather easily made. It was a much more difficult task to define the hierarchy of needs and to establish priorities. But this task was relevant to the social objectives considered in long-term planning. To some extent the hierarchy of needs could be built on the basis of income level, which indicated the probable weight of different groups of needs. For example, the share of nutrition need was decreasing with the rise of income level, while the share of housing, durables and other needs was increasing. A similar analysis could be applied to public needs which required a correlation between the social objectives, the level of development already achieved regarding production forces and national income. But he believed that such general analysis required further research for application to long-term planning in all socialist countries, and that it represented a challenging task for economists. Here he was not contradicting but supplementing what Professor Porwit had said in his paper.

Professor Malinvaud (France) agreed with Professor Porwit on the usefulness of a model for planning that used a decomposition procedure as a representation of the optimal organisation of planning. He wanted to clarify what was the purpose of the theory of planning procedures, which to his mind did not make it its purpose to identify some particular computing scheme, or to shape precisely the administrative structure of planning, but rather to understand the operation of planning better. It was thus never intended to be applied without more consideration of particular needs. When he had entered this field, his idea had been that theory was too remote from practice and that that needed to be changed. One of his motives was to emphasise the necessity to use models to plan the production sphere. He thought he had come to appreciate this. On the question of the allocation of production between collective and private needs, he was not satisfied with the decision-making process implicit or explicit in the theories of Eriklind and Samuelson. He thought it was necessary to study procedures closer to common experience. This research should indeed have implications for the administrative functioning of planning, but these implications were neither direct nor simple.

6 Long-term Overall Planning in Hungary

I. Hetényi

I. THE NOTION OF A LONG-TERM PLAN

Long-term planning forms a part of the system of economy-wide planning, in the framework of which long-term, medium-term and short-term plans are being drawn up in Hungary. The development of the economy has been determined in Hungary for the past twenty-five years by medium-term, generally five-year plans. The five-year plan of the economy comprises:

(a) the problems relating to the growth rate and the major proportions of the economy;

(b) the central decisions relating to development, especially in the fields of investment, the training of labour, technological development and living-standard policies;

(c) the instruments and economic regulators necessary for implementation of the plan.

Economic policy and planning has to tackle many problems the implementation and essential effects of which cannot be restricted to a single five-year period. Among these are the major investment projects, the main directions of scientific research, certain problems of raw material supply, education, qualified manpower training, housing, the social security system, etc. Thus, the policy for progress needs to be determined in a number of fields by means of longer perspectives.

Since 1961 this requirement has been met by the working out of technico-economic conceptions for various fields of the economy. These conceptions serve as a foundation for economy-wide planning. The technico-economic conceptions are studies on the possible effects of technical progress, worked out by reliance on many-sided analyses, on the policies that may be practicable under the conditions of our country, and on the measures to be taken for their implementation. These conceptions are drawn up for the development of individual groups of products, a branch of industry, or for a vertical sector of problems. The technico-economic conceptions are worked out for longer periods in the light of the particular features of the field in question. They also indicate quantitatively, between likely limits, the development deemed desirable and also suggest various possible variants. A similar role to these technico-economic conceptions is performed by long-term studies and other prognoses showing the social impacts of development.

The five-year economy-wide planning and the separately prepared long-term technico-economic and similar conceptions provide many bench-marks for planning the long-term development of the national economy. It is true that various uncertainties emerge in the context of long-term development. But the relative determination of these conceptions makes it imperative for us to work out the comprehensive outlines of development for a longer term. Thus, the central comprehensive long-term planning:

(i) harmonises the longer-term conceptions in the framework of a uniform strategy;[1]
(ii) systematically maps out the more distant future and thereby identifies the expectable pivotal points of development, helping their solution.

The long-term economy-wide plan brings together the long-term trends of the essential factors affecting social and economic development, determines the objectives to be attained by deliberate social action and the main ways and means of attainment. Thus, long-term planning in part lays the foundations for long-term decisions on processes with long gestation periods and which are practically irreversible; in part it formulates the requirements of long-term development in concrete terms for the purposes of medium-term planning. The system of plans for different terms, including long-term planning, helps us to assess the requirements and possibilities of development for a longer term. It also facilitates making the decisions on the development of the economy at an optimal date and in relation to the relevant period.

The long-term plan is not of a type that will be immediately obligatory for the executive organs concerned. Nor does it pretend to fix the whole future state of the economy down to the end of a fifteen-year period. The emphasis is placed on establishing the socio-economic requirements, on attaching priorities to the objectives that can be set, on determining the structural changes leading to them, and on developing the strategies and formulating the long-term decisions to meet them. This view of the plan is related to the idea of revising the long-term plan every five years, always extending the time-horizon by another five years. This involves a continuous checking and increasing precision of the long-term objectives.

At present, the time horizon of long-term economy-wide planning is fifteen years. In some fields the working out of conceptions with an even longer horizon is possible, but for the time being we do not

[1] For an explanation of this and other terms see p. 135 below.

think it possible to formulate comprehensive plans for a period beyond fifteen years.

We consider the long-term, fifteen-year planning as an autonomous link in the planning system. In the light of Hungarian experience it is not expedient to link up fifteen-year and five-year planning organisationally in the sense that the first five-year stage of the long-term period should be considered immediately as a five-year plan. Five-year planning has many problems beyond the scope of ideas dealt with in fifteen-year planning. Rather than intertwine them, it is more expedient to secure links between the plans.

II. LONG-TERM PLANNING IN PROCESS

The first attempts at working out a long-term, fifteen-year plan were made in Hungary in 1959. In fact, the computations remained at the level of prognosis and did not become strategies of economic development. Only the fifteen-year plan for residential construction was formally approved. For this, such practical considerations as the uneven development of the Hungarian economy in the fifties, making a well founded forecast difficult, and the lack of adequate planning co-operation between the member countries of the CMEA were partly responsible.

In 1968 we started to work out a long-term plan covering the years 1971–85. We have made efforts to meet the requirements created by practical considerations for long-term planning as well as to underline the specific long-term features. This means an increased emphasis as compared with earlier planning, particularly in the fields of accounting for interdependences between social and economic progress and in establishing the connections between branches.

Long-term planning is directed by the Planning Office, and any other overall studies are the responsibility of that office. To assist in planning, the president of the Planning Office has formed committees of representatives of responsible bodies and of scientists. Committees have been established for manpower and living standards, regional planning, protection of the environment, international economic relations, industry, the food economy, construction, and transport and communications.

To aid the president of the office, a central consultative committee has been appointed, composed of the chairmen of these committees and of distinguished scientists. And to help in the planning of wider economic problems, an economic committee is also available.

The committee form, despite all the familiar difficulties associated with such organisation, helps to mitigate the departmental loyalties and to repress any particularist approach to the problems that the committee faces; it also provides opportunities for regular exchange of opinion between specialists from administrative bodies, universities and other institutions. Hungarian long-term planning thus relies more extensively on scientific research institutes than has hitherto been the case, and at the same time provides incentives for their work.

As a first stage of the long-term planning work, long-term analyses, covering 1950–67, were prepared. These were followed by the elaboration of prognoses and hypotheses[1] to serve as a basis for long-term planning. After a many-sided discussion of the hypotheses, partial conceptions were worked out for diverse fields of the economy. Based on the conceptions, variants were also worked out in most cases. The next stage of the work is the evaluation and co-ordination of ideas, in the course of which dialogues take place between the centre and the partial planners, as a result of which the partial concepts can be brought together into a single conception.

III. SPECIAL METHODOLOGICAL PROBLEMS OF LONG-TERM PLANNING

The long-term approach has brought scientific work on prognoses to the fore the world over. In the literature, however, attention has been focused mostly on working out the prognoses and less on the problems of using them in planning. Thus I shall make a special effort to make the connections between prognostication and planning clear and meaningful.

The planning centre insists that those working on the partial schemes shall make deliberate use of the prognoses. It requires that support for essential features in any proposals shall be explicitly judged on the basis of the material made available. We make efforts to ensure that the prognoses shall constitute a system capable of serving as a foundation for long-term planning. Thus the following requirements emerge:

(i) *Completeness.* This is not meant in any absolute sense, but requires that the plan data shall be supported by an adequate number of prognoses on which the data are based and that these prognoses shall be of satisfactory quality.

(ii) The system must be *free from contradictions.* This means that, on the one hand, individual elements of a plan variant shall not be based on two versions of the prognoses of the same process and, on the other hand, that the various partial prognoses shall not be mutually exlusive.

[1] For the explanation of terms see the Annex.

(iii) *Hierarchy of prognoses.* It will be explained that one of the reasons for drawing up plan variants may be to show the differences in alternative prognoses taken as a basis – that is, the effects of different assumptions about the same process or phenomenon. It is, therefore, advisable to start planning with some comprehensive prognoses which are only loosely interrelated, for instance regarding the state of the world economy and regarding population growth, and various further prognoses should be drawn up in terms of each of these.

The long-term plan describes the process of change, the path of development, its course over time and not merely the final destination that is regarded as desirable. For present purposes the best solution seems to be to divide the period planned into five-year stages. Thus, technically speaking, the established methods of five-year planning can be employed, for lack of better ones, to show the time path of planned development. In terms of content, however, we are working not on three consecutive five-year plans but on a single fifteen-year plan. This will show itself chiefly in the mutual inter-actions of the sub-periods. In long-term planning the first two periods should indicate the path leading to the objectives defined for the third five-year period. Of course, in this way requirements may emerge for the initial years which can be seen not to be feasible. If this happens, the path must be covered again in reverse. And this process must be repeated several times until a development path is found which seems both realistic as regards achievement and desirable from the viewpoint of future objectives.

It seems inevitable that one must make the computations both at constant prices and at the predicted current prices. Prognoses are drawn up for the tendencies of world market prices, and separately for the C.M.E.A. market prices, for the impact of technical progress on the input pattern, and for the changes in relative per capita wages required to reflect economic policy. These prognoses are taken into account in the course of the co-ordination of the plan. It must be noted that the prognoses of price and value relations can be used only for the formulation of major trends. For concrete long-term development decisions it seems inescapable that one must work out separate price prognoses relating to the particular circumstances of the given problem.

IV. COMPREHENSIVE AND PARTIAL CONCEPTIONS: VARIANTS

Planning comprises two essentially different types of problem. First, for individual selected aspects of the national economy, such as industries or sectors, partial conceptions are worked out. These show as precisely as possible the expected and desirable directions of development and the outlines of a policy to promote this development, and they comprise computations to establish these partial conceptions. The computations are used for co-ordinating all the various conceptions into the long-term development trend of the whole economy. Second, an overall conception is worked out and summary computations are made which express the major objectives of the national economy and the development of its major constituents. This serves as a framework for co-ordinating the partial conceptions and for determining the paths and steps which will best secure the long-term objectives of the national economy. Emphasis is laid on planning the structural changes of the economy. The growth rate of the economy is a computation, consistent with the structural changes, which reflects not only the framework of the changes but also their results.

In working out the partial conceptions to be planned for the long-term, the main criteria are the length of the period necessarily involved in reaching a decision and the time needed for the implementation of the decision. The most important conceptions worked out in the course of planning for 1971–85 are as follows:

(a) Prognoses and conceptions relating to social and human factors and to living standards: population, employment level and composition; changes in working hours; the special problems relating to the young, women and old people; income policy; personal consumption, with special respect to the development of leisure time, the impact of motoring, tourism and urbanisation; education, health, housing and public utilities; and finally sports and adult education.

(b) Expected trends of international economic relations, with particular respect to integrations in the world economy: including the integration of the C.M.E.A. countries; the opportunities for an export-oriented foreign economic policy; the economico-geographical endowments of the country and international supplies; the problems of technico-scientific co-operation.

(c) Conceptions regarding the regional development of the economy: regional prognoses of population, the regional distribution of the natural resources of the country, the trends in the geographical distribution of population; the problems relating to protection of the environment.

(d) Conceptions of the development of productive and service industries; and as aspects of that: the directions of structural changes in industry; the conceptions for the development of energy supply, metallurgy, petro-chemistry, engineering technologies, the food economy, forestry, transport, communications, water management.

The working out of these partial conceptions requires various methodologies. It is our experience that the substance of development can be expressed with the aid of indexes in the fields of manpower and infrastructure, though any quantitative estimate reflects the strategy only imperfectly. In other fields the relation between strategy and quantified estimates is rather nebulous. The quantified estimate is an expression of the objective of economic policy or a prognosis of the consequences or requirements of a proposed strategy, always within wide limits and not indicating all the essential features of a policy. This is true, for example, of many of the foreign trade and regional development estimates.

This double character of quantitative planning is also reflected in the long-term planning of production. In some branches which are capital intensive and do not suffer from rapid changes in technology or in product-mix, such as power, animal husbandry, or rail transport, planning has to be conducted to serve as a basis for quantitative decisions. In other fields, where technological and market changes are frequent, an estimate of the changes in the production pattern has to be embodied not so much in quantitative production targets as in working out scientific and technological policies and policies for research institutions and, in general, proposals for economic policy.

This second group includes a considerable proportion of all that manufacturing which is decisive from the viewpoint of dynamic development. If we identify the main lines of development in this field and formulate accordingly our scientific, technological, institutional and other measures of economic policy, for example regarding preferences or decisions on organisation, this does not amount to limiting the contents of planning but represents a peculiarity of all long-term decisions. The fixing of the usual production and investment targets in this field will continue to be a function of five-year planning.

In the long term an interdisciplinary approach, involving the planning of selected complex problems by cutting across the responsibilities of branches, is of particular importance. In part such problems have to be planned in the same way as they are planned in the short-term by separate branches, either because responsibilities are ill-defined or because changes are slow, as with the relation of the stock of cars to road building. But in part the planning of new types of problems becomes necessary, as with the protection of the environment. An interdisciplinary approach is possible where considerable long-term interdependencies exist. On the other hand, planning is made much easier if problems are selected in such a way that the degree of interdependence is small.

It is a basic concept of our planning procedure that the partial conceptions must be co-ordinated for the long term. The co-ordination must take place in conceptual terms, implying that the objectives of the partial conceptions and the methods for attaining them must be made consistent with the criteria established for the economy as a whole. On the other hand, quantitative co-ordination is also necessary. As regards methods of quantitative co-ordination, various views have emerged. According to some, it is sufficient if those working on the partial conceptions are guided by a few general assumptions constituting a framework for the computations. Our accepted methodology is more formal. It attempts quantitative co-ordination. The core of this is a uniform system of indexes worked out for forty-six sectors and a system of models based on it. To be able to use it, the partial conceptions worked out by methods suited to the particular problem, or rather the elements in these conceptions relating to the reproduction process (such as production itself, labour requirements, investment, material consumption) must be quantified by sectors within the defined framework of this uniform system of indexes. These are known as variants. These partial computations supply the input parameters for the central models. Several different models are used, representing the special problems of various stages in planning and showing the problems that may emerge at the various stages. For examination of the most general macro-economic problems, aggregate growth models are used; to co-ordinate the partial conceptions and to select from among possible combinations the variant that is best from some given point of view, a moderately-sized linear programming model has been constructed; other models again are used for analysing the temporal interrelations, the time paths of economic processes, and, above all, the problems of investment. For the time being, there is no formal relation between the models; the collation and combined evaluation of the various computational results from these models is the task of qualitative economic analysis.

The fact that several models are used, and each of them is solved with variants expressing different assumptions, shows that none of these results is considered as a self-contained 'optimal' plan variant. These series of computations are useful tools of economic analysis and for formulating conceptions, since they reveal interrelations which may remain hidden in a 'traditional' plan co-ordination process, restricted to a single variant. On the basis of these general computations, the ways in which to improve the partial conceptions for the branches can be defined. Thus the working out of the conceptions and the work related to the comprehensive computations are carried on in various stages, in the form of a dialogue between the centre and the branches and involving iterative computations.

Co-ordination can mainly help in defining the policy to achieve structural changes, but at the same time the resulting growth rate plays an essential part in the formulation of economic policies. Structural changes take place, that is to say, as essential elements in economic growth but at the same time closely dependent on the latter.

Whether structural and growth-rate variants can be related in any precise fashion depends very much on the state of development of planning. The better the interactions between the two can be estimated, the more can we plan growth-rate variants. Unfortunately, economic knowledge in this field is rather limited. In other words, our co-ordination methods can account at all accurately only for the effects of inter-sectoral structural changes; the effects of structural changes within a sector on its input–output relations, and particularly on inputs per unit of output, can be only roughly estimated. Since the changes in the sectoral input coefficients have the greatest effect on the rate of economic growth and on the choice of the desirable structure, the relation between a given general development strategy and the growth rate can be only established by inference.

To turn to the possibility of formulating a comprehensive conception, we must start from the fact that this is closely related both to permanent and to variable factors affecting a given national economy. The permanent factors in the development of the Hungarian economy are the socialist social system of the country and the small size of the country. The factors that vary over time are the level of development of the economy, and 'time' itself and the consequent changes of conditions in the world economy and in technology.

Depending on its situation, size and other characteristics of a given country, a comprehensive conception and strategy can be defined:

(i) in terms of the principal political objectives depending on economic development, such as social objectives, reaching the level of more advanced countries, strengthening of international standing, balanced growth;

(ii) in terms of the economic objectives required to meet these political aims, such as industrialisation, world market competitiveness, diversification of economic structure, or selective development;

(iii) in terms of the fundamental instruments of economic development, such as the rate of investment; the relative values attached to material and moral incentives.

The variants of any comprehensive conception may differ in several, though not necessarily in all these elements. In our experience, that is to say, there are objectives, tasks and paths which are virtually identical in all comprehensive conceptions, while for other objectives and policies, alternatives can be identified.

In various fields long-term planning follows basically a single and uniform set of guidelines. For working out the plan conception for 1971–85 there are:

(a) the fundamental requirements of social policy, including increasing the security of life, enhancing the open character of our society, developing a cultured and healthy way of life, achieving economic development by reliance on the growth of labour productivity, associating Hungary's economic development with the consolidation of the economic community of the socialist countries, strengthening the socialist social relations of production;

(b) certain general assumptions regarding the trends of the world economy, such as peaceful coexistence and the expected power relations between socialist countries, developed capitalist countries and developing countries;

(c) certain general economic features in longer-range economic development extending beyond the fifteen-year horizon, whereby, after the industrialisation of the last twenty years and after creation of a large-scale agriculture, the general economic problem will be to rearrange, reconstruct and structurally transform the technology and organisation of production, in the light of world demands and of world market relative values, and to raise the levels of infrastructure and urbanisation to reflect the new productive basis.

In other fields alternative conceptions are studied which differ from one another in the importance or otherwise attached to developments designed to satisfy certain requirements of social policy; in the assumptions made for purposes of planning about circumstances that are outside our control and can thus be foreseen only with a high degree of uncertainty, so that plans must be worked out for both favourable and unfavourable conditions; in the objectives and means of achieving them we forecast for those problems that are undecided and which, with the scientific knowledge available, are incapable of decision.

A further problem in the decision of certain alternatives is the weighing of the risk involved in their implementation. This risk depends not only on the 'probability' of the variant adopted but also on how we can change, if conditions change, from one conception to another without loss or with small loss. We regard as organic parts of the comprehensive conception only those important factors that can affect considerably the main directions of economic progress. In our experience, these are:

(a) in the productive sphere, the opportunities for sharing in the international division of labour, the extent of protection given to production and of selective development, the preference to be given to more rapid development of branches in the vanguard of technical progress or to reconstruction of traditional branches, the infrastructural requirements related to production policies;

(b) alternative developments of infrastructure and urbanisation from the point of view of the desirable degree of geographical concentration of the forces of production and the extent to which we wish to see a change in the geographical pattern of production and the labour force;

(c) alternative policies to improve living conditions, reflecting different ideas as to what we consider to be most important problems to solve during the next decade and a half, such as improvement of housing, improvement of the material and cultural conditions of the young, more active protection of the environment, reduction of the legal working week, and so on.

In the light of studies of the needs, endowments, possibilities of international co-operation and after assessing the rate of technical progress and the growth of efficiency, development variants for different productive branches with long gestation periods can be worked into the plan consistently with the comprehensive conception.

It is an absolutely necessary requirement that, in addition to solving current problems, the plan shall also make provision for the likelihood of the emergence and required solution of new problems and shall also contain incentives towards those activities on which the necessary proportion of the national income available for developments and for dynamic maintenance of existing productive capacity should be spent.

V. TRENDS IN THE STRUCTURE OF PRODUCTION

During the past twenty years per capita national income has roughly trebled. In all branches of the economy the socialist sector has become predominant. National income per head in 1970 was U.S. $900 and G.D.P. per head was U.S. $1,150. The structure of the economy has been most affected by industrialisation. The proportion of industrial employment reached a level characteristic of a developed economy, 37 per cent, in 1970. In twenty years the proportion of agricultural workers has fallen from 52 per cent to 26 per cent. Employment in services is about 4 percentage points lower than in most countries at a similar level of development.

This contrast between a moderate development level and the proportions of activities characteristic of an advanced country reflects the relatively low efficiency of production. The growth of productivity of labour has not exceeded over the past decade that observed in developed countries. If one looks at the growth of production from the point of view of fixed assets, it can be seen that investment was concentrated mainly in industry, construction and agriculture. The share of all other productive and non-productive branches in the total of fixed assets has fallen from 84 per cent in 1950 to 71 per cent.

During the next decade and a half the sources of growth are expected to change. In a few years' time, employment will practically cease to grow. Nor does it seem possible to increase the share of national income and expenditure devoted to investment in primary and secondary production. Thus, the fundamental problem for the planning of production is to work out technological strategies, strategies for international co-operation, and, consistently with these, production strategies that will contribute more to the increase of efficiency than those of the past. To this end, productive capacity must be modified to correspond with world market requirements and world market values, and the planning of changes both in respect of main branches and in micro-structure must be designed to support these strategies.

The necessity for policy changes is shown by the relevant figures. Between 1950 and 1970 gross output, inclusive of material consumption, increased on average by 6·2 per cent a year. The total output of industry and construction grew at an annual rate of 7·4 per cent, agricultural output at 2·4 per cent, and services at an annual rate of 5·1 per cent. From the point of view of production a growth of 0·9 per cent a year was provided by the growth in total employment, 1·3 per cent was the result of transfers between main branches,[1] and 4 per cent could be attributed to the growth in productivity within the main branches themselves. According to the manpower prognoses, during the next fifteen years the annual growth in activity will not be more than 0·2–0·4 per cent, having regard to reductions in the working week. Assuming an approximately unchanged employment

[1] The main branches are: industry, construction, agriculture and forestry, productive services, transport and communications, trade, management, and non-productive services.

in industry, an annual decline of 2·5–3·5 per cent in agricultural employment, and an annual 2·0–2·5 per cent growth in employment in productive and non-productive services taken together, and on the assumption of continued growth in labour productivity at the rate of the past ten years, gross output can only be expected to grow by 4·3 per cent annually. Thus to maintain the current rate of production growth, labour productivity in the main branches will need to grow at an annual rate 1·9 per cent higher than hitherto.

If one looks at growth between 1950 and 1970 from the point of view of fixed assets, gross investment amounted to 29 per cent of G.D.P., while the value of fixed assets increased by 4·3 per cent annually. The changes in proportions between the main branches reduced total capital intensity by 0·4 per cent a year. In industry capital intensity increased by 0·4 per cent annually, in agriculture by 2·4 per cent, while in services, chiefly as a consequence of fuller utilisation, capital intensity declined at an annual rate of 1·8 per cent.

If we base the prognoses of the growth of fixed assets on the productivity and capital intensity trends of the past ten years and on the prognosticated manpower available, the result that emerges is that, even to achieve the indicated 4·3 per cent annual rate of growth in production, the value of fixed assets will need to be raised by an annual rate of 5·1 per cent, that is, the rate of investment will need to be considerably increased. Investment requirements will be raised not only because of the necessity for increasing productivity, but also because the reduction of capital intensity in the service branches cannot continue at the present rate.

The most important conclusions to be drawn are these. It must be regarded as one important element of strategy to develop the structure of production in terms of branches, range of products and technologies that will be efficient by international as well as domestic standards and make possible economy both of capital and labour. The development of both productive and non-productive service branches must be more rapid than in the past but, because of their high capital intensity, their development cannot be speeded up to the point where their share in total fixed assets becomes constant. No more than a reduction of the rate of decline of their share can be set as a target for these fifteen years.

In the long-term planning of production we must take account of these factors. With the exception of agriculture, the traditional requirements for building materials and aluminium, our natural resources are inadequate to cover demand, so that production must rely on external sources to a potentially dangerous extent. And owing to the small size of the country, it must depend, for a scientific background of production in most branches, entirely on adaptation of foreign research results. Only in a few branches of industry is it possible to develop fundamentally new techniques and thus achieve an exceptional advantage in production. Moreover, since both increase of production and technological progress require close international co-operation, a flexible policy adjusted to the conditions of the international economic situation is an absolute necessity.

From all this two essential conclusions may be drawn:

(i) Apart from the appropriate development of the various domestic sectors, we must concentrate our development policy on a few industries capable of selling exports, devoting to them, without too complete commitment, all the resources necessary as preconditions of successful development. This conception is reflected in the long-term plan for scientific research in Hungary, which is composed at the national level of five priority research tasks and eleven priority research projects, each with a definite objective. The research tasks related to technical progress are: research into solid states, research into mechanisms for regulating life processes, and research into biologically active chemicals. The research projects with a definite objective in the field of production relate to the aluminium industry, petro-chemistry, computer technology, light structures, manufacturing technologies, electronic components, communications systems, methods of increasing soil fertility, new methods of meat and other food production, and investigations concerned with improvement of the human environment.

(ii) Long-term international co-ordination of plans is an indispensable condition of the efficiency and stability of our development policy. In the light of our endowments and of existing international plan co-ordination, certain development programmes have already been formulated that are equally relevant for the longer term. These include programmes for the supply of the country with natural gas, the development of the aluminium industry, petro-chemistry, manufacture of buses, production and application of computers, wider use of light structures in building. If the programmes could be supported by international agreements for their development and export, further important fields for development might be communications equipment, containerisation, production of medical, educational and commercial equipment. A long-term programme may also include development of grain and meat production, of viticulture and horticulture, and of forestry.

VI. SOME GENERAL CONCLUSIONS

At the time of writing, the overall computations have just begun. They show that the quantified variants of the different development policies differ in their patterns of trade, in their relative investment proportions of productive and service branches, and in the inputs per unit of output of the individual branches.

There is a clear trend for the share of industrial output to be growing slowly and for the share of services in the total fixed assets of the economy to be slowly declining. Structural changes can be more rapid and move between wider limits in the case of agricultural employment, investment proportions and foreign trade patterns. The decline in the share of agriculture and the growth in the shares of the chemical industry, engineering and productive services are trends of which the extent is fundamentally determined by what are the realistic rates of change in the pattern of foreign trade. The effect of rapid change in the production pattern appears primarily not in the growth rates of productivity and output, but in those variants of distribution of national income in which the share of national income devoted to consumption and development of infrastructure are increasing, as compared with those variants in which the structural change is slower. Thus, rapidity of structural change serves chiefly to reduce the difficulties of developing production.

I have tried to present the results of the long-term planning hitherto achieved in Hungary. Inevitably, this review has been rather sketchy and rather incomplete. Thus, to take one example, for lack of time I have not been able to deal with the problems of geographical planning nor with those of living-standard policy. As may be seen from this paper, planning has had to face many new problems, for which we cannot claim always to have found a final solution. We welcome, therefore, any comments and criticisms and any suggestions that we may be able to adopt in our future work.

ANNEX: Brief explanation of some technical terms

Prognosis: An analytical study based on domestic and international data enabling us to judge the future social, scientific, technical and economic processes with satisfactory probability, to discern their expectable new features and to characterise with their aid a situation developing by some future date.

Hypothesis: If some prognosis does not enable the judgement of some process or state with satisfactory probability (and, therefore, several different expectable processes and states have also to be reckoned with), the different prognoses relating to identical phenomena are called hypotheses.

Conception: A systematised long-term idea relating to the whole of the national economy or to one of its partial fields. A conception must comprise the necessary features of a long-term idea in a logically closed framework. Generally, it is an intermediary idea developing in the process of planning; after the approval of the plan the conceptions adopted and built into the plan are called plans themselves.

Variant: Quantified form of some prognosis or conception suited for being fitted into the national economic plan.

Strategy: A guideline for action concentrated on the attainment of some long-term objective and in a field of decisive importance for the objective, determining the path of desirable development and the general framework for action (its ways and forms).

Discussion of the Paper by
Dr Hetényi

Professor Augustinovics (Hungary) in opening the discussion said that one of the major points stressed in this paper was that long-term planning had to be taken seriously not only from a theoretical and scientific but also from a practical point of view. When making everyday economic decisions one really needed a strategy of economic policy worked out at a series of different planned horizons, and it was necessary that we should be prepared to put considerable and continuous effort into it.

The paper had two parts. The first dealt with certain basic methodological problems as they envisaged them in Hungary. That had to be stressed because in 1968 when they started this work there was practically no experience of the kind in Hungary, and they had to work out the basic principles and the basic methods of this work. These were outlined in the first part of the paper for the precise reason that they would like to have the comments of others on them. These principles involved what he would call the philosophy of planning, and also its methodology in a limited sense.

The points he would emphasise were these. First, they called it a long-term plan, and not a long-term projection, forecast or prediction. They did so because they wanted to emphasise the decision element in the long-term plan operation, to emphasise that the purpose of the work was not simply to foresee what might happen in the future without any action on their part but to enable long-term decisions to be taken, and this was the major element in the long-term plan work. On the other hand, a long-term plan was a specific kind of plan, wholly different from an annual or five-year plan, in that it had no direct executive function and did not include decisions concerning some remote future. It did not contain decisions which were not necessary in the immediate future. It should be a strategy for economic policy in the future, but it should influence economic development through later actual decisions and five-year plans. They also thought that the long-term plan should be reviewed and extended every five years so as to make it a continuous plan.

Second, certain special features of the long-term plan determined the organisation of long-term work. They believed that long-term planning should be done by the usual planning machinery. This was not a task for a scientific institution but for the regular planning machinery, since it would be impossible to draw up a relevant and realistic plan without all the experience and expert knowledge of their shorter-term planners. But they believed that no planning machinery, as normally constituted, possessed adequate intellectual capacity for a task of this magnitude and all the intellectual capacity available in the country should be mobilised. Thus the long-term plan was a task not simply for the ordinary planning organisation but should be regarded as a more democratic process than normal planning usually was.

Third, long-term planning was essentially an iterative procedure. There should be multi-step iteration between basically social goals and the feasible growth path of an economy, between goals and objectives on the one hand, and practicalities on the other. There also needed to be iteration in the dynamics of long-term planning, so that what was visualised and what already existed would be continuously compared. The long-term planning could not be limited to defining some final situation. Equally important was to show the path which would lead from the present to that situation. Existing prices and projected changes in prices should be compared. They did not think that long-term planning at constant prices was practicable, nor planning at future prices only, so they could not see any other solution than to iterate alternative prices.

Fourth, two types of general approach had been known at the beginning of this work in Hungary, which could be referred to as 'either–or'. One was a macro-economic growth-rate-projection approach; the other was a selected-individual-project approach. They had come to the perhaps ambitious conclusion that they would like to have selected individual projects for all those sectors of the economy which were essentially of a long-term character, but at the same time to fit them into a broader macro-economic context.

Fifth, when one was concerned with alternative schemes expressed in quantitative forms, one could speak of variants and alternatives, and their evaluation was a task of some centrally located synthesising body. Selection between these variants and alternatives should be made in such a way that overall social and other needs were kept in mind and under the constraints of economic equilibrium. Technically, this would lead one to optimisation models, yet the problem was not merely technical. It was that the selection of possible alternatives for each different sector of the economy had to be made in terms of the aggregate benefits.

Finally, they were trying to construct a unique framework for quantitative long-term planning. That is, they did not propose to have separate input systems for traditional methods of planning and for mathematical models. They had a unifying framework, which meant that different methods could be applied to different problems, but would depend on a single and unique set of data, so that the different results would be comparable.

The second part of the paper dealt with the results and experience obtained in the course of this work in Hungary. The Hungarian economy faced one peculiar situation, that was that the total number of employed could not be increased from 1976 on. Since the working hours might be expected to decrease, they had to face the situation that the total number of man-hours in, for instance, 1985 would be less than it had been in 1970. This situation would remain till the middle 1990s when a demographic change was expected.

Another unusual thing was that a shift was necessary in investment towards the service industries which had been lagging behind for the past thirty years. These unusual features meant that if they tried to forecast labour productivity or capital formation on the basis of past trends, they would inevitably decrease in the future, together with the rate of growth of the economy. Obviously, the latter was not an objective in itself but it was a very necessary condition for the increase of standards of life and for planning consumption. Thus a principal task of long-term planning was to discover some additional sources of growth.

Investigation had shown that they had certain resources and possibilities in the micro-economy, such as improvement of the quality of labour by increasing education or by training people to higher levels of professional skill. Another way might be to improve the general economic functioning and the ability of enterprises to adopt optimum solutions of their problems. But they had to look also for additional resources in the macro-structure, in a better structure of the Hungarian economy and its industries, in speeding up structural change in the sense that in framing plans priority should be given to industries consuming less labour and capital, while industries with fewer technological possibilities for growth would be expanded more slowly or even contracted.

Obviously, such macro-structural changes in the economy were closely related to foreign trade. In a country such as Hungary one of the major opportunities of changing the structure of the economy and of using resources more effectively was through foreign trade and the advantages it provided. From this point of view international economic co-operation would certainly affect their future development to a very considerable extent.

In conclusion he wanted to mention three points where experience had shown that even elaborate planning methods were perhaps not elaborate enough. One was the problem of alternatives. The real difficulty was not to select between an astronomical number of alternatives but for those with the responsibility for decision-making to envisage the alternatives and to select between them. Decision-making and planning were separable procedures in theory, but in their country at least and in his experience they were absolutely inseparable. This seemed to suggest that long-term planning should not be separated from ordinary planning. But if so, where were expert knowledge and information about current conditions to be found?

His second point was that it was sometimes said that individual growth-oriented projects should be identified for sectors and industries which were of a long-term character, while less attention could or should be given to all others. It turned out in practice that long-term objectives of the government such as the improvement of transport facilities, housing and the like, depended on the growth rate, which in turn depended on industries that were long-term in their strategies.

His final point was the problem of the single approach and of the development of mathematical models. Experience had shown that it was not sufficient to create a channel of communications between the traditional thinking of planners and those constructing models. It was also necessary to create a channel of communication in the reverse direction so that the results of the models became incorporated into the thinking of the planners. It was fully as difficult to use models as to construct them.

Professor Khachaturov (U.S.S.R.) thought that it seemed to follow from the paper that the long-term plan in Hungary was a plan which imposed no compulsory obligations on the executive bodies, and being revised every five years was purely of a conceptual character. At the same time it seemed to include various quantitative parameters. This raised two questions. First, how far were these parameters aggregated or did they remain differentiated? In particular, were the quantitative dimensions of the plan embodied into general output indicators for the whole economy or for various of its branches, or did the plan include certain more specific target figures and projects which were to be regarded as determining the growth of the national economy? And second, the long-term planning provided for several variants to be outlined, which was a sensible approach. Nevertheless, it was obvious that some recommendations in respect to the optimal variant had to be made. How was that optimal variant selected from among other variants presented in a planning operation? Were some calculations of economic effectiveness made, so as to make cost-benefit comparisons possible?

Mr Topala (Roumania) said that he had been asked to take this opportunity to contribute something about their experience in Roumania. He wanted to comment on two factors considered in economic growth models, namely, labour and capital. The labour problem took different forms in different countries. In Roumania there was still a surplus of manpower in agriculture, so special problems had to be solved to make possible the shift of some of this labour force into industry and services, including appropriate training. He wished, however, to comment particularly on their problems of capital supply which had received considerable attention in Roumania. The first question they were asking themselves was how the trend of capital effectiveness was to be estimated within a certain perspective of development. Should they expect a growing effectiveness of capital in general, or that it would remain at the same level, or that there would be a decrease in effectiveness. Several opposing factors were affecting this trend. On the one hand expenditures on replacement or maintenance costs of existing capital were increasing, which resulted in reduced effectiveness. On the other hand, productivity, innovations and organisation were improving, which produced favourable effects. The aggregate result of these factors was, however, a decrease of effectiveness in certain sectors of the Roumanian economy.

Another factor should be added, the annual increase of basic capital, which firstly represented capital of higher effectiveness, and secondly was large in relation to the existing total of productive capital. From this point of view econometric models could make an important contribution in the study of the future volumes of productive capital.

They had made several studies of this kind, which were not yet completed. The questions that these studies sought to answer, were these: what had the effective volume of new capital formation to be in order to maintain the present general level? To what industries should allocations be made to in order to achieve it? And what alternative distributions of allocations should they be considering if these were to correspond to the general strategy of development, maintain overall equilibrium of the national economy, and contribute to the objective of raising living standards? These studies led them to think that the same norms of effectiveness that were used in forecasting could be used also in planning. This made it possible to determine not only a general strategy of development but also perspectives for specific alternative lines of development. The question he wished to put to Professor Augustinovics was how did he handle the future trends of capital effectiveness and, as one important aspect of it, the problem of capital modernisation?

Professor Kantorovitch (U.S.S.R.) was anxious to distinguish two important features of the work described by Professor Augustinovics. One was that prediction made use of a dynamic mathematical programming model with some 800 different parameters relating to various periods. The use of a dynamic programming model allowed greater flexibility and insight and made it possible to introduce greater variety of conditions and to do this more conveniently than did linear-programming models.

Another feature was that mathematical models and their formulation were very well adapted to traditional planning methods. Some branches of industry could readily be described by mathematical models, while others, with more sophisticated structure, more complex interrelationships and a wide range of products, could not. In such cases models were made for various traditional plans, such as a plan of rapid growth of the industry, of slow growth, capital-intensive, labour-intensive, and so on. Comparison of these traditional plans compensated for the difficulties of mathematical modelling. He thought that such a comparison and combination of alternatives was sufficiently accurate and effective for the representation of one particular industry in the economy in general, even if such a combination was sometimes unrealistic. When such parameters as volumes, rates, norms of capital effectiveness, and the rest had been obtained from the general plan, it was possible again to use traditional methods to frame a working plan. This approach also provided a methodology for the endogenous determination of the norm of effectiveness, and, to return to Professor Topala's comments, optimal planning theory required that capital investment should be made where it was most effective and, of course, was most needed. But this was not always true if constant prices were used. This was why he wished to ask whether dynamic evaluation was used in compiling the general plan?

Professor Bénard (France) said that in a small country foreign trade was very important for the efficient allocation of resources, but it was also greatly affected by uncertainty, especially from a long-term point of view. A very interesting and important conclusion regarding international specialisation and plan co-ordination had been advanced in the paper. The question he wished to ask was how the problem of forecasting foreign trade and foreign trade conditions was tackled? There was mention of conclusions but not of a methodology. As regards the reluctance of some economists to elaborate alternatives, a possible explanation could be that this was due to the fact that these economists were engaged in policy-making for the sector they were actually working in, and thus felt a duty to defend that sector. In such a situation of conflict it was a good strategy not to reveal possible alternatives to possible competitors.

Professor Augustinovics (Hungary), in winding up the discussion, said that as regards Professor Khachaturov's question, it was their view that a long-term plan should in effect have no directive character but should be primarily qualitative in character. But of course, it was very difficult in economics to define quality otherwise than in terms of quantities. They expected that a plan document would contain certain quantitative indicators. But they also regarded it as more important that the wide-ranging quantitative analysis which had been made was affecting policy, so that the qualitative ideas expressed in the long-term planning documents would considerably affect the actual decisions embodied in subsequent five-year plans. The long-term plan would not record decisions on specific individual projects, which would be dealt with in five-year plans as they had been in the past.

As regards optimisation, it was obvious that decision-making bodies could not be provided with an infinite number of variants and alternatives. They needed just two or three practicable alternatives to select from. In spite of the use of optimal models, they had certain solutions that, though optimal from a technical point of view, were neither optimal nor capable of being made so from a qualitative point of view. Optimality always remained a feature of a given model, depending on how aims and constraints were specified in it. Thus optimisation techniques were in practice used to supplement the working of the human mind, with the final solution made by the human mind, and not by computers. Selection made in this way was not of a mathematically defined optimal but of a realistic variant. Finally, there were very few reliable methods for planning capital allocation so as to take account of technological and other developments. He meant to 'plan', and not just to 'foresee'. They had no unique method of evaluating prices and quantities simultaneously. They planned to get their quantity figures from optimal models and then to define price systems with the help of dynamic input–output models, and then went back to the optimisation model and repriced it. They hoped that these procedures would converge.

7 Problems of Long-range Planning in Yugoslavia

R. Stojanović

I. CHARACTERISTICS OF THE ECONOMY WHICH AFFECT THE SYSTEM OF PLANNING

Comprehensive systems of planning and forecasting in Yugoslavia – and by the same token long-range planning and forecasting – are built-in organisms which are characterised by three basic features of the Yugoslav socialist society and economy: Yugoslavia is a small country; it is a multinational country; there is an unlimited supply of manpower. Only a closer examination of these three dominant characteristics of the Yugoslav national economy will permit a complete understanding of the basic lines and methods of planning and forecasting in this country. Therefore we shall give special consideration to the implications of the fact that Yugoslavia is a small and multinational country, while the problem of an unlimited supply of manpower will be considered throughout.

II. YUGOSLAVIA IS A SMALL COUNTRY

It is a recognised fact that a small country is not just a large country in miniature, but rather a completely different system, with different goals and priorities, with a different strategy of development, and with a different system of directing trends and development.[1] We shall mention only a few of the most salient characteristics of Yugoslavia as a small country which directly affect its planning methods.

The Order of Basic Priorities in Economic Development

The list of priorities in Yugoslavia is certainly headed by foreign trade, employment, the training of professional cadres and external economies taken very broadly, i.e. enhancing the positive and diminishing the negative effects of the functioning of the principal feedback couplings of a large economic system. Foreign trade and employment are its two principal and long-term priorities with which all other priorities must be accommodated.

The rate of economic growth of every small country is a direct

---

[1] See for example the papers presented at the International Economic Association Conference published in *The Economic Consequences of the Size of Nations*, ed. E. A. G. Robinson (London, 1963).

function of its *foreign trade*, since every percentage of its growth in output depends on the importation of producer goods and equipment. There can be no economic growth without imports, and constantly growing imports postulate constantly growing exports. Hence, present efforts to control imports as rigorously as possible while at the same time stimulating exports must certainly be continued in the long-term development of Yugoslavia. The balance of payments deficit is a problem that will be around for a long time to come.

New employment is not only a very important economic problem, but also a social problem in a country with an unlimited supply of manpower. It is a combination of social solidarity and the most important factor of improvement in the standard of living. This unlimited supply of labour force, another long-term Yugoslav problem, makes the adoption of decisions on substituting manpower with new technology a very delicate matter.

Trained manpower is all that a small country can have in a satisfactory quantity; viz. knowledge is the only 'national capital' which need not be in short supply. Nor need its quality be significantly below the level of large advanced countries. It is true that Yugoslavia must train a large proportion of highly skilled personnel herself but experience has shown that this is a good thing. Personnel trained in large countries find difficulty in adjusting to the conditions of a small country in many spheres of activity, since they have been taught to think on a different scale. What might be a negligible quantity for a large country is not only a very worthwhile magnitude for a small country, but is often even the best that it can do.

In the realm of *external economies* – which according to the terminology of Novozhilov largely correspond to costs arising from effects of the feedback couplings – the most important sources have proven to be in the system of management, i.e. primarily in the proper functioning of the following two feedback couplings of a large economic system: information – decision-making and plan – market.

These four basic priorities of Yugoslavia as a small country naturally differ greatly from the leading priorities of large countries. These would never have foreign trade as their top priority. This difference in priorities has inevitably affected the degree of planning and market flexibility in Yugoslavia, as well as breadth and flexibility in decision-making, i.e. in giving greater freedom to various decision-makers.

The lack of the so-called 'critical mass'

As modern production techniques are developed, the size of the 'critical mass' increases, so that the number of countries which are not able to develop various industrial branches in today's world is rapidly growing. The largest and the most advanced countries already hold a complete monopoly in some fields of electronics (e.g. electronic computers), engineering (e.g. the aeronautics and increasingly the automotive industries), or the chemical industry, not to mention the great expense of research in these branches. What is true for production also holds true, even to a greater extent, for scientific research activities.

This constant and rapid loss of required 'critical mass' for autonomous development of various industries causes small countries to resort to close production co-operation with other countries. Starting with the purchase of licences for new products, a small country goes on to take over entire technological procedures and methods of managing enterprises, finally, through various forms of co-production, to become ever more dependent and practically change its own enterprises into subcontractors of large foreign firms.

This process of satellitisation, as Professor Perroux puts it, is unavoidable for a small country, but it can be made much more tolerable, with far less prejudice to the country's freedom to pursue its own policies of economic development, or choosing the type of economy and society to which it aspires. The effects of the introduction of foreign techniques and technological processes which have been geared, first, to a large country, and second, to the forms of management and administration in that country, must on no account be underestimated. They can cause major upheavals in a small country. The effects of these dislocations will greatly depend on how developed a country's own 'defence system' is, i.e. on the manner in which a small country prepares and undertakes co-operation with large countries. A long-range plan of development is of vital importance here.

The close proximity of the zero point

A small country is very conscious of the constant proximity of the zero point (the point at which investment and its results are equal) in all their important decisions. All its investment and all its efforts, because they are on a small scale, are rapidly exhausted, so that the falling curve of utility and the rising curve of total expenditures meet, i.e. reach the zero point, in a much shorter time and at a much lower level. When this point is passed, negative effects begin to prevail, i.e. there is a reduction in the overall rate of economic growth. Every positive result in every economy has a declining function, and every investment has a rising function, since there is no large economic system without numerous constraints. This means that every country must take the zero point into consideration when making decisions and planning development. This is of particular importance for a small country, since it is cramped within very tight limits. The zero point is very close, and it is reached very quickly in all spheres of economic life and in the whole of society as well. For this reason small countries must often, e.g. always in foreign trade, content themselves not with optimal foreign trade effects expressed as the greatest distance between the rising curve being additional investment for exports or import-substitutes, and the falling curve of results expressed in the growth of the national income (in Figure 7.1 the distance between A and B), but with any positive effect, up to very close to zero point (C).

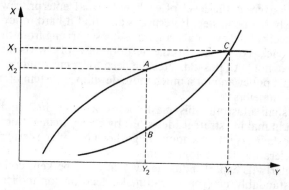

FIG. 7.1

For this reason even if the small countries did not have an unfavourable position in international trade, even if principles of non-discriminatory trade were observed to the letter, a small country would still have a lower rate of effectiveness of foreign trade, since in this area it would have to aim not at the optimum (in Figure 7.1, $X_2 - Y_2$) but deliberately at a point beyond the optimum (going towards $X_1 - Y_1$), as the total achieved foreign trade effect is important for it is the precondition making possible its further economic growth. Its economic growth – because of its small scale – must be paid for at a higher price, and its cost is growing all the time.

Real possibilities for co-ordinating individual and public interests in strategic decision-making

There is another phenomenon closely connected with the proximity of the zero point (regardless of whether we are talking about foreign trade, employment, or some other variable affecting the rate of economic growth), and it is particularly marked when there is a very developed system of decision-making at several levels. The range of real possibilities for co-ordinating individual and public interests, i.e. the interests of lower and higher levels of a large economic system, then appears in a special light. In the Yugoslav system, enterprises try to maximise earnings per employee as their basic objective, which means that their decisions tend to centre on the optimal ratio of investment and its result at the enterprise level. Yugoslavia as a whole seeks to maximise total or overall results, thereby exceeding the optimum for enterprises, primarily because there is an excess supply of manpower in the country. The highest rate of overall economic growth and the highest earnings per employee at the level of each individual enterprise will then obviously not be in step. Enterprises also find it hard to foresee the total effects of the external economies ('costs arising from the effects of feedback couplings' in the terminology of Novozhilov and Kantorovitch). All this indicates the need for a much more complex economic policy and for a much more developed system of management parameters.

We shall illustrate this clash between individual and public criteria in making strategic decisions by a very frequent occurrence in Yugoslavia. Without a doubt Yugoslavia has a long-term problem of accelerating technological modernisation of all its industries, particularly its export industries, which must be kept competitive. Understandably, enterprises will make decisions on modernisation according to the size of their resources, taking into consideration the time and the scope of modernisation which best suits them, their main objective being to maximise earnings per employee in a given work collective. If we express the effect of modernisation as a growth in fixed assets (Fk), a given rate of employment (r_2) and a given rise in labour productivity per employee (p), Figure 7.2 shows the various possible effects of modernisation on total employment.

At a selected level of technology which raises labour productivity from the level of p_t to the level of p_{t+1}, in a country with an unlimited supply of labour force, the absolutely lowest permissible overall level of modernisation of the economy as a whole is $Fk_3 - r_{z_3}$, since then in spite of a growth in fixed assets from Fk_1 to Fk_3, employment is not increased at all (the earlier ratio was $Fk_1 - r_{z_1}$) but at least it stays at the same level, which can also be only a short-term and stop-gap policy. The growth of fixed assets from Fk_1 to just Fk_2 would increase unemployment, whereas employment would begin to grow – a necessity in both medium-term and long-term

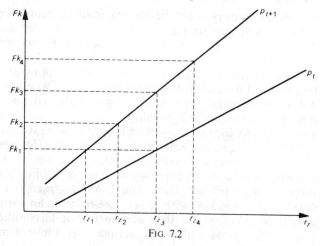

FIG. 7.2

plans – only when the level of investment into fixed assets topped Fk_3 (in the graph shown as $Fk_4 - r_{z_4}$).

For enterprises to know this socially permissible limit, they must be included in the medium-term and long-term plans (in the latter given in very rough terms as 'from – to'). The medium-term plan will contain a somewhat more clearly defined zone of permissible solutions in terms of which enterprises will make their investment decisions, while the long-term plan will only lay down guidelines which will be more closely defined in each medium-term plan. In short-term plans this zone of permissible solutions is increasingly clear-cut. A programme of modernisation for the entire economy must be worked out over a long period, with a setting of priority industries for modernisation but also with due regard for the Yugoslav problem of unemployment. Unless there is such a social programme, the individual decisions of enterprises may clash with the interests of the national economy and may have a negative effect on the long-term rate of economic growth, not to mention the threat to social solidarity as a result of unemployment, which is no less important.

III. SPECIAL PROBLEMS IN FRAMING A MIXED DEVELOPMENT STRATEGY FOR YUGOSLAVIA

In economic theory there is still no accepted classification of possible pure strategies, a combination of which would produce a mixed strategy as the only realistic one. However, on the basis of the main features and basic priorities of the Yugoslav economy and society, a mixed strategy could be formed from elements of the following alternative pure strategies:

(1) a strategy of extensive or the strategy of intensive economic development;[1]
(2) an accumulation-oriented development strategy or consumption-oriented development strategy, a variant of which is the well-known division into the strategy of balanced and the strategy of non-balanced growth;
(3) an outward-looking strategy or an inward-looking strategy;
(4) a strategy of development oriented to a given long-term objective, to which all other short-term objectives are subordinated (or in the terminology of Inagaki, 'Utility Maximisation over Infinite Time'–the U.M.I.T.-strategy) or a development strategy with a set time-horizon for desired objectives and efforts for their implementation (according to Inagaki, 'Marginal Utility Equilibrium over Finite Time'–M.U.E.F.T.-strategy);[2] and finally,
(5) a strategy of development based on a deliberate stimulation of polarisation, and a strategy of development which, avoiding polarisation, is based on organised efforts to reduce polarisation, i.e. to facilitate an even development of all spheres of the economy and society, of all strata of the population, with the least possible urging of individual parts at the expense of others.

The final mixed strategy chosen, which alone is possible in social systems with many levels and many goals, is influenced by the size of the country in addition to the different interests of various social groups, industries and regions. Previously the opinion was widely held that the size of a country largely influenced the structure of production through the available factors of production. However, today it is quite clear that the size of a country also largely determines how many elements and from which form of possible pure strategy will be present in the mixed strategy which is finally selected. The strong priority for foreign trade in Yugoslavia postulates an outward-looking strategy, i.e. a strategy of intensive development with a concentration of modern technology on the most important export branches and also a strategy of a finite time-

[1] Many questions concerning the differences between the strategy of extensive economic development and that of intensive economic development in a socialist country at a medium level of development have been given a thorough consideration in the collection of papers, *Strategia intensywnego rozwoju gospodarki*, ed. Albin Plocica (Warsaw, 1969).
[2] M. Inagaki, *Optimal Economic Growth–Shifting Finite versus Infinite Time Horizon* (Amsterdam–London, 1970).

horizon, and a consumption-oriented strategy. On the other hand, the large supply of unemployed labour calls for many elements of the inward-looking strategy, i.e. the strategy of extensive development, and also elements of the strategy of infinite (in practical terms very long-term) time-horizon and the accumulation-oriented strategy of economic development. The great dispersion in production orientation greatly reduces final effects, but these same effects may be reduced in a small country by too strong an emphasis on specialisation which would exclude many natural resources from use, as well as large contingents of the labour force. Hence, the optimal development strategy in Yugoslavia can obviously only be a carefully selected mixed strategy of development which will avoid both extremes and will select industries and regions in which the elements of some forms of pure strategy will be more prevalent, and those industries and regions in which elements of other forms of pure strategy will be encouraged. This must always be done in such a way that the overall results for Yugoslavia as a whole are the best possible. Every insistence on elements of just one type of pure strategy for the country as a whole would be very wrong, and indeed unpracticable. Our two central problems, and at the same time our two central priorities in development policy – foreign trade and employment – are so overriding that they almost take on the character of fixed goals, i.e. goals which must be promoted to the utmost and which cannot be compromised to further some other goals. Large and advanced countries can never have such firm priorities which subordinate everything else and in terms of which everything else is decided.

While discussing the basic characteristics of Yugoslavia, we have mentioned only a few of the specific circumstances of small, underdeveloped countries which make them differ so radically in their selection of a development strategy from the large advanced countries. Although none of these special circumstances of the small countries is unknown, it must be said that in practice they have not always been sufficiently taken into account and that practice much more than economic theory has caused us to diverge from the experiences of the large countries. It is not easy for small countries, including Yugoslavia, to shield themselves from the scientific achievements and the practice of economic development of the large countries, from their voluminous technical literature which is conquering the world, from their advanced institutions of higher learning where so many people from small and underdeveloped countries are pursuing their education. The entire complex process of adapting the achievements of the large countries to the conditions of a small country has naturally been **entrusted to** the professional cadre of the small country, to their own 'defence system' against whatever is not suitable for such a small country. And the large countries cannot help the small ones in this kind of thing. In this respect there is a better outlook from the joint co-operation of scientists of the small countries themselves.

IV. THE SPECIAL PROBLEMS OF A MULTINATIONAL STATE

Although it is a truism that there is no need to explain what a multinational state is like to someone who has lived in one, and that it is almost hopeless trying to explain it to someone who has not experienced it, nevertheless we shall touch upon this phenomenon only to give an idea of the lines along which Yugoslavia is building its system of planning, particularly long-range planning.

Of all the types of conflicts in a socialist society, undoubtedly the most persistent and the most complex is that between the various nationalities which comprise a state (as a rule a federation). Yugoslavia's experience in this respect has been exceptionally rich, not only because there are many nationalities within it, but also because such a proportionately large number of nationalities live together in a relatively small area.[1] This combination of small size and multinationality undoubtedly complicates the selection of an optimal development strategy and planning. Even though unemployment is also one of the considerations for choosing a strategy, nevertheless there is a basic difference between these three restricting factors. Whereas the size of a country and its multi-nationality are constants, the problem of unemployment is subject to changes, especially in the course of long-range development. However, even though the size of the country and the unlimited supply of manpower are a very severe handicap in Yugoslavia, conflicts are most keenly felt in the sphere of nationality relations.

There is a theoretical tendency in a small country to greater specialisation, especially in export industries. However, in a multi-national country this process of specialisation is greatly hindered by another tendency – that of the creation of separate national economies of the various nationalities. This latter tendency in Yugoslavia is quite marked, hence the problem of finding adequate methods of management and management parameters

---

[1] In addition to the five main national groups in Yugoslavia there are a number of minorities. The Serbian republic contains the highest number of minorities; Albanians followed by Hungarians are the most numerous minority groups. The two republics of Slovenia and Montenegro are relatively the most nationally homogeneous.

which would counter this tendency is a very real one. Each of the six republics is trying to develop the same industries (even when this is not justified from the standpoint of a need for given products), all in the desire to maintain their relative ranking in development, and of course there is a secret desire to go one rung higher.

Lest this tendency turn into a conflict between the various nationalities, which would threaten the stability not only of the economy but also of the entire society, every means must be used to relax these conflicts and to seek ways of fostering coalitions between national partners. This problem thus gives a strong imprint to the basic method of planning. In fact, in efforts to minimise all conflicts in society, and primarily the most severe – the nationality conflict – the economic plan takes on the significance of a social coalition at the highest level. This is the first basic assumption in elaborating long-range plans in Yugoslavia.

The second basic assumption is the systems approach, i.e. treating the economy as a very complex multi-level multi-goal system; within this system the interests of the whole (in this concrete case the national economy) and of all its parts must be so co-ordinated as to allow optimal development, both of the national economy and of its parts, acknowledging the priority of the national economy and the relative autonomy of its parts.

V. A SYSTEMS APPROACH TO PLANNING IN YUGOSLAVIA: THE SO-CALLED CONVERGENCE METHOD

In forecasting future development, the degree of uncertainty grows in proportion to the length of the period under consideration, i.e. it is greatest in long-range planning. The measurability of the various factors affecting the rate of economic growth also differs, so that the influence of completely immeasurable factors is too great to be ignored.[1] The span between very different degrees of constraint on various factors of economic growth is no less large, just as conflicts between the various parts of a large economic system and the whole of its complex scope are similarly strong. Of everything

---

[1] Whether we take as an example of attempts at comprehensive measurements the results of the expanded production function of Mikhalevski and Soloviev for the Soviet Union, or the results of the specific factor analysis made by a team at the University of Chicago for seventy-four capitalist countries in the world (forty-one factors were studied), it is clear that the political system has the greatest effect of all the non-economic factors. However, the management system and the political system are still immeasurable factors, in spite of the first attempts made to calculate their enormous influence. See Irma Adelman and Cynthia Taft Morris, *Society, Politics and Economic Development – A Quantitative Approach* (Baltimore, 1967).

that we have mentioned, by far the most complicated is the task of reconciling conflicting interests; it requires a parallel development of a very elaborate system of information (particularly of what is called 'the alarm system') and, in connection with this, of various methods of making strategic decisions.

The problems connected with various degrees of uncertainty – unmeasurability, limitations and, above all, conflicts – do not begin the moment we start elaborating a medium-term or long-range plan of development, but when a strategy of development is selected. And here arises the question for whom a strategy of development is being sought and, accordingly, for whom a plan of development should be made.

Such questions would be quite superfluous in systems with one objective; in systems with a number of objectives but without any conflict among them, the answer would be easy; the problem of finding an answer arises when there are many conflicting objectives, such as is the case in all social systems. The more the conflicts, the more difficult it is to find the best strategy of development and work out a plan of development, since a larger number of conflicting objectives with different possibilities for co-ordination must be kept in mind. Selecting a development strategy and working out a development plan for a large economic system is a very complex task, since it requires a very complicated procedure of translating lower level optima into higher level optima: from work collectives and their associations to industries and regions, or in the case of Yugoslavia, to provinces and republics, all the way to a development strategy and the plans of a large economic system as a whole.[1]

Selection of a development strategy and elaboration of a development plan are carried out in two basic stages in Yugoslavia.

In the first phase, each selects his own optimal strategy (i.e. one of the most acceptable variants), which is only a partial optimum from the standpoint of higher levels, or of greater entities. Hence on the basis of the elaborated variants, the individual enterprise, the individual industry and region, and the economy as a whole each seeks the best variant for itself, but in the first phase without knowing the optima of all its parts. This preliminary

---

[1] We mean optima at various levels, the optimal strategy of development, the optimal plan, etc., even if the entire theory of optimisation is still not ready for practical application. Nevertheless, it seems to us that the very aspiration to optimise the system and apply what is known about optimisation today justifies this terminology: all practical efforts in the world in this field have shown that even partial results can have considerable value. Their application in practice, furthermore, is one of the important prerequisites for the further elaboration of the theory of optimisation.

individual selection of variant plans, i.e. without co-ordinating the interests of the whole and the partial interests of the parts, is a necessary procedure for reaching a final optimum which contains within itself, again up to an approximate optimal limit, the best possible co-ordination of interests of the whole and its parts.

In the second phase, the optima of the lower levels must be translated into optima which suit higher levels. First, the optimal variants for individual enterprises must be turned into optimal variants for industries and for regions. However, as experience has taught us, this is far from a simple search for compromise solutions in cases of conflicting interests; behind these partial interests at various levels are different groups of the population and their different interests, which, of course, can never be adopted in their entirety, but neither can they be completely rejected.

This *convergence method* in seeking optima is in fact a guarantee for the best possible consideration of the whole and the parts. The fact that the individually calculated optimum for each individual partner is known, without consideration of other partners, makes it possible in this second phase to find solutions which suit everyone; they suit everyone to the extent that, although no one gains everything, at least they do not lose everything, when it is clear to everyone that they cannot exist alone and that they gain most when best integrated into the whole and when their interests are in line with its interests; the whole, again, gains most because individual goals and their individual optimal solutions are respected to the maximum. Hence the convergence method of finding social optima (which do not have the substance of mathematical optima, and hence must be clearly differentiated from them)[1] means the seeking of 'social interests' at various levels, so that in the process 'social criteria' and 'social interests' are not an impersonal statistical average or the impersonal interest of some amorphous society, but rather the common interest expressed at various levels, up to the highest. In other words, this is a coalition formed at the level of a large system, with maximum relaxation of social conflicts.

The convergence method is not only the best possible expression of individual optima (i.e. optima of lower levels in the 'social

---

[1] In fact, it is necessary to differentiate three types of optima in economic systems: the narrowest, i.e. mathematical optimum (including the technical optimum), next the economic optimum, and finally, as the broadest, the social optimum. In practice, of course, this last optimum, being the most realistic, must be the main goal. Such a distinction between the three types of optima is very reminiscent of the division of a development programme into three parts by Oskar Lange: the optimal programme; next, more broadly, the field of permissible programmes; and finally, as the broadest of all, the field of programmes that satisfy marginal conditions. Oskar Lange, *Optymalne decyzje – Zasady programowania* (Warsaw, 1964).

language' of a large economic system; it is also a means for finding the optimal relation among various types of priorities at different levels. An optimal variant of development of a multinational system implies seeking a common scale of priorities. But a common scale of all the most important social values implies limiting the freedom of decision-making and, finally, implies the entire concept of the future society. With this method it is important to know the basis for evaluating individual criteria, the basis for deciding the extent to which each individual part of the large economic system can influence the final optimum of the system. It has long been known that in human society the mere strength of numbers of various parts of a given whole are worthless for determining all optima at higher levels. All enterprises are not of the same importance for economic development, nor are all economic branches, or even all population groups. The influence of social strata is not the simple result of the strength of their numbers. Nor do all parts of a large social system have the same influence on the development of the economy.

Because of the very complex and dynamic treatment of these hierarchies – different levels, different priorities, different influences and their changeableness in the process of development of the system – and because of insistence on maximum co-ordination of interests between the whole and its parts, the convergence method is of first-rate importance for socialist countries. And for multi-national countries it is of even greater importance. This method contains in a far clearer and more comprehensive form what is also contained, for instance, in the method of strategic games – recognition of the rights of all partners to take part in decision-making on optimal development of the system. No one's goals and criteria can be completely neglected. Everyone has the right to formulate what is best for him and later, in the second phase, to take part in deciding on what is best from the standpoint of the highest level – the largest economic system (the national economy) – remaining a partner to the end, with the possibility of interpreting his own interests and their place among all the social interests until the final decision is made. The convergence method, as a typically systems approach to planning, is essentially democratic and humanistic. However, because of its complexity it is certainly one of the most difficult and most complicated to put into practice, as shown by the experience of Yugoslavia.

VI. THE PLAN AS THE BROADEST SOCIAL COALITION

Compromise or coexistence of opposites

The process of working out a plan of economic development for the entire country starts from coalitions at the lowest levels and works up to the highest levels, i.e. from coalitions at the enterprise level through their associations and entire economic branches and regions (as far as Yugoslavia is concerned, provinces and republics) to the highest level. But how are coalitions at these various levels formed? There are two basic methods, and our experience already permits us to assess them in terms of their effect on the rate of economic growth. These are the method of compromise, which has so far been the most prevalent in Yugoslav planning practice, and the method of coexistence of opposites, which the country is trying to use in view of the serious inadequacies of the first method.

In fact, it is difficult to say to what extent the method of compromise has been a consciously selected and elaborated method. This method was forced upon us by practice, primarily the practice of co-ordinating plans adopted at regional levels, which means at levels of the nationalities. According to this method, when the objectives of the various republics as contained in their regional plans of development are confronted, compromises for all conflicting objectives are always sought. Of course, there are a rather large number of them; at the same time it is over the most important strategical objectives that conflicts are strongest. This means that no one can obtain all of what he seeks for any one objective, or at least not in a given time period, since with each individual objective there must be at least a modicum of renunciation in favour of the other members of the community. These fatal 'middle-of-the-road solutions' made all participants dissatisfied, since each had the impression that he was giving up more for others than he gained in return from belonging to the social community.

The method of coexistence of opposites means finding another way to a coalition, a way which, at least as it seems so far, instead of the eternal 'middle-of-the-road-solutions' with their adverse effect on the solidarity of the members of the social community and on the general rate of economic growth, would mean ensuring the fulfilment of the first objectives in the list of priorities of each region, i.e. objectives on which each republic places the most insistence, which in its opinion are the most vital for its further development. If some objectives must be renounced in favour of others, it is easier if these are less important objectives and furthermore, the desired line of developments and the desired rate of growth are less injured. The object of this method is that everyone should retain his most essential priorities, and that compromises are made on the less important, lower-priority objectives.

There is a prerequisite necessary for carrying out this method; the republics must make their plans of development bearing in mind that they are part of Yugoslavia, and within the framework of Yugoslavia as a whole they must seek their place in the future economic and social development. Unless this Yugoslav component is admitted, there is a danger of creating national economies within the republics, there is a danger of duplicating factories, of fragmenting and miscellanising production. The success of this method also depends on a broad elaboration of rules for co-operation between various republican partners in the case of complete or practical identity of priority objectives of development.

Indifference curve or zone of optimality

For optimalisation of the relative autonomy of the parts in relation to the greater whole to which they belong, the system of decision-making and its corresponding system of information must be organised so that the optimal levels for adopting various decisions can be found within them. It is essential for effective decision-making that decisions be made at optimal levels, which in practical terms means at the level at which a given decision can be fastest and most fully implemented. Often these are enterprises. Associations of enterprises are competent for some types of decisions, and for others republican or federal economic organs or republican assemblies or the Federal Assembly as the highest administrative levels in the country, are appropriate.

However, for those decisions which enterprises adopt within their own jurisdictions, as well as for expanding their powers, it is necessary for the plan of economic development to provide guide lines on future trends in the economy and society; i.e. the basic rules of behaviour of enterprises must be incorporated in the plans. First of all, the enterprises must know the most important economic variables between whose lower and upper limits their operations are permissible, in other words how much 'manoeuvre ground' they have. This 'manoeuvre ground' should of course be sufficiently wide to allow an enterprise to select its optimal development strategy (taking optimality with certain qualifications). But this room must not be so broad as to endanger a co-ordinated development of the whole. The space in which some variables can move, without upsetting a co-ordinated development of the whole, is called the zone of optimality.

The taking of a decision which must be within the zone of optimality is basically distinct from the taking of a decision which must be on the indifference curve. In the first instance, the 'manoeuvre ground' of the enterprise (or whoever makes the decision at lower levels) is much wider. Figure 7.3 shows the extent of the 'manoeuvre ground' in the zone of optimality.

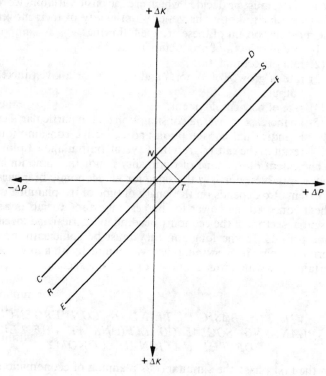

FIG. 7.3

Here $R - S$ is the mathematical optimum for $K : P$; $N - T$ is the zone of optimality in which decisions concerning the ratio between capital (C) and production (P) can move; $C - D$ is the permissible minimum for growth of P; $E - F$ is the permissible minimum for the growth of C.

When defining the zone of optimality, enterprises may make any decision within the limits $C - D$ and $E - F$, or within the space $N - T$. This means that with the same amount of available capital, enterprises can invest so as to gain different volumes of production. If the indifference curve is adopted instead of the zone of optimality, the enterprise with a given volume of available investment resources must acquire the same volume of production, i.e. must adopt a certain ratio between C and P (a determined point on the indifference curve), reducing their 'manoeuvre ground' only to a choice between technical procedures which give the same capital coefficient, i.e. the same coefficient of effectiveness of invested resources.

Finally, it must be decided which are the basic variables for which it is necessary to know the zone of optimality of their movement. The most important of these are the following:

(1) rate of growth of production (G.N.P.);
(2) rate of accumulation;
(3) rate of growth of imports and exports for a given increase in output;
(4) rate of new employment;
(5) an increase in overall consumption and in particular a growth in individual consumption and collective consumption as a result of the rate of growth of overall output and employment.

The extent of the zone of optimality is not the same for all the above variables, nor is it the same for all economic branches, and its extent also depends on the length of time of the planning period. These zones are narrower for higher important variables and for essential sectors of the economy (leading industries) and for shorter time periods. In the long run they must be sufficiently broad to permit changes in everything that was planned with a low degree of certainty, or which was unknown or even unexpected.

VII. THE BASIC OUTLINE OF CONVERGENCE PLANNING – SOCIAL COALITIONS AT THE LEVEL OF THE NATIONAL ECONOMY

In the first phase the simultaneous planning of economic development in terms of the enterprise and of society as a whole, and next, in the second phase, the finding of a final form of social coalition (as the maximum possible relaxation of the important conflicts in Yugoslav society) can be demonstrated in Figure 7.4.

General social priorities in long-range economic development set by the chosen line of development and the basic philosophy concerning long-range social values and objectives cannot be viewed in the same way from the perspective of enterprises as from the perspective of society. This also holds true for the direction of scientific and technological progress in the world, for methods of the best utilisation of available resources and the given geographical position of the country in respect to future centres of development.

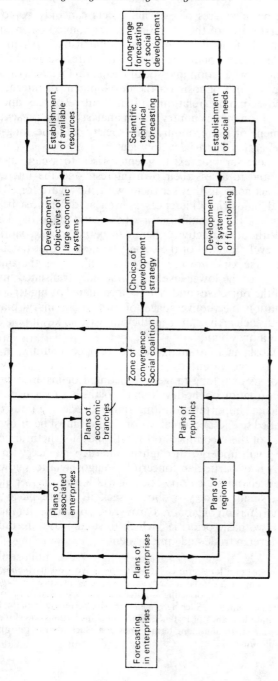

Finally, the basic sources of external effects can only be covered from the perspective of the overall large economic system and its environment. The following information is particularly pertinent for this type of long-range planning: (1) scientific forecasts on the future development of production and social needs; (2) forecasts of demographic trends; (3) prognosis on the development of international political and economic relations; (4) natural resources and geographical position of the country; (5) an analysis of the present level of development of the economy and society and the long-range problems generated by this development.

But it is necessary for existing enterprises to weigh up their possibilities and to assess their own interests and the interests of the national economy as they see them, with due regard for all local, regional and industrial differences as well as differences between various parts of the population, as the second stage of planning activities. Without this activity there can be no social coalition at the highest level, the level of the society. Here it is that conflicts of the most diverse kind are gradually reconciled and the interests and objectives of the lower levels are gradually translated into the language of the objectives and criteria formulated at higher levels.[1]

Confrontation, i.e. convergence of two preliminary plans of development, each arrived at in a different way, makes it possible to hammer out a final plan.

Since Yugoslavia is a small, semi-developed country, it must depend to a large extent on forecasts made in large advanced countries for its own long-range forecasting. For instance, it alone lacks the information on the development of the basic sciences, which are of particular importance in long-range forecasting (much more so than applied sciences). Similarly, conclusions must be drawn from the forecasts of these countries on what kind of structural changes its economy will undergo through its interdependence with other countries. It is of particular concern for Yugoslavia to know what kinds of new economic co-operation it will have to undertake and where as a small country it should seek its future place in the international division of labour. Throughout, of course, it must keep in mind its two basic priorities, which in some ways are mutually exclusive – foreign trade and employment.

[1] As a guarantee of a long-term coalition, i.e. for a more secure foundation for long-range planning, in Yugoslavia there is an increasing practice for large enterprises (as direct co-producers or acting as purchasers and sellers) to make long-term agreements with one another. Such agreements are also becoming common between economic organisations and, for instance, educational institutions which must train highly skilled personnel (quite a long-term proposition). Such contracts are also made with research institutes.

VIII. OUTSTANDING PROBLEMS

In conclusion, it should be stated that the procedure for working out a plan of economic development in Yugoslavia as described above is still largely in an experimental stage. There are three unsolved problems that are worthy of particular note:

(1) One of the leading problems concerns methods of putting deep-lying and rather permanent social conflicts into their proper perspective, and of setting up a network of institutions to deal with them. What are the methods for making major long-term decisions which will make possible a relaxation of conflicts? At one time this was considered to be the method of strategic games (especially the so-called co-operative games) and it was thought that its importance was enormous in solving nationality conflicts. Attempts to apply this method in making regional (i.e. national) plans of development made it immediately obvious that this philosophy of strategic games might certainly be useful, but that for Yugoslavia some other methods for making strategical decisions might be more suitable, taking into consideration immeasurable factors and factors of different levels of certainty. Similarly, the network of institutions authorised to identify conflicts and take part in solving them is not suitably developed. Some of these institutions do not have a methodology for spotting and solving conflicts, but rather work on an *ad hoc* basis. And it goes without saying that for implementation of long-range plans of development it is of the utmost importance to foresee possible conflicts and their implications and to make timely preparations to cope with them.

(2) The proper organisation and functioning of the so-called alarm system is also a problem which is yet to be dealt with. In a country which wants to implement the general objectives of the long-term plan in the medium term, and to work out operative plans for putting them into practice in the short term, while at the same time preserving multi-level decision-making with relative autonomy of its parts, the alarm system must be in good working order. The proper functioning of an alarm system implies an immediate signalling of changes which may upset the economy and the entire society, regardless of whether these changes arise from the external environment (the appearance of new foreign trade competitors, changes in international economic and political relationships which alter the previous status of the country, etc.) or from the country's own course of development (upsetting of social solidarity, dislocations in nationality relationships, the proximity of the zero point in some important industry, etc.).

(3) Finally, the relationship between objectives and management

parameters is another insufficiently studied field of our activity in the planned guidance of long-term economic and social development. Every long-term strategical objective must be backed by at least one management parameter, but in such a way that all these parameters taken together form a logical system, just as all strategic objectives should form an integral system. However, the still insufficiently elaborated new system of management of the Yugoslav economy, and particularly the multi-level decision-making, does not facilitate the rapid development of a system of management parameters, especially those appropriate for each level of management. Even though the number of these parameters has considerably increased, the parameters have not been reduced to a logical, coherent system.

We have limited our discussion to just three problems, although obviously the list is a long one. The working out of a new method of planning, i.e. a systematic approach to planning in a small, multi-national country, is a field which requires much more theoretical and practical work and experimentation.

Discussion of the Paper by Professor Stojanovic

Dr Fels (F.R.G.) in opening the discussion said that Professor Stojanović gave a clear and comprehensive picture of the planning process in Yugoslavia and of the problems which required to be solved in this process. He started with the analysis of the three basic characteristics of the Yugoslav economy – that Yugoslavia was a small country, that it was a multinational country, and that it had at present an unlimited supply of manpower. He then dealt with the process of planning, with the social stresses that needed to be overcome, and with the techniques that were used to find an optimal solution at each planning level.

The small-country consideration implied two points which made the planning process more difficult. The basic priorities of Yugoslavia differed significantly from the dominant priorities of larger countries. And secondly, there was a process of satellitisation which had its source in the fact that most of the advanced countries had a monopoly in certain technically leading industries. To avoid the disadvantages which might arise from dependency, a specific 'mixed development' strategy had to be worked out.

This appeared to become rather complicated in a multi-level and multi-national planning system. Professor Stojanović had stressed all these difficulties. For instance, a considerable impediment to specialisation and the building up of export industries was created by the attempts of each of the six republics to develop the same industries, even if this were not justified from the standpoint of social needs or demand for a given product. Another difficulty for consistent national planning lay in the built-in conflict between the national employment objectives and the interests of labour-managed firms.

Dr Fels had an impression that one was here confronted with a severe problem for a labour-managed economy. There was neglect of employment objectives at the firm level. This had to do with the fact that the earnings per worker were being maximised. One could also say that the profit rate per worker was being maximised since these profits were distributed among existing workers, in contrast to a capitalistic capital-managed economy, in which the firms were maximising the total amount of profit. Thus there existed no incentive to extend employment in the firm even if their products were highly demanded.

In regard to the structure of incentives, Dr Fels thought that Yugoslavia was facing the same difficulties as many of the developing countries in which the structure of incentives was not in line with the needs of development, especially when the needs were for creating new employment. In these countries industrialisation was stimulated artificially by low interest rates, high depreciation allowances and investment premiums. That meant that the use of capital was subsidised more highly than employment of labour. The employment objective seemed to require subsidies dependent on the number of jobs created. Perhaps Professor Stojanović could tell them whether it might be possible in Yugoslavia to bring the structure of incentives more into line with the employment objectives. This could possibly be managed as part of a national investment policy.

Turning to the proposed mixed development strategy, Dr Fels said that Professor Stojanović had listed the choices which had to be made by the planning decision-makers. These choices covered extensive or intensive development: an accumulation-oriented strategy or a consumption-oriented strategy; an export-seeking strategy or an inward-looking strategy; an infinite time-horizon or a finite time-horizon; and finally, polarisation or balanced development.

Professor Stojanović had not indicated exactly how the optimal mixed-development strategy was to be designed. She had stated that the strategy had to be carefully worked out and must avoid extremes. The overall results for Yugoslavia as a whole had to be the best possible. She claimed priority for the foreign trade and the employment objectives. She accepted, however, that there was conflict between these two objectives. On one hand, a strong priority for foreign trade in Yugoslavia would postulate an outward-looking strategy with concentration on modern technology in most export branches. On the other hand, the large supply of the unemployed labour would require an inward-looking strategy. He was not himself very familiar with the situation in Yugoslavia, but on the basis of general considerations he doubted whether there was in fact strong conflict between these two objectives. As long as there was plenty of labour it seemed that the country had comparative advantages in labour-intensive lines of production. To exploit these comparative advantages meant to create new jobs in labour-intensive export industries in which there were handicaps from high wages in more advanced countries. This gave Yugoslavia the chance to enter more advanced markets, to earn more foreign exchange, and at the same time to create more jobs. Similar strategies had been successfully adopted by Italy and Japan after World War II.

The second part of the paper dealt with the techniques of planning under the particular conditions which prevailed in Yugoslavia. It was a process of planning from below. The optimum was a plan achieved by the so-called convergence method, which was a guarantee for the best possible harmony of the whole and the parts. It also formed a means of finding optimal relationships between various priorities at different levels.

The plan was considered to be a product of social coalition. The coalition was one of two basic methods: first the method of compromise which had been used hitherto, and second a method of coexistence of opposites which the country was now trying to use because the first method had proved inadequate in several respects.

Dr Fels's first question on this second part of the paper was what was the role of the national investment policy in the planning process? Secondly, did the central planning authorities provide guidelines to steer the planning process towards a satisfactory solution? How did they do so? And thirdly, did the method of coexistence of opposites imply that there was opportunity for a sort of competition between the republics?

Professor Stojanović (Yugoslavia) asked if she might intervene to clarify the questions put in the opening by Dr Fels. The experiment with convergent planning system had not yet been completed, and in a way all socialist countries had convergent planning, in the sense that it was not the central planning bodies alone that made the national decisions. It was difficult to say at the moment just how this experiment would continue in the future, for the Yugoslav problem was that of six national republics and a large number of small enterprises in an economy which was still in the first stages of integration. With so many small enterprises making independent decisions the major problem became that of investment policy for Yugoslavia as a whole.

The other two principal issues for Yugoslavia were foreign trade and employment, and she would hesitate to say which of them had greater priority for a small country, though employment was not only an economic but also a social problem. Export of labour, though a temporary solution, was not a solution in the long run. She agreed with Dr Fels that if some practicable solution was to be found, it should be based on developing some key industry capable of solving the problem, such as electronics or some suitable transportation industry. However, there was an associated problem, which was that Yugoslavia had certain mining and extractive industries which were labour-intensive. Under all these conditions it was not easy to change the structure of the economy, and the scheme of planning was designed to take account of this structure.

Similar problems, as she knew, arose in respect of the national republics of the U.S.S.R. But there was the additional problem of size. Yugoslavia was equal in size to just one republic of the U.S.S.R., and it was much more difficult to solve the problem of historical failures of economic development of different parts of a small country. For this involved the relative independence of peoples some of them numbering less than a million, and thus created political problems which could not be solved quickly. And in respect of optimal planning areas, this meant a degree of independence of republics, organisations and enterprises, and made investment policy difficult.

As for competition, this did not take place between the national republics, but between enterprises and industries. Coexistence of opposites did not exist at the republic level. Had it been so, the national problem would have been even more acute than it was in Yugoslavia.

As to the choice of an optimal strategy, that currently adopted for Yugoslavia was a strategy of consumption, not of accumulation. With decisions made independently by individual enterprises, a strategy of accumulation would be most dangerous, for either accumulation at the enterprise level would be inadequate or choice as to how to use it would be the responsibility of the enterprise, which was not desirable in a country with surplus labour. They in Yugoslavia were encouraging arrangements that would fix the accumulation level for whole industries.

Professor Khachaturov (U.S.S.R.) said that he was not quite clear what Professor Stojanović meant when she spoke of small-country disadvantages. Was a small country defined in terms of area or population or level of economic development? In terms of area, most countries in Europe were small countries, including even Great Britain. Thus area could hardly be the criterion of a small country. Moreover, countries which were not large in terms of area, sometimes had a high level of economic development, of labour productivity, and of accumulation. Thus, small area as such was not necessarily a handicap as regards development of production. He wanted to suggest that low level of development coupled with great opportunities for expansion was also no handicap. Availability of cheap labour and opportunities for development were, on the other hand, factors contributing to rapid growth, provided that technology available in other countries could be transferred and used. So his first reservation was that the fact of being a small country by no means explained what Professor Stojanović had called 'satellitisation'.

He wished to turn next to the use of convergent planning in Yugoslavia. Convergent planning as such was a considerable advantage; it permitted better allocation of resources of the economy, because central planning agencies working in isolation were not always aware of the opportunities existing on lower levels.

As for the conflicts of interests of different republics, he thought it was very important to avoid a tendency to 'compromise' which usually satisfied nobody. It was obvious that certain lines of progress should be defined and given priority over others. This was precisely the task of central agencies, and perhaps it was possible to overcome some of the tendencies to compromise by increasing the power of the central planning authority. The opportunities presented by central planning could thus be better used to establish the strategy most beneficial to the country. And this applied also to the problems of accumulation and of the distribution of investible resources, which could also be dealt with centrally.

Professor Marczewski (France) wished to comment on the small-country effect and also on the question of co-ordination of individual and public objectives. Unlike Professor Khachaturov, he believed that there was some thing which might be called a small country. The definition could be made in approximate terms as the relation between the national market of the country and the optimal sizes of national firms. He thought it would be agreed that the size of a firm in a small country tended to be significantly smaller than in a large country. If we accepted that there was no such thing as perfectly free foreign trade – and in current circumstances foreign trade was not free although there might be progress towards freeing it – there did exist such a phenomenon as the small-country effect, for it was much more difficult for a small country to enter world markets with enterprises which were smaller than those of the larger trading countries.

He did not however completely agree with Professor Stojanović's presentation of the 'zero point', or balance between new investment and its results. It was argued that a small country reached the 'zero point' much earlier than a bigger country. But if one introduced a foreign market this was not so, and there was practically no theoretical difference between a small and a large country from the optimisation point of view. The practical difference was that if the domestic market was narrower, the country was forced to seek the foreign market earlier, and as that market was not free, as usually happened but not always, this could be achieved at less favourable conditions compared to home market.

He had two questions regarding co-ordination of public and individual interests. He thought that it was a weakness of the system of workers' councils that, first, the enterprise did not really exist as an independent economic unit, because in its most important decision – the investment decision – this decision reflected not the time preference of the enterprise but the time preferences of the workers. Thus in this sense the enterprise did not exist as an independent unit. Shorter time preferences of workers compared to those of an enterprise probably explained why accumulation was likely to be insufficient.

His second point was that there was no real labour market as such. Yugoslavia had reintroduced the market for goods and services, but had not restored the labour market, since there was no bargaining between the enterprise as such and labour as such. Their interests were confused, with two consequences: first, there was no inclination to enlarge the enterprise and go ahead with the necessary investment because the existing staff of workers had no interest in increasing the number of workers; a second and contrary result was that the existing staff had a kind of solidarity which was a good thing from a human point of view, but it was opposed to any reductions of the number of workers employed, even if this might raise individual wages.

Professor Porwit (Poland) said that his first question was concerned with planning technique. When Professor Stojanović was speaking of long-term planning, had she in mind really long-term planning horizons of some fifteen years, or did she mean medium-term horizons, more directly related to capital investment and to cycles of investment? It had been emphasised that the economic structure of Yugoslavia included a large number of small enterprises, and even in terms of a long-term horizon he doubted whether much could be done regarding share and structure of the markets, the structure of demand, and so on.

Second, if he had understood right, the operations of planning from below, from the enterprise level, and from above were going on simultaneously. He had not discovered at what stage these two operations became fused. It seemed to him that in many cases some initial knowledge of the basic strategy and assumptions embodied in the general overall approach might be very valuable for the decentralised programming. Thus his next question was how far and to what extent this initial information was being made available?

Professor Bruno (Israel) agreed with those who had said that such a thing as a small country did exist, and that it existed not in terms of area or population but in terms of economic activities, that is, total G.N.P. One could identify differences in characteristics of countries by size, such as openness to international trade which went with small size. One got the impression that being small was a disadvantage. But there were also certain advantages in being small. The disadvantages were usually connected with economies of scale, but a small country could overcome these at least in part by specialisation. The question was whether it was easier or more complicated to plan in a small country? On the whole one could find good reasons why it should be easier. For instance, prices for at least some products were given. Secondly, there was easier access to capital inflow. But a point that was not easily quantifiable was the question of managability of the economy from the point of view of planning. Even if there were no good formal planning procedures, in a small country there was a small number of decision-makers who could be consulted informally, and access to information was also easier.

Professor Majminas (U.S.S.R.) felt that it was far from clear how two planning processes – state planning from above and a whole hierarchy of local planning – republic, industry, enterprise – were actually interrelated in Yugoslavia. He thought that the confronting of these two processes somewhat narrowed the problem of convergent planning, because apart from the conflicts of interest between representative bodies – state interests on one hand, and republic and industry interests on the other – there were two other conflicts of interests, between enterprises and republics, and between enterprises and industries. Interrelations seemed necessary not only between the republics and the state, but between enterprises and industries as well. So his question was how did Professor Stojanović visualise the whole mechanism of convergent planning in relation to all the levels of this hierarchy?

Another question which arose in this context has been put by Professor Marczewski. Could enterprises as systems really be reduced simply to the interests of their employees? There were surely the interests of individual workers, of enterprises, of groups of enterprises and of a state as a whole – in short a hierarchy of interests. Could Professor Stojanović throw light on the mechanism for defining, for example, state interests or those of other groups under the conditions of convergent planning? This problem was being discussed in the U.S.S.R. also, and it was actually a question of basic levels of planning and of the fact that the interests of one level could not be directly conveyed to another, so that there was need for some organ to represent them at other levels of planning. Finally, to what extent was convergent planning possible for long-term planning, say for about a fifteen-year period? It seemed possible in the downward direction from the state to the enterprise, but what about the bottom to top direction?

Professor Machlup (U.S.A.) was anxious to return to the problem of the relevance of small size of a country, and to raise two points that had not been mentioned. The first had to do with decision-making at the level of the firm as against decision-making at the level of some supra-firm agency. Assuming that in a socialist country firms were free to purchase goods from one another, it could readily be seen that a small country was limited in doing this because the number of enterprises that could do it would be limited. The larger the area or the larger the number of enterprises, the greater the opportunity to decide to buy the products needed, quite apart from any bureaucratic decision-making, or any decision at a higher level. This assumed, of course, that imports were controlled as they usually were in a socialist country. The decision to buy, if it was made at the enterprise level, presupposed comparison of two prices: the price at which it could purchase, and the exchange rate. The more the sources of supply were invoicing in foreign currency, the greater the bearing of the foreign exchange rate. If both the domestic price and the exchange rate should be very different from what one might call the competitive norm, the greater the problem involved. The firm might decide that on the basis of the prices quoted and the exchange rate it would be best to import. The higher agency was in a position to prohibit this, and this brought one to Professor Stojanović's statement that present efforts to control imports as rigorously as possible while at the same time stimulating exports must certainly be continued in the long-term development of Yugoslavia; the balance of payments deficit was a problem that would be around for a long time to come. But that meant that the exchange rate of Yugoslavia was wrong, and the true reason was not given.

Professor Kozlov (U.S.S.R.) said that if one was concerned with planning for a period longer than five years, the central problem was the allocation of capital investment which could create the necessary conditions for the fulfilment of the plan. With this in mind, if one took the whole of the investments of Yugoslavia as 100, what fraction of them was determined by the central authorities? What fraction was decided by the republics? What fraction by the enterprises themselves? What he was concerned about was not the sources of finance, which did not matter in this case, but what fraction of the investment decision-making was controlled directly by the state. If it was a major share, as it was in the U.S.S.R., then the state always has the opportunity to implement the decisions it wanted. But if a major share in the decision-making lay with the enterprise, and the enterprise controlled the money to be spent, then conflicts of interest between the state and the enterprises could become rather important. So, who had what share of decision-making in Yugoslavia?

Professor Bénard (France) said that Professor Stojanović was advocating coexistence of opposites instead of a middle-of-the-road solution and she had defined it as a method which retained the top priority objectives of each region, so that every region suffered minimal restrictions. But how was a decision to be reached if these priorities were strongly contradictory or if their total exceeded the resources of the national economy? His second question referred to the concept of optimality zones. How did one define what Professor Stojanović called 'the indifference curve' of an enterprise? There might well be a combination of circumstances in which the 'optimality zone' would actually become a restriction on the freedom of choice of an enterprise.

Professor Stojanović (Yugoslavia) in replying to the discussion began by commenting that a majority of those who took part in the discussion had been concerned with the effects of small or large countries. Thus she agreed with Professor Khachaturov that planning in a small country is not a special problem in itself, but nevertheless planning, decision-making and their functions were significantly different in a small country. To a greater extent the problems of a small country were simultaneously problems of optimal organisation and structure not only of the economy but also of the society as a whole. Perhaps in the case of Yugoslavia the establishment of their system involved certain losses of time and money, but as an economist she was in favour of such a system, for multi-stage decision-making had its own advantages. Thus the problem of the optimum had not only economic but also social and democratic dimensions.

She agreed with the comments made by Professor Marczewski. In respect of the zero point, she had meant that there were, of course, benefits, but any such effect was exhausted very much sooner in a small country, so that the sources of these benefits had to be renewed and multiplied much more often.

As regards the problem of interests and the need for special consideration for state or national interests, there was inevitable conflict between the interests of the employed and the unemployed, so that the solidarity which had been mentioned had to be extended to include the interest of the working class in general, that is to say to be extended so as to coincide more closely with national interests.

Convergent planning in Yugoslavia was to be regarded more as an experiment than as accepted practice, and actual planning work was divided between three levels: the planning commissions, the political system (that is local councils, including workers' councils), and the economic chambers. The choice of the strategy of development, the extent of participation in international trade and other similar basic questions were decided by the political system, and the nature of any particular question determined whether it would be decided at the state or at the republic political level.

To turn to techniques or technologies of planning, these were designed on a multi-level basis by the planning organisations of the enterprise, the industry, the republic or the state. But their function was simply that of designing the technology of planning necessary to implement the strategy chosen at the political level.

Thus, the most important planning work was done by economic chambers. This was a new development and it had been introduced in order to avoid further specialisation of planning commissions. These economic chambers were organised on an industry basis and included representatives of enterprises, of the state and republics, as well as economists. Thus they were proper forums for discussing matters of conflict and for the resolution of situations of conflict. These chambers were well aware of the general strategy of development and familiar with the techniques of planning, but their basic tasks were concerned with relations between enterprises.

Various parameters were used in the process of planning; the principal was the accumulation parameter. Accumulation was controlled by means of the turnover tax, customs tariffs, credit policy, investment credits, and the like. In addition, there were such parameters used as the prices of production factors. It was accepted for the time being that the minimum–maximum production factor ratio was not to exceed 1:5, and the specific interpretation was set by the state. That implied that there was some kind of price control by the state, that is by the economic chamber which set the ratio. The economic chambers possessed all the relevant economic information and provided guidelines for the enterprises.

With regard to the differences in economic development between different republics, their relative unemployment rates and so on, it had been asked whether it was possible for production factors to move from one area to another? In a multinational area this was extremely difficult and required a substantial time. Everyone preferred to invest not only in one's own republic but also one's own enterprise and community, and inter-republican investment was not easy to organise. She wanted to emphasise again that convergent planning was still an experiment which was in progress.

8 Some Problems of Long-term Forecasting of Living Standards in Yugoslavia

E. Berković

I. INTRODUCTION

The standard of living in Yugoslavia is of a special significance for two main reasons: because the process of differentiation of wages and salaries, attended by a high rate of inflation and balance of trade deficit, escaped reasonable public control, and because Yugoslavia is about to define a long-term policy of socio-economic development in which the vision of a future standard of living assumes an important place. This work is dedicated to the second group of questions, but in order to understand the situation it is necessary to have some knowledge of the present tendencies with which any long-term programme of development of living standards must count.

II. CURRENT TRENDS IN LIVING STANDARDS

As we know, Yugoslavia has abandoned centralised planning in order to allow considerable scope to the mechanism of the market. At the same time, the process of development allowed for changes in the distribution of income in which personal consumption received an increasing share. From the wage levelling, which lasted until 1956, a gradual progress was made toward increasing differentiation. Coincidental with increased incomes and a higher share of personal consumption in their distribution, the standard of living recorded a relatively rapid growth. As a result, the problems which for a long time featured exclusively on the supply side, now began appearing on the demand side.

These tendencies were fully substantiated in the 1965 economic reform. The aims of the reform were mainly to stimulate skilled labour, which is very largely responsible for production, to give full initiative to the enterprises, including freedom of decision in apportioning income between consumption and investment, to adopt a capital-intensive policy of production and in this connection, to halt temporarily the high growth of employment, which caused inflation. The emphasis on the standard of living, which used to be strong even before the reform, now became even more so. It was believed at the same time that the market mechanism would take care of the elimination of stocks and that the balance of payments would thus be put right. To enable the market mechanism to perform its function, the earlier strongly pronounced price disparities between industrial and agricultural products including raw materials were removed. World prices were taken as a criterion, but they were liberalised for only about one half of the products.

Of all the achieved results, the most conclusive were those in arresting the growth of unemployment. However, as the expulsive factor in agriculture was very strong, the number of emigrants increased dramatically, and within a few years, reached a figure of 700,000. Wage differentiation was also introduced, but it soon became evident that within a very short time it had grown far bigger than was expected or was socially tolerable. This is what undoubtedly rendered more difficult the realisation of other reform targets. The rapidly altered aggregate demand as a result of increased differentiation in incomes created within one population group a relatively larger demand for durable consumer goods which imposed a pressure on imports, thus bringing the balance of trade into disequilibrium. On the other hand, the lower purchasing power of the bulk of the population resulted immediately after the reform in the creation of stocks of mass consumption products, such as textiles and footwear. Nevertheless, production adjusted relatively quickly to the new aggregate demand, among other things because the real incomes of all categories of the population had increased in the meanwhile. Yet the fact remains that wage differentiation was viewed only from the aspect of stimulation of production, underestimating the effects of a suddenly changed aggregate demand on production and the balance of payments.

There are different opinions among the Yugoslav economists as to why the implementation of the reform had run into difficulties. Whereas some believe that the market mechanism was given more scope than it should have in the current conditions, others took the view that, in shifting to a market economy, a stop was made midway. There are opinions that the aims of the reform are not consistent. This view is again countered by other opinions that there is nothing wrong with the aims of the reform, but that the measures for their implementation were not adequate. While these controversies are still raging, Yugoslavia has undertaken a series of measures which, according to official interpretation, does not constitute a return to an administratively managed economy but a necessary adjustment for the implementation of the spirit and aims of the reform.

The dinar devaluation has in the few recent months eliminated the deficit in the balance of trade. Prices are temporarily frozen. The social compact on wages and salaries, whose introduction is on the way, practically regulates relationships between the wages and funds while maintaining the stimulative factors. It should also help to fight the major sources of inflation. These measures will again tend to change the aggregate demand. It is probable that readjustment to this demand will not be very easy. However, there is no doubt about the justifiability of these stabilisation measures. This is a factor to be reckoned with at the beginning of the realisation of a long-term conception of development of living standards.

Independently of these dynamic changes, which Yugoslavia has undergone since the war, and particularly after abandoning central planning, there were certain tendencies with which any long-term development of the standard of living must cope. Because of its geographical position and openness, Yugoslavia tends to imitate in consumption the developed western countries. This demonstration effect is strengthened by the following factors:

(1) a mass movement into the cities of rural labour force which is materialistic and as such constitutes an exceptionally suitable agent of a consumer society;

(2) a very large number of economic emigrants who are susceptible to influences from the environment;

(3) the long-standing restriction of personal consumption to accelerate industrialisation, which created a hunger for consumer goods; and

(4) official insistence on personal consumption.

The coincidence of these influences resulted in a distorted order of priorities, probably most evident in the motorisation which has taken far larger proportions than is warranted by the real incomes of the Yugoslav citizens. This clearly pronounced tendency toward a consumer society constitutes a special difficulty in making a long-term forecast of living standards.

III. PROBLEMS OF FORECASTING LIVING STANDARDS: METHODOLOGICAL QUESTIONS

A number of economic institutes were engaged to produce a conceptual plan of Yugoslavia's long-term socio-economic development. In elaborating the portion concerning the standard of living, the author faced many dilemmas. Some of these dilemmas will be discussed further on in this article.

We shall begin with the difficulties arising from purely methodological issues. Different quantitative methods, which are often subtle, will not be used as the basic approach in forecasting future consumption. The most frequently applied method of extrapolation is based on the assumption that as their incomes increase, the consumers will adopt the level and manner of consumption which were characteristic of past development. To comprehend tendencies in development of consumption, two kinds of statistical material are most frequently used – inquiries into family budgets and time series. Coefficients of elasticity obtained on the basis of family budgets have an analytical value but also are static in character, because they reflect relationships of a given period with its own peculiar technical level of production, price structures, income levels, etc. Reliance on time series in estimating demand also runs into difficulties. They do have a more dynamic character, but they are also not suitable for estimating long-term development of consumption since they reflect demographic, economic, social and other relationships and trends which cannot be reasonably extrapolated in the future. Even with some corrections they could not be acceptable as the only method, since they usually use analogies with the development of consumption in other countries having a higher standard of living, but where the motive of development of the standard of living is based on different values.

This does not mean that quantitative methods are useless in fixing long-term projections. The short-term and medium-term estimates in which these methods are successfully applied are the stages of a long-term development. Here is where the significance of these methods comes to the fore – as an auxilliary means in setting up long-term estimates. Quantitative methods are also used as a control instrument, as a global quantitative framework for qualitative contents which the standard of living must have over a long period.

The forecasting of future living standards must be approached with due regard for the historical moment. If economic and social developments are inseparable in real life, if we do not want to continue reducing human terms to economic terms, then standards of living cannot be viewed exclusively from an economic aspect. We have had very good lessons from history in this respect. The granting of privileges to the economy resulted in all the other realities being regarded as something secondary. We had to face the pollution of air and water, mankind had to become physically threatened before realising that what was long considered as secondary is now in many places primary. For this reason we often wonder what the sense of progress is and how accurate our earlier notions about the effectiveness of investments were, if enormous social expenditure for the rehabilitation of natural conditions, increasingly indispensable today, has been neglected. The problem is actually much broader. We face the problem of human environment not only in the physical but also in the humanitarian sense. The concept of a welfare economy, as has been shown by some of the more developed countries which implemented it consistently, can hardly survive with its hedonistic philosophical base, incapable of escaping social pathology.

In other words, the concept of the future standard of living, if it is to be an active factor of a future style of life, must be prepared to face the difficulty in selecting among different roads of our civilisation. The socialist countries, including Yugoslavia, belong to this civilisation and share in its dilemmas. It is true that owing to a set of historical circumstances the European socialist countries have been late in forming the industrial type of economy and society. However, this fact, although in itself a historical handicap, also offers considerable possibilities of creating an industrial society which will avoid excessive urbanisation and social pathology, well known in the developed countries. The socialist countries must think of creating their own type of industrial society, if only because of the stage they have reached in their development. The problems which were exclusively on the side of production are more and more being transferred to the side of consumption. In this connection, the question arises whether and to what extent such a consumption will have a humanitarian character.

This approach obviously contains certain value implications. Leaving aside the present ideological division of the world and values which inevitably arise therefrom, there is a set of values which are more or less accepted as ideals of a major part of mankind. For an insight into the future living standards, highly important are: equality (viewed as a process of creating equal chances for all men), social security in all its aspects, and a real popular participation in the adoption of vital decisions in society. Another important value is the development of the personality. It is assumed that even the developed countries are today relatively undeveloped in the number of rounded and authentic personalities created; or rather that the present-day development has produced an imbalance between material and cultural development. Put in other terms, future evolution in the developed countries will focus more and more on the development of the personality and its intellectual and creative capabilities.

Closely connected with this is the question of the needs which no concept of living standards can avoid. They are a separate subject of study. In a realistic approach to the search for an optimal relationship among the elements of the living standard, the question of what are authentic needs is usually placed in the foreground. However, this is a question to which it is hard to supply a definitive answer, but which for that reason cannot be altogether overlooked.

If we are to establish reliable fundamentals in this matter, then in material consumption it would be to satisfy essential needs. The problem is more difficult in the sphere of non-material elements of the living standard. Yet even here scales of values which are not subject to dispute can be established. One such constant would be social values or, more precisely, creation of conditions for their realisation. Another would be the introduction of man to a higher order of necessities.

The scale of lower and higher needs is known. Marx, too, believed that as a natural being man must first satisfy his biological and physiological needs, but that it was not a purpose of life but rather a precondition for an all-round development of man.[1] Instead of abstract discussions on what constitute authentic needs, it seems that we should start by trying to establish which needs are of a lower or a higher order. It would not be amiss to recall here the observation of J. Fourastié, who, discussing the utilisation of leisure as a problem of generations, argued that the first leisured generation tries to kill time by indulging in some kind of activity (gambling, bowling, etc.). The next generation is prone to eating for the sake of eating, drinking for the sake of drinking, and susceptible to pre-occupations with sports and senseless travelling. It is only the third generation that is obsessed by real passions, intellectual and artistic preoccupations. Leaving aside whether and to what extent the lower and higher orders of needs are a question of generations, the fact is that the scales of lower and higher orders are actually known and are not challenged.

This approach to forecasting the standard of living is obviously too broad and does not content itself with just the material side expressed in personal consumption. It must be that way if it is to implement the long-term aims of the socio-economic development. The standard of living is not only a sum total of consumer goods and services; it is a constitutive element and possibly the most important factor in creating a life style. For this reason it must assume a more important role in the realisation of the aims of a long-term socio-economic development. It is also no less important in long-term predictions to bear in mind the predilections of the present young generations for which such a standard is being created. The thinking part of that generation has made a sufficiently clear option in favour of the creation of a humanitarian society. There is reason to suppose that such a tendency will only grow and acquire a mass basis.

[1] K. Marx: *Ökonomisch–philosophische Manuskripte aus dem Jahre 1844*, Marx–Engels Werke, Ergänzungsband I (Berlin, 1968) p. 544.

IV. PROBLEMS OF FORECASTING: PERSONAL AND COLLECTIVE CONSUMPTION

One of the basic questions in framing a long-term concept of the development of the living standard is the relationship between personal and collective consumption. Division into these two large groups of elements is based on the nature of needs which are being satisfied. Income serves to cover the expenditure for food, clothing, housing, the purchase of different consumer durables, as well as a certain number of services. The funds of collective consumption cater for the needs connected with the building of a person and ensuring his place in the society. This includes education, culture, medical and social welfare, standard of hygiene, social and personal security. What priority will be given to either of the two groups of elements, which can be termed material and non-material, will depend on several factors: level of economic development, type of society, historical development, cultural traditions, scale of values. These factors have a strong interaction and wield a very strong influence on the pattern of needs in a society.

The relationship between material and non-material elements of the living standard is extremely complex at all levels of economic development. At a low level, difficulties arise because of limited means and because of the priority given to the satisfaction of the essential needs. Too much attention on material consumption may remain greatly pronounced even at a higher level of income, which otherwise widens scope for the development of the other elements of the living standard. For this reason it is necessary to have a conception of the development of society and the personality and to insist on a *continuity of values* even though at a low level of incomes the material base for satisfying the needs of this kind may be extremely small. Otherwise the development of the material standards becomes one-sided and leads to the creation of a consumer society with all its known aberrations.

Material consumer goods which satisfy the needs for food, clothing, housing and for a number of industrial goods and services, whose usage is gradually becoming general as wages increase and material production and technical progress develop, undoubtedly constitute an important factor of the living standard, and their importance can never be denied. It is also not possible to establish the saturation point with the material consumer goods since the structure of consumption of different groups is subject to changes. As income grows, so better and more expensive products are consumed, and the development of material production makes it possible for all needs to be more efficiently satisfied.

The trouble is that material consumption need not always be an expression of real needs. It may also be the result of a status-seeking in society, which influences consumption in various ways. We know, for example, that consumers avoid purchasing the goods that sell fast because of their low prices. At the root of such behaviour is the desire to stand aloof from the other consumers, and it is known as the 'snob effect'. Similar motives lie at the base of the so-called 'Veblen effect', which is seen in a close positive correlation between the consumption and prices of some consumer goods. In other words, for prestige reasons only those articles are bought which, because of their high prices, are accessible to only a small number of consumers. As the number of consumers increases, the consumer ceases to buy those goods and looks for other, more expensive products. Phenomena such as this promote needs and in certain conditions serve as a model for a type of consumption.[1]

Since the consumption of material goods, if left to follow spontaneous development and the effect of demonstration, practically never becomes saturated, and since the available means are at the same time limited, we are faced with the question of structuring consumption between material and non-material elements. Is it dependent on a given level of income, or a level of supply with material consumer goods? In our opinion, non-material needs must be present at all levels of the living standards. The essence of the problem is that man must adopt a given structure of needs as his own at all levels of the development of consumption. Even the basic needs of existence should be viewed from this angle. In the past they implied a minimum of goods needed for biological survival. Socialism, which appeared almost as a rule in the underdeveloped countries, had to overcome the population's material poverty as its high priority goal. This is achieved by satisfying such essential needs as food, shelter and clothing. All the other needs depend on the scale of values, personality profile, acquired preferences, etc. However, the overcoming of the biologically imposed needs does not mean in every instance that the essential needs have also been satisfied, since those depend on the degree of economic and social development. Namely, as the biologically conditioned needs are satisfied, the notion of the essential needs is extended. In a relatively more developed society, essential needs include a certain number of the

[1] Thorstein Veblen, *The Theory of the Leisure Class* (London, 1899); H. Leibenstein, 'Bandwagon, Snob and Veblen Effects in the Theory of Consumers Demand', *The Quarterly Journal of Economics*, vol. LXIV no. 2 (May 1950); G. Scherhorn, *Bedürfnis und Bedarf. Sozialökonomische Grundbegriffe im Lichte der neueren Anthropologie* (Berlin, 1959); H. Kreikebaum, G. Rinsche, *Das Prestigemotiv in Konsum und Investition* (Berlin, 1961).

so-called social needs. The higher the average level of life, the larger is the number of minimum social needs. How many of the non-material needs will enter the concept of the minimum and even the average standard is a question of the level of economic development, balance of social forces and affirmation of a certain scale of values.

The relationship between the material and non-material element of the living standard is not predominantly dependent on personal incomes, since non-material elements are generally satisfied from the means of collective consumption. Consequently, this relationship depends on the distribution between personal and collective expenditure within the means which are earmarked for the standard of living. The complexity of the problem also stems partly from the fact that increased personal consumption is at the expense of the collective consumption and vice-versa, and when the available means are relatively low, it is not easy to find an optimal relationship between personal and collective consumption. It is true that this balance is lacking in many countries where the shortage of the means for living standards is not an overriding concern. The point is whether or not society has an active role in structuring the material and non-material elements of the living standards. This is precisely the reason why the balance between personal and collective consumption may be regarded as a parameter which leaves its imprint not only on the living standards but on the entire society.

The understanding of what non-material elements imply may help to establish adequate relationships between the personal and collective consumption. This involves two main preoccupations. The first is to establish those fields where the principle of equal needs must unconditionally be applied, and to assess how far the elements of collective consumption influence the development of moral and intellectual values. The second is to establish the influence which this type of consumption has on the creation of preferences for certain needs and on the structuring of personal consumption. It seems that such an approach to the formation of the structure of personal consumption, i.e. insistence that it should develop parallel with the formation of personality, constitutes the crux of the entire problem.

V. PROBLEMS OF FORECASTING: TYPE OF SOCIETY

The type of society is the greatest dilemma which overshadows all others. Selection of the type of society should be such as to achieve a consistency of goals and solve the conflicts which may arise among them. There are of course different types of societies ranging from the consumer society to the humanitarian society.

The standard of living is today very clearly defined in a society which has the distinguishing features of a 'consumer society'. In such a society there is an exaggerated preoccupation with material consumer goods, while the other social needs of man and all the values contained in these needs are suppressed either for objective or for subjective reasons. Experience has shown that a consumer society distorts the optimal relations between relative material prosperity on the one hand and the cultural development of the personality and its social fulfilment on the other. In his observations on the traditional economic concepts of consumption in advanced capitalist countries, J. Galbraith points out the phenomenon of an abundance of consumer goods produced by private manufacturers, whereas there is a dearth of goods and services provided by the government or community (schools, medical centres, parks, recreation facilities, etc.). In his opinion the entire economy is based on one portion of minor human needs.[1]

Erich Fromm, analysing the position of man and his needs in modern society, came to the conclusion that the bourgeois life of prosperity which satisfies all material wants causes boredom, which in turn is relieved by social pathology. He asks if this is not a drastic illustration of the fact that man does not live by bread alone and that modern civilisation does not fulfil man's needs. Fromm wonders whether there is something wrong with the way of life and the goals to which they aspire when it is the populations of the countries of western Europe and the United States, which have made a materially comfortable life the goal of overall socio-economic activity, that are showing alarming signs of mental derangement.[2]

Irrespective of the fact that socialism implies a humanitarian orientation, it is possible that in practice, through a number of pragmatic steps, it might incline toward one or the other type of society. The question that seems to arise at this historical juncture is whether socialism must pass through the phase of a consumer society, even temporarily, or avoid it.

Opinions are divided on this question, which preoccupies not only economists but also philosophers and sociologists. This controversy perhaps became sharpest in the debate about private automobiles carried on a few years ago in virtually all the socialist countries. These discussions became academic overnight when factories were built for the manufacture of passenger cars, but misgivings about the wisdom of such a move have remained, especially since problems of air pollution and urban noise have become so acute. Subsequent realisa-

[1] J. Kenneth Galbraith, *L'ère de l'opulence* (Paris, 1961) p. 286.

[2] Erich Fromm, *Zdravo društvo* (Zagreb, 1963) pp. 35, 36.

tion that the private motor car is not such an efficient means of transportation and that it serves secondary more than primary needs has increased doubts as to the justifiability of these factories. However, these doubts assail intellectuals more than they do manufacturers of automobiles which are taking an increasingly important place in the economy. From this standpoint the step that has been taken seems irreversible.

We have cited the example of a typical consumer article which symbolises the dilemma of whether to opt for a consumer civilisation and the pragmatism which can lead a society up the garden path of a consumer civilisation in spite of general trends to the contrary. Here again the propensities of transitional societies conflict with some of the values on which socialism insists.

There can be no doubt that potential inclinations toward a consummer society are very strong in socialist countries. These preferences can be traced to the first generation of peasants who left the village and came to the cities where, after generations of deprivation, they have the historical hunger for all material goods. The expansion of all social services, especially education, in the socialist countries has brought other needs as well. This no doubt has been a sound policy, but the aspiration for material consumption could not thereby be fully extinguished, particularly since the model of economic development required enormous resources, leaving relatively little scope for personal consumption. Furthermore, the desire to imitate the consumption of the advanced capitalist countries was also very difficult to neutralise. Finally, the slogan 'catch up and surpass' would seem not always to be limited to the sphere of production and contains the effect of emulating the living standard of the advanced capitalist countries. If all this is true, then it would seem that the floodgates have been opened for the rush of the consumer civilisation. Protagonists of the view that socialism cannot avoid a consumer civilisation further argue that people must satisfy some of their cravings so as to realise through their own experience that a consumer article is not the end-all of human endeavour.

There are also views that it is possible to skip a consumer civilisation since it is incompatible with a humanitarian orientation. It is thought that after a relative saturation with such necessities of life as food, clothing and housing, a person's living standard is largely structured on his own scale of values, and this implies the development of the personality, of man's intellectual potential and sensibilities so that he can appreciate the true values of this world. One important and certainly novel argument along this line is that resources are limited. This fact must be reckoned with and careful study given to the view that, because resources are limited, the underdeveloped countries can never reach the material consumption of the advanced countries. The question is whether such concern is warranted, not only because a consumer society is basically wasteful, but also because of its scale of values which determines its nature of consumption. People with a higher order of needs require relatively fewer material resources. It follows that there should be greater investment in people, not just for the sake of greater labour productivity but also to create consumers with higher orders of needs. Needless to say, the proponents of this view feel helpless before certain trends which have already gone far, such as private motorisation. They do not advocate asceticism, and in so far as the automobile is concerned it could be argued that instead of serving man as a simple means of transport, the car has enslaved him and is dictating his life style or has become a prestige symbol. The most cogent arguments are that consumer society is undergoing a crisis in the advanced capitalist countries as well, hence it is a historical paradox that the socialist countries are its extension. Of course the achievement of a fully humanitarian society requires adequate means, which will be discussed separately.

VI. PUTTING A CONCEPT OF LIVING STANDARDS INTO EFFECT

Every conception can simply remain an intellectual exercise unless suitable ways and means are found for its realisation. The freedom of choice of the consumer is usually cited as the greatest difficulty. Of course no one can deny the consumer his freedom of choice in the technical sense. But there is considerable agreement that a consumer's decision is determined by his scale of values. Accordingly, influence should be brought to bear on the scale of values and not directly on the decision itself. The reverse effect should not be lost sight of, viz. a certain structure of consumption influences the scale of values.

In this sense, the structuring of production is highly important for the shaping of consumption and consumers. The demonstration effect does not exist only in the field of consumption but also in that of production. It may even be claimed that the elements of a consumer civilisation penetrate through those channels possibly even more than through imitation in consumption. Social decision whether priority in production will be given to the manufacture of houses or motor cars, or whether (there being a housing shortage) the building of luxury apartments should be permitted, has different consequences on social relations, particularly on social differentiation.

Imitation acts in several directions. It is usually qualified as a negative factor to which some economists such as J. Duesenberry ascribe very far-reaching economic effects. However, imitation need not be a negative factor. It is certainly not where application of technical progress in production is concerned. Even in the field of consumption it may be used in a progressive sense. In every society there are social groups whose life styles serve as models for the broad masses. It depends very much on the behaviour of these groups whether this type of consumption, with corresponding values, will be used as a model which will be followed by the broad masses.

Certainly it is the governments and the ruling ideologies that have the most important role. In our opinion, the question is rather whether the ruling social forces are sufficiently resolved to follow a conception of needs than whether they are capable of realising it. First of all, there is the policy of income distribution. Sweden has shown that even with capitalism it is possible to have a high participation of collective consumption in the distribution of income and thus establish a relative balance between the material and sociocultural developments. Those possibilities are all the greater in the socialist countries where influence not only on income distribution but also on the structure of production and other relationships is far greater. Speaking of the influence of the ruling social forces, it should be remembered that ideology is very strongly present there, but ideological factors in this sphere must not be excluded.

VII. SOME CONCLUSIONS

In the presentation of some of the dilemmas that the author has encountered in working on the long-term development of the living standards in Yugoslavia, a deliberate endeavour has been made to select those spheres where economics comes up against other realities. It now seems a thing of the past when every theory of economic development started from the growth of per capita income in order to eliminate in this high-handed fashion the other objectives which must be present in making a long-range estimate of the living standard.

The economy cannot be separated from other social realities; nor can it define its own objectives. This is possibly most obvious in the sphere of targets which principally take the form of living standards. A justifiable demand for accuracy and facts must not imply that nothing that cannot be measured exists.

In an attempt to make a long-range forecast of living standards, it is useful to employ quantitative analysis, either as an auxiliary means of discovering structural changes, or as a control of the real economic framework in which the standard of living is formed. However, the crux of our investigation is to try to create an authentic standard of living dependent on all the relevant factors. In this light, the question is more and more persistently being asked whether the developing countries should uncritically follow the model of the developed western countries. In our opinion the same question arises not only for that group of countries but for all other countries individually.

Discussion of the Paper by Professor Berković

Dr Deaton (U.K.), opening the discussion, said that Professor Berković raised some very difficult questions which, though they might be answered in different ways, were of significance for socialist and market economies alike. In the first part of the paper there was a description of living standards in Yugoslavia, and this provided a good example of something which had come up a number of times both in papers and in discussions. This was the impossibility of adequate planning without adequate forecasting. However good might be one's intentions, planning must fail if it was based on an incorrect forecast. This was true not only of wrong forecasts but also of forecasts that were incomplete. In the case of Yugoslavia the introduction of wage differentials to stimulate production had unforeseen effects on the structure of consumer demand, and hence on the balance of payments. This was not in itself a surprising result. Nevertheless, it was of a type which was easily missed if incomplete forecasting models were used.

Dr Deaton thought that one general point, frequently raised in this conference, had not been adequately discussed. It could perhaps be summarised as follows. Long-term planning, long-term forecasting or long-term guessing – whatever it might be called – was not possible in any useful sense without an adequate understanding of the behaviour and trends of the production, consumption and distribution of the economy in the medium term. He was saying medium term rather than short term because one could probably afford, in this conference, to abstract from cycles and immediate supply difficulties as essentially short-term phenomena. He did not think that understanding of this yet existed in sufficient measure for us to be able to speak very meaningfully about the even greater difficulties of long-term analysis. All this was even more true for a non-centrally-controlled economy than it was for a socialist economy.

Nevertheless, no economy was controlled to the last act of the last agent, and actions in one sphere, as could be seen from Professor Berković's paper, could have unexpected consequences on other parts of the economy. It would thus seem to him that the first and immediate priority for long-term forecasting was a continued development and study by the quantitative methods of economics and econometrics of the structural relationships of both socialist and capitalist economies. He felt that it was perhaps the absence of an accepted body of knowledge in the form of a general model of what makes an economy function in the short run which had accounted for many of the generalities of this conference. As Professor Marczewski had said, nobody in either East or West was actually doing long-term planning, and this was perhaps because, except in a few well-defined areas basically connected with demographic planning, where the short term was measured in decades, the basis for a long-term plan just did not exist.

Professor Berković had gone on in her paper to discuss the other factors which had been important in influencing consumer behaviour recently in

Yugoslavia, such as urbanisation and emigration. The very richness of her description of what had happened in Yugoslavia, and of the interaction of social and economic factors in the consumption sphere was perhaps an indication of just how difficult was the projection of what would happen.

These social factors, difficult enough to identify in the past, were much more difficult to project into the future. And since it was so difficult – and since he himself was one who believed in the principle of maximum simplicity of explanation – he would be very interested to know just how much of the pattern of consumer demand in Yugoslavia since 1956 could be explained in terms of the more conventional variables such as income and prices? Indeed, the rapid growth of the demand for consumer durables, especially motor cars, at times of rising real incomes was something which was common enough in many countries and for which explanation existed, largely in terms of real income. This was not to say that he did not himself believe that other factors which Professor Berković had discussed had not been important or would not be important in the future – clearly they would. But if only one could quantify their relative importance in the past it could help one to assess the reliability of future forecasts in the face of the great uncertainty in the movement of variables over long distances of time.

Another part of Professor Berković's paper dealt with long-term forecasting of living standards. Here she raised some very fundamental questions indeed, extending so far as the whole nature of society, which was, of course, if the term of projection was long enough, itself a variable. Plans became more qualitative and more metaphysical and less quantifiable the further one went. Nevertheless, as Professor Berković had emphasised, the extrapolation of past trends, either from one's own country or from a more highly developed neighbour, was a very weak response indeed to the challenge presented by the possibility of planning the structure of demand of the future. Professor Berković was quite right to point out here that statistical methods were not appropriate in this context. Econometric investigation of either the family budget or the time series type revealed the structure of consumer behaviour as it had existed within a particular environment. But the aim of long-term planning might well be to change that environment, including the structure of consumption as a part of it. How the consumer behaviour was to be modified depended on one's basic necessities plus, perhaps, a few basic luxuries, and on what goods should be produced and consumed.

In this context Professor Khachaturov had discussed the hierarchy of wants – personal, social, cultural and so on. If such a hierarchy could be established and become a matter of general agreement, then it could form a basis for long-term planning of consumption, at least in a socialist state. Professor Berković herself seemed to think this was so. She suggested that scales of values that were not subject to dispute could be established. He himself did not feel nearly so sure. It would not be easy to explain to a family without a car that because 50 per cent of all families owned cars, and the roads were fully used and cities had become polluted, production was now ceasing and they would never have one. And if one put cars in the necessity category of the hierarchy the same problem would occur when some families had many cars, and others only one. He felt that any scale of values imposed from outside would encounter distribution problems between families of this sort.

Professor Berković had realised this when she discussed the imitation factor. But it had to be realised that this imitation made it impossible to impose a scale of values independently. First of all, the distribution of goods and services existing or traditionally existing in the economy, and secondly, the values or the scale of values which prevailed in neighbouring or other comparable economies, and thirdly the theoretical difficulties of combining individual preferences, all presented acute practical difficulties in this sort of context.

Nevertheless, a decision of what the hierarchy of consumption should be was of great importance, for if the economists or planners failed to make these choices, an optimal solution could not be achieved merely by chance. In a western economy the forces and technological conditions of production, the managerial and market environments required by modern industrial production, all had a very great momentum of their own. In the absence of strong outside control – and it was indeed very arguable how much of this was provided by the market while government control in this field was very weak – the forces of production would be largely responsible for the structure of production and hence the structure of consumption.

Professor Berković had illustrated some of her points, using automobiles as an example. To take the United Kingdom, there had been very strong reasons from the side of supply and production, why more and more cars should have been produced. It was certainly true, at least in the short run, that consumers preferred to buy more cars and the government seemed prepared to build more roads to accommodate them. The alternative for the government was to legislate that some people could not have cars – and this was a very difficult decision, much too difficult for most western governments. So the end to car consumption would come when motoring became unpleasant and not worthwhile – a situation which could hardly be called the optimum but rather the pessimum. It was less encouraging to hear from Professor Berković that this problem was being seriously considered in the socialist countries. It would be unfortunate if a decision were indeed made on the basis of what had happened in western economies, a possibility that she had suggested.

There must certainly be production forces in the socialist states militating towards a similar structure of production to that which they had in market economies. Perhaps participants from other socialist countries could say how they had dealt with this problem in the past, and how in the future they saw consumer demand evolving in a way distinct from that in the market economies.

Professor Khachaturov (U.S.S.R.) thought that the central idea of Professor Berković's paper was a model of an ideal structure of consumption. In the first stages, planning in the socialist countries had mostly followed the lines of allocation of resources for economic growth. This must have been the consequence of an insufficient level of development of the productive forces. At the same time, with the advance of the socialist economies, the necessity to reconcile both the planning of production and the planning of consumption was becoming more acute, thus emphasising the urgency of determining what were to be considered the human needs in a socialist society.

He thought that these needs, both material and cultural, could be determined on the basis of certain norms and used as an ideal consumption model. Some economists in the socialist countries had already tried to make such projections, although a complete ideal model had not yet been compiled. He believed it was quite possible to put forward the aim of designing such a model. Starting from knowledge of the aehieved level of consumption and of the possibilities and the rates of economic growth, it should be feasible to plan the stages and the rates of demand satisfaction on the basis of an ideal consumption model.

At present they could speak of this not as something already done but rather in terms of practical steps which could now be taken to solve this task. He thought that Professor Berković's paper outlined these steps, giving full consideration not only to material and cultural needs but also to protection of the environment, to the economical use of resources, and similar factors. In this context he himself thought it was essential that when determining the prospective consumption structure, attention and consideration should be given to some of the negative after-effects which had appeared in those western economies in which the structure of consumption was more advanced. Dr Deaton had rightly suggested that these harmful consequences of western experience did not necessarily need to be repeated in socialist countries.

Professor Marczewski (France) said that Professor Khachaturov had raised the very important question of what criteria should be used for planning individual consumption, with particular accent on the necessity to establish certain norms of what he had called the ideal structure of consumption. In the opinion of most western economists there was no reason why a society should impose such rigid norms of consumption upon the individual. They believed that social prosperity would be maximised when the choice between different patterns of consumption was in the control of the individual consumer. They also thought that the consumer maximised his satisfaction when he chose the products and the quantity of those products to be consumed. It was likely also that any kind of norm would result in a black market, outside the official distribution network, in order to adjust the actual distribution to the ideal one. All that required, of course, two constraints or reservations. The first was that society, in their opinion, had the right and even the obligation to impose certain limits on the total volume of consumption and in particular on the choice between consumption and investment, the latter being fixed by an economic sovereignty responsible for expressing collective preferences. Thus, the first limitation was that the balance between collective future needs and individual immediate needs had to be fixed on a global level; this could easily be done even in western economies by and through the state control over the disposable incomes of consumers. The second limitation was that there were certain types of consumption which were obviously harmful from both individual and social points of view. He had in mind consumption of alcohol, drugs and so on, where public intervention was necessary. But western economists were, he believed, fully convinced that outside of those two limitations, which were unquestionably important, an individual consumer should be free to express his preferences and that there was no scope for imposing any set of norms upon him.

Professor Bénard (France) said that Professor Berković had raised the important question of why a government should interfere – if it had to interfere – in the range of individual preferences. Neoclassical economists in western countries usually considered this to be an artificial problem, thus refusing to deal with it and relegating it to the periphery of their studies. He himself thought that even from the neoclassical point of view the problem deserved much more consideration. At least three reasons were usually given to justify this intervention of society or a government upon the individual consumption. The first was the objective of redistribution of income, including, of course, allocation of goods to meet this redistributed income. The second reason – externalities – was also familiar and the example of pollution illustrated it well enough. The third reason, which in his opinion was the most important, was the poor information available to all or most consumers. Some years ago he had made a study in which he had introduced the idea of a 'technology of consumption', and in which ordinary consumer goods were considered to be the inputs, and intelligence and the cultural, personal, and other aspects of human capital, represented the outputs. He had discovered that most people did not have the best information they could have had in the current state of knowledge about consumption technology. Thus if it could be assumed that the government or some group of experts had better information on consumption technology, their modifying influence upon the quality and quantity of consumption could be justified.

This raised the question whether the government was really better informed about consumption technology than individual people were? It might be true for certain particular areas of consumption, such as health services, but it might be dangerous to go too far with such an assumption because freedom of individual choice might be utterly destroyed. Another point was that even if the government was indeed better informed than the public at large, it still had to choose between greater control and diffusion of the information. This brought one to the question of how to combine and optimise both control and information. It often seemed that information had a considerable cost in terms of the manpower and resources it required, while control cost nothing. But this was an illusion, for control also involved the cost of the administrative machinery as well as the social cost because people were reluctant to accept control. The best solution remained to be found.

Professor Khachaturov (U.S.S.R.) believed there was some misunderstanding. He had not meant to suggest that rigid norms should be imposed on the individual customer. He should certainly retain his opportunity to choose. But some possible general norms were required if one wanted to establish what an overall level of consumption would be. So he would want to define the task as being to find the general volume of consumption, given the abundance of choices and freedom of the individual consumer's choice.

Professor Porwit (Poland) thought that the meaning of what they had been calling 'norms' needed to be clarified. He felt that these should not be treated very mechanistically because quantifiable directive norms could be set only in certain fields of consumption. What he thought one had in mind was the probable future consumption pattern of a society. This involved numerous studies of a sociological and similar kind, dealing not only with material consumption but with different aspects of life in the society concerned.

As regards the question of how to make use of the resulting picture of the future, it was not a matter of forbidding anything but that the freedom of individual consumer choice was always exerted in a certain environment and this included not merely the distribution of income and the effects of price determination, but also many sociological and psychological effects influencing his choice. The possibilities of exerting influence related, he suggested, to influencing the factors that in turn influenced the choice of the consumer.

Finally, he fully agreed with Dr Deaton's conclusion that what we needed was a better understanding of the medium-term functioning of a society. He would only add that it was not only a question of a practical and quantifiable science of this functioning but also of taking into account the problems they had just discussed.

Dr John (Hungary) said that in Hungary the planning of living standards was not merely a form of planning activity, nor was it just a prediction of the future. It covered also the form of their future society and their future conditions of life. When discussing living standards some economists thought of them purely in terms of material consumption. But living standards had a wider meaning that perhaps justified talking about the planning of the socio-economic conditions of life. In socialist countries, and even in market economy countries, governments and planning bodies had, in his opinion, not only the right but also the obligation to intervene whenever such intervention was necessary to shape the future conditions of life and the future structure of consumption.

In making long-term plans in Hungary they gave priority to the social aspects. That meant that in all planning procedures they wanted first to picture their future society and its needs as a whole, including both their material and their non-material needs. They had formulated a set of objectives, the ultimate and most abstract of which was the building up of a communist society, while the others were more specific and special, such as to ensure security of life in the wider sense (an income policy, health policy, and the like) or to strengthen the open character of the society (embodied in the educational system and its flexibility, as well as in equal opportunities for men and women). A further aim was to have an income distribution which would combine the two objectives of providing incentives for higher productivity and at the same time diminishing the gaps between different groups in the population. They sought also to avoid social conflict by influencing consumption and the means to it so as to solve the problem of autonomous functioning of the different structures of consumption. And last and most important was the role of infrastructure in determining the style of life and its qualitative elements.

9 Planning Development of Population and Manpower Resources in Bulgaria

D. Bradistilov

I. INTRODUCTION

The reproduction of population and the actively occupied sector of it together with the use of the nation's labour resources have an important place in Bulgaria's social and economic development plan. Population and labour resources represent on the one hand a vital factor in economic growth and on the other they represent the ultimate purpose of all production. With state ownership over the means of production the full satisfaction of the nation's material and cultural needs and the psycho-physiological and intellectual development of the individual form the content and purpose of the plan-directed economic and social activity of the nation.

A satisfactory solution of this problem involves both the quantitative and qualitative replacement of the nation's manpower resources in terms of number, composition by age, sex and qualification, and also their efficient use – their appropriate distribution in terms of occupations, experience, education, skill and so on. That means that the objectives and policies for national economic development must be set after taking account of the needs and problems of making full and effective use of the manpower resources. The efficient use of the nation's manpower resources, with suitable provision for their general development, directly affects the nation's social and economic standards, and its capacity to satisfy its material and cultural needs. This involves the working out of an economic policy that reflects the distribution of capital investment, the regional distribution of the manpower resources, and the probable effects of mechanisation and automation on the growth of labour productivity. This emphasises that the efficient use of the nation's active population and the social problems involved in it require the attention of scientists as well as of administrators.

The growth of population and manpower resources is not and cannot be an end in itself. The quantitative and qualitative changes that occur or may be achieved during a given planned period are determined by the extent to which various economic and social problems are satisfactorily solved during this period by the country and the socialist state. Starting from this concept, the principal public and state organisations have formulated in a number of programme documents and decisions regarding the economic policy which must be adopted in this field during the years of building up a fully developed socialist society in Bulgaria. This policy may be outlined in the following terms: by using the achievements of science and technical progress, and by creating conditions for a fuller and more complete satisfaction of the nation's material and cultural needs, to ensure an optimal employment for the active population of the country in such a way as will raise the indicators of quality, such as improvement of education, of occupation, of distribution and technical and professional training.

This in its turn implies a corresponding policy in the demographic field and, during the coming years, the carrying through of those social, health, educational policies; other measures must be ensured that are necessary to modify the demographic processes in such a way that they reflect the national economy's needs for professional and administrative manpower; in the meantime conditions must be created that will raise living and cultural standards throughout the country. The interrelations between the quantitative population growth and its qualitative aspects – the change of the age composition and the net reproduction rates in the given social system – exert their influence on the growth and composition of manpower resources not directly but indirectly. This influence occurs mainly through factors affecting the living and social conditions of the society – the level of incomes, the extent to which the population's material and cultural needs are met, the qualitative and quantitative trends of urbanisation and so on. This leads to the second aspect of these problems and the methods to be used for their planned regulation. In working out a long-term perspective plan, not only must quantitative and qualitative forecasts be made of these demographic factors and of the growth on this basis of future manpower resources, but the changes must also be planned in those elements of the social environment which influence directly and indirectly all the factors which are susceptible to direct influence by planning.

For discussions of policies designed to affect these demographic factors and to influence changes of the nation's manpower resources both in quantitative and qualitative respects, forecasts have to be available. The complex dynamic and probabilistic character of these demographic processes and of the factors which influence them, and which can increase or diminish the likelihood that the expected results of the various policies of the plan will be achieved, implies a directly proportional decrease of the reliability of the forecast with extension of the time-horizon and suggests the techniques that can best be used by planners for this purpose. The planning in this field can be of no more than a forecasting character.

Forecasting is an organic part of the long-term planning. The nature of the demographic processes which form the basis of the growth of population and labour resources represent one element in the long-term planning. The forecasting of these elements provides a scientific basis for the planned foreseeing of one factor in the production processes and one object of social policy for the organisations concerned with social and state functions. These in their turn represent the social objectives of forecasting.

II. FORECASTING MANPOWER RESOURCES

One direct concern of forecasting is the national labour resources, their qualitative and quantitative composition, as well as their utilisation in the national economy. This implies that the potential active population and its efficient distribution between the various production and non-production fields must be considered. The forecast has to provide an answer not only regarding the quantitative changes of the active population and of the labour resources, but also regarding their demographic composition, their qualifications and the participation rate of the potentially active population. This implies that the forecast of the future growth of the labour resources must start from the general policy for the development of the national economy and be conducted in close relation to the trends in the demographic factors.

The forecasts of the qualitative and quantitative indices of the population and its active sector have to be made in direct relationship to the expected changes in economic, social, urban and other fields during the period covered. These forecasts have to take account of the dynamic indicators of the national economy, such as the growth of the gross national product and national income, the volume of accumulation during the various planned periods, the branch and regional distribution of capital investment. These factors constitute the quantitative and qualitative determinants. At the same time they make it necessary to examine these problems as a single social complex. When speaking about planning policies of the nation and the state organisations designed to affect the growth of the population and the active labour force, two things have always to be borne in mind. First, one is discussing a very complex and slowly changing social phenomenon, changes which take place under the combined impacts of economic, social, biological, psychological, aesthetic and other factors, including factors of an irrational character such as religious standards, manners of life, traditions and so on. This is an essentially probabilistic phenomenon. Nevertheless the size of the population, the dynamics of its growth, its geographical distribution, its general and professional education, and the associated manpower resources are social phenomena subject to relevant economic and social laws. These create the social environment in which the demographic processes and the associated determination of the labour resources operate. This environment is in turn affected by the forms of ownership of the·means of production and the social relations that emerge on this basis.

The reproduction of the active population, as a very important element in the productive capacity of the country, is entirely subordinate to the economic and social laws that govern these reproduction processes on a national and regional scale. The change in the structure of the national economy and the consequent changes in demands for labour with different skills and qualifications involve an active policy in regard to these factors. But socio-economic forces, and especially the economic laws which operate during a planned period, their production qualification, affect the branch and territorial distribution, as well as the labour productivity. Thus the existence of a general policy regarding the development of the national economy over a longer period of time is one of the necessary conditions for producing a reliable and scientific forecast of the country's labour resources and population. The quantity of manpower that may be expected and its composition in terms of age, sex and qualifications is a starting point for forecasting the qualitative and quantitative indexes of the population.

III. TECHNIQUES OF MANPOWER FORECASTING

The social and economic determination of demographic processes and the influence which these factors exert on the dynamic indexes of the population and on its labour resources largely establish the limits within which the planning organisations can forecast. The state through its economic policy can do something to improve the methods of forecasting. A contribution to this has been made by the use of correlation and factorial analysis, by the possibilities of measuring, even if only approximately, quantitative effects of different factors, and by the possibilities for mathematical modelling of the assumed processes. The use of economico-mathematical models and modern computer techniques contributes greater reliability to the forecasts being made. With planned direction of such socio-economic factors as the level of income, the building of places of education, the solution of housing problems, the planned regional distribution of productive capacity, the processes of migration and urbanisation, social policy designed to raise the birth rate (child allowances, maternity leave and the like), all have an effect on the forecasted trends and in some degree contribute to the achievement of the expected outcome.

These processes are so complex and so far from permitting simplification that estimates either on a national or a regional scale are difficult to present at the level of popular exposition. The forecasting must always keep the whole range of factors in mind and remember the complex and uncertain character of the processes being estimated, and the possibilities of change in conditions affecting them in the future, if a reasonably reliable estimate is to be made of the final outcome.

The number of factors which affect the demographic processes, the changes in the operation of these factors during the different phases of the period covered, as well as the possibility for their interaction help to explain the main variants of the forecasts in this social field. The number of variants is determined by the different factors and conditions that may be used to influence the processes covered by the objectives in view, and by the criteria adopted to evaluate the different variants. This gives a hypothetical character to all the proposed variants. The optimal variant will be that which ensures the highest probability of achieving the required solutions of the problems of the national economy during the plan period, and which provides the necessary manpower resources in the production and non-production spheres, thus contributing to the improvement of the country's economic potential and the living standards of the population.

The stage which the development of the Bulgarian economy has reached and the problems to be solved during the next two decades in industry and agriculture give a special emphasis to the importance of forecasting. As an important addition to the methods and instruments used hitherto for the planning and management of the country's economic and social development, forecasting has to take its place in the scientific shaping of the nation's long-term development in terms of its industrial and territorial composition. By careful analysis of the forecasts for branches of industry, for geographical regions and for the whole economy, the problems of manpower resources have been discovered together with the qualitative and the quantitative changes which are required in this field of the national economy. The effective use of the active manpower has to take into account the changes which will take place in the branch and territorial organisation of production, which in turn assumes the occurrence of various changes in the number, age and sex structure of the population and in its geographical distribution. The limited experience gained during recent years in this new scientific field suggests that for forecasting the branch, social, territorial and other structures it will be necessary not only to use the familiar methods of extrapolation, but also to make wide use of expert estimates, hypothetical models, inferences from analogy, and normative methods, as well as some of the more elaborate economico-mathematical models with which we have to experiment. The alternative or simultaneous use of these methods is determined by the special features of the systems or phenomena being estimated and especially by the actual dynamic changes in the conditions under which the demographic processes and the creation of the manpower resources will operate during the ensuing years in the Bulgarian economy.

IV. RECENT TRENDS OF MANPOWER SUPPLY

During the past two decades a policy of industrialisation of agriculture on a co-operative basis has been carried out in Bulgaria. This policy was applied progressively from 1956 onwards. This led to fundamental structural changes in the economy and was reflected in the industrial and geographical distribution of the occupied population. Industry became a major branch of the economy. Co-operation and rapid mechanisation of work in agriculture led to the release of manpower and the need for its transfer to industrial occupations. Within the short period 1948–71 the balance between urban and rural employment changed from 26:74 to 58:42. During this period more than 1,300,000 workers were moved from rural villages into the developing industrial centres. There was thus a rapid change in the balance between the industrial workers and those in agriculture. The number of industrial employees rose to 1,260,000 in 1971 as compared with 251,000 in 1948. The urban population went up nearly 3·5 times, and in 1971 amounted to 4,679,000, with a growth of total population by 35·4 per cent as compared with 1939; the rural population decreased by 21 per cent, and amounted only to 3,879,000.

The more rapid development in the various industrial branches implied a change not only in the balance between different industries but also in the geographical distribution of activity. The building of large industrial enterprises, and the creation of what in Bulgaria represent large industrial centres in Sofia, Plovdiv, Varna, Russe, Bourgas, Stara–Zagora, Pernik, Gabrovo and other places led to an increased dynamic of migration. Large numbers of workers previously employed in agriculture headed for the rapidly growing towns. Urbanisation became much more rapid. The number of major towns grew to 172. While before the war only three towns had more than 100,000 inhabitants, now their number is increasing rapidly. The population of Sofia, the capital, is more than 1 million. Those of Plovdiv and Varna are above 300,000. Among towns with more than 100,000 are Russe, Bourgas, Stara–Zagora, Shumen, Pleven and others. The demographic structures of urban and rural areas have changed greatly. It was mainly the young and fertile groups that came out of the villages. The age structure of those still employed in agriculture was adversely affected. This had repercussions on the rural birth rate. It has now not only reached equality with the urban birth rate but has actually fallen below it. While in 1941–5 the urban birth rate was 23·9 per 1,000 and the rural rate 25·2 per 1,000, by 1970 the urban birth rate was 17·9 and the rural rate was 14·6. The great changes in social conditions, the universal availability of free medical care and other social measures of the last twenty-five years have led to a sharp decrease of infant mortality and an increase of average life expectation. In 1935–9 the average expectation of life was fifty-two years. By the end of 1970 it was over seventy years. With present knowledge of the techniques of public health and of biology and medicine it is believed that life expectation in Bulgaria has reached or is closely approaching the biological maximum.

V. THE USE OF MANPOWER

During the period discussed there has been improved use of the nation's manpower as well as a rise of living standards. Compared with 1939, population in 1971 was 35·4 per cent higher. Although some decline in the average rate of population growth has occurred, it has remained during recent years within the limits of 0·8 to 0·9 per cent. In 1970 the rate was 0·85 per cent. As a result of certain social improvements in recent years, there has been a slight rise in this figure.

An important contribution to the national economy has come from the complete elimination of the concealed under-employment of manpower resources that always existed in pre-war Bulgaria. The research of one of the country's best authorities on this, Professor Ianaki Mollov, shows that before the socialist reconstruction of the economy, there was in Bulgarian agriculture the equivalent of not less than 1 million man–years of unemployed able-bodied workers. These were occupied only in periods of peak agricultural activity. This phenomenon has disappeared for more than two decades. Development of productive activities in various branches of industry has ensured the effective use of the nation's manpower and has contributed to the improvement of standards of living and culture, not only for those working in industry but also for those remaining in agriculture. An analysis of these processes just for the period since 1952 will show what has been happening. For the period 1950–5 the average annual growth of population amounted to 15 per 1,000. Over the same period the volume of industrial production increased annually by an average of over 10 per cent taking 1952 as a base; it had increased by 1971 more than eight times; agricultural production, more than four times. This has created conditions for a steady increase of the population's nominal and real incomes, and a rise of living standards.

The problem of the effective use of the nation's manpower and the improvement of the standard of living has been analysed and estimated not only on a national scale, but also in terms of regions. This ensures a high degree of practical realism in the social, urbanisation, cultural and other measures that have an influence on demographic trends and the development and geographical distribution of the population and its labour resources. The planned allocation of the investment programme between different activities and regional units makes it possible to introduce new productive capacity into the areas where, first unemployed labour resources with suitable qualifications are available, and second, where there are suitable natural resources and geographical conditions for the efficient development of a given product. Simultaneously with improving the regional distribution of labour and its geographical specialisation and with improving the regional and industrial organisations in the various production–territorial complexes, it was also necessary to solve the problem of the efficient utilisation of the increasing output of the raw materials and other resources available in the areas of the different regional production units, and above all to ensure a more effective use of the available labour of both sexes.

The social conditions and parameters and the socio-economic factors which have affected the demographic trends and the growth of population and labour resources during the last two decades will continue during the coming years. But more and more clearly certain trends are appearing in the national economy and the social sphere which may significantly modify them. The country has entered the phase of building up a developed socialist society. Objective and subjective conditions exist for the successive manifestation of the features and parameters characteristic of this phase of a national economy's development which affect fertility and the quantitative and qualitative indexes of population and labour resources.

In the early stages, the increasing influence of these forces will lead to a more rapid development of productive capacity and an improving geographical distribution of it, with new directions and conceptions being worked out for the national economy's long-term development and the widespread application of the results of scientific and technical research to material production and to the intellectual activities of the nations. It may be expected that under the influence of these factors the character and the productive capacity of the labour force will gradually be changed and the relative proportion of highly skilled labour will grow. In particular the technical qualifications, organisations and remuneration of agricultural workers will be brought more and more in line with those of industrial workers and their work will be more similar to that in industry. The level of education of the labour force will rise. The already common integration of the work of research and design staff with that of the administrative staff in various enterprises and in public services indicates the character of a new type of economic activity – that of the all-round workers as Marx once called them. With state ownership of the means of production and the absence of competitive conflicts the importance of this group for production as well as relative income will increase.

In the second place, the economy of Bulgaria will develop during the coming years principally as a result of the intensive use of resources, the better use of the investment capital, the introduction of improved technology, and the consequent increase of labour productivity. This growth is determined by two main factors: the opportunity provided by technical progress, and the conditions created in the Bulgarian economy during recent years. The effects of the first factor are well known. The second factor deserves closer attention by economic researchers and administrators. It must now be assumed that the considerable labour reserves available in the initial period of the socialist industrialisation and of the reorganisation of agriculture on a co-operative basis are near to being exhausted. The available agricultural labour and its age and sex composition correspond to the needs, with such mechanisation of production methods as exists or is likely in the near future in the arable and cattle-breeding branches. Increased mechanisation during the coming years must offset the decline of the labour force resulting from those leaving agriculture through reaching retiring age. The national economy's other requirements for manpower will have to be met from the growth of the active population. The labour requirements for the new and dynamic developing activities such as mechanical engineering, electronics, the chemical industry and non-production activities will have to be met mainly through redistribution of the existing labour resources. Improved mechanisation and automation of production methods in Bulgaria's traditional industries, such as food and textiles, wood-working and others in which new techniques are being introduced, will make it possible to transfer some of the skilled and administrative personnel employed by them to the new industries and to the non-production activities in accordance with the plan.

VI. EXPECTED GROWTH OF THE ACTIVE POPULATION

Lack of adequate empirical data makes it somewhat difficult to estimate completely the effects on the forecast trends to be expected to result from the future growth of money incomes and the increase of social funds as well as from gradual change to the principles of distribution according to the rational needs of the different individuals. But one can hardly doubt the positive effects that a drastic improvement of housing conditions, planned control of urban development, the shortening of the working day, the lengthening of paid holidays, the improvement of school facilities, the improvement of maternity facilities and so on will exert on population and labour resources. In step with the quantitative growth of these services certain qualitative changes must be expected which will affect the demographic trends and the various factors connected with them.

By studying the combined effects of all these factors, the forecasting of the demographic processes and the growth of the population and its active sector has been begun during the last few years. It has to be mentioned, that as regards the forecasting of demographic processes such forecasts have been made before. It is expected that during the next two or three decades changes in the Bulgarian economy will take place, which will create the economic, social and other preconditions necessary for a gradual advance from the lower to the higher phase of the socialist society. Forecasts of population and labour resources are based on the work of the planning organs, the information organs, the scientific research institutes, the medical care organs, as well as the local government organs. The preparation of a general policy for the expansion and territorial distribution of the nation's productive resources as between districts and economic regions, prepared by the District People's Councils and their planning commissions, tackles this problem. The forecasts prepared by them hitherto, although implying minor differences in levels and details, are very close to or identical with the basic indexes.

Time series extrapolation is conducted by taking account of the fertility of women of child-bearing age and birth and death rates adjusted for any foreseeable changes in socio-economic factors.

The statistical organisations have worked out three hypotheses regarding natural increase of population. The first of them assumes that the rate of natural increase will decline to 6·1 per 1,000 by the year 2000 from the 8·2 per 1,000 of 1972. It allows for a slight increase of birth rate (from 16·19 per 1,000 in 1970 to 17·3 per 1,000 by the end of the forecast period) and some increase in the death rate as a consequence of the increase of the proportion of the population over retiring age. The second version assumes a decline in the rate of natural increase from 7·8 per 1,000 in 1975 to 5·2 per 1,000 by the year 2000, with the present birth rate unchanged and a slight increase of the death rate. The third variant also supposes an increase of the death rate and a decrease of the birth rate. The natural increase of population would thus lie within the limits of 7·4 and 4·1 per 1,000 inhabitants. A series of social measures decided during recent years and assumed to be carried out by the responsible organisations give a reason to expect that the growth of population during the forecast period is likely to be within the estimates given in the fifth and sixth five-year plans.

The higher estimates of natural increase also indicate the figures expected for the various five-year periods covered by the forecast. The optimistic variant predicts an increase of the population of Bulgaria from 8,534,000 in 1970 to 10,245,000 by the end of the period; with the second, the increase by 1980 is estimated to amount to 9,140,000 and by 2000 to 10,072,000; with the so-called 'pessimistic variant', the figures are estimated to be 9,113,000 and 9,901,000.

Throughout the whole period the active population will be growing in absolute numbers. The differences in proportion to population between the variants are insignificant. By 1980 the active population in all three variants levels off, and by the end of the fore-cast period a difference of 58,000 is estimated between the first and second and of about 100,000 between the first and third. In relation to total population they represent insignificant differences. But in all three variants a continuous trend is found for decrease in the relative proportion of the active population. While the active popu-lation at the beginning of the period is 59·7 per cent it falls with the first variant to 54·7 per cent, with the second to 55·0 per cent, and with the third to 55·5 per cent.

The accelerated rates of development of the Bulgarian economy of recent years will continue throughout the period covered by the forecast. For this various circumstances are favourable: the increase of the volume of capital investment and of the investment oppor-tunities in the economy; the increase of national purchasing power; the development of closer economic relations with socialist and other countries. Despite the change of the 'accumulation-consumption' ratio in favour of public and personal consumption, the absolute volume of capital investment is still growing. With an optimum ratio of technical modernisation of existing productive capacities to the creation of new working jobs, it will be possible for the latter to keep pace with the natural growth of labour resources. The results of technical progress will be broadly applied to all branches of the economy and of production. This will make it possible to improve the utilisation of the country's labour resources during the five-year and long-term plans in three ways.

First, with a general increase in the number of employees in industry some of the labour resources will need to be transferred to new branches. This, together with their contribution to raising the general technical level, will ensure an increase of labour productivity both at the individual and the national level. With an average annual rate of growth of productivity of 5–8 per cent in different branches of industry, in transport and in building it becomes possible to achieve a total increase of industrial production of 7–9 per cent. This increase can be secured in all cases through an increase of the capital and energy equipment of the workers engaged in industrial production. The average growth of industrial production that is planned is expected to result from the best use of the labour resources and from their increase by about 10 per cent before 1980, by another 12 per cent before 1990, and by a further 11–12 per cent before the end of the period. In other words, with an increase of labour resources by 32–3 per cent during the whole period covered, as compared with 1970, the necessary labour force is ensured to provide the productive resources needed in the various industrial branches and to carry out the planned production policies.

Second, a further reduction has to be made in the total number and proportion of Bulgaria's labour resources employed in agriculture. The expected trend is the result of an assumed continuation of the processes of concentration, specialisation and introduction of industrial methods in arable farming and animal husbandry. Thus the problem of increasing productivity in agriculture requires a radical solution. By establishing this objective one is adopting analogies from other industrially developed nations. Bulgarian agriculture will, however, continue to have an important part in the national economy. This is favoured by the soil and climatic conditions, the long experience of those engaged in this branch of the economy, and the export possibilities of a variety of important agricultural products. The progressive solution of the problems of mechanical harvesting of many labour-intensive crops on which Bulgarian agriculture specialises, will permit the reduction of employees in these branches. By 1980 it is expected that there will have been a 20 per cent reduction of the agricultural labour force, with 20 per cent of the active population still engaged in agriculture. By 1990, the total labour resources in agriculture will have fallen by 30 per cent, and only about 9·2 per cent of the active population will then be engaged in agriculture. By the year 2000 the numbers will have decreased by 40 per cent, and will by then represent 5·9–6·0 per cent of the active population. With such a figure, Bulgaria will be in line with nations with high industrial capacity.

Third, the growing importance of non-material activities makes it necessary to direct the planned capital investment and labour resources towards this field, which is particularly important for the nation's balanced development and its response to the growing needs of society. It is necessary to take into account the development of science, arts and other activities which mainly satisfy the intellectual needs of the country. For this purpose the numbers of those engaged in this field and their proportion to total employment are expected to increase continually and steadily. Some 504,000 were so engaged in the base year. By the end of the period their number will double and will represent about 20–2 per cent of the total labour resources.

The forecasts of labour resources and their distribution by branches in the material and non-material activities provide for employment of 80 per cent of the active population of the nation. Over the past twenty years the employment of labour resources has varied between 77·8 per cent and 84·1 per cent. The remaining proportion is accounted for by the numbers of students, invalids, pensioners who are of normal working age, and so on, who, because of their position or inability to work take no part in production or other economic activities. The employment ratio stated may be assumed to represent the optimum for the Bulgarian economy. It makes possible the normal conduct of the national economy and the expansion of production.

Discussion of the Paper by Professor Bradistilov

Professor Porwit (Poland), opening the discussion, said that the paper was divided into four main sections. The first dealt with planning and the role of forecasts in respect to population and labour resources and described the scope of the work in this field. The second presented an outline of the changes in the demographic structure of the population and in employment during the past twenty to thirty years of tremendous change for Bulgaria. The next section examined the main lines of the work on forecasting and planning being done at present, and finally, the fourth part gave some examples to illustrate the preliminary results of such forecasts, and suggested the assumptions to be made for the next twenty or thirty years.

As far as the first section was concerned, the main points made by Professor Bradistilov, as he saw them were these. First, it was emphasised that two approaches needed to be combined in planning and forecasting, one of them starting from the social and cultural aims of development, with people as the beneficiaries of the policy, and the second beginning with population and employment and considering their use as production factors. These two approaches should ultimately form a single whole.

On the basis of this approach it was suggested that policy assumptions, planning and forecasting in the field of demographic conditions and employment should be regarded as an integral part of the overall social and economic policy. The objectives of that policy were defined as the use of the achievements of science and technological progress for the creation of conditions permitting fuller and better satisfaction of the society's material and cultural needs and for ensuring an optimal employment of the able-bodied occupied population in such a way as to raise the quantities and qualities of education, employment and production of the population.

This brought one to the third main point, which was that this complex and integrated approach should be treated as the basis for formulation of a national demographic policy aimed at modifying the future demographic background. Two aspects of this were emphasised. First, it was the probabilistic nature of the processes being studied, and Professor Bradistilov warned one against any simplistic popularisation of these processes, as well as against hopes of them being at all easily planned in quantitative terms, but at the same time indicating possible ways of influencing them indirectly.

Attention was drawn to the fact that demographic conditions, such as the age, sex, and occupational composition of the population should be, and were being, considered in terms of the relative changes in the parameters relating to other changes in the structure of the economy, both as regards branches of the economy and the various regions of the country. The application of mathematical models and computerised techniques were especially useful for this. The major changes in Bulgaria in the past two or three decades concerned a substantial shift of population from rural areas to urban employment, with the latter accounting now for 58 per cent of the country's occupied population. This in turn had been a consequence of progress with the creation of industrial centres. An interesting feature of this, contrary to experience in most other countries, had been that the birth rate in urban areas had been higher than in rural areas of the country.

The main lines of planning and forecasting in the demographic field fell into two categories. One related to particular problems that had been identified in Bulgaria. They were concentrating on increasing the educational levels and professional skills in all fields, not only technical but also managerial and of other kinds. The second issue was how to solve the problem that in future the greater part of any increase in output would have to be secured through a growth of productivity and not a growth of the number employed. What was of considerable importance was that any major shift in the structure of the national economy would depend on inter-industry shifts of those actually employed, and that more rapid growth of some branches of industry would be impossible without such actual shifts of labour.

The final part of the paper drew attention to the three basic versions of demographic forecasts which they had prepared – one which represented an average view, one which was optimistic about population growth, and one of which was rather less optimistic, with corresponding conclusions made on the basis of each of the three. One assumption, common to all of them, was that in the next twenty or thirty years Bulgaria would definitely become a highly industrialised country, with agricultural employment absorbing less than 6 per cent of the total occupied population by the end of this period.

Professor Porwit's own first question related to the formulation of the demographic policy and its indirect influence. To what extent could these policies be deduced from other elements in the analysis? What should be the basis for their evaluation or for considering the processes desirable in the assumed conditions of a country? His second question related to the use of mathematical models and computers. Did Professor Bradistilov have in mind some particular models of demographic processes? Or were they using various kinds of models, for occupations, for social structure, and so on? His third question was on the regional aspects of the problem. On one hand, there were various biological reasons for needing to forecast the regional distribution of population, including the influence of migration on the structure and distribution of population. But these problems were related to those of the equalisation of incomes in different parts of the country and to the effects of population density on the problems of meeting the socio-cultural needs of the population. Would Professor Bradistilov comment on that?

Professor Malinvaud (France) said that the conference had two papers on the planning of a labour force, this one by Professor Bradistilov for Bulgaria, and another by Professor Maier for the G.D.R. It would be interesting if Professor Bradistilov could be persuaded to compare the methodologies used in the two countries. He would also like to ask about the fact that until recently Bulgarian economy had been developing in conditions of rapid growth of urban population, which was expected to slow down in the future. How was the national planning being adapted to that new situation?

Professor Oelssner (G.D.R.) was interested in what had been said in the paper about higher birth rates. But did Professor Bradistilov regard this as a long-term or a temporary phenomenon. He personally believed it to be temporary. With development of agricultural technology and introduction of new methods, agricultural jobs were becoming as attractive to young people as industrial jobs. This could be seen currently both in the U.S.S.R. and the G.D.R. General socio-cultural conditions in urban and rural areas were also converging, so that he thought that one could expect equalisation of the birth rates in the future. What would be Professor Bradistilov's views about this?

Mr Topala (Roumania) asked whether structural changes in industrial distribution of the occupied population had been studied in Bulgaria in their relation to per capita income? They in Roumania had made comparative studies for countries with per capita incomes of U.S. $200 to $4,000 a year and had found a decline of agriculturally employed and an increase of service employed population with rising incomes. At an income level of about U.S. $4,000 per head the share of population employed in manufacturing industries did not exceed 30–5 per cent. This was important for planning of the labour force and its training.

Professor Khachaturov (U.S.S.R.) thought that, as in the case of any planning, a balancing of input and output in demand for and sources of labour should underlie demographic planning. In regard to demand one could distinguish demand in the production and non-production spheres, with that in the latter increasing more rapidly in all socialist countries as the result of the levels of development achieved. In this context, how were the demands in the two spheres being calculated? As for means of meeting the demands for labour, various internal sources of labour might increase as a result of changes in the age structure of population. Students, retired people and housewives, employed full-time or part-time, represented substantial internal reserves of manpower. Could Professor Bradistilov comment on the labour balances which formed the background for their labour planning?

Professor Denison (U.S.A.) thought that the U.S. experience was relevant to any discussion of shifts in labour structure. They in the U.S.A. had been seeing an outflow of labour from production sectors and an inflow into services. Two factors might be contributing to this process; one related to the sharp decline of agriculture as an employment area, and the other a result of higher wage levels in service industries. Yet if one compared the number employed in services in 1929, 1948 and 1969, it could be seen that the number of people employed in the public services was decreasing, while employment in corporation services was growing. These trends were not visible if one operated with aggregated data.

Professor Aganbegyan (U.S.S.R.) said that there was something that was dozens of times more important than purely demographic phenomena *per se*, and that was the quality of labour force, both in terms of general education and of professional training, and this accounted for about 10 per cent of all expenditure in the socialist countries. In some countries these expenditures were two or three times the allocations for scientific research and development and made the determination of strategy in this field their absolutely first problem in long-term planning. Moreover, expenditure on improving professional skills and the educational background were the most efficient way to raise the production output. Professor Bradistilov had rightly stressed that population was not only a source of labour supply but its needs were the final objectives of the production process. Creating better conditions for the human being was a primary goal of socialist production. From this point of view, qualitative changes in the nature of labour processes, such as overcoming the after-effects of changes in the professional division of labour, were of great importance. Unfortunately, these qualitative aspects were not given enough consideration in planning labour resources, and the very instruments of planning, such as labour resources/demand calculations, failed to consider the qualitative parameters. He thought that, in long-term planning and forecasting, the qualitative aspects of labour resources should be given priority over their quantitative dimensions.

Mr John (Hungary) thought that Professor Denison, when speaking of the necessity of minimising shifts in service employment, had excluded organisations, so far as they were non-profit organisations. This was a significant omission, because almost all non-government non-profit organisations operated in the sphere of education or scientific research. The chief characteristic of the twentieth century had been shifts in the field of mental, non-manual labour.

There were some 400 or 500 types of activities in material production. If one attempted to divide them according to the intelligence and knowledge demanded, they fell into six categories. His analysis was not yet complete, but his hypothesis was that there was not only a shift from manual to mental labour, but that the rate of this shift was increasing.

Moreover, the planning horizons for labour planning and for population planning were not the same. It was possible to plan labour requirements for a period of about twenty years, but this horizon was quite insufficient for the planning of population growth. Any results of a twenty-year plan affected not the already existing labour force, but the one which would appear in another ten or twenty years. In addition, it was necessary to use other methods as well as mathematical methods. Their experience had shown that in the initial stages of planning it was essential that social attitudes and phenomena and the sociological sides of labour planning should be considered. They had also learned that in respect of future resources it was not enough to raise the average income of the population, but the distribution of income between families had to be considered. Perhaps the Hungarian case was not universal, but they had found that distribution of income between families in relation to average size of families and numbers of dependants was a more important factor in manpower equilibrium than birth rates. As a result of their studies they had come to recognise that in future they would have to distinguish between the incomes which provided an incentive to production and those which had a purely social character, thus ensuring future population growth by equalising family incomes by means of family allowances, differentiated free services, and the like.

Dr Grove (U.S.A.) said that one striking thing was the remarkable growth of productivity in the service industry. Concern about the shift of the labour towards the service industries generally reflected a concern that this would lead to a fall in average productivity. But in many services, though not in all, the rate of productivity growth was at least equal to that in manufacturing. He thought that in any labour force, increased participation of pensioners, married women, and others, as suggested by Professor Khachaturov, deserved very special attention, first because it was a good source of labour supply, and second, because it was capable of being encouraged very much through public policy in a number of ways. There was another implication to be considered. If the authorities wanted to increase the labour participation rate, this had a significant implication for the production of the consumer goods. In other words, more durable consumer goods of a labour-saving type would need to be produced to make it possible for many married women to be able to participate in a labour force.

Professor Marzcewski (France) wanted to come back to the question raised by Professor Aganbegyan. The usual procedure for planning human resources consisted in starting from the final demand for goods and services, deriving from it the necessary volume of production, and then at the next stage trying to find the necessary structure of the manpower. This procedure was absolutely inescapable, of course, if one was seeking to adjust the future structure of the available manpower to the needs of production. But he thought that at the same time human development and training represented an objective in itself and ought to go into final demand as such, an objective independent of production, requiring its own production structure and appropriate professional qualifications. In this way they should be able to deal with the two-fold quality of manpower: with education as a final objective and as a means to production.

Professor Bradistilov (Bulgaria), replying to the discussion, said that, when choosing the subject of his paper, he had thought that he could scarcely hope to make any personal contribution to solving basic theoretical problems of planning and forecasting. He himself was more interested in certain issues which were immediately relevant to the Bulgarian economy. Mathematical models were still relatively little used in planning in Bulgaria as compared with some other countries, and were applied mostly to optimisation of the distribution of productive resources. He thought that the problems of labour resource planning and the developments in this field were of great practical and theoretical importance, since they were simultaneously objectives and factors in the production process. As for their approach to these problems, he thought it was different from that of most other countries. It was a small-country approach. They regarded the Bulgarian economy as an open system, developing in close co-operation and integration with the economies of other socialist countries.

When writing his paper, he was not trying to formulate principles for the guidance of demographic processes in socialist countries. Thus when discussing the trends and qualitative features of demographic development and of the use of labour resources, he thought he should say that he had found no evidence to support a view often held in his country that population growth would lead to higher income per head. Population growth in Bulgaria had remained about constant and recently had been slightly increasing. This was an interesting phenomenon, and the explanation might be found in Hegelian logic, namely, that qualitative changes in Bulgarian life had not yet resulted in quantitative population growth. An additional point was that they had already achieved an optimal demand for labour, which at present was at the maximum practicable level of 89–90 per cent of the able-bodied population. And a third point was that the increase of living standards in the country as a whole extended to all its regions.

He completely agreed with Professor Aganbegyan that improvement of the qualitative aspect of labour resources was the most essential element in demographic policy, and one which could lead to better quantitative demographic parameters. These parameters needed to be improved in his country, and the structure of population which had emerged during the last decade needed to be changed. They had a stationary demographic pattern, with a growing proportion of higher-aged groups, a lower proportion of young people, and a decreasing proportion of able-bodied people. In this sense they did not plan demographic parameters directly, but by taking indirect measures of a social nature, such as better housing, higher wages for certain categories of the employees, child-care facilities, and the like. Mathematical models were used only to assist in the use of labour resources, not with regard to the demographic processes.

As for regional demographic policies, he thought they had one that was yielding some positive results. They had inherited different levels of economic development in different provincial areas of the country. The problems were mostly felt in agriculture, and they had not yet overcome them. Overcoming the remaining inter-regional differences was one of the major goals of their long-term planning, and the means they were using included capital investments, improvements in infrastructure, as well as emphasis on more rapid development of larger villages. Of the latter they now had about 4,500 with more than 5,000 inhabitants. The objective in the villages was to establish industries which would keep the labour in the village and at the same time solve various social problems. There had earlier been a migration from rural to urban areas and from small to bigger cities; in recent years they had found not only a decrease of this migration, but to some extent even a reflow, when people returned to their villages.

As regards comparison of the two methodologies used in this paper and that by Professor Maier for the G.D.R., he thought they were remarkably similar. As regards compensation for inadequacies in demographic adjustments, he thought the way to handle it was by introduction of technological innovations and stimulating the growth of labour productivity. In agriculture, for example, it was hoped both to attract young people and make it possible for them to stay. They had studied their population and labour-resource structures in relation to national income. The productivity of labour in industry appeared to be three to four times that in agriculture, and the outflow of agricultural population was one of the factors in their economic growth. In respect to labour resources, they did use inter-industry balances and were trying to make use of internal reserves such as students, pensioners and married women. But a more radical solution needed to be established on a more solid basis and on better inter-industry and regional distribution of the available manpower, as well as on general increases in labour productivity.

H

10 Long-term Planning and Forecasting for Education in the German Democratic Republic[1]

H. Maier

I. EDUCATIONAL LEVEL AND QUALIFICATION STRUCTURE IN A SOCIALIST SOCIETY

The general development and education of the working people is, under socialism, one of the main objectives of social development, and is at the same time an important factor in developing society itself. Thus, long-term planning of the educational and qualification level of the working people will be of great importance in planning and forecasting the general development of a socialist society.

Given social ownership of the means of production, the socio-economic contents of a plan will be to eliminate, step by step and to the extent permitted by the level of economic progress achieved, the fundamental difference between physical and mental labour, to diminish permanently the proportion of heavy physical and mentally monotonous labour, and, thus, to create the conditions in which the social, productive, mental, physical and cultural gifts and abilities of all the members of society may develop – 'this full individual development [as Marx wrote] being the mightiest productive force and, thus, reacting itself on the productive force of labour'.[2] As regards forecasting and controlling the process of *economic reproduction*, this results in the problem of how to allocate social labour to the production process, to the educational system, to the development of science, and to the other spheres in the process of social production, so as to ensure that to the greatest possible extent the material and intellectual wants of all members of society shall be met. Of progress towards this, the rate of growth and the structure of the national income will be the best indicator.

It will, I think, be useful to distinguish between educational forecasting, long-term educational planning, and medium-term and short-term educational planning, each of which fulfils specific tasks and employs specific methods.

[1] The models of planning represented in this paper are based on ideas first developed by the author and elaborated by Dr Udo Ludwig and Dr Juergen Wahse. See U. Ludwig, H. Maier and J. Wahse, *Education as Economical Power under Socialism* [in German] (Berlin; Dietz Verlag, 1972).

[2] K. Marx, *Outlines to a Critique of Political Economy* [in German] (Berlin; 1953) p. 599.

II. EDUCATIONAL FORECASTING AND PLANNING

Starting from the socio-economic and scientific-technical processes prevailing in the period to be covered by the forecast, *educational forecasting* will not only have to estimate the development of educational requirements, of levels of qualification, and of levels of education, but will also have to show the resulting qualitative and structural requirements to be met by the socialist education system as well as its capacities, thus leading to long-term and medium-term decisions on educational policy. With the aid of educational forecasting, several variants for meeting the educational requirements of the socialist society will have to be indicated and their contribution to the development of the personality and to economic efficiency will have to be examined. Thus, educational forecasting must, above all, seek to discover new policies for the improvement of the educational level and of the qualification structure as well as improvements of the educational system itself, its main task being to furnish in advance a maximum of information to be utilised in long-term planning.

Long-term educational planning will aim at selecting from the possible forecasted variants that which will be most appropriate for the objectives of the socialist society and will indicate the most efficient method of achieving the objectives. Even at this stage it will be necessary to secure a balance between the desired educational measures. And these measures will, already at this stage, have to be co-ordinated with and adjusted to the development needs of the other activities of the national economy, and priorities will have to be established between the various economic objectives.

Medium-term and short-term educational plans will have to ensure that the objectives and rates of progress of educational policies established in long-term educational plans will be reached by efficient employment of the available resources during the appropriate space of time.

In this paper, I shall deal primarily with the problems of forecasting and of long-term planning of the educational processes. In my discussion of them, I shall be principally concerned to describe in detail a number of planning models, examining them from the aspect of how they can help to interrelate the socio-economic, scientific-technical, and pedagogical evidence in such a way as will be relevant to the long-term decision-making process, thus securing efficient development of the educational and qualification levels as seen from the objectives of a socialist society.

The tasks to be solved by the long-term planning and forecasting of education are, therefore, as follows:

(1) determination of the long-term educational requirements of

members of the society concerned and of those components which will, at the given level of socio-economic and scientific-technical development, affect the manpower and professional requirements;

(2) starting from there, the supply of trained persons will have to be estimated according to the level of education (professionals trained at universities or upper technical schools; skilled workers; semi-skilled workers), to special fields of competence, and to the employment possibilities of the professional manpower;

(3) on the basis of the established educational requirements and of the required supply of leavers from the various educational establishments, the actual structure of education, the level, profile, and duration of training at all the various stages must be determined; in doing so, the efficiency of the various educational channels represented by direct studies, of extramural studies, of education combined with simultaneous professional training will have to be established, and the best balance between them will have to be discovered;

(4) starting from the fact that technical knowledge and qualifications will become obsolete as the result of economic, scientific and technical progress, the requirements for subsequent retraining of the professional cadre will have to be decided both in terms of scope and timing;

(5) a major problem of long-term planning of education and manpower supply will be to find the conditions under which the levels of skills acquired will be fully utilised in the processes of economic production, so as to ensure the employment of the trained labour force in the most efficient way and to create a climate of intensive training and education within the working environment itself.

A main feature of educational planning is its strategic nature, as fundamental decisions of educational planning will often become effective directly and fully only ten or twenty years later. Its effects will continue indirectly over even longer periods if one remembers that pupils who started going to school in 1972 will still be working by 2026 or 2031, and that the last pupil to be taught by those teachers that are just beginning that responsible task will still be working by 2063 or 2067.

The fact that educational processes are long-term ones will have far-reaching consequences for educational planning. On the one hand, it obviously implies that one must abandon exaggerated ideas of the possibility and desirability of estimating in precise detail the demands for professional staff or the precise contents of training and education. On the other hand, it emphasises the need to increase the adaptability of future workers by a training that aims at the acquisition of fundamental knowledge.

Third, educational planning will in consequence need to function in such a manner as to make it possible to organise it as a process of learning.

Educational planning so organised will continuously teach itself by absorbing all the fresh knowledge gathered in the course of carrying out the plan and relating to the educational requirements of a socialist society, to the interrelations between the various growth factors in the process of economic production, to the relative weights of the various skilled groups in relation to each other, and to the practical relations between different stages of education. In other words, educational planning as a process of learning must, thus, include a comparison between the theoretical and the actual values, this being the crucial feedback and link between the phase of making a plan and of carrying it out.

The fundamental problem that long-term educational planning will be facing is primarily, and with regard to content, the determination of efficient quantitative and qualitative ratios between education and economic production, and at the same time the similar issues within education itself. The method of balancing adopted for the other branches of economic planning provides the basic methodological pattern. On one side of such a balance, the long-term growth of the demand for labour force with a given level of qualification is covered, at least tentatively. The long-term forecast of the demand for qualified labour, calculated on the basis of the natural population growth, will have to be set against the actual and projected capacities of the educational system. The object of such a procedure is to simulate future bottleneck or surplus situations and to disclose efficient educational paths in order to be able to deal beforehand with any waste of educational expenditure.

III. LONG-TERM MANPOWER REQUIREMENTS

The main problem of long-term educational planning, if conducted in a realistic manner, is how to determine correctly the required rate of growth of the labour force in terms of the various groups of skills and professional qualifications. Carelessness or wishful thinking over this will have disastrous effects on human happiness and lead to loss of economic efficiency. This task cannot be solved by simply aggregating the labour demands estimated by individual factories, by combined undertakings, and by other institutions. The reason is that, in such cases, the time-horizon for decision-making is very much shorter than is required for long-term educational planning, and that the educational process will be regarded, at this level, rather from the viewpoint of the requirements of a particular set of different job assignments than from that of securing a high degree of technical and professional adaptability and of ensuring a general education of the available manpower. This does not, of course, deny the need for making careful analyses of the requirements that may result from the progress of mechanisation and automation of the working process, and which may affect the levels of skill required. On the contrary, since such analysis is fundamental to long-term educational planning, it has to be included in the estimation of the basic components of manpower demand to be expected from economic growth as a whole. For this purpose, it has proved useful to subdivide the national production process into five demand components. As the various fields of production differ as regards the exact part they play in total national production, estimation of their labour demands will require the employment of different methods.

These components of manpower demand are:

(1) that which results from the growth of the workers' educational needs and from their improved working and living conditions (including cultural needs, improved public health, extended services, and so on);

(2) that which results from the increase of material production and the creation of the material preconditions for meeting the material and intellectual wants of the working people;

(3) the specific demand resulting from the growth of science and technology;

(4) the demand for professional manpower required for public administration and economic management;

(5) the demand for trained professional manpower required by education itself to enable it to meet the manpower demands in the four preceding categories.

IV. A SKELETON MODEL FOR LONG-TERM PLANNING

These five components of the demand for trained manpower and of their fields of employment will form the basic pattern of the skeleton model for long-term planning. This model makes possible the integration of the methods hitherto available for calculating the demand for professional manpower and emphasises, at the same time, the need to develop specific models and techniques for those components of manpower demand which have not as yet been thoroughly investigated.

In utilising this skeleton model, I shall proceed by three main stages, in the course of which the claims made by the different elements of the social production process on the capacity and on the pattern of training of the socialist educational system will be estimated.[1]

First of all, the total numbers of workers needed in each category to achieve the tasks imposed on them will be estimated in purely quantitative terms. At the second stage, the total manpower requirements of the nation will be calculated and will be set against the available manpower resources (the manpower balance). Both these stages are represented in Figure 10.1. At the third stage, there will be a separate estimation of the future labour structure by types and levels of qualification.

On the basis of the total demand of the socialist society for trained manpower, balanced against the labour supply, and of the quantity of labour available (i.e. active throughout the planning period), the demands of the various groups of skills for replacements and additional labour can be calculated. From this, we shall derive the initial information necessary to estimate the requirements for the development of education.

The quantitative and qualitative manpower demands in the various spheres of production will in each case have to be determined by appropriate methods. Here, I shall confine myself in detail to the case of material production. The manpower demand for material production as a whole depends mainly on the expected level of labour productivity and on the total volume of the national income envisaged. As, however, not all material production contributes fully to the production of national income, we must estimate the total manpower demand from material production by establishing the demand of each of the various sectors of the economy. As regards industry, handicraft production, the building industry, and agriculture, we must start from the existing relationships between the net product of these sectors and the level of labour productivity measured in terms of net product per worker in the branch concerned. But since a majority of spheres are composed of a number of sectors and branches of the economy, the required educational level of the manpower (which is what we are primarily interested in) will not be identical in all sectors and branches of the economy. Thus, the actual demand for education can more easily be estimated for smaller economic units, if this is done correctly. We shall, therefore, further

[1] See U. Ludwig, H. Maier and H. Stiller, 'Socialist Educational Planning as Part of the All-social Activities of Forecasting and Planning' [in German], in *Sozialistische Bildungsökonomie* (Berlin, 1972) p. 64 ff.

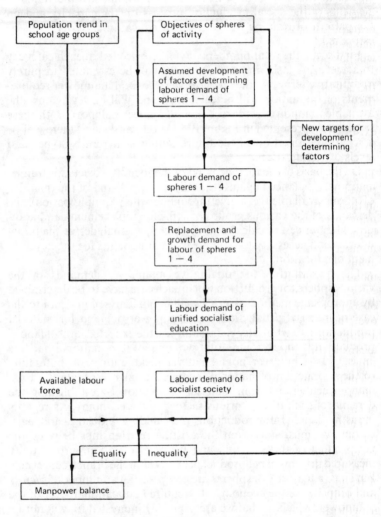

FIG. 10.1 The Manpower Balance

subdivide the manpower demand of the various economic spheres into sectors (e.g. industrial spheres within the general economic sphere of industry), and these sectors into branches (e.g. industrial branches of each industrial sphere), so far as such subdivision will make sense. The growth of net product and of labour productivity will have to be estimated separately for each of these various parts.

Figure 10.1 represents the functioning of the skeleton model for the determination of labour demand. The main factors influencing the results obtained by this model are as follows:

First, there is inadequate knowledge of the actual relationships existing between the various social spheres that will not be covered by this model. These are, however, very important for a rational allocation of the total available manpower to the industrial spheres. This is particularly evident when one attempts to estimate the manpower demands of the spheres after taking account of improvements in their material and technological efficiencies in order to obtain a manpower balance. In doing so, it must be remembered that it will be necessary to achieve, in addition to the manpower balance, a number of other balances (e.g. conformity of types of jobs with available labour; of accumulation with planned investments; of materials required; and so on).

Second, to forecast accurately the growth of national income and of social labour productivity is a particularly difficult task. Moreover, the level of labour productivity will also depend on the number and qualification of workers which will have to be determined by means of this model. The procedure presented in this paper presupposes, therefore, a high degree of knowledge of the ways in which scientific-technological and socio-economic factors, as well as various types of mechanisation and automation will affect the growth of labour productivity and the skill-requirements of labour.

Third, the trends of growth of the non-material spheres of social reproduction and their effects on labour demand have hitherto been very inadequately investigated.

The demand of a socialist society for manpower with various kinds of training may, to a certain extent, be forecast by using simpler models. In what follows I shall attempt, on the basis of assumed growth rates, to estimate the course of manpower demand in the period covered by a forecast by taking into account the changing numbers of skilled workers and graduates from universities and higher technical schools. It is the object of the model designed for this purpose (a model of difference equations) to show, on the basis of given assumptions as to the growth of the above-mentioned supplies of labour available, the consequences that changes in these numbers will have for the expansion of the total capacity and the

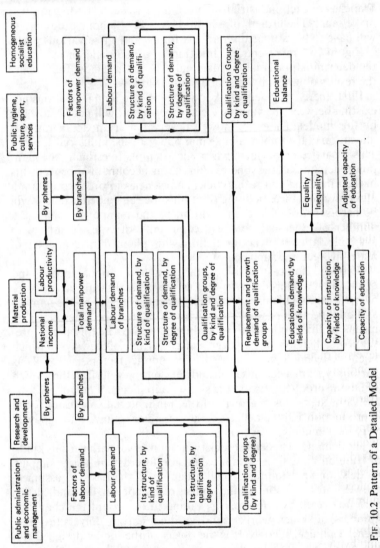

FIG. 10.2 Pattern of a Detailed Model

pattern of training in the socialist educational system of the G.D.R. (i.e. upper secondary school, secondary technical school, technical college and university). The model of difference equations makes it possible:

- (i) to determine by variants the development of the number of skilled workers and graduates from technical colleges and universities;
- (ii) to establish for each variant the number of students required for the four parts of the educational system; and
- (iii) to analyse the expected future numbers of skilled workers and graduates from technical schools and universities to make sure that these expected numbers are mutually consistent and that they are consistent with the trend of population.

V. DESIGN OF A MODEL

In constructing such a model, I shall start by estimating the increase and decrease in the numbers of skilled workers and of graduates employed in technical colleges and universities, the decreases being the result of death or of retirement due to old age or sickness. Another relevant factor is the need for higher teaching qualifications resulting from a shift to a higher educational level indicated by the working of the model. In the model itself, we shall take into account only the shift from the level of a skilled worker to the level of a technical college graduate.[1]

The decrease in numbers from all different causes will be summed up by a loss rate (or rate of leavers). The additions to the various levels of qualifications are composed of graduates from the corresponding educational stages. Skilled workers will be former apprentices. The newly graduated professional manpower will have been trained at technical colleges and universities. The number of those leaving the corresponding educational establishment will, in turn, depend on the number of those who have entered a secondary technical school, technical college or university, as well as on the date of admission and on the number of those who have passed the relevant examinations (the success rate). The number of entries in colleges and universities will, in its turn, be determined by the numbers of those leaving upper secondary schools. The number in the last-named group will be determined by the number of those admitted to the upper secondary school and the date of admission, and by the success rates in the various examinations. The number of

[1] A detailed discussion of the problems connected with basic instruction and continued professional training will be found in Section 9 (dealing with basic questions) of 'Socialist Economics of Education' [in German] (Berlin, 1972).

those admitted to the upper secondary school or starting an apprenticeship training will ordinarily be limited by the size of the corresponding age groups. These capacity relations existing between the different educational stages can be represented clearly and quite accurately by an equation system whose single equations (difference equations) cover (*a*) the development capacity of each educational stage as a function of the corresponding lower one and (*b*) the trends in the numbers of those leaving the relevant educational establishments as a function of the number of those admitted and of the duration of the actual educational process.[1]

The different stages in the unified educational system provide a different degree of advance in education, this being dependent on their distance from the end of the chosen path of education. The greater this distance, the greater will be this advance. As regards the course of these educational processes, the periods and dates of completion of them are, thus, very important. I shall, therefore, treat the growth of the number of skilled workers, technical college and university graduates as well as the number of those leaving and entering the various educational establishments in all cases as a function of the time *t*. The time *t* is subdivided into units of time. Since the periods of time are comparatively long, having regard to the duration of educational courses and of professional life, I shall for this model take, for purposes of the average duration of attendance at upper secondary school and of apprenticeship training, two years as the unit of time *t*. The equation system representing the relationship between the growth of the number of skilled workers and graduates of technical colleges and universities as well as of the number of the corresponding accessions and separations and of the transitions from one educational stage to another, will thus be as follows.[2]

$$B_4(t) = (1-\alpha_4)B_4(t-1) + m_4(t) \qquad (1)$$

t = index of time period ($t = 0, 1, \ldots$);

B_2, B_3, B_4 = number of available skilled and professional workers trained at secondary technical schools, at colleges and universities;

m_3, m_4 = number of new graduates of technical colleges and universities;

---

[1] As to the first attempts to model the gradual course of educational processes by means of difference equations, see *Economic Models of Education* (Paris, 1965) and *The Residual Factor and Economic Growth* (Paris, 1964).

[2] For a detailed explanation of the model see U. Ludwig, 'On dynamically proportioning socialist education and social reproduction process' [thesis, in German] (Berlin, 1970) pp. 95 ff.

m_2 = difference between those leaving secondary technical school and those entering technical college;

n_1, n_2, n_3, n_4 = number of those admitted to upper secondary school, secondary technical school, technical college or university;

$d^{(t)}$ = numerical strength of age group reaching age of sixteen and seventeen years within the period covered;

$\alpha_2, \alpha_3, \alpha_4$ = loss rate of skilled workers and of graduate staff, determined by death, advanced age or sickness;

k = relation of number of those leaving upper secondary school to that of students of same age group.

The actual number of graduated professional staff will, thus, in the given time period be composed of those remaining from period $t-1$ and of the number of new graduates of colleges and universities of time period t:

$$m_4(t) = n_4(t-2) \qquad (2)$$

The number of those leaving college and university in the time period t will, on account of the four years of education, be determined by the number of those starting college or university education within period $t-2$.

$$n_4(t) = \frac{1}{k} a_1(t-1) \qquad (3)$$

The number of those starting college or university education within period t will depend on the number of those starting upper secondary school education within period $t-1$ and on the proportion of upper secondary school leavers who, for various reasons, do not start college or university education ($k > 1$). Those, however, will not be included who will do so later because of military service or because of previously taking a course of practical work. I shall start from the assumption that the resulting reduction in the number of school-leavers of period t will be approximately compensated for by the number of those who have finished their military service during that time.

$$B_3(t) = (1-\alpha_3)B_3(t-1) + m_3(t) \qquad (4)$$

The actual number of graduated professionals available in period t will be composed of the proportion remaining from period $t-1$ and of those who have left technical college within period t.

$$m_3(t) = \tfrac{1}{2}[n_3(t-1) + n_3(t-2)] \qquad (5)$$

As a course of study at a technical college will take three years, on the average, we shall, on the basis of the two-year duration established for each period, have to assume that approximately each half of the number of graduates leaving technical college in period t will consist of those having started technical college education[1] in the periods $t-1$ and $t-2$.

$$a_2(t) = d(t) + \frac{k-1}{k} a_1(t-1) - a_1(t) \tag{6}$$

The number of those starting to be trained as skilled workers will depend on the numerical strength of the corresponding age groups $d(t)$, on the number of those entering upper secondary education, of those members of these age groups $a_1(t)$, as well as of those having started upper secondary education in period $t-1$, who have not started college/university education and who will not do so within a reasonable space of time. The latter group will be included among those starting other vocational training, as everybody is required to learn a trade, according to the constitution of the G.D.R. In doing so, however, we assume that these leavers of upper secondary education will not have passed their examination at the same time as finishing a vocational training.

$$m_2(t) = a_2(t-1) - a_3(t) \tag{7}$$

The total number of skilled workers in the period will increase by the number of those having finished their vocational training in the given period, the number of these being equal to the number of those who have started their vocational training in the period $t-1$. The number of skilled workers will, on the other hand, decrease by the number of those starting a technical college education in the period t. The difference of both these opposing developments will be summed up by the term $m_2(t)$:

$$B_2(t) = (1-\alpha_2)B_2(t-1) + m_2(t) \tag{8}$$

The total number of skilled workers available in period t will be determined by the residue of the number from time period $t-1$ and by the number of those who have finished their vocational training, and those ready to begin study at the technical college. In this way, the capacity relations between the number of those entering and

[1] To keep our presentation as clear as possible, we shall in what follows neglect all those leaving an educational stage before examination as well as those repeating a one-year course of the corresponding educational stage (i.e. we assume a success rate = 1). Furthermore, we shall make the qualifying assumption that all those leaving these educational stages will start working immediately if there is no further education. The qualifications made could, at any time, make it possible to improve the results produced by the model, if the corresponding coefficients were introduced (success rates; portion of those starting professional life).

those leaving the four educational stages as well as the growth of the total numbers of skilled workers and of graduates of colleges and universities have been represented in an equation system.

We can now ask how the various educational stages will have to change on the basis of the interrelationships given by the model, if these numbers are to increase with reasonable regularity. This question corresponds to that put at the beginning of a forecast, but does not, as will be seen later, stop there. To solve the problem, we shall make use of certain features of our equation system.

The system of the equations (1)–(8) can be split into three groups of equations, i.e. the equations (1)–(3), (4)–(5), and (6)–(8). The first two groups, relating respectively to the growth of numbers of university trained staff and those still studying, and of the technical college trained staff and those still studying there, are self-contained equation systems. If both these equation systems have been solved, the resulting values of $a_1(t)$ and $a_3(t)$ can be substituted into the third system. Thus, there is no difficulty in solving the whole equation system. The equation systems (1)–(3) and (4)–(5) consist of difference equations. Supposing that the rates of trained staff leaving college or university and also the growth rates of the demand for university and college trained staff remain constant during a given time period, the solution of the equation system will show that, taking into consideration certain conditions of the basic period ($t = 0$), the numbers of those leaving and entering the respective educational stages (e.g. those starting upper secondary education and finishing it) will necessarily increase by the same growth rates as the numbers of the group to which they will belong after finishing the corresponding course of education. This result will become more realistic as we succeed in synchronising the time-conditioned limitations on a steady numerical growth of available labour with the limits imposed by the assumed constancy of the loss rates; in order to simulate this steady growth as the best possible approximation to the unsteady growth rates of the numbers of university or college trained professional staff which are still largely unknown, we are forced to estimate these parameters by calculating the variants. On the basis of assumed growth rates of the numbers of university and college trained professional staff, we can calculate the growth of the capacity of the relevant educational establishments, this capacity development being necessary to achieve the growth rates concerned. Next, it will be possible by substituting successively the results thus obtained into the equations (6)–(8), to estimate the growths of the number of skilled workers available and of the apprentices to be trained.

From the multitude of such calculations of different growth rates it will be possible to exclude all those the results of which appear absurd. The criteria of absurdity are any pattern of labour allocation involving such numerical relations between the numbers of skilled workers and of college and university trained staff as are unlikely and as will be contrary to experience and any oscillations in the supply of skilled workers. It is precisely these oscillations that will make evident at what time a given growth strategy regarding university and college trained staff will cease to be appropriate to population growth which, in this case, is reflected in the possible number of new apprentices to be trained. This will not, of course, yet provide the necessary criterion for selecting from the remaining multitude of variants the one which seems the most likely, or even the optimum.

VII. AN INPUT–OUTPUT TABLE FOR EDUCATION

The results obtained from the model of labour demand outlined above will, within the framework of a balance for socialist education as a whole, have to provide the initial data for establishing an input–output table of education itself. Such a model of the interrelationships of education itself, which will help to establish its internal proportionality, attempts to answer the question as to how the estimated demand for trained manpower can be met at the lowest possible cost. By means of such an input–output table it will, therefore, be attempted to represent education as a system of processes that are interconnected and interdependent. In order to ensure that education shall expand while maintaining its internal proportionality, it will be necessary to conduct the work of education at each stage in such a way as to meet the demands of the following stage. The expansion of the different stages and branches of education will, thus, have to be made to accord with the timings characteristic of education as a whole and of the social demand for education. Within the framework of the input–output table and by means of rates of transition from one stage of education to the next, it will then be possible to analyse the effect that changes in such transfers will have. With this, the various transition rates (rates of transfer to the next class; rates of leavers and of those repeating the course) will be important instrumental variants in educational planning.

To establish such a model of the input–output relations governing the internal structure of education, we can compile a table in which each of these elements (class, study year, educational stage, etc.) is represented in the preceding column as well as in the box heading. Those boxes in the table which are interconnected on account of the legally established relationships between the various parts of socialist education will be marked separately. The present table includes the compulsory general polytechnic secondary school (classes 1 to 10, comprising what elsewhere is called a primary school), the upper secondary school (classes 11 and 12), the three possible forms of craft training, the school of engineering and the technical college (four years of study as a maximum), and the university or the academy (six years of study as a maximum; the duration depending on the different fields of study and taking account of extra-mural studies). Technical college and academy education is, in addition, subdivided by the types of studies.

In addition to the various forms of education there are included in the table not only columns and lines for the various totals, but also boxes with the numbers of those leaving the educational course after or before the examinations and starting to work, as well as boxes with the numbers of those admitted to the various classes or educational stages as entries from outside. The last-named group includes beginners (entering class 1) and also those who enter the educational system from outside (e.g. from professional life or military service). The totals of the lines and the columns will, respectively, show the actual number of pupils in the corresponding classes at the times t and $t + 1$. The line indicated by 'other leavers' includes those pupils who leave the unified system of education in the course of the school year without starting to work (due to sickness, death, change of residence, transfer to school for backward children, and so on). It will be noted that the table is a representative cross-section showing how many pupils will move from class i to class k (at time $t + 1$). A further subdivision, the pattern of unified socialist education (e.g. by showing more fully the various levels of qualification, the social origins, the division by sexes, branch patterns, and the sources of the entries from outside) would be possible and would result in refining the conclusions reached.

In conformity with the possible and actual transitions provided by the general survey of the table, a matrix of transitions (D) is constructed, showing the absolute numbers of students. In this matrix, there will be:

S_{ik} = number of transitions from class or educational establishment (i) to
    (1) class or educational establishment k: S_{ii};
    (2) same class i (repeaters): S_{ii};
    (3) professional life: S_{ia}
between time t and $t + 1$.

The main diagonal of the matrix will thus show the number of repeaters (S_{ii}), while the diagonal situated directly above the main diagonal will give the number of those passing over to the next class

(S_{iii}). Now, we shall introduce the vector of the class strength $S^{(t)} = S_1^{(t)} \ldots S_n^{(t)}$. Its ith component $S_i^{(t)}$ shows the number of all the members of the classes i (representing a definite educational stage) at the time t. Then, on account of the data given by the matrix of transitions (D) for the number of pupils of classes k, at the time $t+1$, we shall have:

$$S_i^{(t)t} = \sum_{k=1}^{m} S_{ik} \quad (i = 1, 2, \ldots n)$$

$$S_k^{(t+1)} = \sum_{i=1}^{n} S_{ik} \quad (k = 1, 2, \ldots m).$$

From the matrix of transitions D, the matrix of transition quotas Q will be developed. As, in general:

$$q_{ik} = \frac{S_{ik}}{S_i^{(t)}},$$

the specific quotas will be:

(1) $q_{ik} = C$, if $k = i$; this representing an upper triangular matrix. Only in exceptional cases, which may be neglected here, will there be an additional qualification at a lower stage of qualification (e.g. a university graduate additionally studying at a technical college);

(2) $q_{ik} = q_{ii}$, if $k = i$; the main diagonal of the matrix will, where occupied, represent those pupils who will repeat the course, i.e. return to the same class in the next school year;

$$q_{ii} = \frac{S_{ii}}{S_i^{(t)}}, \text{ being the quota of repeaters;}$$

(3) $q_{ik} = q_{iii}$, if $n-1 = ki$; there will be two possibilities:
   (a) $k = i+1$, this meaning the quota of transitions to next class of same type of school, and
   (b) $k = i+z [z = 2, \ldots n-(i+2)]$; this quota meaning the transition to upper school systems; $q_{iii} = S_{iii}/S_i^{(t)} =$ quota of transitions;

(4) $q_{ik} = q_{ia}$, if $k = n-1$, n; this quota stating what portion of pupils will leave socialist education (before or after examination); $q_{ia} = S_{ia}/S_i^{(t)} =$ quota of leavers.

The sum of the quotas of one line will be equal to 1 for all columns.

Starting from this representation of the passage of students through the system of education, the total distributed between the various parts of the educational system at the time $t+m$ can be calculated by matrix arithmetic if (a) this number is known at time $t+m-1$, if (b) data of the size of the age groups due to enter school and of the entries from outside the system are available, and if (c) the coefficients of the transition matrix remain constant. If we indicate by $f^{(t)} = (f_1^{(t)}, f_2^{(t)}, \ldots f_n^{(t)})$ the vector of the entries from outside, its ith component $f_i^{(t)}$ will furnish the increase in number of the ith classes by those entering from outside, at the time t (e.g. $f_2^{(t)}$ being the number of beginners in the year t). The vector of the strength of the classes $f^{(t+1)}$ will be at the time $t+1$:

$$S^{(t+1)} = S^{(t)}Q + f^{(t+1)}$$

Accordingly, the number of those being instructed at the kth educational stage $S_k^{(t+1)}$, i.e. the kth component of the vector $S^{(t+1)}$, will be calculated by the following formula:

$$S_k^{(t+m)} = \sum_{i=1}^{n} q_{ik} \cdot S_i^{(t+m-1)} + f_i^{(t+m)} \quad (k = 1, \ldots m)$$

The rule for calculating the vector of the strength of the classes is a recursive formula. By means of this formula, the future strength of the classes can be calculated for the subsequent years in succession. In doing so, however, no year must be left out:

$$S^{(t+2)} = S^{(t+1)} \cdot Q + f^{(t+2)} = S^{(t)}Q^2 + f^{(t+1)}Q + f^{(t+2)}.$$

In general, this will take the following form:

$$S^{(t+m)} = S^{(t)} \cdot Q^m + \sum_{j=1}^{m-1} f^{(t+j)} \cdot Q^{(m-j)} + f^{(t+m)}.$$

The object of the calculations done with the aid of the input–output table is to determine that degree of internal proportionality of socialist education which will ensure the preservation of its external proportionality. This is done by simulating the number of passages through socialist education within the forecast period with the aid of the known number of pupils and students in the base year t_0, the known number of those entering the system within the forecast period, and by means of the matrix of transition quotas which will at first be kept stable. If, none the less, there are shown to be discrepancies between the numbers of those leaving education and the manpower demands, a complex of measures affecting the actual contents of education itself and the construction of new educational buildings must be worked out, which will, in the end, result in such changes of various figures in the matrix of transition quotas as will eliminate these discrepancies. In this way, the method of meeting the demand for trained manpower can be discovered which will involve the least possible cost. For each variant method of meeting the national requirements it will, moreover, be possible to estimate the demand of national education for teachers, school rooms and other purposes if coefficients of the relation of teachers to pupils and of the relation of pupils to school rooms are taken as a basis.

The advantages of such a model will be:

(1) that the movements of pupils and students through the educational system will be shown to be interdependent, and in consequence decisions on the method to be chosen for meeting the estimated demand for trained manpower will be further clarified;

(2) alternative policies for expanding the various stages of education can be tested as to their feasibility, on the assumption that the present structure of education is maintained;

(3) the effects of given changes in the structure of any part of the educational system on the system of education as a whole can be demonstrated.

VIII. APPLICATIONS OF THESE MODELS

The models discussed for achieving balance in the planning of a development of education that is proportional to the social reproduction process and at the same time gives a balance in the internal proportions of the educational system, will, as they now exist, help in identifying the conditions necessary for securing the proportionality of education. We shall, however, require certain additional criteria for discovering from the multitude of such conditions of equilibrium the particular variant which, from the point of view of the objectives of the socialist society, is likely to be the most efficient for the development of the various qualification levels of the working population. Lack of such information is, in my opinion, the critical 'information lag' affecting the making of educational decisions.

For years past, extensive investigations have been made in various countries to solve this problem. Thus, the attempts made by S. G. Strumilin in terms of the Soviet wage system,[1] and in the U.S.A. by Denison[2] and Schultz[3] with the aid of production functions and the concept of 'human capital', are familiar. We in the G.D.R. have, on the other hand, tried to approach the problem of quantifying the productive power of labour with different levels of qualifications by starting from the Marxian concept of reducing complex labour to

[1] See S. G. Strumilin, 'The Economic Significance of National Education in the USSR', in *The Economics of Education*, ed. E. A. G. Robinson and J. E. Vaizey (London: Macmillan for the I.E.A., 1966).

[2] E. P. Denison, 'Measuring the contribution of education to economic growth', in *The Residual Factor and Economic Growth* (Paris, 1964).

[3] Th. W. Schultz, 'Education and Economic Growth', in *Social Forces Influencing American Education* (Chicago, 1961).

simple labour by taking into account the production costs (educational and living costs) of such labour.[1]

The main objection to be raised against these methods is that the results obtained with them will, by their inner logic, depend directly and solely on increasing the number of workers with higher qualifications. In fact, it is assumed that the contribution made by the increased level of qualifications to economic efficiency will be indicated by the quantitative increase in the proportion of highly trained manpower. A high quality of training, the right ratios between the different qualification levels as well as the efficient employment of such trained staff, are taken for granted. As these are, however, the precise problems to be solved by making the appropriate economic decisions, we still remain without the adequate criteria for a solution. In addition, in the actual process of estimation it is precisely these components that are likely to counteract each other, so that to neglect them involves a danger of misleading the decision-making.

If there should be a great demand to secure highly trained labour and it is therefore urgently necessary to raise their number quickly, the bias caused by these assumptions and the effects on the estimates will not be serious. The effect of the bias is likely, however, to be greater at the moment at which vigorous expansion of the corresponding factor in educational growth will become important, i.e. the raising of the qualitative level of training at all stages of qualifications, the more efficient employment of trained manpower, the preservation of a continuing policy of further education of the working population, and so on.

It is these new and more qualitative factors in raising the qualification level of the working population that will not be identified by the methods used hitherto. This is confirmed by a test of the best recognised methods to measure the contribution made by education to the national income of the G.D.R., using the data forecast down to the year 1990. This test resulted in the conclusion that, as a result of the diminishing effect of the component which involves extensive development of the qualification level, the contribution of educational growth would also become smaller and smaller, since the effects of increased education of the working population were not included in these calculations.

It is important, however, to recognise here that the unsatisfactory results obtained by using this procedure were principally caused by the fact that we could not adquately cover the conditions of optimum proportionality relations either between education and the other

[1] H. Maier, 'Tasks and Problems of Socialist Economics of Education' [in German], in *Sozialistische Bildungsökonomie* (Berlin, 1972) pp. 46 ff.

spheres in the production process or within education itself, by these methods. The limitations imposed by the use of methods which employ index numbers to measure the activities of such forms of non-material production as education are obvious.

Under socialism, the effects produced by education cannot be expected to behave like commodities. The policy of development for education cannot, therefore, be calculated rationally by methods which make use of index numbers, because these are based on firm and numerically precise calculations of inputs and outputs and will use value categories. In order to evaluate the expenditure and yield of education, new methods must therefore be developed that will take account of the fact that the problems confronting socialist education are of various dimensions. That will help us to improve the process of making decisions on the allocation of social labour to the various spheres in the social reproduction process and, in that way, the realisation of the basic law of socialist economics as well as the law of economy of time.

A practicable way of tackling this seems to be to refine the input–output analysis of educational processes and thus create a method for investigating progressively the various elements of costs and benefits of various educational measures, so as to make them comparable with each other and to make it possible to compare them, and select that variant which may seem most advantageous for the increase of economic efficiency. By benefits we mean, in general, the contributions made by the various educational measures to the achievement of the objectives of socialist society. The making of input–output analyses of socialist education assumes the existence in detail of objectives fixed for each branch as well as of alternative policies for the attainment of such objectives. On the basis of these, a comparison of input and output may be made. In selecting the variants for developing education within the framework of the process of economic reproduction, we shall, in general, have to deal with three types of variants:

(1) variants showing in practice comparable outputs but different costs; here, the variant with the most favourable relation of costs to benefits can be defined without much difficulty, by using the criterion of costs; though this type of variant is rather infrequent, it is often considered as a general case, thus causing from the outset the danger of misleading decision-making;

(2) variants that, in practice, will involve the same costs but will have different results which must then be estimated and made comparable for the different levels of decision-making;

(3) variants of incommensurable input and output which will have to be estimated separately and which will have to be made

comparable and weighed against each other at the various levels of decision-making.

It will thus be important to define and estimate those components which have to be included in the input–output analysis when evaluating educational activities. Such components are:

(1) inputs; and here the relation of once-for-all to recurrent expenses, as well as of actual to target labour costs;

(2) parameters of quality and performance;

(3) the dates at which results of educational measures or policies will be effective;

(4) general social benefits.

In this context, we shall have to take account of the opposing effects of particular components which will need to be estimated and assessed accurately when making decisions. For example:

(1) a given level of quality and performance parameters may be reached earlier if in return greater expenses are incurred;

(2) a given quantitative raising of the qualification level may be achieved with a given input if the requirements for quality and performance have been lowered.

It is very dangerous to take into account, in evaluating educational measures, individual components of the input–output analysis, since these individual objectives will nearly always be reached at the expense of the others. The still widespread uni-dimensional evaluation of measures and projects in education (e.g. one made by means of the criterion of costs or of general concepts of social benefit) will, therefore, have to be replaced by a multi-dimensional evaluation made within the framework of input–output analysis.

The improvement of the input–output analysis and its application to the process of decision-making will naturally depend mainly on investigating the significance of the interrelations existing between the educational system and the other spheres of the process of social reproduction, and on investigating the internal efficiency of the whole educational system. It will depend, in addition, on the development of economic and mathematical instruments capable of connecting the information resulting from analysis made on the basis of political economy, with the decision-making process in such a manner as to make the interconnection relevant. Moreover, the efficient employment of highly trained manpower and the intensive utilisation of their knowledge and ability, as well as the creation of a permanent scheme for further re-education of trained manpower, must form part of such a policy.

Discussion of the Paper by Professor Maier

Professor von Weizsäcker (F.R.G.) in opening the discussion of Professor Maier's paper said that as economists we were used to treating education as a part of capital formation and calling it human capital formation. This was unquestionably one of the most durable capital assets in the economy. This was shown by the fact that the schoolchildren of 1972 would still be members of the labour force down to the year 2031. The last pupil to be taught by a teacher who at the moment was just starting a teaching career would be a member of labour force until the year 2067, almost a hundred years from now. If one remembered these time dimensions, it was no wonder that in East and West alike education and manpower planners were particularly concerned to take the long-term planning of education seriously. If he understood it correctly, the model described by Professor Maier was actually being used in manpower planning in the German Democratic Republic. A matrix of pupils going through the education system was considered, as well as the flows from the educational system to the outside world. Both the educational system and the outside world could be classified into different categories, and these criteria of classification were of the greatest importance. The model also took account of the influence of the outside world on the educational system.

Professor Maier's concept was that each row of the matrix represented the sum of the pupils of a given category. Coefficients were introduced for movement of pupils from one category to another and as structural parameters of the model for forecasting purposes, the coefficients being fixed in time. This made it possible to forecast the movements of pupils between given categories and the outflow from the education system to the manpower system. Not all of this outflow, of course, went into the labour force; some of it was lost through migration, death, and other things. The inflows could be predicted from a demographic model, otherwise the model under consideration would not be of much use.

At the same time, there was a matrix of labour requirements, differentiated according to qualifications. That meant that if a plan involving production vectors were provided in a planned economy, it was possible to forecast the labour requirements. Such a labour requirement computation was basically in reverse, in the sense that it represented a computation from the future into the present.

Professor von Weizsäcker's first question was concerned with what happened if the two models gave inconsistent results. There was no reason why the number of trained persons coming from the educational system should be consistent with the labour requirements emerging from a long-term plan of the economic system. Professor Maier had mentioned this problem in a few sentences and had said that what had to be done in such a case was to change the coefficients of movement so as to adapt the education system to the labour force requirements. Could Professor Maier be more specific on this point and tell the conference how this was done in practice? Naturally in a country like

West Germany they were rather reluctant to make such alterations and this implied a problem of the long-term consistency of the education and the production systems which was a complicated political as well as economic issue.

His second point was that we were engaged in discussing long-term planning; how precisely could they predict individual coefficients in these models and the whole structure of coefficients over a period of ten, fifteen or twenty years or more? Was there not a high degree of uncertainty involved? And how was one to deal with this uncertainty?

His third question was whether they were using a satisfactory model? He had in mind the principle of substitution and he believed, on the basis of experience in several western countries, that there was a large degree of substitutability between differently qualified manpower. In a long-term planning model this substitutability ought to be taken into account explicitly, and one might need to have a more complex model of what labour requirements really were. The model might become more complex, but the practical problems might become easier as a result.

His final question embraced to some extent the first three and related to the flexibility of the system. He thought it was important to realise that the greater the uncertainty about the future, the more necessary it became for a system to possess inbuilt mechanisms of flexibility, which could themselves be an object of long-term planning. In other words, the requirements were not given but were malleable, and in this sense education was a sphere in which flexibility was of extreme importance.

Professor Vangrevelinghe (France) wanted to ask whether people already classified under manpower were able to re-enter the educational system in this model or not? There was the problem of the difference of capacity between the man when he is just out of the education system and twenty or thirty years later, and this difference was very difficult to forecast. How were the needed qualifications defined? He would himself prefer to define them not as certain sorts of technological abilities but as the abilities and capacities to learn and acquire successive new technologies in a given field. Were not the qualifications he had suggested a way out of the problems of substitutability and of the need of flexibility that had been discussed by Professor von Weizsäcker?

Professor Robinson (U.K.) said that on an earlier occasion some ten years previously, the I.E.A. had organised an international conference on education. That conference had been concerned with the same problem of the degree of fineness with which it was desirable to try to make estimates of manpower demands, and particularly high-level manpower demands. In one sense it was not sufficient to ask what the total high-level manpower demand might be, because all industrial groups really needed a mixture of different types of qualified manpower: certain amounts of high-level managerial, research and administrative manpower. And when it really came to employment of high-level manpower, it was not enough to show that so many chemists would be wanted. In practice, it would be so many chemists working on oil, so many on dye-stuffs, and similarly on the whole variety of products. Had Professor Maier gone into further detail in order to make some sort of ideal manpower-demand estimates? It seemed to Professor Robinson that the difficulties would be immensely greater than was suggested either in Professor Maier's paper or in Professor von Weizsäcker's introduction to it, because the demand for high-level manpower was not at all a simple function of the output of particular industries. As he had said, a substantial part of the high-level manpower would be employed on research and development, and here there were periods when horizons opened and considerable manpower was wanted to do the research, while at other times this might happen not in this particular industry but in other industries.

A further problem was the question of the obsolescence of high-level manpower. The needs of particular industries very much depended on whether they needed to replace some portion of their manpower within a specific time period because their existing manpower had become obsolete. Most of us acquired our educational capital once and for life. In the past it had been assumed that that capital would be sufficient for one's whole life, but today it was increasingly doubtful whether this was the case. In his own country they were giving very hard thought indeed at present to whether a second round of human capital formation was going to be necessary at some later stage in life, in order to replace the obsolescence of one's first round of education.

But coming back to the problem of classification, education became increasingly specialised as one reached its final stages. For most of the purposes of educational planning, what was wanted was not a very fine division but the very broad division within which the education itself operated. He thought it was relevant to ask the question, to what degree of fineness did universities – which were the decision-making units in this case – normally work? Professional education was not broken into narrow fields until very late in the educational process, and these broader divisions were really enough for educational planning. He would want to argue that one should not try to do high-level manpower forecasting in extreme fineness, first because it was not really necessary, and second because the users of these estimates were very well aware of the perils and uncertainties of such forecasting, so that the more one was trying to provide a precise forecast, the more sceptical the users were likely to be. He did not think that one needed greater fineness in such estimates than the one used in planning universities.

Professor Chenery (U.S.A.) suggested that there were two possible approaches to educational planning: an input–output approach and the one of valuing different kinds of education at their market value, or computing rates of substitution for different kinds of education. Both the input–output and the substitution approaches had been well tested and showed that there was a great degree of flexibility in the form of substitutability of different kinds of education. The question he wished to explore was the implication for planning.

We at least knew that the input–output system gave us a feasible solution. Not improbably, the coefficients represented in the present system might be reproduced in the future. Another approach might be more flexible and specific; but the question arose as to what was the cost of such specification. At the end of his paper Professor Maier had mentioned having tested several alternative variants, and this was what he would like to hear about. Did it turn out that if some constraints were relaxed, it became possible to reduce costs or obtain a more flexible output?

For poorer countries there had been a tendency to apply the input–output methodology and to end up spending a very large proportion of the budget on education, which turned out later to have been an over-investment in certain kinds of education which the country could not really afford.

At the end of his paper Professor Maier had indicated that he had tried several alternative approaches allowing for different patterns of budget allocations and for changing the balance between various fields of education. Could Professor Maier tell them more about these alternatives?

Professor Bénard (France) commented that Professor Maier had said that one had to choose between a large number of solutions that one could obtain from the model. What criteria would be used for making such a choice, and what would the methodology be? At the end of his paper Professor Maier came to variants, comparisons and measurability on the basis of what he called 'general social utility'. Did this refer to methods already used by anybody in East Germany, or to some future methods which were just being worked out? Why did they not use such methods as linear programming, for instance, which in his view very well combined input–output with optimisation or cost–benefit approaches, or the human capital approach? So far as he could understand it, Professor Maier's model seemed to him to be essentially of the transition matrix type. It was a good and useful type, but sometimes it was dangerous because it led to too mechanistic and inflexible an approach. For instance, such models tended to forecast a big increase of demand for graduates coming from technical, vocational schools. But if other methods – such as an optimisation model – were used, either in the partial or the more general form, it could be found that this type of education was not really worthwhile, for in terms of economic cost it did not provide a sufficient return. Apart from the uncertainty regarding the required skills and the rate of obsolescence of skills, one had to be even more cautious about this type of excessively specialised education. Professor Maier's model did not, he thought, automatically include risk in a forecast, but it involved risk, and he himself did not quite see how it was possible to avoid it.

Professor Fritsch (Switzerland) said that the possible inconsistencies between the education and the production sectors seemed to be crucial to Professor Maier's paper. What happened if these two sectors were not consistent? It was argued here that the educational system should attempt to meet increasingly higher needs for substitution by providing more flexible training, so that this adjustment could ultimately be effected within the production system itself. It would be interesting to know what practical solutions Professor Maier could envisage for making the adjustment between the two systems. He himself thought that these two systems were by no means independent, and at a sufficiently high level the production sphere itself could take care of this adjustment. This happened in the market economies where industrial enterprises were training their staff accordingly, to meet their requirements.

Dr Grove (U.S.A.) said that Professor Robinson had mentioned the likelihood of a growing need for a second round of education because of educational obsolescence. It might be interesting to give the example of a large American firm, presumably influenced by, indeed primarily influenced by, market forces, which was thinking of moving in this direction in its own self-interest. It had found that as people approached the age of fifty, they were really not as productive (because this was technologically a very progressive industry) as the younger technical people that could be hired, who had acquired their Ph.D.'s fairly recently. Yet the people approaching fifty were generally far more costly in terms of the salaries they received than the younger people who could be hired. The company had the prospect of the older people continuing until the age of sixty-five, with appropriate salary increases from time to time, and really not being able to contribute proportionately. There was concern that this might tend to drag down the average level of technical competence. So the company was seriously exploring the possibility of giving people an option to retire at the age of fifty and subsidising a second education for them in whatever field they might wish in order to encourage them, as they approached the age of fifty, to decide whether they preferred to refurbish their skills in their already chosen specialism or try to make a second career, perhaps in an area that would not be quite so demanding from the educational standpoint. No decisions whatsoever had yet been made, but preliminary calculations showed that it would be profitable for a company to make it worthwhile for many technical people to accept this opportunity. This was an example of how the problem of a second education was being considered by a private industry.

Dr Velikov (Bulgaria) found himself in agreement with the general treatment of the problem by Professor Maier. But if it was assumed that the objective of a socialist system was the all-round satisfaction of the material and cultural needs of people and the development of their capabilities, and if wider opportunities were being created for changing jobs, was it right to suggest that those two factors would have new and substantial effects on all planning and forecasting both of educational requirements and of the structure of skills required, far exceeding the narrowly defined production needs for socio-economic development? And would it not be reasonable to expect that in the future both the educational level and the qualifications of manpower would to some degree be in excess of these narrowly defined social needs for production?

Professor Denison (U.S.A.) wished to start from the question of projecting the distribution of labour force by level of education or type of qualification. The standard procedure used by the Bureau of Census or the Bureau of Labour Statistics in the U.S.A., and used also in studies for other countries, was the so-called cohort method. This method relied on the fact that for most working age groups education had been completed, that is that people in the forty-five and over age group had had the same education as people in the thirty-five to forty age group. Calculations could then be made merely on the age distribution basis, taking account, of course, of differential changes in retirements and the like. Professor Denison's question was whether this approach had been tested as an alternative in East Germany?

His second question was concerned with the rationale behind the interpretation at the end part of the paper, which dealt with the impact of changes in education on the production sphere. In that section there was a suggestion that the benefits of education should be compared with its costs, which Professor Denison interpreted as something of the type of rate of returns calculations. It was not quite clear from the paper exactly what calculations were involved.

Finally, it was suggested that the objectives of education should be concentrated on non-economic aspects, and that efforts should be made to change the structure of education and content of work in such a way as to eliminate hard labour and to increase intellectual labour as a deliberate policy. Was such a policy, which was in fact a general world-wide trend of development, envisaged? And if so, then how did it fit into the general approach described in the paper?

Professor Bruno (Israel) said that the discussion had centred on how the education system might adjust to the needs of the production system, and *vice versa.* He would like to point out that the education system was one of the most important redistributive devices in any economy. Sometimes there might be objectives which would call for more equal distribution of human capital as between different sectors of the population. So it was not only in terms of the objective function to be used, but sometimes also in the technique of the education system itself, that particular adjustments might have to be sought.

Professor Maier (G.D.R.), replying, said that so far as the relationships between different types of education, they in the G.D.R. had a ten-year compulsory education. That meant that ten-year education set a limit for further planning of specialised education. He thought he had been slightly misunderstood, because he was not strictly an economist and did not believe that education should be considered only from the point of view of economics. The major objectives of education were social, and education should not be – and was not in G.D.R. – adjusted to the needs of production.

He did not want to argue that his model was the best one, nor had it become a routine instrument of the state planning committee. There were other approaches to the subject, and other ways to apply such models in the work of state planning which were being discussed. There were different concepts as to how education should be structured: one of them was the fixed quota approach. During the past few years 20 per cent of those who graduated from ten-year schools continued their education in establishments of higher learning. They thought that if this continued there would be inadequate manpower available for professional technical education. The conclusion was that such a development was not in the interests of society as a whole, and ways and means of changing that ratio would have to be considered.

The effectiveness of education was another important problem, particularly in relation to the changing structure of the national economy. Ten years ago there were 700 basic specialities in the G.D.R. At present they had 300, and they were working towards an even smaller number of basic professions, from which people could easily move into more specific specialisations. These basic professions were to have a major role in their education.

He thought that obsolescence of education could be met by systematic advanced training of the already trained groups. They believed that all skilled workers should refresh their knowledge once in every five or ten years. As regards the people already in production who would like to go on with their education, they had the chance of advanced training courses or evening or correspondence courses to help them to get degrees.

The question of the criteria for choosing the optimal education policy was a difficult one, and he did not think it had been answered anywhere in the world. He did not believe that very elegant mathematical models could be of very much use here. Perhaps one should take a step back and analyse the impact of the various specific components of education and their effects, both in the production and in the social spheres.

Part Four

Long-term Forecasting and Planning
in other Economies

11 Sources of Growth Accounting as the Basis for Long-term Projection in the United States[1]

E. F. Denison

I. INTRODUCTION

All long-run projections of total output combine pieces of information pertinent to the future with guesses and with extrapolations of past trends or associations, and no method can assure accuracy. A projection based on the sources of growth technique is no exception.

This technique nevertheless has advantages. It provides a framework within which to fit and appropriately weight some types of information that do not fit systematically into other approaches, and it goes somewhat further than most in introducing causal relationships as distinct from mere associations. In comparison with other techniques familiar to me, it also reduces the fraction of the projection that must be based upon past trends or associations. I believe sources of growth analyses also provide information about the past that is more pertinent for a projection into the future.

In essence, the technique requires allocating past growth rates of output among sources, projecting the contribution of each source to a future period, and adding the projected contributions to secure the projected growth rate of output. In this paper I illustrate the technique with a projection of United States output to 1980, because an example will be more informative than a mere description. The projection unfortunately had to be made in haste because the historical analysis from which it starts was completed only shortly before the deadline for this paper. The techniques used for the projection of most components could be improved with more work.

II. ESTIMATES FOR THE PAST

Use of this method of projection requires a breakdown of the past growth rate of output among the determinants of output which changed and which caused output to change, that is, among the 'sources of growth'. I have just completed such an analysis for the

[1] The views expressed in this paper are those of the author and do not purport to represent the views of other staff members, officers, or trustees of The Brookings Institution.

I

United States.[1] It provides data for every year from 1947 through 1969, as well as for 1929, 1940 and 1941. The methods cannot be described here in detail, but the general approach is sufficiently similar to that followed in *Why Growth Rates Differ* to allow the reader familiar with that book to understand this paper, even though the detailed statistical procedures have been improved for almost every detailed component.[2] The output measure analysed is national income (or 'net national product valued at factor cost') valued in constant prices of 1958.[3]

Two procedural changes from *Why Growth Rates Differ* are of sufficient importance to require mention at the outset.

(1) In *Why Growth Rates Differ* income originating in the 'services of dwellings' industry (as the term is used in European national accounts statistics) and net property income from abroad (here labelled 'international assets') were isolated for separate treatment because (*a*) changes in output in these sectors are directly related to changes in a single input, and (*b*) the output attributable to that input is directly available from the national accounts. Similar considerations led me also to isolate national income originating in 'general government, households, and non-profit institutions' in the new study. Output in this sector is ascribable solely to labour input. It is, in fact, quite conventionally measured by use of employment data. About one-fourth of all employment is in this sector. Its separation leaves a much more homogeneous universe, the non-residential business sector, which comprises the remainder of the economy. Each of the four sectors was then separately analysed. In the new study all components of labour input in non-residential business are measured by use of data that refer only to persons employed in that sector.

(2) A completely different, and I believe much better, procedure to measure the effects of short-run changes in the intensity of demand upon the intensity of utilisation of employed resources and hence upon output per unit of input was developed. The previous procedure used the unemployment rate as an indicator of demand

[1] It will be published in a study tentatively titled 'Accounting for United States Economic Growth, 1929–69', which will include a full description of the estimates.

[2] Edward F. Denison, *Why Growth Rates Differ: Postwar Experience in Nine Western Countries* (Washington: Brookings Institution, 1967). The book is also available (without the appendixes) in the Russian language.

[3] Aside from some minor adjustments, the series is derived from the Department of Commerce series for gross national product valued in 1958 market prices by (1) adding the statistical discrepancy in the national accounts to secure a series more comparable with employment data used in the analysis; (2) deducting depreciation valued in 1958 prices to secure net national product at 1958 market prices; and (3) extrapolating the 1958 factor cost value of each expenditure component by the index of its value at 1958 market prices.

intensity. The new procedure uses departures from trend in the non-labour share of corporate national income, with allowance for differential wage–price movements. By the old method, the cyclical peaks and troughs in productivity were coincident with troughs and peaks in unemployment. By the new method, unemployment usually lags cyclical movements in productivity.

The new study also has a completely new feature, an annual series for potential national income in 1958 prices derived by sources of growth techniques. Potential national income in any year is defined as the value that national income in 1958 prices would have taken if (1) the unemployment rate had been 4 per cent; (2) the intensity of utilisation of employed resources had been that which would *on the average* be associated with a 4 per cent unemployment rate;[1] and (3) other conditions (including the size of the capital stock) had been those which actually prevailed in that year. Potential national income is obtained each year by making two adjustments to actual national income in the non-residential business sector. (1) Output per unit of input is adjusted for the difference between actual and potential intensity of demand. (2) Total input is adjusted for the difference between actual and potential labour input and resource allocation. The two adjustments are often in opposite directions. In 1969, for example, potential national income of $607.0 thousand million was obtained from actual national income of $599.6 thousand million by addition of $10.3 thousand million because intensity of utilisation of employed resources was below the potential level, and subtraction of $2.9 thousand million because actual labour input was above the potential level. The study includes estimates of the sources of growth of both actual and potential national income.

The annual series for potential national income shows that the United States experienced periods of fast growth of potential output in the early and late post-war periods separated by a longer period of much slower growth, and that the periods are clearly divided at 1953 and 1964.

Table 11.1 shows actual and potential national income, by sector, for selected years and growth rates during the three post-war periods and over the whole period from 1948–69.

Table 11.1 also shows the projected value of national income in 1958 prices for the year 1980 whose derivation is described in this paper. *The projected value is that of potential national income, as already defined. I make no forecast of actual national income.* I have

---

[1] Intensity of utilisation, and hence productivity, in a year in which employment is at 4 per cent depends to a great extent upon whether output is rising more, the same, or less than the trend rate and upon the extent of labour hoarding. 'On the average' refers to the average of these conditions.

Table 11.1

Actual and Potential National Income in Constant Dollars, by Sector: Amounts and Growth Rates

(Amounts in thousand millions of 1958 dollars; growth rates in per cent per annum)

| Year or period | Actual National Income | | | | | Potential National Income[a] | |
	Total	Non-residential business	General government, households and institutions	Dwellings	International assets	Total	Non-residential business
Amounts							
1948[b]	270·1	225·9	36·6	6·5	1·2	264·6	220·4
1953[b]	337·3	274·5	50·8	10·7	1·3	337·6	274·8
1958[b]	363·6	293·2	53·6	14·8	2·0	391·2	320·8
1960[b]	399·4	324·7	55·6	16·8	2·3	417·4	342·7
1960	400·8	325·8	55·9	16·8	2·3	418·9	343·9
1964	480·1	391·2	62·8	22·3	3·9	479·0	390·1
1969	599·6	488·1	77·2	30·3	4·0	607·0	495·5
1980[c]	935·8	771·0	95·4	62·3	7·1	935·8	771·0
Growth rates							
1948–69[d]	3·85	3·72	3·59	7·64	6·02	4·02	3·92
1948–53	4·54	3·98	6·78	10·62	1·65	4·99	4·51
1953–64[d]	3·23	3·24	1·89	6·90	10·67	3·20	3·20
1964–69	4·54	4·52	4·23	6·35	0·62	4·85	4·90
1969–80	4·13	4·24	1·94	6·79	5·31	4·01	4·10

[a] Potential national income is the same as actual national income in sectors not shown separately.
[b] Excluding Alaska and Hawaii.
[c] All figures for 1980 refer to projected potential national income.
[d] Adjusted to exclude the effect of adding Alaska and Hawaii to the series.

nevertheless entered the 1980 values in the actual national income columns in order to show the change that would take place from the actual 1969 situation *if* actual national income in 1980 should happen to be at the potential level.

The estimate was derived by estimating changes from actual 1969 to potential 1980 conditions. A later year than 1969 could not be used as the base point for the projection because my historical analysis terminated with 1969. Use of a more recent base would, of course, have been desirable.

III. PROJECTIONS OF LABOUR FORCE AND EMPLOYMENT

In 1970 the Bureau of Labor Statistics (B.L.S.) of the U.S. Department of Labor published a rather complete and internally consistent projection of the United States economy which included the year

1980.[1] Estimates of the total labour force, by sex and age, were based upon the expected population and expected labour force participation rates.[2] A distribution by highest school grade completed of the civilian labour force, by sex and age, was derived for older age groups by the cohort method and for younger groups from estimates of school attendance, etc.[3] The study also provided employment estimates by detailed industry and by other breakdowns. These were obtained by allocating final demand by components and using input–output analysis to derive labour requirements.

Because I could not undertake my own detailed projection of labour force and employment, I have relied heavily upon that of the B.L.S. I introduced two changes in components, then based my initial estimates of labour force and employment upon these data.[4]

Developments and further analysis since the projection was made have led B.L.S. analysts to conclude that the total female labour force in 1980 was substantially underestimated and the male labour force overestimated, though by a much smaller amount. The B.L.S. has not yet revised its projection, but George L. Perry of the Brookings Institution has made a recent projection of the potential labour force, by sex and age, which has this characteristic but which is not accompanied by employment detail. I have used it to introduce a summary adjustment to the original detailed projection.

The first three rows of Table 11.2 show, by sex, my estimates of employment for 1969, estimates for 1980 based upon the B.L.S. projection which I shall refer to as the 'original' 1980 estimates, and estimates for 1980 based upon the Perry projection which I shall refer to as the 'adjusted' 1980 estimates. All are available also by age. The 1980 employment estimates assume unemployment is at a

[1] *Special Labour Force Report 119*, Sophia C. Travis, 'The U.S. Labor Force: Projections to 1985'; reprint 2673 from *Monthly Labor Review*, vol. 93 (Feb 1970) pp. 3–12, with supplementary tables added. *Special Labor Force Report 122*, Denis F. Johnston, 'Education of Adult Workers: Projections to 1985'; reprint 2685 from *Monthly Labor Review*, vol. 93 (Aug 1970) pp. 43–56. *Patterns of U.S. Economic Growth: 1980 Projections of Final Demand, Interindustry Relationships, Output, Productivity, and Employment*, bulletin 1672 (1970). *The U.S. Economy in 1980: A Summary of BLS Projections*, bulletin 1673 (1970).

[2] Data are for persons sixteen and over. I added persons fourteen and fifteen for comparability with my historical series.

[3] The published projections refer to persons twenty-five years of age and older. Unpublished projections for persons eighteen and over were generously provided to me for comparability with data used in the past.

[4] Data used are those from the B.L.S. '4 per cent basic model'. I cut the total armed forces in 1980 from 2,783,000 to 2,400,000 (about the present level), while raising their female component to 100,000. I sharply reduced private household employment in 1980 because the B.L.S. projection implied an increase whereas the series has fallen persistently and continued to fall since the B.L.S. projection was made.

TABLE 11.2

Employment by Sector and Sex

(Thousands of persons, aged 14 and over)

	1969	1980	
		Original	Adjusted
Total	83,614	97,980	100,766
Male	53,613	62,140	61,777
Female	30,001	35,840	38,999
Non-residential business	63,062	72,892	75,688
Male	41,482	47,812	47,449
Female	21,580	25,080	28,239
General government, households and institutions (*total*)	20,552	25,088	25,088
Civilian	17,089	22,688	22,688
Male	8,707	12,028	12,028
Female	8,382	10,660	10,660
Military	3,463	2,400	2,400
Male	3,424	2,300	2,300
Female	39	100	100

4 per cent rate and include fourteen and fifteen-year-olds who are excluded from the B.L.S. and Perry projections.

The next step was to divide the 'original' 1980 employment estimates between the 'non-residential business' sector and the 'general government, households, and institutions' sector (Table 11.2); to divide employment in the non-residential business sector among non-farm wage and salary workers, non-farm self-employed and unpaid family workers, and farm workers (main headings of Table 11.4); and to divide employment in general government, households and institutions among about fifteen industry groups needed for analysis of that sector (not shown, except the military component which is given in Table 11.2). This division was based upon the movement of the detailed employment estimates in the B.L.S. projection. I then divided all the 1980 'original' estimates of employment (except the detailed breakdown of civilian employment in general government, households, and institutions) by sex. This division was based on past patterns, controlled to the overall division of civilian employment by sex.

With these employment estimates completed, I was ready to project national income in each of the four sectors.

IV. PROJECTION OF OUTPUT DETERMINANTS IN THE NON-RESIDENTIAL BUSINESS SECTOR

My study for past years allocated changes in output in non-residential business among a large number of determinants. These determinants were projected to 1980 and combined to secure a 1980 estimate of national income originating in the sector.

Table 11.3 shows past 'actual' values and the projected 1980 potential values of the determinants in index form (1958 = 100).

TABLE 11.3

Non-residential Business: Indexes of Output Determinants and Total Output

(1958 = 100)

	1948	1953	1964	1969	1980[a]
1. TOTAL FACTOR INPUT	90·54	99·98	109·80	125·48	157·54
2. Labour	94·71	102·93	108·68	122·40	147·43
3. Employment	97·39	102·85	106·35	121·08	139·95
4. Hours	103·83	103·26	99·80	98·05	95·70
5. Average hours	106·15	103·77	99·45	96·18	93·08
6. Efficiency offset	99·00	99·87	99·49	100·25	100·43
7. Inter-group shifts	98·80	99·64	100·87	101·69	102·37
8. Age-sex composition	99·80	100·33	98·91	96·62	95·77
9. Education	93·85	96·60	103·51	106·71	112·17
10. Correction to 'adjusted' basis	—	—	—	100·00	102·47
11. Inventories	75·19	91·95	119·05	153·72	234·49
12. Non-residential structures and equipment	69·68	84·32	118·16	148·72	246·48
13. Land	100·00	100·00	100·00	100·00	100·00
14. OUTPUT PER UNIT OF INPUT	85·09	93·63	121·09	132·21	166·33
15. Advances in knowledge and n.e.c.[b]	87·21	94·45	109·64	117·60	137·03
Improved resource allocation					
16. Farm	96·85	98·79	101·50	102·69	103·64
17. Non-farm self-employment	99·81	100·24	100·58	101·52	102·02
18. Economies of scale	95·35	98·14	102·45	105·99	112·58
Irregular factors					
19. Weather in farming	100·35	100·16	99·98	100·07	100·05
20. Labour disputes	99·98	99·99	100·01	99·98	99·98
21. Intensity of demand	105·51	101·86	105·61	101·71	103·86
22. Anti-pollution costs	—	—	—	100·00	98·15
23. TOTAL SECTOR NATIONAL INCOME	77·04	93·62	132·96	165·89	262·04

— = not relevant.

[a] Projected under potential conditions. Line 10 is a summary adjustment of labour input for the difference between the 'original' employment projection, used in lines 3 to 9, and the 'adjusted' employment projection.

[b] n.e.c. = not elsewhere classified.

When a number of years are shown, this is more convenient than the growth rate form with which it is interchangeable. The growth rate of any series between any two dates is easily computed from the index values. I now describe briefly the lines in this table.

The index of *total sector national income* (row 23) in past years is computed directly from the output data (as given in Table 11.1, column 2). In 1980 it is the product of total factor input (row 1) and output per unit of input (row 14). The 1969–80 movement of this index provides the 1980 national income figure shown for the sector in Table 11.1.

Total factor input (row 1) in all years is the weighted average of the inputs of labour (row 2), inventories (row 11), structures and equipment (row 12), and land (row 13). In past years the series is a linked index of annual percentage changes obtained by weighting the changes in the four inputs by their cyclically adjusted earnings in the two years linked. A 1969–80 growth rate of total factor input (used to obtain the 1980 index value) was obtained by weighting the growth rates of the indexes by their 1968–9 weights. The 1968–9 weights in non-residential business are: labour, 80·00 per cent; inventories, 3·90 per cent; structures and equipment, 12·04 per cent; land, 4·06 per cent. Changes in weights have had only a trivial effect on the index in the past.

Output per unit of input (line 14) is obtained in past years by dividing sector national income by total factor input. In 1980 it is the product of lines 15–22.

Labour input (line 2) is measured as the product of its component indexes, rows 3, 4, 8, 9 and 10.

Employment (line 3) is an index of the total number of persons employed in the non-residential business sector. The 'original' estimate for 1980 from Table 11.2 is used here. The remaining components of labour input are introduced to take account of changes in average hours and in employment composition that prevent employment from providing an adequate measure of labour input. Before describing them I must digress to discuss Table 11.4.

Distributions of employment and average hours

Table 11.4 provides a breakdown of employment and average hours in the sector that is used in the estimation of several output determinants. Total hours for any group of workers, and hence total and average hours for any combination of groups, can be calculated from these data. Total employment is first divided among non-farm wage and salary workers, non-farm self-employed and unpaid family workers, and farm workers. Each is then divided by sex. (These 1980 estimates have already been described.) Finally,

TABLE 11.4

Non-residential Business: Employment and Average Weekly Hours by Detailed Components

(Employment in thousands; hours in units)

	Employment		Average weekly hours	
	1969	1980	1969	1980
All non-residential business (total)	63,062	72,892[a]	38·8	37·5
Non-farm wage and salary workers (total)	52,647	62,860	37·6	36·4
Full-time male	30,567	35,602	42·4	42·0
Part-time male	3,193	4,844	17·2	17·0
Full-time female	14,351	15,993	38·0	36·8
Part-time female	4,536	6,421	18·4	18·5
Non-farm self-employed and unpaid family workers	6,852	7,348	44·9	44·9
Full-time male	4,145	4,458	53·1	53·1
Part-time male	653	702	16·7	16·7
Full-time female	1,232	1,312	50·9	50·9
Part-time female	822	876	17·1	17·1
Farm workers	3,563	2,684	44·6	44·6
Full-time male	2,268	1,711	55·5	55·5
Part-time male	656	495	16·7	16·7
Full-time female	319	239	48·8	48·8
Part-time female	320	239	20·2	20·2

[a] Based on 'original' estimate from Table 11.2.

each of these six groups is divided between full-time and part-time workers and average (and total) hours worked by each of the resulting twelve groups are estimated. For past years these estimates were developed by the writer from B.L.S. data; the 1980 projections are described next.[1]

Non-farm wage and salary workers. The percentages of both males and females who work full-time have been declining persistently, with the annual decline since the early 1960s much greater than

[1] Since the end of the Second World War changes in average hours in the sector as a whole have chiefly reflected changes in the weights of these twelve groups rather than changes in the average hours of the separate groups. Hence average hours in the sector are best projected by projecting hours for each group and combining them with 1980 employment weights. However, this is not the chief purpose for separate projection, as will become evident when remaining output determinants are described.

I*

previously. A sharp rise in the numbers of employed students working part-time contributed heavily to this movement for both sexes. More important for females was the rise in labour force participation rates for adult women, which resulted to a large extent from acceptance of part-time employment by women who would not have taken full-time jobs.

The increase in the part-time proportions is projected to continue, but at a slower rate than in the 1960s because (1) the change in age distribution will dampen the shift whereas in the 1960s it accelerated it and (2) continuation of the previous rate would imply an increase in part-time female employment that probably exceeds the sector's capacity to create part-time jobs. The 1980 full-time figure for each sex is the average of estimates obtained in the following two ways, both based on estimates for the past under potential rather than actual conditions. (1) The yearly decline in the full-time percentage from the 1967–9 average to 1980 is the same as the yearly decline from 1957–9 to 1967–9. (2) The net increase in employment from the 1967–9 average to 1980 was distributed between full-time and part-time workers in proportion to the change from 1957–9 to 1967–9. The second method yields more full-time workers in 1980 than the first. Starting the calculation for the past later than 1957–9 would yield fewer full-time workers in 1980 on either calculation. The full-time percentage for males drops from a 1969 'actual' figure of 90·5 to 88·0 in 1980, the corresponding female percentage from 76·0 to 71·4.

From my new study the average hours of full-time workers of each sex are available on three bases for each year from 1947 to 1969. They are: actual hours; potential hours, which are equal to actual hours adjusted for the difference between actual and potential demand conditions; and 'trend' hours, which smooth out irregularities in potential hours. The 1969 figure for each and the projected 1980 figures are:

		Males	Females
1969			
	Actual	42·41	37·97
	Potential	42·64	38·05
	Trend	42·38	37·96
1980		42·03	36·79

Average hours of full-time workers are notoriously hard to project because they tend to change by appreciable amounts or not at all. Male hours dropped about 0·3 hours from 1947–50 to 1953–65 and 0·55 hours from 1953–65 to 1967–9, with almost no change within these periods. The projection assumes an annual drop in trend hours from 1969 to 1980 equal to that from 1953 to 1969, with 1980 equal to the trend. Female hours have dropped more gradually and by a larger amount than male hours. The projection assumes 1969 trend hours will drop by the average yearly amount experienced from 1953 to 1965.

Average hours of part-time workers of each sex in 1980 are assumed to equal their 1967–9 average.

Other groups. In non-farm self-employment and in farm employment (which together account for only one-eighth of 1980 employment in the sector) the percentage of workers of each sex working full-time is assumed to be the same in 1980 as in 1969. Average hours in each of the eight detailed employment categories are also assumed the same in 1980 as in 1969. Neither the percentages working part-time nor the average hours of any detailed group have changed much in recent years, though there are minor irregularities in the series.[1] The average hours assigned to full-time workers in these groups have almost no effect on the projection because they do not affect labour input.

I now resume description of the rows in Table 11.3.

Hours (row 4 of Table 11.3) measures the estimated effects of changes in average hours upon labour input per worker. The index is the product of rows 5, 6 and 7. The estimate is not based upon a supposition that a given percentage change in the average hours worked by all employed persons in the sector, combined, changes labour input proportionately and therefore has the same effect on output as a percentage change of the same size in employment.

Only if that assumption were made would the index of *average hours* of all workers in the sector (row 6) measure the effect of hours changes. Only in so far as a change in average hours results from a change in the relative numbers of full-time workers and part-time workers, from a change in the average hours of part-time workers, or from a change in the relative numbers of male and female workers do I make that assumption. If the change in the combined average results from two other types of change it is judged to reduce labour input less than proportionally or not at all. The two remaining sub-components of the 'hours' line implement these judgements.

In so far as a change in average hours in the sector results from a change in the average hours of full-time non-farm wage and salary workers of either sex, it is estimated to be partially offset by a change in output per hour (currently, to the extent of nearly 30 per cent). Changes in average hours of full-time farm workers or of full-time

---

[1] There is one exception: the percentage of male farm workers employed part-time has been rising. A further increase was not projected.

non-farm self-employed and unpaid family workers of either sex (which consist chiefly of irregular fluctuations) are estimated to be fully offset by changes in output per hour. Inclusion of line 6, *efficiency offset*, implements these judgements.

Average hours may also change because of a shift in the distribution of full-time workers of either sex among the three labour-force categories distinguished in Table 11.4. Such changes are not considered to change labour input at all; otherwise similar individuals are counted as the same amount of labour input if each works the average full-time hours of persons of his or her own sex in the category in which he or she is employed. The effects of such shifts upon average hours are offset in line 7, *inter-group shifts*.

The next component, *age–sex composition* of total hours worked (line 8), is introduced in order to count hours worked by individuals in ten age–sex groups as different amounts of labour input. Hours worked by each group are weighted by average hourly earnings in 1966–7. The distribution of total hours worked in 1980 between the sexes is calculated from Table 11.4. The 1980 distribution by age of the aggregate for each sex was based on changes in total civilian employment by age, the past division of employed persons in each age group between sectors, and past differentials among age groups in average hours worked.

The *education* component of labour input (line 9) is introduced to count persons at each of nine levels of 'highest school grade completed' as different amounts of labour input. Both the weights for the nine groups of employed persons (earnings in 1959 of persons differing only in amount of education) and the distributions of persons among education groups to which the weights are applied refer only to persons employed in the non-residential business sector, and are computed on a full-time equivalent employment basis. The 1980 distribution is derived by adjustment of the B.L.S. projection already described. The series includes an allowance for past changes at the elementary and secondary levels in the average days of attendance per school year. The projection implies that the education index will rise at a slower rate from 1969 to 1980 than it has in the past. Both the upward shift in the distribution by years of education and the adjustment for days attended per year of school will taper off. The lessened rise in the education index occurs even though education is projected to rise as fast in the business sector as in the whole economy, whereas in the past it has risen less (mainly because teaching absorbed a disproportionate share of new college graduates).

The entry for *correction to 'adjusted' basis* is a summary adjustment for the difference between the 'original' and 'adjusted' employment estimates in Table 11.2. For simplicity, all of the difference between the two estimates was placed in non-residential business. 'Adjusted' employment exceeds 'original' employment in the sector by 3·84 per cent, but the increase is concentrated in age–sex groups with the shortest hours and the lowest earnings per hour. If employment in each age–sex group is multiplied by average hours and average hourly earnings, the aggregate calculated from the 'adjusted' employment estimates is 2·47 per cent larger than the aggregate calculated from the 'original' employment estimates. This estimate is used to correct labour input, so an entry of 102·47 is made in 1980.[1]

Inventory input (line 11) is measured by the quantity of business inventories valued in 1958 prices. Input of *non-residential structures and equipment* (line 12) is measured by a weighted average of indexes of the gross and net stock of business-owned capital of this type, with gross stock weighted 3 and net stock weighted 1.[2]

The stock of the two types of capital in 1980 will be determined by the present stock and the amount of investment from now to 1980, so one (perhaps the best) way to project the 1980 stock is to estimate investment during the intervening years. Such estimates are provided by an unpublished projection for these years by the Bureau of Economic Analysis of the Department of Commerce, based on a modification of the Thurow model.[3] It provides estimates for additions to inventories from which the 1980 stock of inventories can be calculated. It also provides fixed investment and a derived series for the gross stock of non-residential structures and equipment (separately), though on a slightly different statistical basis from the series I use; I have attempted to adjust these estimates to conform with my input series for non-residential structures and equipment.

These estimates imply 1969–80 growth rates of 4·33 for input of inventories and 5·04 for inventories of non-residential structures and equipment. I regard these as probably too high because the model's projection of 1980 potential output is above most others, including mine; because the model was run on the assumption of below average unemployment during the 1970s; and because substantial expenditures for pollution control were added to fixed investment

[1] The correction can be partially allocated among the labour input determinants. The employment index is raised by 3·84 per cent, from 139·95 to 145·32. Use of corrected employment would scarcely change the education index. The product of the 'hours' and age–sex' indexes would therefore be lowered by 1·31 per cent (from 91·65 to 90·45). This partial breakdown is used in the derivation of Table 11.5.

[2] Reasons for my choice of this weighting scheme have been described in various places, most recently in the *Survey of Current Business*, vol. 52, pt 2 (May 1972) pp. 101–4.

[3] The model is described in Lester C. Thurow, 'A Fiscal Policy Model of the United States', *Survey of Current Business*, vol. 49 (June 1969) pp. 45–64.

on the assumption that they would be wholly an increment to, rather than in part a substitute for, investment that would otherwise be made. The results also look high in historical perspective. Unable to rerun the model on different assumptions, I have simply substituted moderately lower rates. These assume that the 1969–80 growth rate of inventories per person employed in the sector will be the same as the 1953–69 rate, and that the growth rate of structures and equipment input per person employed would exceed the 1953–69 rate by 0·2 points in the absence of new pollution control requirements and these requirements will add nearly another 0·2 points.[1] The resulting 1969–80 growth rates are 3·93 for inventories and 4·70 for input of structures and equipment.

Land input (row 13) is estimated not to change significantly.

The first entry under output per unit of input is *advances in knowledge and n.e.c.* (line 15). In past periods this is the residual in the estimates; the index is obtained by dividing the index for output per unit of input by the indexes for all its other components. It grew at the following annual rates in some past periods: 1929–41, 0·55; 1941–8, 1·02; 1948–53, 1·61; 1953–64, 1·37; 1964–9, 1·41. Thus it has a record of substantial change if one goes back a long way in time. However, since 1950 its growth rate has been quite stable at about 1·40. The series picks up the effects of all unmeasured determinants of output in the sector, but in my judgement it provides a reasonable measure of the changes in output per unit of input that were due to the incorporation into the process of production of new managerial and technological knowledge of all types and from all sources.

No information about the future is brought to bear for projection of the state of knowledge because I have none that I consider pertinent. I simply project the post-war growth rate of 1·40 to the 1969–80 period. This could, of course, be wide of the mark.[2]

The next two indexes refer to gains in output per person employed in the sector that result from reallocation of labour. The reallocation of labour from farming (line 16, *farm*) is calculated on the basis that at any date a 1 per cent increase in labour input (not employment) in the non-farm portion of the non-residential business sector would raise non-farm national income in the sector by 0·80 per cent and a

[1] The 'adjusted' employment figure for 1980 was used in the calculation of 1980 capital inputs by use of these procedures.

[2] Some observers fear that the cessation of the fast growth of expenditures for organised research and development which has already occurred will reduce the contribution of advances in knowledge in the 1970s, but it is not clear to me why this should be so (since the level of such expenditures will remain above the average post-war level) nor what its quantitative importance would be if it were so.

1 per cent decrease in labour input in farming would reduce farm national income by 0·33 per cent, and that such changes occur as the percentage of labour input devoted to farming declines. The re-allocation of labour from non-farm self-employment (line 17, *non-farm self-employment*) is calculated on the basis that, as the percentage of self-employed and unpaid family workers in non-farm business employment diminishes because of the elimination of fringe enterprises, an increase in wage and salary employment only one-fourth as large as the decline in self-employment is required to obtain production of equal value. Table 11.4 provides the estimates of projected shifts in employment which are the main ingredient of the 1980 projection for these indexes.

All determinants considered thus far are measured as if the economy operated under constant returns to scale. Economies of scale are estimated to add 15 per cent to the growth rate of sector output that changes in other determinants (except irregular factors) would provide under constant returns to scale. This estimate was used to project the *economies of scale* index (line 18) to 1980.

The next three indexes measure the effects of irregular factors upon the annual series for output per unit of input in the sector. The 1980 indexes for the effect of *weather in farming* (line 19) and *labour disputes* (line 20) were placed at their average values in the 1948–69 period. The 1980 index for the effect of fluctuations in *intensity of demand* on the intensity of use of employed resources and hence on output per unit of input (line 21) was assigned the value that had been determined in the historical analysis to be its level under potential conditions (103·86 when, as in these indexes, the lowest post-war year, 1958, is taken as 100).

Anyone making a projection must ask whether changes in conditions will introduce some new ingredients into future growth. I shall not tire the reader with my views about such new ingredients or caveats about how they may invalidate the projection.[1] However, new legislation for control of air and water pollution seems sufficiently certain to significantly affect the growth rate of measured output per unit of input to require an estimate. On the assumption that annual costs *imposed on business* to prevent pollution without giving rise to measured output will increase by about $16 thousand million in constant prices from 1969 to 1980, I estimate that this will subtract 1·85 per cent from the sector's measured 1980 output. Hence I introduce in 1980 an index of 98·15 for *anti-pollution* costs.

[1] Most plausible possibilities would adversely affect the growth rate. However, one special fact about 1980, that it is a leap year consisting of fifty-two weeks plus two weekdays, will lift measured output in that particular year.

V. PROJECTIONS OF OTHER SECTORS

Separate projections for the three other sectors will now be very briefly described.

General government, households, and institutions

In this sector, the Department of Commerce obtains output in 1958 prices by extrapolating the 1958 compensation of employees in every component industry or employee group by full-time equivalent employment, or by an equivalent procedure.[1] I use the same procedure, based on projected employment, to secure 1980 output. From 1969 to 1980 total output is projected to rise at an annual rate of 1·94 per cent while employment rises at an annual rate of 1·83 per cent. The difference results from a slower projected growth of full-time equivalent employment than of total employment (which may be construed as an effect of changes in hours) and from changes in the weights of components among which compensation per worker in 1958. Because of the method by which output is measured, the entire change in the sector's output must be counted as a contribution of labour input.

Dwellings

The crucial figure required for the 1980 projection is consumer expenditures for space rent, valued in 1958 prices. I have used the B.L.S. estimate, which was obtained by adjustment of a figure secured by use of estimating equations for consumption items that were developed by Hendrik Houthakker and Lester D. Taylor. The projected increase is large but not unreasonable, especially in view of recent great strength in residential construction. Expenses, including depreciation, are deducted from space rent to secure net national product, and the percentage change in net product is applied to national income.

My historical analysis divides the change in national income in this sector between the change which would have occurred if the percentage of dwellings occupied had been constant (which is classified as a component of capital input) and the change that resulted from fluctuations in the occupancy ratio (which is classified as a component of output per unit of input). The division does not affect the projection, but to complete a sources of growth table in the following section I estimate that the occupancy ratio will be the same in 1980 as in 1969.

International assets

The projection is based on the level of the series in the first half of

---

[1] National income, gross national product, and net national product are the same in this sector, and for past periods are obtained directly from the national accounts.

1972; examination of the movements of the current-dollar components of receipts and expenditures of interest, dividends, and branch profits; and a guess at the future change in import and export prices.[1] I had access to two projections of related data by experts in this field, but stress that projection of this small item is hazardous at any time and doubly so now because of exchange rate fluctuations.

VI. SOURCES OF GROWTH IN THE WHOLE ECONOMY

The sources of growth technique of projection requires that the contribution of changes in each output determinant be projected. These contributions are then added to secure the growth rate of total national income. Table 11.5 presents the projection in this form.[2]

For comparison the table also presents my estimates of the sources of growth of actual national income from 1948 to 1953, from 1953 to 1964, and from 1964 to 1969. The figures for the projected period refer to changes from the actual 1969 situation to the potential 1980 situation. The 1969–80 estimates are applicable to the growth of actual national income in this period only if 1980 should happen to be a year which corresponds to the conditions stipulated in the definition of potential national income.

Measured in percentage points, the contribution of any source to the growth rate of total national income is the product of (1) its contribution in percentage points to the growth rate of national income originating in the sector in which it appears and (2) the percentage of the growth rate of total national income which originates in that sector. Of the output determinants distinguished, only labour input appears in more than one sector. In Table 11.5 I have separated the contributions of labour employed in the two sectors in which labour input is present.

Table 11.5 brings out very clearly, and quantitatively, the detail of the changes between past periods and the future period that are projected to occur. Space limitations bar pointing out these changes verbally but the table makes such a review unnecessary.[3]

Estimates for past periods of the sources of growth of potential national income, similar to those presented for actual national

---

[1] See n. 1, p. 256 above.

[2] Total projected output can also be obtained, as was done in Table 11.1, by using the same estimates to project national income in each sector and adding the sectors.

[3] In calculating the 1969–80 contribution of employment in non-residential business I have incorporated the 'adjusted' employment series. The adjustment of −0·08 points to the hours and age–sex composition components of labour input is left unallocated (see n. 1, p. 253 above). However, it is clear that the contributions of both hours and age–sex composition would be reduced (i.e. be made larger negative figures) by some fraction of this amount if the allocation were made.

TABLE 11.5

Sources of Growth of Actual National Income, Selected Periods

(Contributions to growth rate in percentage points)

	1948–53	1953–64	1964–9	1969–80[a]
NATIONAL INCOME	4·54	3·23	4·54	4·13
TOTAL FACTOR INPUT	2·95	1·30	3·08	2·39
Labour	2·07	0·60	2·15	1·37
General government, households and institutions	0·96	0·27	0·55	0·23
Employment	0·91	0·31	0·51	0·24
Hours and shifting weights	0·05	−0·04	0·04	−0·01
Non-residential business	1·11	0·33	1·60	1·14
Employment	0·72	0·20	1·75	1·12
Hours	−0·06	−0·21	−0·24	−0·15
Average hours	−0·29	−0·26	−0·45	−0·20
Efficiency offset	0·12	−0·02	0·10	0·01
Inter-group shifts	0·11	0·07	0·11	0·04
Age–sex composition	0·07	−0·09	−0·31	−0·05
Correction to hours and age–sex composition[b]	—	—	—	−0·08
Education	0·38	0·43	0·40	0·30
Capital	0·88	0·70	0·93	1·02
Inventories	0·18	0·08	0·18	0·12
Non-residential structures and equipment	0·38	0·29	0·45	0·47
Dwellings	0·31	0·27	0·29	0·39
International assets	0·01	0·06	0·01	0·04
Land	0·00	0·00	0·00	0·00
OUTPUT PER UNIT OF INPUT	1·59	1·93	1·46	1·74
Advances in knowledge and n.e.c.[c]	1·34	1·13	1·15	1·16
Improved resource allocation	0·41	0·24	0·34	0·10
Farm	0·33	0·21	0·19	0·07
Non-farm self-employment	0·08	0·03	0·15	0·03
Dwellings occupancy ratio	−0·03	−0·01	0·01	0·00
Economies of scale	0·48	0·32	0·56	0·46
Irregular factors	−0·61	0·25	−0·60	0·16
Weather in farming	−0·03	−0·02	0·02	0·00
Labour disputes	0·00	0·00	−0·01	0·00
Intensity of demand	−0·58	0·27	−0·61	0·16
Anti-pollution costs	0·00	0·00	0·00	−0·14

— = not relevant.

[a] Change from actual national income in 1969 to potential national income in 1980.

[b] See n. 3, p. 257 above.

[c] n.e.c. = not elsewhere classified.

income, are available from my new study, and such estimates could be calculated for the 1969–80 projected period. For the 1969–80 period they would differ from those shown in Table 11.5 in two main respects. The contribution of 'intensity of demand' would, by definition, disappear; it would therefore be cut from 0·16 to 0·00 percentage points. The contributions of labour input and improved resource allocation would be changed; their sum would be raised by 0·04 percentage points. Other components would be the same. The projected growth rate of potential national income, 4·01 per cent, is therefore 0·12 percentage points lower than the projected growth rate of 4·13 per cent calculated for the change from 1969 actual to 1980 potential national income.

All aspects of the projection refer only to national income measured in 1958 prices. I have not attempted a conversion to G.N.P. measured in 1958 prices, but note that simply substituting 1969 G.N.P. weights for 1969 national income weights for the four sectors shown in Table 11.1, and using the same growth rates for each sector, would raise the 1969–80 projected actual-to-potential growth rate from 4·13 to 4·26. This happens to be very close to the 4·32 per cent growth rate from 1969 actual G.N.P. to 1980 potential G.N.P. which the B.L.S. projection, based on a quite different approach, implies.[1] My allowance for anti-pollution costs reduced my growth rate by 0·14 percentage points whereas the B.L.S. projection (which is presently being reviewed and revised) made no such allowance. On the other hand, my projection incorporates an upward adjustment of the 1980 labour force that B.L.S. used.

It is even more necessary than usual to caution that if, as is likely, the base year for deflation is changed from 1958 to a recent year, this will require a change in the projected growth rate. This is because the relative sizes in 1969 of the four sectors distinguished in Table 11.1 are substantially different when measured in current 1969 prices than when measured in 1958 prices, and projected growth rates differ greatly among the sectors.

---

[1] If it were not, it would be necessary to revise the 1980 projection for space rent and perhaps also some of the detailed employment estimates that I have used (all of which emerge from the B.L.S. projection) and re-work my own projection to incorporate the changes.

Discussion of the Paper by Professor Denison

Dr Rivkin (U.S.S.R.), in opening the discussion, said that as a mathematician he naturally welcomed an axiomatic approach to economic studies. The building of a mathematical model was of the greatest value if it made it possible to go deep into the essentials of the economic mechanism and if it contributed to showing relationships which could not be traced by means of informal analysis. The builders of such models had usually been content to achieve results that were no secret to economists with a broader approach to economic analysis. Yet 'truth was something more than knowledge' and to obtain economic truth, that is knowledge verified by genuine statistics, was an extremely difficult task, demanding courage, wisdom and caution. Successful long-term forecasts based on econometric models were not frequent and always created considerable interest among economists.

There had been a period of general interest in the West in big regression models for simultaneous prediction of a large number of variables. It seemed that such models did not correspond to the opportunities provided by the apparatus by which they were evaluated. Studies made in Uppsala had proved that gigantic monsters of forecasting models were extremely unreliable. With increase of the number of correlation equations, relationships between endogenous variables became too numerous and their simultaneous evaluation too difficult. Moreover, such models had no single theoretical base and were extremely eclectic in nature, with some equations rooted in the assumptions of one theory, and others in quite a different one. Perhaps this was what Professor Malinvaud had meant by pretentious models.

Professor Denison's aim has been different. It was to obtain conclusions while remaining within the framework of the statistical information available, and without designing monsters of this kind. It certainly took courage to use the one single methodological concept throughout the whole work, but as a result of this his analysis came out solid in form. The methods developed by Professor Denison earlier for studying rates of economic growth were in this case to be used as a basis for long-term projection.

In his view, the most substantial innovation introduced by Professor Denison was the calculation of potential national income on the basis of the sources of growth analysis. Together with the potential national income, real indicators were forecasted, the latter differing from the potential ones as a result of possible variations in the intensity of the use of labour or in its inflow. By considering intensity of use of labour as an independent factor Professor Denison had managed to avoid the mistake of those researchers who used the unemployment level as the major criterion of economic pressure.

Corresponding parameters for the 1960s showed that direct relationship between the level of unemployment and the rate of economic growth had disappeared. Thus, the period of unusually high rates of growth for the U.S. – 1961–6 – was at the same time a period of rather high unemployment. Slowing down of the rate of growth in 1967 and the low rate in 1968 led to no increase in unemployment, which increased only slightly during the crisis year of

1969–70 and continued to rise after the end of the crisis in 1970 and in early 1971.

Using his method of evaluation of potential output, Professor Denison showed that there was a gap in the trend of unemployment compared to the cyclic movement of the productivity index. Dr Rivkin did not think that within the framework of this survey more delicate relationships were necessary.

The idea of the total of income as deriving from certain specific sources was basic to Professor Denison's paper. He understood that a great deal of argument had been going on for some time on the identification of these sources and the weights or shares of the corresponding factors and the effects of changes in real factor prices and changes in final products. This could be explained by the desire to interpret conclusions reached on the basis of a simple static model in a much wider way than such a model actually permitted. Some economists who could see the limitations and inadequacies of an imputational approach were apt to criticise the models themselves, rather than their inadequate application.

He thought the matter became clearer if one turned from a static balance model to a two-factor dynamic model of the production process. Such a model allowed two alternatives: either to postulate a dynamic relationship between final production output and factor weights, or to accept a permanent savings rate hypothesis. The first alternative was equivalent to the adoption of the 'golden' savings law suggested by Phelps, according to which the norm of savings should equal the production elasticity for the corresponding resource. The second alternative could be used when analysing an economy in terms of a fixed savings rate. It could be proved that the result would be a system capable of reproducing the given conditions of growth over an unlimited period of time.

It was true that a deviation from the 'golden law' would result in a decrease of the minimal rate of growth which was stable for such a system. Yet there was no reason to believe that the growth of the economy under consideration was achieved as a result of internal factors only. As a consequence, an economist who attempted to determine the weights of different factors of growth faced additional and perhaps insoluble difficulties. It seemed that a dynamic model could, at least in theory, clarify the problems involved in the use of final products as weights.

One other point concerned the rates of growth. In forecasting it was always important to remember the meaning of the parameters chosen as a basis of analysis. But rates of growth measured at constant prices did not always achieve this objective, even if the recalculation into constant prices was most accurately done. Thus it was not possible to say that a country with a higher growth rate was developing more efficiently than one with a lower rate of growth. It was even more difficult to speak of adequate comparability of different sectors within one economy.

There were countries with a stable savings norm and low rates of growth which continued over a long period, which nevertheless had a high level of personal consumption: for example, Sweden and Belgium. The hypnotising effect of growth rates on forecasters showed one of the basic methodological faults of forecasting, the limited nature of forecasts based on unrelated analyses of individual national economies. The paradox of wealth with low growth rates could be explained only by considering a system of countries as a whole. One other difficulty had to be overcome in order to forecast properly: that was to learn to forecast not only growth rates of output or incomes at fixed prices but the dynamics of prices themselves so as to evaluate the true position of an economy or a region in comparison with other economies or regions.

Professor Marczewski (France) said that Professor Denison stated in his paper that economies of scale were estimated to add 15 per cent to the growth rate of sector output that changes in other determinants would provide under constant returns to scale. He wished to ask how this rate had been determined or estimated? Why should the rate be the same for all sectors? Was there no kind of law of diminishing returns to scale when the degree of concentration of a sector increased?

Professor Osadchaya (U.S.S.R.) pointed out that in Table 11.5 and the conclusions derived from it regarding the contribution of different factors both for the past and for the forecast growth, the author had attempted no interpretation of the table and of the trends which it suggested. He had himself made certain calculations on the basis of the table, which led to some interesting conclusions. According to the table there was a decrease in the contribution of labour, which accounted for 45 per cent of growth in the first period, for 18 per cent in the next, and was expected to be 33 per cent in the 1969–80 period. Other changes included a decrease in the contribution of inventories from 8·13 to 7·5 per cent, of greater capital investments (up by 25 per cent in the planned period), and a higher contribution from productivity per unit of input. Would Professor Denison comment on these changes in the structure of basic sources of growth? What exactly was the meaning of 'advances in knowledge'?

Professor Kozlov (U.S.S.R.) said that the fundamental assumption of Professor Denison's paper was that there were certain determinants of economic growth by weighting and adding which it was possible to arrive at the total resource input index, and thus at general output indicators. It was known from planning experience that methods involved in statistical analysis were not necessarily applicable in planning. For example, in the case of intersectoral models, analysis of past development was conducted with one kind of method, while the planning of future growth was conducted with quite a different method which in no way resembled the first type and in practice reflected the different nature and purpose of the studies. Did Professor Denison believe that it was both possible and advisable to use some other approaches to forecasting also, for example, general indexes of economic growth, different from the approach suggested by the paper? It was difficult to understand the criteria for weighting certain factors in the planned period. For example, the use of the weights appropriate to the late 1960s produced a difference of 30 points for 1948, which is twenty years before 1968, and of 150 points for 1980. It seemed obvious that, in the case of 30 points difference, whatever weights were chosen, they did not practically influence the final result. But in the latter case a different choice of weights would produce substantially different results. This raised the question of the criteria for the choice of weights, and of how one justified the forecast of the determinants of the parameters being weighted? He thought that the assumption that the rates of growth which actually took place in 1968–9 would remain the same until 1980 was reasonable only as a first approximation, but left much to be desired from the point of planning.

Professor Khachaturov (U.S.S.R.) asked whether it would be possible in Professor Denison's approach to distinguish factors of growth relating exclusively to material production, so as to make it easy to make comparisons of different national economies, for example, between the economies of the U.S. and of the U.S.S.R.

Professor Porwit (Poland) was interested in the fact that the results obtained by Professor Denison were very close to the B.L.S. forecast. Could this be because Professor Denison's forecast was partly based on the information and forecast of the Bureau of Labour Statistics, and that the two forecasts were close to each other because of the use of the same or similar information?

Professor Robinson (U.K.) was interested in the fact that whereas in 1948–53 a very large contribution to growth of output per unit of input came from improved resource allocation, mostly from transfer from farm work to other work, that source had almost disappeared, according to Professor Denison's estimate, by the period 1969–80. This was surprising, because in the European countries there was still much redeployment of resources going on not so much from farm work but rather from the early industrial revolution industries to more modern industries with higher product per head. Had the United States completely exhausted that second source of gain in productivity through transfer?

Professor Denison (U.S.A.), replying to the discussion, said that his projections of capital stock and capital input were consistent, he believed, with a reasonable estimate of the saving rate in the period concerned. The only stable relationship he could find was in the long run on the savings side and in the growth of the saving rate which was reasonably stable. This did not translate directly into investment because the government surplus and deficit had to come into the calculation.

Economies of scale were of course a very rough estimate. In fact the figure was obtained not by pure assumption but statistically through a correlation of productivity series with changes in output using successively four, five, six and seven-year time periods in several ways: for example, by comparing the change in productivity with the change in output determinants independently measured. It had always been his belief that in principle a coefficient remained stable over time if everything remained constant. He did believe, however, that if one moved to a different type of market and to a different size of a unit, technological progress was such that opportunities for scale economies were constantly replenished.

As regards the changes in the sources of actual national income growth, he thought that it was not as useful to consider contributions to growth as percentages of the total of change as it was to do so in the actual percentage points themselves. For example, when put in terms of percentage points, the contribution of education to growth had been remarkably constant in the past right back to 1929. It was, however, perfectly true that for the projected period the labour force projection by level of education did clearly indicate a reduction in the increase of the educational level, at least as indicated by earnings rates for different levels of education. This was a most interesting point which he had not really anticipated before he made those calculations, and it occurred despite the fact that there was one thing that would tend to make it go the other way round. These calculations were based on education distributions for the sector of the economy concerned, which excluded, most importantly, teachers. Throughout the post-war period teachers for all levels of education had been absorbing a disproportionate part of the increase in college-trained people. This had been particularly true for women. This trend was not expected to continue in the future. Despite this fact we had a projected decline, even in the business sector. His estimates in terms of percentage points indicated that from approximately the middle of the 1950s the contribution of education had been virtually constant, and projections simply assumed that it would continue at about the same rate. For the particular time period shown in Table 11.5, the figure appeared a little higher before the year 1953, but that was an early post-war period, and he would not put any emphasis on it.

By 'advances of knowledge' he meant all changes in our knowledge of how to produce, technical or managerial or organisational, that affected output per unit and unit costs. He was unable to divide this estimate further by type of knowledge or by where it came from. This was the greatest challenge to future growth analysis.

In respect of weighting, he would assume that in this case it was rather a matter of terminology. This work had nothing to do with planning except as providing a projected estimate of future aggregate growth in output. In general, this approach did not lend itself to other types of output, for example, to projections of output by industry or type of product. It could provide an estimate of the total amount to be allocated between those disaggregations but could not indicate such disaggregations. Might he stress that the weights refer only to the compositions of the inputs. He had computed the total output and weights for the whole period of 1929–69, and they did not really affect the total very much.

He could not deal with material production separately but he would point out that he could deal separately with what he had called the non-residential business sector. This excludes all income originating in general government, households and institutions, and also excluded housing services. In a new study he was intending to provide a complete estimate separately for that sector. This, of course, was not quite the same as material production but it came a great deal closer to it, and it would certainly provide a better estimate for certain purposes of comparison.

It was true that he had relied on B.L.S. projections for the labour force and employment to a considerable extent. But the main point was that all the detail of the B.L.S. projection for short-term estimates was not used. The B.L.S. projections of labour by age and sex or by education were not used for output projection, or used only to a limited extent.

He could not agree with Professor Robinson's suggestion that some redeployment of labour from obsolescent to modern industries might be a significant source of growth in the U.S.A.

12 Prospects of Economic Growth in the Federal Republic of Germany

G. Fels

I. INTRODUCTION

This paper deals with long-term economic growth forecasts for the West German economy, the methods used or which ought to be used, the results yielded, and hypotheses about factors determining the pattern of the future growth process. Long-term forecasting with respect to economic growth is a rather recently established activity in West Germany. For a long time during the post-war period, policy makers regarded economic growth merely as a spontaneous result of the market mechanism which descended like manna. There seemed to be no reason to consider it as a matter of economic policy. Moreover, economists who have taken an interest in quantitative long-term forecasts have run the risk of being suspected of smuggling planning elements into the free market economy. As long as growth rates were sufficiently high, the public interest in growth analysis and growth prediction was very low.

Thus it was not until the recession of 1967, when the G.N.P. growth rate became negative, that growth was discovered as a target of economic policy. In the Stability and Growth Law which was enacted in 1967, 'steady and adequate growth' is enumerated as one of the main goals. In an official projection of overall economic development for the period 1969–73 the 'adequate' growth rate is defined as a 4 per cent increase of real G.N.P. per annum. In 1968 the Federal Ministry of Economics presented a so-called perspective projection until 1980 [1],[1] somewhat in between a probability forecast and a target projection. The growth rate of G.N.P. projected for 1968–80 was expected to lie between the 3·8 per cent and the 4·8 per cent growth paths. In 1970 the official growth projections, the methodology of which is discussed below, was extended to 1985 [2]. It implies between 1970 and 1985 an annual real G.N.P. growth rate of 4·8 per cent according to the medium variant, and of 4·3 and 5·3 per cent according to the lower and upper variants, respectively. Since the projection is widely accepted as a basis of all kinds of private and public planning, one can characterise it rather as a target projection than as a probability forecast.

Though widely accepted in its results, it does not rest on a widely accepted methodology for forecasting long-term economic growth,

[1] For all references see p. 275.

because such a methodology does not exist for a decentralised economy. Growth theorists have produced an immense intellectual display of the equilibrium conditions of hypothetical growth paths, and empirically oriented growth analysts have devoted hard guess-work to the identification and the quantification of the factors determining actual growth rates. Although from a policy-maker's point of view the latter's activities have proved to be more fruitful than the former's, they were not able to put forward the techniques for forecasting growth rates in more than an incremental fashion. This is because the insight into the determinants of growth gives only information regarding how to shift the forecasting problem from one variable to one or more others, i.e. instead of future output the future supply of capital, labour and other input factors has to be predicted exogeneously. Thereby, the forecaster's business becomes easier only if the exogenous variables have proved to be more stable over time than the endogenous ones.

As economic growth is not only a concern of economists but also an important goal of economic policy, there exists a demand for predictions of how the economy will function in the future. And what is demanded in a market economy is also supplied. Therefore, long-term forecasts are provided regardless of the methodological short-comings. The basis of forecasting is mainly extrapolation of past or cross-country trends combined with plausibility of adjustments in a more or less intuitive manner. The tools of theoretical and empirical growth analysis are used to break down the output variable into its main components and to take care of formal consistency. The pattern of the breakdown depends on the forecaster's opinion about the relative predictability of certain components and about the factors which limit economic growth in the future. Thus, the fore-caster's business seems to be more a matter of speculation and imagination than of positive science. However, economists are credited with having comparative advantages in this field.

II. LONG-TERM PROJECTIONS AVAILABLE FOR THE WEST GERMAN ECONOMY

The main features of eight attempts which have been made to predict long-term economic growth in West Germany can be surveyed in Table 12.1. In addition to the information presented in the table, the two following points are worth noting:

(i) Apart from the E.C.E. projection, all projections are supply oriented; this means that output growth is considered to be limited either by the supply of labour or the supply of capital and the efficiency in which these factors can be used, whereas overall demand is always assumed to exhaust the available capacities.

(ii) In all projections at least the exogeneous variables are pre-determined intuitively; this means in most cases an extrapolation of past experiences is adjusted (or not adjusted) after its plausibility was checked.

To relate growth projections to the supply of productive factors means to predict potential rather than actual output. Apart from a decline in capacity utilisation which may arise from an overall and voluntary shortening of working time, the operating rate of the economy is held constant. In particular it is abstracted from cyclically caused under-utilisation of resources, the prediction of which is regarded to be a matter of short-term forecasting. In the medium and long run one assumes that the demand management of the government provides full employment of labour force and physical capital. Although the supply oriented procedure is the conventional method of handling growth projection problems, during recent years doubt has arisen whether it does not obstruct the view on the growth pattern of an open economy like West Germany. In such an economy which allows the immigration of foreign workers as well as the inflow of foreign capital in all forms, including foreign direct investment, the supply of labour or capital can hardly be considered as a limiting factor in the growth process. As the economy absorbs the resources which it needs from other countries the magnitude and the structure of demand becomes the main determinant of growth. Demand itself depends not only on domestic expenditure behaviour but also on the overall international competitiveness of the economy, which can be measured by the real rate of exchange, and on the specialisation pattern of the economy in the system of international division of labour.

The open-economy-aspect questions are all supply oriented projections. The O.E.C.D., indeed, has avoided calculating potential employment figures for West Germany in the sixties 'as it is difficult to define potential employment because of the influx of foreign workers' [13, p. 44], but does not hesitate to show a 0·2 per cent increase in labour supply during the seventies [13, p. 77]. The E.C.E. projection which is partly demand oriented indicates the change in labour demand in addition to the change in labour supply. This projection can be regarded as a first step in overcoming the conceptual shortcomings of the supply oriented method. What seems to be adequate for an open economy is to pre-estimate overall output growth and output growth by sectors as exogenous variables and to estimate the supply of labour and capital endogenously. The method of pre-estimation, however, has to be more sophisticated than the

TABLE 12.1

Long-term Growth Projections for the West German Economy

Author or Institution	Year of Origin	Coverage of		Technique of Analysis	Projected Annual Percentage Change		
		Historical analysis	Projection		G.N.P.	Labour productivity	Labour force
1. Gehrig–Kuhlo [5, 12]	1963	1925–38 1950–61	1962–70	Simultaneous equation model consisting of functions for production, private consumption and investment – time series	4·7	5·7	−0·9
2. Federal Ministry of Economics [1]	1968	1950–67	1968 80	Functional breakdown into labour force and labour productivity and into capital stock and capital productivity – time series	3·8–4·8	3·9–4·5	0·0–0·2
3. Economic Commission for Europe (E.C.E.) [3]	1969	1953–67	1965/7–80	Industrial breakdown with special emphasis to the relation between per capita income and manufacturing growth and the elasticities of other sectors against manufacturing growth – cross-country data and time series	4·6	3·3–3·4	1·2ᵃ–1·1ᵃ
4. Prognos [14]	1969	1958–66	1965–85	Breakdown according to national accounts categories – time series	4·4	4·3	0·1
5. O.E.C.D. [13]	1970	1955–68	1970–80	Functional breakdown into labour force and labour productivity and industrial breakdown – time series	4·6	4·4	0·2
6. Schatz [15]	1971	1950–68	1970–80	Breakdown into investment ratio, investment structure, labour force, and marginal capital/output ratio – cross-country data	4·6	—	—
7. Federal Ministry of Economics [2]	1971	1950–70	1970–85	Same as in projection no. 2, supplemented by production functions of the Cobb–Douglas type – time series	4·8	4·5	0·4
8. Görzig [7]	1972	1954–69	1970–80	Functional and industrial breakdown. Consistency test in respect to the capital and labour requirements of projection no. 7 – time series	5·3	4·6	0·7

ᵃ Change in labour 'demand'.

extrapolations applied in the E.C.E. study. As to the level of overall demand, one would have to make alternative assumptions about the future exchange rate policy in relation to wage pressure and to relative price level increases, i.e. assumptions about the real rate of exchange. The structure of demand, which changes due to rising per capita income, innovations, and trade structure shifts, could be pre-estimated by econometric methods. A recent study for the West German economy which is based on the analysis of inter-country and over-time development patterns has lead to encouraging results [4]. Given the level and the structure of demand, a bridge has to be constructed from output growth to productivity growth, a field in which Verdoorn has done pioneering work [17]. Along these methodological lines a growth model is going to be worked out in the Institute of World Economics.

The exogenous variables which have to be forecasted in a demand oriented model are other than those in a supply oriented model but, in principle, there arise the same methodological difficulties as in the forecasts enumerated in Table 12.1. The method of forecasting there applied can be labelled as intuitive extrapolation: the past trends were extrapolated into the future somewhat mechanically, but after having taken into account certain expected tendencies which deviate from past tendencies. These adjustments are based partly on information about more or less firm commitments on future behaviour and partly on qualitative judgements on the main forces or impediments of the growth process. An example is the expectation that, due to a drastic shift in favour of more public investment, the marginal productivity of total investment and total capital is going to decrease more than is indicated by the trend of the past. The task of the forecaster is to transform rather vague information or widely held expectations into quantitative predictions of the exogenous variables, a process which can hardly be checked by other persons. Therefore, there is plenty of scope for mixing positive judgements with value judgements. The danger of subjectivity is greater the less competition exists between the forecasters and the more forecasters are associated with the organisation which follows up particular aims. There is only one case in which the lack of objectivity is unimportant, i.e. if the prediction is supplied by the government and accepted by the relevant authorities as a target projection, the value judgements become a part of a political target function.

In order to discuss the specific characteristics of the projections it is advisable to subdivide the eight attempts according to three different techniques of analysis:

    (i) The Gehrig–Kuhlo approach is based on time series estimation of a simultaneous equation model.

(ii) The approach of the Federal Ministry, Prognos and the O.E.C.D. is also based on time series but the technique of analysis is essentially a non-econometric one.

(iii) The projections presented by the E.C.E. and Schatz are based, at least partly, on an inter-country analysis.

Difficult to classify is the Görzig projection because it is based on time series and uses econometric techniques but does not apply a simultaneous equation model. As it can be regarded as a supplement to the Federal Ministry projection, it is considered with that.

The Gehrig–Kuhlo approach

A first attempt to project economic growth in West Germany by econometric methods was published by Kuhlo [12] and Gehrig [5] in 1962. On the basis of historical data covering the periods 1925–38 and 1950–61, Kuhlo estimated production functions of the Cobb–Douglas–Tinbergen type. Gehrig supplemented this supply model by adding a private consumption and an investment function and re-estimated the equations of the model simultaneously. The predictions of the model are classified as projections, in contrast to prognosis or forecasts, because the authors excluded the forecasts of the exogenous variables, i.e. *inter alia* labour supply, imports and technical progress, from their own analysis, and refer to intuitive forecasts of these variables provided by Hahn [8]. Although the model includes demand elements in form of the consumption and investment function it leads only to a projection of potential production because a full use of capacities is always assumed. Recently the authors published *ex post* projections of their model for the period 1963–9 [6]. If the actual values of the exogenous variables are employed, the projection errors proved to be tolerable, which may partly result from the fact that all variables are trend-affected; the projection errors were the least with respect to potential output (0·6 per cent for the whole period) and the greatest with respect to investment (4·9 per cent). However, the exogenous variables which were used in 1962 could not have been forecasted very exactly, so that the rather satisfactory performance of the model with respect to the endogenous variables could not be brought to bear. This econometric attempt gives evidence of how stable some structural relations have been over time. Yet it leaves the forecasting problem virtually unsolved. This may be the reason why the econometric approach on the basis of time series has hardly appealed to other forecasters.

The non-econometric time series approaches

In the four essentially non-econometric projections nearly all variables are forecasted exogenously. Regression analysis is sometimes used in order to supplement the intuitive forecast or to calculate elasticities of sectoral growth with respect to overall growth. The intuitive forecasts are checked both by plausibility considerations as well as by a consistency test in terms of national accounts.

Figure 12.1 gives estimates of the development of the main growth components according to the governmental projection which seems to play the rôle of a parent projection with respect to the Prognos – and O.E.C.D. – projections as well as with respect to the Görzig projection. This can be concluded from the observation that all four projections imply nearly the same growth rate of labour productivity. And, indeed, the trend of labour productivity has proved to be rather stable, not only in the case of West Germany but also in the case of other countries [10]. Figure 12.1 shows that growth rates of labour productivity of about 4·5 per cent fall nearly together with the actual trend of this variable since 1955. At that time the phase of extensive growth passes into the phase of intensive growth, in which the increasing scarcity of labour became an important incentive for the adoption and development of labour-saving techniques. This labour-saving process is reflected in an increase of the overall capital/output ratio (which can be interpreted as the relation between labour productivity and capital intensity) from 3·4 in 1955 to 3·7 in 1970; in the governmental projection a further increase to 4·0 before 1985 is implied.

The later the projections originate the higher the rate of growth of labour force is pre-estimated. Before 1971, no (or very slight) increase of labour supply was expected for the seventies. During the boom of 1969 and 1970 the West German economy experienced an influx of foreign workers, which was unexpected in its actual magnitude. As a result, forecasters revised their predictions about labour force growth in the upward direction. Comparing the growth rates now expected with those expected before, one has, in addition, to take into account the employment effect of the educational programme which was announced in 1971. According to government estimations, through intensified education 600,000 employees are going to keep aloof from immediately productive employment until 1985. The negative employment effects are expected to be offset by additional foreign workers so that the physical capacities which will be created can be used optimally.

The Görzig projection does not have, as mentioned above, the character of an autonomous forecast of growth but of a consistency test of the governmental projection with regard to the implied factor requirements. Thus, from 1970 to 1980 Görzig's G.N.P. growth rate equals that implied in the governmental projection. For each sector

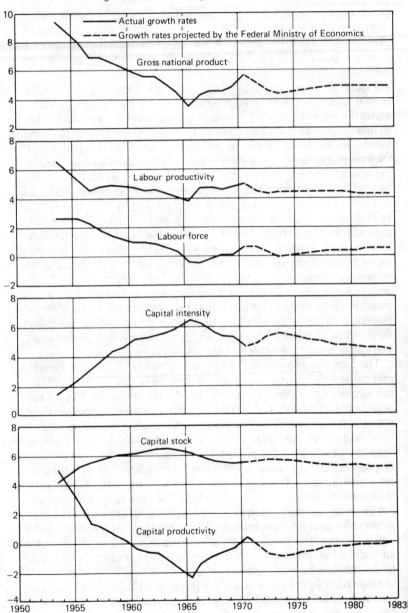

Fig. 12.1 Growth of Output and its Main Components

potential output growth is broken down into labour requirement, capital intensity, a component reflecting the productivity effects of changes in the inter-sectoral factor allocation, and a residual component representing technological progress. In combination with an independent forecast of inter-sectoral output mix, these variables were extrapolated in an iterative process in order to determine labour and investment requirements of the economy which grows along the lines projected by the government. The result of this test is that both the investment requirements as well as the demand for labour will be higher than the governmental projection assumes, if the economy is to be running with a growth rate of 5·3 per cent in the seventies.

The inter-country approach

In contrast to all other projections those worked out by the E.C.E. and Schatz use inter-country regressions. The E.C.E. study refers to inter-country data in order to estimate elasticities between manufacturing growth rates and income per capita, between manufacturing growth rates and other sectoral growth rates, and between output growth rates and productivity growth rates. The elasticities computed by this method, representing a kind of common international pattern, are then, by intuitive compromise, combined with elasticities derived from national time series in order to find out growth rates and elasticities which are employed for extrapolation.

The Schatz study is in its analytical part based on cross-country regressions alone and deals mainly with the rôle of the investment ratios in the growth process. According to this analysis, the investment ratio has proved to be an important determinant of output growth in the past. From a sample covering fifteen industrialised western countries it follows that 74 per cent of the variations in net output can be explained by variations in the net investment ratio. Applied to the case of West Germany the explanation range of the net investment ratio for the period 1950–68 covered even more than 90 per cent of growth rates variations. The inter-country analysis was extended to additional growth components like investment structure, incremental capital/output ratio, growth of labour force, and trade union behaviour from which only the investment structure, i.e. the relation between investment in the secondary sector to other investments, seems to have a significant influence on the output growth rate. The prediction of future growth is derived from an intuitive assessment of the investment ratio and the incremental capital/output ratio.

One might be inclined to venture somewhat more with a cross-country analysis. In principle, such an analysis of growth rates and its

K

components like investment ratio, capital/output ratio, etc., seems to promise not only insights into the interactions of variables of the past but also information about how an economy is going to run in the future. There exist inter-country differences in the stage of development, measured, for instance, by income per capita, which might be associated with different constellations of growth components. If the constellations vary with the per capita income in a regular way – this may be found from a cross-country analysis – one could, under certain conditions [11], predict the development of growth components under the preliminary assumption that per capita income grows at a given rate. After transforming the predicted change in growth components into a predicted change in output – in the next step – one has to check the predicted growth rate of output against the originally assumed growth rate in order to adjust both to each other in a process of iteration.

A projection along these lines requires a careful analysis of possible future information which can be obtained from countries which have already reached a higher development level. In the case of West Germany, by per capita income standards, these are the United States, Canada, Sweden and perhaps Switzerland. This admittedly small sample for general analysis purposes has to be extended also to countries with a lower development level than West Germany. For instance, one should try to find out how the investment ratio or the capital/output ratio behaves if per capita income goes up. As to the behaviour of the investment ratio, Sommers and Suits [16] have recently published results which seem to indicate that, from a certain development level on, it becomes a decreasing function of per capita income. Similar analyses are needed for other components.

III. FINAL COMMENTS

After having discussed the several attempts at growth projection, one might inquire about the relative merits of the different projections. But in the field of forecasting there are no objective *ex ante* criteria of what is wrong or right or good or bad. The only objective criterion to assess the quality of a projection is an *ex post* test of whether it approximates the actual development. Economists can improve the techniques of forecasting by exhausting all possibilities of positive science which seem to lead to information relevant for the future. In the case of West Germany especially this means to work out a demand oriented projection, which seems to be an alternative to the supply oriented ones already available, and to intensify the analysis of cross-country regularities.

REFERENCES

[1] Der Bundesminister für Wirtschaft, 'Perspektiven des Wirtschaftswachstums in der BRD bis zum Jahre 1980', *Die wirtschaftliche Lage in der BRD*, III (Bonn, 1968).

[2] Der Bundesminister für Wirtschaft, 'Perspektiven des Wirtschaftswachstums in der BRD bis zum Jahre 1985', *Die wirtschaftliche Lage in der Bundesrepublik* Vierteljahresbericht III (Bonn, 1970). In addition, unpublished background papers containing detailed information about assumptions.

[3] Economic Commission for Europe, *Structural Trends and Prospects in the European Economy, Economic Survey of Europe in 1969*, I (New York, 1970).

[4] G. Fels, K.-W. Schatz and F. Wolter, *Der Zusammenhang zwischen Produktionsstruktur und Entwicklungsniveau, Versuch einer Strukturprognose für die westdeutsche Wirtschaft*, Weltwirtschaftliches Archiv, band 106 (1971) heft 2.

[5] G. Gehrig, *Ein makroökonomisches Modell für die Bundesrepublik Deutschland*, Schriftenreihe des Ifo-Instituts für Wirtschaftsforschung, no. 56 (Berlin–Munich, 1963).

[6] G. Gehrig and K. C. Kuhlo, *Überprüfung der ökonometrischene Projektion von 1962*, Ifo-Studien, 18. Jgg. (1972) heft 2.

[7] B. Görzig, *Die Entwicklung des Wachstumspotentials in den Wirtschaftsbereichen der Bundesrepublik Deutschland, Analyse und Projektion bis 1980, Beiträge zur Strukturforschung* (Berlin, 1972) heft 18.

[8] H. Hahn, *Vorausschätzung des Bruttosozialprodukts bis 1975* (Munich, 1961).

[9] T. P. Hill, 'Growth and Investment According to International Comparisons', *Economic Journal* (June 1964) pp. 287–304.

[10] J. W. Kendrick, *National Productivity and its Long-Term Projection. Long-Range Economic Projection. A Report of the National Bureau of Economic Research* (New York–Princeton, 1954) Studies in Income and Wealth, vol. 16, pp. 98, 67.

[11] E. Kuh, 'The Validity of Cross-Sectionally Estimated Behavior Equations in Time Series Applications', *Econometrica* 27 (1959) pp. 197–214.

[12] K. C. Kuhlo, *Die Wachstumsprognose, insbesondere auch die Prognose der Produktivitätsentwicklung*, Schriften des Vereins für Socialpolitik, band 25, N.F. (Berlin, 1962) p. 258.

[13] O.E.C.D., *The Growth of Output 1960–1980* (Paris, 1970).

[14] 'Prognos', report no. 3, *Westeuropa 1985*.

[15] K.-W. Schatz, 'Wachstumsbedingungen in der Bundesrepublik Deutschland im internationalen Vergleich', *Die Weltwirtschaft*, heft 1 (1971) pp. 202, 215.

[16] P. M. Sommers and D. B. Suits, 'A Cross-Section Model of Economic Growth', *The Review of Economics and Statistics* (1971) pp. 121–8.

[17] P. J. Verdoorn, 'Complementarity and Long-Range Projections', *Econometrica* (1956) pp. 428–50.

Discussion of the Paper by Dr Fels

Professor Majminas (U.S.S.R.), in introducing the paper, said that Professor Fels had rightly begun from the history of the concept of growth which for a long time was regarded not as an objective of economic policy but as something given. It was now generally agreed that G.N.P. growth should be regarded not as an aim or phenomenon in itself but as a means to achieve other goals. This methodological view of G.N.P. growth as a means and as one component in economic policy as a whole was of great interest and significance.

The paper was concerned also with the development of methods of long-term forecasting of economic growth, the most common way being that of extrapolation of certain trends with various corrections introduced intuitively. Dr Fels had pointed out that hitherto all models for long-term growth forecasting had been concerned primarily with inputs – capital investments, labour resources, and so on – while assuming that output was produced in some way or another. This assumption was not always valid, and Dr Fels was right in pointing out that output analysis was no less important, especially for an open economy with high dependence on exports. This was an interesting theoretical point which provided some guidance for further development of forecasting models. He himself would also consider collective consumption (education, health service, other fields of social policy) to be a no less exogenous factor. Thus he would suggest that consumption should be extended to include all social needs and social consumption as an exogenous factor; the question was how this could be done. It seemed to involve greater attention to international trade and to international and interregional analysis, which would go beyond national limits, and to include studies in the fields of national interest, national aims and goals, and their formation.

Reviewing models of economic growth forecasting, Dr Fels had divided them into two categories, one being that of 'traditionalist' extrapolation models, and the other – that of the Economic Commission for Europe – being based on international comparisons, a series of still pictures for several countries simultaneously instead of a motion picture for just one of them. He agreed with Dr Fels that future development of forecasting needed to merge these two approaches, which would be of even greater interest in that a more developed country was to a certain extent a model for the future of a less developed country.

One of the most challenging problems was how to model future structural changes and explosions. Dr Fels had pointed out that models were good at forecasting productivity of labour, but were rather ambiguous as to demand for specific types of labour. In cases when factors involved were not scarce (for example the supply of foreign workers), it might be possible to forecast the growth of an economy. But under conditions of scarcity for one or more factors structural shifts might powerfully influence the resulting parameters.

Professor Majminas thought that the usual practice of some people building models, others collecting information, and still others applying this information to the models was not likely to produce the desired result. It was also the case that forecasters bore a heavy social responsibility, for state policy to a significant degree depended on their forecasts. This brought one to the problem of combining different methods and different techniques in the process of planning and forecasting.

They in the U.S.S.R. had to pay close attention to these problems, and they did not think of long-term forecasting apart from the planning system. To them long-term forecasting was simply a preliminary stage which should make use of formal models such as economic growth models or dynamic inter-sectoral balance models which were useful for a period of up to five to seven years, but worked poorly for a period longer than about fifteen years, precisely because they were unable to foresee the magnitudes of structural changes. To compensate for this, various heuristic and expert evaluation methods had to be used in parallel with the modelling, though their mutual compatibility was very far from being clear.

When all this had been done, the next stage was to formulate a hierarchy of national goals and to identify the major trends in economic development, leading up to the formulation of long-term national programmes aimed at the maximisation of one or several social objectives of the state. It seemed obvious that because of the many uncertainties, long-term planning could only be adaptive in character.

It seemed clear that certain volumes for groups of products could be estimated, these products being essential for the growth of the economy during the planned period, whatever methods of production of these products might be adopted. If this could somehow have been done, target resource programmes could be compiled and co-ordinated into a single plan not only for the whole of the period but for the specific shorter periods as well.

Mr Vangrevelinghe (France) said that Dr Fels emphasised one point of great importance. It was related to long-term projections for an open economy, especially with regard to consumption as well as production. It was clear that national sources of production could easily be replaced by imports, either of capital or manpower. This created an entirely new problem for nearly all western economies. The foreign demand was itself affected by other factors, such as competitiveness and rates of exchange. It appeared that governments had now to be more prepared to make necessary internal adjustments to stimulate foreign demand. At the same time authorities seemed to be reluctant to dampen down inflation by slowing economic growth. It might be asked whether it was true that actions taken to combat inflation by slowing down the economy were having the consequence of making the rate of long-term growth less than might have been expected, especially when one considered the rates of growth of France and in Germany.

Professor Denison (U.S.A.) commented that if indeed the availability of labour and capital from abroad was as unlimited as Dr Fels seemed to suggest, then projections became almost impossible. It seemed to him that the situation was similar to projecting the output of a country where future boundaries were completely unknown, for example, if one had tried in 1942 to project German output for 1973. This was not true, however, if the output measure was domestic product or net domestic product. The term used in the paper was G.N.P. Professor Denison's question was whose output was being projected?

If in fact it was that of the German people, then a reasonable measure of national income or G.N.P. would exclude the earnings of foreign workers and make adjustment for earnings and capital that came in and went out, in which case the problems might not wholly disappear but would become much more limited.

His second question concerned a suggestion that one might make long-term projections from a demand side. It was difficult to understand the postulated conditions, since if the resources were indeed unlimited and if one did interpret domestic product as a geographic area product, then as a result one could get all the demand and all the supply one might want. There must be some limitation to the output which is to be included. His question was how was this to be determined.

Professor Maier (G.D.R.) wanted to know what socio-economic goals Dr Fels considered to be especially important for long-term planning and what their influence might be upon economic growth in terms of accelerating it or slowing it down.

Dr Shibanov (U.S.S.R.) had the impression that Dr Fels underestimated such factors as labour and capital supply. Did he consider the possibility of their exercising a restrictive influence upon the growth of F.R.G. economy at some stage? And secondly, did Dr Fels believe that the inflow of foreign labour would remain almost guaranteed in the future? There had been some criticism in the F.R.G. in recent years of the importation of substantial amounts of foreign labour instead of developing production in the areas of excess labour. He was anxious also to know whether Dr Fels assumed that future West German participation in the international division of labour would continue along the same lines and rates as at present, or was the F.R.G. interested in some kind of stabilisation and control? Finally did Dr Fels believe that there was a possibility of a shift in the F.R.G. from the present capital-intensive form of growth to another capital-saving form?

Professor Fritsch (Switzerland) said that forecasting for an open economy was very difficult if not wholly impossible, and in the case of Germany one saw that, as a result of the close interconnections between the national economy and external economies, a shift had been occurring from the use of women's labour to the use of foreign labour and finally to the use of foreign production facilities. Similar changes could be observed in Switzerland. He was anxious to know how far one could anticipate these developments and whether they were taken into account in Dr Fel's analysis.

Professor Porwit (Poland) said that Dr Fels had suggested that in the future it would be sensible to approach forecasting from the demand side. Would it be possible in such a case to switch from large aggregations that proved rather difficult to handle to disaggregated parameters, and if so how?

Professor Robinson (U.K.) was interested in the problem of forecasting for a quasi-open economy. He thought it was increasingly doubtful for what areas it would be practicable in the future to do the same sort of programming and forecasting which we had been doing in the past. Inside particular countries fairly good forecasts for a country as a whole were possible. But when one started forecasting for any region, one had to make assumptions about transfers of regional resources, with a resulting accumulation of all sorts of difficulties and uncertainties. Just before coming to this conference he had been discussing whether the time had not come to stop doing United Kingdom forecasts and to begin doing European forecasts, because he believed it would be very much more practicable in the future to try to predict Europe, as a more nearly closed economy, and to foresee the shares of particular regions and countries inside Europe as a total, rather than to make individual forecasts for parts of Europe. He believed that this was the true implication of much that had been said in Dr Fels's paper.

Professor Marczewski (France) agreed that it was now unavoidable, in the present state of development of international trade, to make, if not plans, then at least forecasts on European and even world levels. They were as a matter of fact to some extent doing this in France in the G.P.I. institute, which was working on a model for a medium-term forecast. This model was designed for a world comprised of twenty regional groups. The aim was to forecast international trade as well as economic growth of each region and for eighteen main sectors of the economy. This model had already been used for ten years with some improvements introduced each year.

Professor von Weizsäcker (F.R.G.) said that he had been involved in forecasting manpower requirements for highly trained manpower. This had also been done in other European countries, for example in England, in such a way that identical studies could be made for Europe as a whole. But on further investigation it had turned out that migration of highly qualified manpower, apart from certain countries like Switzerland, was not very substantial, although there was substantial migration of manpower with lower qualifications. They had come to the conclusion that it was premature to attempt a European forecast. But this introduced one kind of limitation on German growth. Obviously, another limiting factor was land, which was reflected in land prices in Germany.

Professor Khachaturov (U.S.S.R.) said that long-term forecasts could be verified by comparing forecasted with actually achieved parameters. Had such comparisons already been made for some of the parameters dealt with in Dr Fels's paper?

Dr Fels, replying to the discussion, said that strictly speaking his paper did not deal with economic planning but with forecasting. That was why many topics touched upon could not be dealt with substantially, and it might be a reason why his paper raised more questions than it answered. He wanted to stress that he had not attempted to determine what might be a desirable policy with regard to international migration or national objectives. Professor Majminas had pointed out that growth was not an end in itself. With that he had no point of disagreement. With regard to structural shifts influencing structural parameters and making forecasting more difficult, he had tried to exclude one such shift due to the influx of foreign workers. Of course, one could not exclude all structural changes, and one had to be aware that they would appear in the future as a permanent source of instability and uncertainty in forecasting.

Professor Majminas had also suggested that consumption should be considered exogenously and should at the same time be included in the prediction. It was indeed exogenous in a very limited sense. Exogenous implied that the government must manage this demand by exchange rate policy as well as by government expenditures, and that the government must determine the structure of demand which will be equivalent to both domestic and foreign resources. Of course, this needed to be taken into account in a projection.

He did not think that a demand oriented approach to an open economy of the West German type was easier to handle than a traditional supply oriented approach, but he did think that the first was more relevant to the problem under discussion and therefore one had to think along these lines. In regard to its use, he thought that a government should first be asked to indicate its intentions regarding exchange rate and demand policies, so as to obtain the exogenous information on which a forecast had to be based.

He thought that in the future the export of services, which was much more like the export of jobs than the export of commodities, would also depend on the real rate of exchange which measured the efficiency of the West German economy in the international environment.

His feeling was that the recession of 1967 had only a short-term depressing effect on growth. What happened in 1967 was a reorganisation of the productive process combined with structural changes, with high productivity increases between 1968 and 1970 as a result of that reorganisation. Thus he did not think that the government anti-inflation policy had any medium- or long-term depressing effects on the West German economy. Moreover, efforts to damp down inflation had always been initiated at the domestic level and employed domestic means, and that had had the effect that the terms of trade and the position of the foreign sector vis-à-vis the domestic sector was improved. The foreign sector was not affected by the anti-inflationary measures and could get a better supply of labour and capital and sell at more favourable prices because of over-supply in the domestic sector. Thus there had been a kind of re-structuring because the domestic sector was as a consequence of this not greatly affected by anti-inflation policy and in fact ran into various bottlenecks, in education, in services, and in the private sector.

To turn to the question of whose output was being projected, he would say the output of the region regarded as a unit of government decision, whether it was for the planning of education or for all types of public planning that this projection was to be used. He would also say that the demand–supply reversal had a certain, but limited application. Among the factors limiting supply even in an open economy such as the West German were, first, the availability of skilled labour (which was not available in the countries of labour emigration). Second was the scarcity of environment and land which in the future was likely to be one of the major bottlenecks. And third was that the integration of foreign workers into the West German society would be a barrier to unlimited growth of the West German economy. Till now there had been only minor tensions, but he thought that in future tensions would increase and labour would have to consider this constraint more than it did in the past.

There were, of course, other social objectives besides the environmental problem which would be affected by economic growth. The main industries in Germany, such as the chemical industry, would be affected in the future by the emphasis on the environment and by the fact that extension of the resources hitherto exploited would become impossible.

He thought that the introduction of foreign workers had not accelerated structural changes in West German economy with respect to the needs of less developed and semi-developed countries. The cheap supply of low-skilled workers had provided opportunities for labour-intensive activities such as leather, textiles, clothing, shoes and the like. In other highly developed countries, in Sweden for example, these industries were already among those declining, but they retained a significant share in West German output, mainly as a result of the availability of cheap foreign workers. If these were not allowed to come, the West German economy would have had to undergo greater structural changes, particularly in the light of the export needs of cheap labour countries, including the East European countries. That was part of the international division of labour.

At the moment they had relatively high wages and scarce labour with resulting emphasis on technological progress. Dr Fels did not believe this could be reversed in the direction of capital-saving, as suggested by Professor Shibanov, but he would admit that labour-saving technological progress would have been faster if it were not for the supply of workers from South Europe. At the same time, the wage level would have been higher without this labour supply. As far as wages in different countries were concerned, there would remain a tendency for labour to move to the north of Europe, whatever might be conditions in other countries.

In principle he agreed with Professor Robinson when he suggested that the West German economy should be forecasted as part of a European region. Yet there were some points of difficulty. In a national projection one had to take into account a parameter which was not present in the regional forecasting, the exchange rate. At the same time social relations between workers of different nationalities could be taken into account in national projections. Thus regional projections had some essential differences from national projections.

K*

13   A Macro-programming Model for the Finnish Economy[1]

R. Hjerppe

I. INTRODUCTION

In this paper some of the experience gained in the construction of an input–output programming model for the Finnish economy will be discussed. The target in the construction of the model was to examine whether at this stage of the collection of data and of developing computing facilities an empirical allocation model could be constructed which would be useful for planning purposes in an economy such as Finland's.

Quite a lot of work has been done in some countries to develop linear programming models for planning purposes. Some of these studies are well-known and documented in the economic literature.[2] No attempts have so far been made in Finland to make use of this kind of approach to planning problems.

I shall first describe the structure of the experimental model and discuss the problems which can be studied with such a model. Then some of the results gained so far will be reviewed. As experiments with the model are still going on, some conclusions for further development of the model are suggested. Finally I shall try to set the model in the wider context of the problems of social planning which can be seen to be relevant at the moment in a society mixed with an economy such as Finland's.

II. SOME SPECIAL FEATURES OF THE FINNISH ECONOMY

In order to provide some orientation to the environment to which the model is to be applied, may I draw attention to certain special features of the Finnish economy.[3] Traditionally the overwhelming share of Finnish exports has consisted of timber, timber products,

[1] The author wishes to thank Professors Jouko Paunio and Olavi Wiitamo for encouragement in writing this paper. Thanks are also due to Dr Rex Wade for reading and criticising a first draft.
[2] Some of these are studies by Chenery and Kretschmer [4], Sandee [14], and Bruno [2], [3]. (For references see pp. 297–8.)
[3] A recent review of these aspects can be found in a document prepared by the Economic Planning Centre [16].

pulp and paper. The growth of the whole economy has very much relied on these products. On the other hand Finland has traditionally had a relatively large agricultural sector. But due to an increase in productivity, a very large part of the labour in agriculture has become redundant since the Second World War. There have been continuous problems to get this surplus labour employed in other industries. During the past decade gross capital formation has been relatively high, nearly 30 per cent of G.D.P. This has not been, however, sufficient to achieve such a structural change that we could manage to avoid unemployment and balance of payments problems. If we add the existence of regional problems, there is a strong desire to secure better allocation of resources in order to make such structural changes that these various problems can be solved or at least mitigated in the future.

With that background, we think there are convincing needs to consider methods which can improve the planning of the structural economic policy.

III. THE MODEL

We have chosen as our problem that of maximising the level of private consumption at some date T subject to constraints describing the structure of the economy.[1] This and certain related approaches have been adopted also in certain other recent experiments to develop economy-wide programming models. I shall try to justify this approach from our point of view in the next section. But before that I shall describe the formal structure of the model:

Thirty-four production branches or industries have been selected for the empirical model. The endogenous variables of the model consist of thirty-four production variables of these industries, thirty-three export variables, thirty-three import variables divided between competitive and complementary imports, gross capital formation by branches and private consumption. Public consumption, labour divided in two categories, and the aggregate existing capital stock were selected as exogenous variables.

The constraints of the model are the following. First we have the product flow constraints:

$$(I - A)X - B - E - C + M \geqslant G \tag{1}$$

where $(I - A)$ is a Leontief matrix (A is a flow–input coefficient

---

[1] In practice we selected 1970 as a target year in the experiments because we could compare the results with the actual figures. The starting point was 1965. All the variables in the experiment are for 1970, and no time paths will be available because of the static model.

matrix of an input–output system. These coefficients include the unit inputs from domestic products and competitive imports).

X = vector of domestic supply
B = industry-by-industry gross capital formation matrix
E = matrix where exports by industries are on the main diagonal, other elements equal zero
M = matrix where competitive imports by industries are on the main diagonal, other elements equal zero
G = vector of public consumption.

In equality from there are thirty-four product-flow constraints. The labour force has been divided into two categories in order to separate various skill or education levels. In the first category wage earners and agricultural labourers are included, and salary earners in the second. The second category represents the more educated labour force. We have the following constraints for this labour.

$$WX \leqslant L \tag{2}$$

where W is (2×34) matrix of labour coefficients and L is (2×1) vector of available force.

In the model we wanted to take into account also the already existing capital stock because that was thought to be an important factor when structural changes are considered in an economy over a medium-term time period (five to ten years). Therefore, the following constraint for the existing capital stock was introduced

$$\sum_j k_j x_j \leqslant K \tag{3}$$

where k_j is the capital used per one unit of product j. K is the amount of existing capital stock. This as well as all other exogenous variables had to be predicted for the time period T where the programme is aimed.

In addition there is a constraint for the foreign trade

$$\sum_j m_j^{mc} + \sum_j m_j^c - \sum_j e_j \leqslant D \tag{4}$$

where m_j^{mc} is non-competitive imports to industry j, m_j^c is competitive imports to industry j, and e_j is exports of products of industry j. D is a predetermined constant for a target value of balance of current payments. This is a kind of target variable which is exogenously given constant in various experiments.

All endogenous variables were in addition constrained to be non-negative. These were the constraints of the first and basic version of the experiments which were carried out with the model. The two other versions experimented with the following additional constraints. To the second version the following constraints were added:

$$x_j \leqslant (1-M).\bar{X}_j \qquad (5)$$

where M is the proportion of the capital stock depreciated during the plan period and $\bar{X}_j$ is the value of x_j at the base year (1965).

In the third version, in addition to the constraints of the second version, the following limits were put:

$$e_j \leqslant E_j, j = 1, 2, \ldots\ldots, n \qquad (6)$$

where E_j is the estimated maximum of the exports from industry j in the target year. The reasons for different types of limitations will be explained in the next section.

In a finite horizon problem it is well known that one also should pay some attention to the further growth of the economy. This is guaranteed through capital formation activities. Therefore, we had to decide how to incorporate gross capital formation into the model.

To make gross capital formation endogenous we introduced a simple assumption

$$B = F(X)$$

and the form of the function was specified as linear.

The investment output matrix of industry by industry was formed and if we call this matrix K then the relationship is

$$B = KX \qquad (7)$$

The theoretical justification for this type of relationship is that X represents the possibilities for financing the investments and in the medium term this relationship is reasonably good to indicate where investments should be directed.

IV. JUSTIFICATION OF THIS SPECIFICATION OF THE MODEL

To select consumption as a variable the value of which is to be maximised is tantamount to assuming a utility function

$$U = U(C)$$

for the economy. Here U is the utility level and C is consumption. This is in line with the traditional thinking of economists. Recent optimal growth theories in particular have used this assumption (see for example [11]). Incorporated into this approach is the assumption that the welfare of the society is a function of its consumption level. This starting point has been very much criticised recently but its use is based on the idea that consumption is still the most essential element in the welfare analysis. We selected the level of private consumption as the variable to be maximised. This starting point can be used also because of its simplicity. Nevertheless, the clear limitation of this simple approach from the welfare point of view should be remembered. I think, however, that the fully satisfactory allocation model should take into account a broader view of the targets of the society rather than simply considering the level of consumption in the way it is measured today in the national accounts. Some of these aspects will be discussed more in Sections VI and VII below.

When deciding on the constraints (1) above, the analysis was started from the assumption that the reallocation of resources can mainly happen through substituting domestic production for competitive imports or vice vera. Therefore, the imports were divided into competitive and complementary. The latter were assumed to be a linear function of the total production of the corresponding industry and there were no substitution possibilities for this. This is of course a simplification. Not all complementary imports are of a kind which could not be produced domestically.

From the approach selected it followed that the input–output coefficients were defined to include both domestic production and competitive import input. The substitution possibilities between these two were free, in other words the competitive imports could be wholly substituted for domestic production or vice versa. In constraints (2) the labour was divided into two categories. For the first there were included the less educated labour force: wage earners and farmers and farm workers. In Finland the latter make up a large labour input. In the second category in principle the more educated labour was included. The operational delineation of these labour groups is, however, in some cases somewhat questionable.

Constraints (3) and (5) take into account the existing capital stock and the speed by which it can be reallocated. When considering structural change this is a factor which should be taken into account. Constraints (5) mean that the production of a certain industry can be reduced at most as fast as the capital stock of that industry is depreciated. This estimate, we think, somewhat exaggerates the possibilities of change because the depreciation estimates were based on the depreciation for business purposes and therefore in some cases the capital equipment fully depreciated can still have some productive capacity left.

The data for the model was derived mainly from the input–output study for the Finnish economy for the year 1965 [7]. The estimates of capital are based mainly on fire insurance values in the annual industrial statistics [6]. These figures were augmented by un-published estimates prepared by Mr Pertii Kohi and myself.

We might present some arguments for a static model because there has been great effort recently to put macro-economic programming work into dynamic terms. First there is simplicity: it is usually simpler to start with a static model. The second reason is compre-hensiveness. When a model with many sectors is constructed as a dynamic one it easily becomes quite extensive, it is difficult to inter-pret, and there is of course much room for undetected errors. Third, given the data problems, it might be that even a static model can give useful information about the functioning of the economy. Fourth, and perhaps most important, is the fact that it is difficult quantitatively to forecast technological change and its effects for input–output coefficients if the model is even medium-sized. The co-efficients may, however, as some evidence has indicated, be reason-ably stable over five years or so, but over that period it is perhaps more valuable to use only quite heavily aggregated models.

Finally, one important justification for the selected approach should not be overlooked. There has been quite well known and very remarkable advancement in the practical computing techniques in carrying out economic analyses, which even though probably known earlier have become practical only with the development of the computing facilities. I think it is worthwhile to consider how to use these possibilities in order to advance theoretical and practical economic science. In fact, at the moment there are possibilities of empirically operating various types of optimisation problems which thus far have been carried out only theoretically for the most part. There are, however, well known problems in the smooth neo-classical non-convex-type problems, but if assumed economic relationships are linearised there are convenient computing facilities available. It has to be remembered that this capacity is available only at the cost of losing some realistic relationships, since the world obviously is not completely linear.[1]

V. NUMERICAL RESULTS

The numerical experiments were planned to give the variables for 1970, the base year being 1965. We think that a period of approxi-mately five years best suits this type of model. It can be thought that this model will serve as a macro-stage model, if we consider a plan setting of a Tinbergenian stages-type.[2]

[1] There is a very interesting study by Baumol and Bushnell [1] about the possible dangers in the linearisation.
[2] Tinbergen [18], pp. 88–9.

To carry out the programme for 1970 required the forecasts for the exogenous variables. These were made principally by using past experiences about the behaviour of the exogenous variables. The labour for 1970 was measured in 'efficiency' units (actual labour input times the estimated change in the productivity).[1] To estimate the amount of efficient labour, the productivity of labour was assumed to develop as in the last ten years. The balance of current payments variable is a kind of policy target variable, and it was in basic alternatives required to be zero. (The current payments were required to be in balance.)

The first experiments were carried on three basic alternatives.

(1) There were no restrictions for the movements of capital and labour between industries (or branches) and no limitations for the export markets. In other words, in the most simple version it was assumed that the foreign markets could absorb all the amounts supplied of various products on the same terms. This could mean that the country in question is so small a supplier in the world market that its supply does not affect the price of the product. In the case of most Finnish export products this is fairly close to the actual case. There are only some products, mainly pulp and paper products, where there might be a noticeable effect on the world market if the supply were to increase by a large amount.

(2) It was more realistic to put limitations to the movements of the existing capital between industries. Therefore in the second version there was a limit put on the movement of capital from an industry. It was assumed that the stock of capital in a sector could be reduced only by depreciation. That factor limits also the movement of production downwards. The cumulated five-year depreciation was the maximum for consumption of capital in an industry. In this version there were no limitations for the expansion of exports.

(3) It is not especially realistic to expect linear export functions to remain unchanged no matter what the amount of supply. Therefore, in the third version limits were added for the export expansion in addition to the constraints of the second version.

We think it is at least theoretically interesting to go through all those alternatives and compare the achieved results. It was hoped to get some insight on the efficiency of different industries and the functioning of the economy by this procedure.

The result to be achieved by the first alternative is theoretically interesting in the following way. We could consider the level of consumption achieved in this version, compared to the level of actual consumption, as a maximum welfare addition achievable by allocative means. It is a measure of potentialities of reallocation policies

[1] This is similar to Phelps' augmented labour ([10], p. 5).

of an economy under static conditions. This is also a measure which is very easy to standardise internationally because input–output in different countries allows some kind of international comparisons. It might be interesting to see whether the results are very similar in different countries. If we denote the level of the consumption achieved in the first alternative by C_I, and the actual level by C, we can define the above mentioned measure as

$$(A) \quad \frac{C_I}{C}$$

If we denote the level of private consumption reached by the second alternative by C_{II} we can define the measure

$$(B) \quad \frac{C_{II}}{C}$$

as a measure of maximum welfare addition achievable by allocative means under unlimited export markets.

In a similar fashion we may define a measure for the third version

$$(C) \quad \frac{C_{III}}{C}$$

and call it a measure of maximum welfare addition achievable by allocative means under limited export markets. Of course, the values of these measures depend on the values given to the exogenous variables. In the experiments which we carried out we reached the following results: measure (A) 1·34, measure (B) about 1·09, and measure (C) about 1·07. That means that in case the existing capital was allocated strictly according to the comparative advantage and there were no limits for expansion of export markets under unchanging price conditions, it would be possible to achieve a consumption level under existing technology and given primary resources, which would be approximately a third higher than the level actually reached by the economy.

When we take into account the available allocation of the capital stock it is obvious that over a five-year period it is a considerable factor in allocation policy. The experiment shows that this in fact constrains quite heavily the possibilities to increase the level of consumption by allocative means. Adding the limits for the export market expansion did not remarkably reduce the consumption level.

In the third alternative the private consumption was about 7 per cent higher than the actual consumption. For G.D.P. that alternative means about 3·5–4 per cent higher level than the actual G.D.P.

If we compare our result with a recent study by Pöyhönen about the effect of liberalising the foreign trade, we get quite an interesting comparison. Using a different methodology he concluded that the effect of liberalising the foreign trade would increase the Finnish G.D.P. about 0·4 per cent a year or about 2·6 per cent in five years. If we conclude that the main effect of the liberalising is through better allocation of resources, his conclusions are not too far away from ours.[1]

This analysis was carried out by using the parametric programming technique of linear programming. Figure 13.1 traces the results of the comparative statics analysis of consumption with respect to the capital stock.

FIG. 13.1 The Level of Private Consumption As a Function of Capital Stock under Various Alternatives

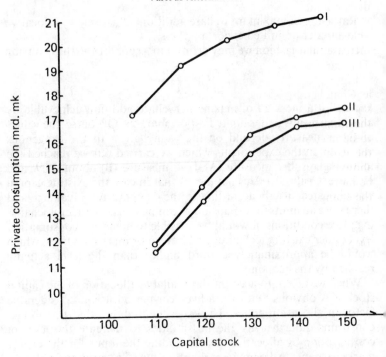

I   = No limits for the movements of capital and exports

II   = No export limits

III = With export limits

[1] Pöyhönen [12], p. 41.

This analysis is interesting first from the point of view of the savings policy. Second, it is also necessary because there might exist a remarkable margin of error in the estimate of the stock. It is therefore helpful to know how sensitive the results are for variations in the capital stock. If the sensitivity is very high the results are of course more uncertain as recommendations for economic policy because of the uncertainties is the estimates of the basic exogenous variables such as capital stock.

In Figure 13.1 there are three alternative consumption paths corresponding to the three different constraint sets. The considerable difference which was pointed out above, between the first alternative and the two others, can easily be seen. This refers to the fact that in medium-term planning the capacity constraint is very essential. Accordingly we see that adding constraints to the export expansion does not affect the resulting level of consumption very greatly.

Rather, the constraints for the export expansion have considerable effect on the structure of the economy. The export constraints increase the number of industries which seem to be socially effective. This can be seen from Table 13.3 below.

Figure 13.1 confirms, as was expected, the so-called Generalised le Chatelier principle mentioned by Samuelson.[1] This is a well known principle in programming which says that the increase in the number of constraints reduces the value of the objective function to be maximised. The sensitivity of the solution to the changes of the capital stock (and consequently to different savings policies) showed that the industrial composition of the production seems to be more sensitive to the existence of the export constraints than to the changes in capital.

TABLE 13.1

The Share of Consumption Goods, Investment Goods and Raw Materials Industries in the Total of Manufacturing under Various Alternatives[a]

	Actual 1970 %	Alternative II (no export limits) %	Alternative III (with export limits) %
Investment goods	12·8	15·3	15·2
Consumption goods	43·6	59·0	52·3
Raw materials	43·6	25·7	32·5

[a] As a basis for measurement gross product has been used.

[1] Samuelsson [13], pp. 36–9.

In Table 13.2 below, the industrial structure of the manufacturing industries generated in various alternatives can be seen.

TABLE 13.2

Distribution of the Gross Product of Manufacturing Industries under Various Alternatives compared with the Actual of 1970

Manufacturing industry	Actual 1970 %	Alternative II %	Alternative III %
1. Food manufacturing	22·6	12·3	25·3
2. Textiles	4·1	2·1	4·2
3. Clothing	2·7	3·4	3·4
4. Footwear	0·6	0·9	0·9
5. Leather	0·3	0·5	0·5
6. Sawmills	4·1	2·5	3·2
7. Other woodworking	2·1	1·4	4·0
8. Furniture and fixtures	1·5	1·9	2·0
9. Pulp	8·4	5·9	5·5
10. Papermills	8·0	5·0	4·6
11. Other paper products	1·9	1·3	3·5
12. Printing	3·5	4·9	4·5
13. Rubber products	0·7	24·7	1·2
14. Fertilisers	1·1	0·5	0·5
15. Paint, varnishes, lacquers	0·4	0·3	0·6
16. Cosmetics, medical products, etc.	1·1	1·9	1·9
17. Other chemical industries	2·7	0·9	0·9
18. Petroleum and asphalt products	2·7	0·6	0·5
19. Non-metallic minerals	2·8	1·4	3·2
20. Iron and steel basic industries	3·4	1·2	2·2
21. Other basic metal industries	5·7	3·0	2·7
22. Metal products	1·2	2·1	2·0
23. Miscellaneous metal products	2·6	3·7	3·5
24. Machines	5·7	9·1	8·5
25. Small electrical apparatus	0·7	1·0	1·1
26. Other electrical machinery	3·1	1·1	1·0
27. Ships and boats	2·6	1·3	1·2
28. Automobiles	0·7	2·8	3·4
29. Other transport equipment	1·4	0·7	1·8
30. Plastic products	1·2	0·3	0·8
31. Other manufacturing	0·5	1·7	1·6
	100·0	100·0	100·0

There are two remarkable features of the results which have appeared in all the calculations. The first is the result that in all calculations it seemed that basic industries or raw material industries got a much smaller share and the investment and consumption goods industries a considerably bigger share of the total production than what has actually happened. This is a phenomenon which is very interesting from the point of view of economic policy since there has been much discussion and criticism against the heavy expansion of basic industries (wood, metals, textiles) in recent years in Finland. The results give some support for this criticism. In Table 13.1 we can see the economic structure of the economy under various alternatives. The industries have been roughly divided into three categories: consumption goods, investment goods and raw materials industries. Also the actual structure of the economy in 1970, similarly calculated, can be seen there. (As a measure, gross

TABLE 13.3

Efficient Industries with the Alternatives II and III

Alternative II (*no export limits*)	Alternative III (*with export limits*)
Forestry	Agriculture
Food manufacturing	Forestry
Clothing	Food manufacturing
Footwear	Textiles
Leather	Clothing
Sawmills	Footwear
Furnitures and fixtures	Leather
Other paper products	Sawmills
Printing	Other woodworking
Rubber products	Furniture and fixtures
Cosmetics, medical products, etc.	Other paper products
Metal products	Printing
Miscellaneous metal products	Rubber products
Machines	Paint, varnishes, lacquers
Small electrical apparatus	Cosmetics, medical products, etc.
Ships and boats	Non-metallic minerals
Automobiles	Iron and steel basic industries
Other manufacturing	Metal products
	Miscellaneous metal products
	Machines
	Small electrical apparatus
	Ships and boats
	Automobiles
	Other transport equipment
	Plastic products
	Other manufacturing

product of industries has been used.) Even though the division into these three categories is rough and not based on detailed product classification it seems that the socially efficient structure of the economy would include relatively more investment and consumption goods industries than has actually been the case.

The other quite interesting result of the experiments is that when there are less restrictions to exports there will be more unemployment. In Figure 13.2 one can see unemployment under various amounts of capital stock. It shows that under the relevant range the unemployment of less educated labour force would be about 30,000 man/years higher in case of no export limits than if there are such limits. This indicates that it might be more difficult to maintain a

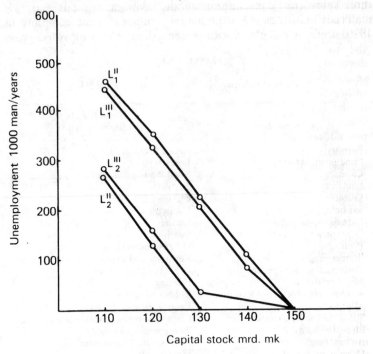

L_1^{II} = Less educated labour, alternative II (no export limits)

L_1^{III} = Less educated labour, alternative III (with export limits)

L_2^{II} = More educated labour, alternative II

L_2^{III} = More educated labour, alternative III

FIG. 13.2 Employment as a Function of the Capital Stock

high employment level if the foreign trade barriers were lowered. It is interesting to find that similar types of results have been achieved by Professor Pöyhönen in a study mentioned above.[1]

For high-level manpower the situation seems to be somewhat different. That category of labour seems to be in a better position as regards employment in the case of a more open trade policy. Further it seems that the less educated labour has a greater probability of becoming unemployed than the more educated labour. For a given capital stock there is considerably more unemployment among the less educated labour. The capital stock should be about 7–8 per cent greater than it is actually estimated to be, in order to employ the whole labour force. This is a considerable amount and corresponds roughly to the gross capital formation of one year.

The results reached indicate that an allocative programming model, even a static one, can provide interesting information about the functioning of an economy. There are many possibilities of developing the model further and making more experiments. Most of the results are, I think, better regarded as qualitative in nature rather than quantitative. The ideas suggested by using a macromodel can be subjected to further, more detailed, study in the subsequent planning stages. The results of vast computational procedures can be quite meaningless, however, if the computations cannot be guided by good theoretical reasoning. On the other hand, what is needed at the moment is to get some idea about the overall relevance of this type of model. That means that we have to develop reasonable ways to test a programming model.

There are also reasons to enlarge the scope of the programming models. These aspects will be briefly discussed in the following section. Finally I shall reflect on the whole approach, namely the optimisation approach to social planning.

VI. POSSIBILITIES OF ENLARGING THE MODEL

The model was constructed to examine questions of the optimal allocation of resources between industries in an economy. Already in this rough form it has given results which are interesting from the point of view of structural economic policy. It has to be remembered, however, that all the aspects and potentialities are not fully exploited and there should still be many possibilities to develop the optimising approach in a more useful direction. The testing of programming models has only just begun, particularly from the dynamic point of view.[2]

[1] See Pöyhönen [12], p. 44.
[2] An interesting testing procedure has been proposed recently by Nugent [9].

It may be necessary to enlarge the scope of the model. There are in particular two central problems which require more attention in economic policy and which are connected with allocation policy. These are the problems of the environment and of income distribution.

In principle the environmental problems, or perhaps it is better to say certain aspects of them, are in principle quite easy to incorporate into activity-analysis-type programming model. We have only to use, for example, the approach developed by Leontief in connection with input–output analysis.[1] It is clear that the environmental repercussions should be taken into account when considering a realistic allocation policy and a policy to change the structure of the economy. The difficulties here, however, are mainly with the relevant data. So far, at least in Finland, there has been no attempt to measure environmental repercussions in the context of input–output analysis. The enlargement of the scope of the model in this direction is therefore dependent on generating the proper data.

It can be also expected that various allocations lead to different distributions of income. Thus, it might be fruitful to examine the effects of allocation policies on income distribution. In the end, I think we shall have to try to develop models which incorporate all the aspects of national economic accounts or a framework from which these accounts, as delineated in the new S.N.A., could be derived. This framework should, however, be enlarged at least with the environmental accounts. It is doubtful whether we should try to incorporate into one major. model all the important aspects of a society.

VII. IS IT REASONABLE TO TRY MACRO-OPTIMISING?

It is not yet well established that we should try to seek some optimising model for the economy. I think the doubts about this type of approach are mainly based on the argument that the complicated structure of the society does not allow the building of a model which is realistic enough for planning purposes and in which the targets of the economy are represented in a balanced way. In a comprehensive model for a society it seems to be really difficult at the moment to build a model where all the most important targets are included and where their relative importance is weighted. The difficulties no longer involve the possibilities of carrying out laborious and complicated calculations. Rather, the real problem is to measure

---

[1] Leontief [8].

and weigh together the target variables of the society and to specify a comprehensive model for the society.[1]

In economic theory there has long existed an ideal world of perfect competition, bringing all the blessings of life without any conscious effort from the Central Planning Board of the economy. This world has been long troubled, however, with problems of inequalities, of externalities, of collective goods, of monopolies and other forms of imperfect competition, of shortcomings in the availability of information, of saving/investment and liquidity traps of the Keynesian theory, and so on.

I think it is now well recognised that it is not possible to succeed in steering a society without conscious effort. It has been pointed out that, in spite of the fact that the problem is very complicated, it can be said that social and macro-economic needs have objective existence.[2] Thus, these needs affect decision-making and they can, at least in principle, be measured and forecasted. In other words, we can consider all human activities as purposeful, and there is consequently some kind of optimising behaviour in human activities. From the existence of social needs it follows that the only reasonable way to practice social planning is to deal with the objectives of the society in some way or other. Research that fails to take social needs into account succeeds only in explaining the phenomena, not in purposeful planning of the society.

When a comprehensive model of a society is not available, the planning has to make use of models which are designed only for certain sectors of the social phenomena. The allocative problem is one of the basic problems of the economy. Given the obvious difficulties of defining the macro-economic targets, there have been few attempts to construct macro-economic programming models. I think it is worthwhile to try to gain experience in constructing macro-economic optimising models, even if rather crude ones to begin with. The reasons for working with an economic allocation model are simple enough: the better allocation of economic resources can give the society better means by which to achieve its goals.

[1] There have been lively discussions about these problems recently in connection with social indicators. There exists a large study of these indicators in Finland [5].
[2] There is a very clear statement about this for example in Smirnov [15], p. 49.

REFERENCES

[1] W. J. Baumol and R. C. Bushnell, 'Error Produced by Linearization in Mathematical Programming', *Econometrica* (July–Oct 1967).
[2] Michael Bruno, 'Optimal Patterns of Trade and Development', *Review of Economics and Statistics* (Nov. 1967).

298   *Long-term Forecasting and Planning in Other Economies*

[3] Michael Bruno, 'A Programming Model for Israel', in I. Adelman and E. Thorbecke (eds), *The Theory and Design of Economic Development* (Johns Hopkins University Press, 1966).

[4] H. B. Chenery and K. S. Kretschmer, 'Resource Allocation for Economic Development', *Econometrica* (Oct 1956).

[5] Elämisen laatu; tavoitteet ja mittaaminen [The Quality of Life; objectives and measurement], Talousneuvosto [Economic Commission] (Helsinki, 1972).

[6] *Industrial Statistics of Finland*, vol. I, 1965, Official Statistics of Finland (Helsinki, 1967).

[7] *Input–Output Study for Finland, 1965*, Central Statistical Office, Tilastotiedotus, No. Kt 1969:3 (Helsinki, 1969).

[8] Wassily Leontief, 'Environmental Repercussions and the Economic Structure; An Input–Output Approach', *The Review of Economics and Statistics* (Aug 1970).

[9] Jeffrey B. Nugent, 'Linear Programming Models for National Planning: Demonstration of a Testing Procedure', *Econometrica* (Nov 1970).

[10] Edmund Phelps, *Golden Rules of Economic Growth* (W. W. Norton & Company, 1966).

[11] *Problems in the Theory of Optimal Accumulation*, A Collection from the Review of Economic Studies, Jan 1967 (Oliver and Boyd, 1967).

[12] Pentti Pöyhönen, *EEC ja Suomen vaihtoehdot I* [E.E.C. and the Alternatives for Finland], Research Report No. 18, Institute of Economics, University of Helsinki (1972).

[13] Paul Samuelsson, *Foundations of Economic Analysis* (Harvard University Press, 1963).

[14] J. Sandee, *A Demonstration Planning Model for India* (Asia Publishing House, 1960).

[15] A. O. Smirnov, 'Problems of Constructing an Optimal Interbranch Model of Socialist Reproduction', in A. P. Couter and A. Brody (eds), *Contribution to Input–Output Analysis* (North-Holland Publishing Company, 1970), I.

[16] *Suomen kansantalouden kehitysmahdollisuudet vuoteen 1980* [The Development Alternative for the Finnish Economy till 1980] Taloudellinen suunnittelukeskus [Economic Planning Centre] (Helsinki, 1972).

[17] *A System of National Accounts*, Statistical Office of the United Nations (New York, 1968).

[18] Jan Tinbergen, *Central Planning* (Yale University Press, 1964).

Discussion of the Paper by
Mr Hjerppe

Dr Leibkind (U.S.S.R.), opening the discussion, said that it seemed commonly accepted nowadays that long-term planning involved primarily the solution of socio-economic problems. Yet there existed no criterion of social progress and development by which one could take full account of all the relevant social factors. Such a criterion could be found if one were to approach the problem either by trying to construct a vector criterion of optimisation or by using heuristic methods to co-ordinate separate social and economic goals in terms of some aggregate goal.

With such an approach, the goals of an economic system proper could be co-ordinated with the other long-term goals of the society concerned, and this was the only approach which made it possible to discuss the application of 'pure' econometrics to long-term planning. None the less the construction of pure econometric models was in itself very difficult, and one could argue about the use of inter-sectoral models for this purpose. That seemed to have been the reason for the choice of a medium-term five-year model, which was regarded as a purely analytical tool, capable of demonstrating the computing techniques and possibilities for economic analysis implied in inter-sectoral model-making.

The model itself was of the classical, Leontiev type and was linear and static, with the traditional constraints on output, skilled and unskilled labour, and on capital – the latter being given exogenously for the final stage of the planned period. The author believed the advantages of this model to be, first, its relative simplicity both in structure, in obtaining the necessary information, and in computation; and second, the fact that such a model made it possible to omit the factor of scientific and technological progress, but thus inevitably preventing the model from being used for long-term planning. This raised the question of whether a relatively small thirty-four-sector medium-term model could be considered stable without seriously depreciating the quality of the calculations.

In two modifications of the model, with capital flow, and with capital flow and export constraints, the resulting effects amounted to 9 and 7 per cent, respectively, which seemed to be somewhat of an indicator of the inadequacy of a model which did not consider about 10 per cent of the factors involved.

The two major conclusions at which the model has arrived were these: first, under any calculations the share of mining and extraction industries was declining in relation to the actual development of the economy; and second, removing foreign trade limitations makes it much more difficult to maintain a high level of employment. A possible explanation of the latter might be that export-oriented industries made faster growth in linear models due to their higher efficiency. Dr Hjerppe believed that further development of this type of model was possible in the form of its transformation into a national accounts model.

Dr Andreev (U.S.S.R.) commented that the work described was a pilot project for Finland, and that was why its results could do much to improve their experience. They were not only of theoretical but also of practical significance for Finland. His first question was whether this work had fully achieved the objects it was pursuing. Second, had any practical recommendations already been made at this stage, and if so what were these recommendations? If such recommendations had been made, had they been accepted either by the government or by the planning organisation? Third, in what sense should the Finnish economy be described as a mixed economy? This was really a question of the applicability and use of the model. And finally, had any calculations or estimates been made of the significance for Finland of the possible increased influence of foreign trade factors, if, for example, there were a free trade zone agreement with the E.E.C.? How useful or otherwise could Finland's participation in such an agreement be?

Professor Yershov (U.S.S.R.) asked what precisely was meant when it was stated that data for 1965 were used? Did that imply that all the coefficients were calculated on the basis of 1965 data, or had some adjustments been made? And what changes had occurred in the growth of the Finnish economy between 1965 and 1970? Having regard to these could the assumption of fixed coefficients really be justified? He was anxious also to know how personal consumption was introduced into the model, and whether the consumption growth vector was different in its composition from the same vector for 1965. He was anxious also to know how far changes in the structure of the sectors described in Table 13.2 could be attributed to the use of fixed coefficients, and how far to the process of optimisation. Again, how had the capital volume been forecasted in equation (3)? Could assumptions be made about changes not in the sectoral structure but in the share of imports in total supply or of exports in overall production? He thought it would be more informative to examine these parameters and to discover the relative redistributions. Finally, if these redistributions prove to be substantial, could fixed coefficients be assumed to remain while the export and import shares in different sectors were changing?

Professor Bruno (Israel) said that since this was an allocation-type model where something was being maximised (he understood this to be total consumption) and which represented a device to obtain the production possibility function of the economy, it was none the less a device to arrive at a price system; yet nothing was said about prices. Was there an attempt to study the price system that was supplementary to this model? And how did shadow prices relate to actual observed market prices for such things as skilled and unskilled labour, foreign exchange, and so on? There was only one consumption aggregate variable appearing in the model. Was there any demand restraint, that is to say a consumption basket restricted to follow certain demand relations, or was demand completely free to adjust to the total maximum, in which case one might get a very extreme solution? And finally, what kind of reasoning lay behind relating gross capital formation to output levels? Did this mean that growth rates in the planning year were assumed, or what other kinds of assumptions were made about the future growth?

Professor Chenery (U.S.A.) was surprised not to see a reference to natural resources in the production function. Was that an omission? Or were they reflected in the lower capital coefficients in the sectors where there were favourable natural resources and in higher capital coefficients in unfavourable sectors? Did the results of the model have practical application? In principle there were three ways in which an economy could adjust. It could adjust by substituting capital for labour directly, but the only substitution allowed was that of capital for labour through trade. It could also adjust by changing the composition of demand. He interpreted this model as having simply omitted the vector of consumption; otherwise he did not see how the equations made sense. There had to be at least a fixed consumption vector. How realistic did the author think his results were if used for planning purposes?

Mr Hjerppe (Finland), replying to the discussion, said that there had been some disagreement about the meaning of planning. He thought this disagreement arose when one came to planning at the social level. He understood that the crucial distinction between forecasting and planning was that a plan involved some element of implementation while forecasting did not. In Finland the only plan which existed was the annual state budget, and that was a plan to be implemented. In this sense there was planning of collective consumption, and that was a feature of all economies. In Finland there was a tradition of economic forecasts as a background to the annual budget. Since the mid-sixties the Economic Council has been preparing economic forecasts for five-year periods using a kind of simulation model based on input–output relations. Thus, this forecasting was not purely theoretical. The role of forecasting in an economy was in any case to provide some basis for social planning. Recent interest in Finland in the problem of long-term social forecasting had resulted in discussion of so-called social indicators. This was only natural in view of the growing importance of human capital in production. Thus, planning should start from social planning.

The main reason for undertaking the study had been structural economic changes which had recently been considerable in Finland. During the 1950s and 1960s productivity in agriculture had increased very rapidly, resulting in a surplus of output and release of substantial amounts of labour. On the other hand a general shortage of available capital coupled with a growing available labour force had led to relatively slow growth of other sectors and increasing unemployment. In the circumstances it was hoped that a mathematical model of the future state of the economy could provide some useful guidance in framing policy. That had been the motivation behind the model, which admittedly was rather crude but which nevertheless provided some valuable guidance. Obviously, there was considerable scope for improvement, and the final objectives of the model had not yet been achieved.

He would not for the moment attempt to decide whether to call the Finnish economy a 'market' or an 'open' one. As to any possible agreement with the E.E.C., it was clear that the existing model was not designed to cover such considerations; yet some of the consequences could be followed through, such as G.N.P. growth. Other problems, the employment situation, for example, were still far from solution. Finland had an exceptionally high share of agriculture in the total G.N.P. as compared with other countries of the same national income level.

He had not been able to take into account scientific and technological progress, although this should be done. But that would require a development of the model. No special price system was included. But he had made various calculations of shadow prices. Skilled labour, for example, was much higher priced than capital. Apart from that, prices in the household and private sectors were also exceptionally high. To his mind this proved that these sectors were not so efficient in relation to the economy as the export-oriented sectors. The consumption function was also very crude, and it could certainly be improved in various ways. He agreed that natural resources could and should be taken into account, as well as the land resources which were important agriculturally. So far as concerned the comparisons possible with this type of model, one needed to begin by establishing the real possibilities having regard to actual resources, which was essential for Finland. These factors determined the production possibilities. At the moment they could not distinguish the factors that were due to the lack of mathematical sophistication of the model from those due to other causes. In further development of the model, more attention should be paid to this fact.

From the point of view of a rather small open economy, a closed model with an internally balanced expansion was not the best to start with. When they considered rapid technological change, the substitution of imports and the expansion of exports, this gave rise to the problem of what might be the most appropriate technology for a small economy. There were in the world firms bigger than whole sectors of the Finnish economy, so that thinking about existing outputs might not always be the best way to plan future growth.

14 Internal and External Aspects of Development Plans and Performance in Aid-receiving Countries

H. B. Chenery and N. G. Carter

INTRODUCTION

International bank for reconstruction and development, Washington

The analytical and philosophical basis for the aid and development programmes of the past decade was formulated in the early 1960s.[1] In outline form it asserts that:

(i) external resources can be used by underdeveloped countries as a basis for a significant acceleration of investment and growth;

(ii) the maintenance of higher growth rates requires substantial changes in the structure of production and trade;

(iii) external capital can perform a critical role in both resource mobilisation and structural transformation;

(iv) the need for concessionary aid declines once these structural changes are well under way although further capital inflow may be needed.

This rather optimistic diagnosis of the possibilities for achieving self-sustaining growth and the potential value of well-timed capital transfers has had widespread effects on the plans of both aid donors and developing countries.

More recently there has been a variety of criticisms of both the performance of countries receiving aid and the basic ideas on which aid programmes have been conceived. It is asserted that aid is largely offset by increased consumption, that aid donors interfere with national priorities, and that aid permits countries to defer difficult policy changes that otherwise would have been taken.[2]

---

[1] Representative academic contributions to this formulation include Milliken and Rostow (1957), Rodan (1961), Chenery and Bruno (1962), Little and Clifford (1965), United Nations (1964). A useful summary is given by Hagen (1968).

[2] A representative set of criticisms are Johnson (1965), Rahman (1967), Hirschman (1961), Griffin and Enos (1970), and Weisskopf (1972). Griffin and Enos assert that 'If anything, aid may have retarded development by leading to lower domestic savings, by distorting the composition of investment and thereby raising the capital–output ratio, by frustrating the emergence of an indigenous entrepreneurial class, and by inhibiting institutional reforms' (p. 326). The testable aspects of these assertions are taken up below.

The policies of the aid donors have been mixed. While aid as a share of G.N.P. has declined continuously in the United States since 1963, this decline has been largely offset by increases in the European contributions. Official Development Assistance (O.D.A.) from the D.A.C. countries as a group now approximates 35 per cent of their G.N.P., and total public and private flows amount to $18 thousand million or 0·8 per cent of their G.N.P., considerably short of the U.N. target of 1 per cent.

Against this background of qualified support for aid, it is somewhat surprising to find that the overall performance of the developing countries for the decade just ended has generally lived up to the expectations of the early sixties. For the decade as a whole, the net amounts of external capital supplied were not far short of the more conservative estimates of the amounts needed for accelerated growth, and market access for L.D.C. exports has improved. Growth rates have accelerated in most countries, and over the decade a number of aid recipients have gone through the anticipated sequence of increased investment rates, structural transformation, and declining aid requirements. On the other hand, several countries have also confirmed the suspicions of the aid sceptics and show little benefit from the assistance received.

In this paper we present a summary evaluation of the interrelations between internal and external policies in the development experience of the past decade, focusing on the needs of policy makers in both developing and developed countries. The problem is complicated by the lack of any tested empirical methodology for determining the sources of growth in developing countries. The factor productivity approach developed by Denison and others[1] to study the performance of the advanced countries focuses entirely on internal factors and cannot accommodate trade bottlenecks and other disequilibrium conditions common to developing countries. At the other extreme, approaches that centre on a comparison of trade performance tend to exaggerate the importance of aid and exports.

Early attempts to treat internal and external factors in a single quantitative framework were derived from the methodology of development planning.[2] The statistical series available in the early 1960s permitted only very crude estimates of the structural relations on which they were based. Ten years later, it is possible to draw on a vastly increased supply of statistics to reformulate the basic relations among import requirements, exports and capital inflow on the one

---

[1] E.g. Abramovitz (1956), Aukrust (1959), Denison (1967), Maddison (1972).
[2] E.g. Rodan (1961), Chenery and Bruno (1962), United Nations (1964).

hand, and savings, investment and growth on the other. This reformulation helps in the interpretation of recent experience.

I. THE ANALYTICAL FRAMEWORK

From plans to behavioural models

An assessment of development performance requires the use of a model which specifies the relationships between policy instruments and economic results. For individual countries the most comprehensive basis for such an assessment is provided by their development plans, in which the need for external capital has been determined by both balance of payments and savings–investment constraints. In countries that use an inter-industry model for this purpose, these aggregate constraints are determined by a detailed analysis of feasible production and export levels and import requirements in each sector.

Despite these advantages, development programmes cannot serve as a basis for a comparative evaluation without significant modifications. In the first place, the published programmes also have a political purpose and take an optimistic view of the rate at which required changes in the structure of production, trade, taxation and other characteristics can be brought about. They also tend to be optimistic about the external economic environment, particularly the markets for exports and the supply of external capital. In summary, although they may be technically consistent, the cumulative effect of a series of favourable assumptions makes development programmes overly optimistic.

The early formulation of two-gap models of aid and development were designed to modify the typical plan results by specifying limits to the feasible range of structural change based on analyses of past behaviour.[1] The disequilibrium system described by these models results from the assumption of separate limits to the feasible values of the principal policy instruments – taxes and savings rates, investment rates, export growth, and capital inflow. The concepts are those of linear programming, although they are usually applied in less formal ways.

Subsequent modifications in the framework for the analysis of aid and development have been of two sorts. The first has been in the direction of designing more satisfactory planning models by specifying more explicit objective functions and determining the optimal capital inflow over time with given constraints on the system. The

---

[1] This was done on the basis of the country's own past performance in the Chenery–Bruno analysis of Israel (1962) and from inter-country norms in the Chenery–Strout projections (1965, 1966).

second has consisted of reformulating the behavioural relationships and policy limits in the models on the basis of the increased statistical information now available.

The present paper pursues the second approach. We will first outline the principal modifications in the analysis of the aid-development relationship that are justified by the econometric studies of recent years. Since there are serious difficulties in estimating these relations under disequilibrium conditions, we will use the general results available as a basis for a less formal evaluation of the development experience of the past decade.

Relations between development and external resources[1]

'Development' can be thought of as the increase in total output together with the transformation of the economic and social structure needed to sustain future growth. In the early stages of development, external resources are largely complementary to domestic resources of labour, capital goods and raw materials; the high productivity of the former results from the low degree of substitutability between them.

The sources of financing of external resources consist of export earnings, net private investment, and net public capital (or official development assistance). Official assistance on softer terms is particularly important in the early stages of development of those countries whose natural resources do not provide a basis for the rapid growth of primary exports and hence do not attract private capital. However, public capital is also likely to be important at a later stage in the transformation of primary export economies after this source of foreign exchange ceases to grow. Since public borrowing is the only source of external resources that is largely under the control of the recipient government, its productivity tends to be high in situations where other sources are scarce.

These aid–development relations were initially formalised in the two-gap models of Chenery and Bruno (1962), McKinnon (1964), and Chenery and Strout (1966).[2] These models are stated in terms of the limits to the extent of governmental influence on the variables that determine the capital inflow required for a given growth of G.N.P.: investment, domestic savings, required imports, and exports.

The Chenery–Strout version of this model is summarised in Table

---

[1] In a broad sense, external resources include imported goods and services plus the services of foreign technicians and entrepreneurs. The net resource transfer is defined as inputs of goods and non-factor services minus exports of goods and non-factor services.

[2] Critiques of these formulations of the aid relationship are given in Hagen (1968), Mikesell (1968), and Bruton (1969).

14.1. It was designed to determine the capital inflow needed to sustain a specified rate of growth of G.N.P. Since the model describes growth as being either investment limited, savings limited or import limited, it is necessary to identify the principal constraint and to specify an adjustment mechanism in order to estimate the relations statistically.

Subsequent studies permit us to introduce several behavioural elements into these relations, thus incorporating statistical results common to a number of countries and presenting the policy choices

TABLE 14.1

Comparison of Growth Models

	A. *Chenery–Strout model*	B. *Extended model*
1. Saving limit	$S_t \leqslant \bar{S}_t = s_1 + s_2 Y_t$	$S_t \leqslant \bar{S}_t = s_1 + s_2 Y_t + s_3 F_t$
2. Trade limit	$M_t \geqslant \bar{M}_t = m_1 + m_2 Y_t$	$M_t \geqslant \bar{M}_t = m_1 + m_2 Y_t + m_3 I_t$
3. Investment requirements	$I_t \leqslant k(Y_{t+1} - Y_t)$	$I_t \leqslant b_1 Y_t + b_3(Y_{t+1} - Y_t)$
4. Export earnings	$E_t = E_0(1+\epsilon)^t$	$E_t = E_{po}(1+\epsilon_p)^t + E_{mo}(1+\epsilon_m)^t$
5. Target growth rate	$Y_t \leqslant Y_{t-1}(1+\bar{g})$	$Y_t \leqslant Y_{t-1}(1+\bar{g})$
6. Capacity limit	$Y_t \leqslant Y_0 + \dfrac{1}{k}\displaystyle\sum_{T=0}^{T=t-1} I_t$	$Y_t \leqslant Y_0 + \dfrac{1}{k}\displaystyle\sum_{T=0}^{T=t-1} I_t$
7. I.C.O.R.	$k = \dfrac{I_{t-1}}{Y_t - Y_{t-1}}$	$k = \dfrac{I_{t-1}}{Y_t - Y_{t-1}}$
8. Identities	a. $Y_t = C_t + I_t + E_t - M_t$	$Y_t = C_t + I_t + E_t - M_t$
	b. $F_t = I_t - S_t = M_t - E_t$	$F_t = I_t - S_t = M_t - E_t$

Definition of symbols (subscript indicates year):

Y_t = gross domestic product
I_t = gross investment
S_t = gross domestic savings, $\bar{S}_t$ = potential gross domestic savings
M_t = imports of goods and non-factor services, $\bar{M}_t$ = required imports of goods and non-factor services
E_t = exports of goods and non-factor services
E_{pt} = exports of primary products
E_{mt} = export of manufactures and non-factor services
F_t = net inflow of foreign capital (resource gap)
C_t = consumption
k = gross incremental capital to output ratio
ϵ = growth rate of exports
ϵ_p = growth rate of primary exports
ϵ_m = growth rate of non-primary exports
$\bar{g}$ = target growth rate

in less aggregated form. This extended form is also given in Table 14.1. It allows for:

- (i) possible limits to the government's ability to channel external assistance into productive uses;
- (ii) the effects of differences in growth rates on both savings and capital requirements per unit of output;
- (iii) the interdependence among the four basic functions in the aid–development relation.

The basic structural equations determining the aid–development relation will be outlined here and then expressed as a dynamic system in Table 14.1. The notation follows Chenery and Strout (1966).

The *savings function* of developing countries has received considerable attention in recent econometric studies.[1] The level of exports, the inflow of external capital, and (to a lesser extent) the rate of growth of G.N.P. have all been shown to have a significant effect on the level of savings in both time series and cross-section analyses. (Typical values found in different studies of this and the other basic relations are shown in Table 14.2.)

TABLE 14.2

Inter-country Estimates of Savings and Investment Functions

Savings functions

(a) $S = a + \cdot183\,Y - \cdot227F + \cdot176E$

(b) $\dfrac{S}{Y} = a + \cdot047 \log \dfrac{Y}{p} - \cdot534 \dfrac{F}{Y}$

(c) $\dfrac{S}{Y} = a + \cdot14 \ln \dfrac{Y}{p} - \cdot004 \left(\ln \dfrac{Y}{p} \right)^2 - \cdot443 \dfrac{F}{Y} + \cdot20 \dfrac{E}{Y}$

Capital requirements

(d) $I_t = 2 \cdot 06 (V_{t+1} - V_t) + \cdot07\,V_t$

Sources:

- (a) Sample of seventeen savings limited countries (Weisskopf, 1972).
- (b) Sample of eighteen Latin American counties (Landau, 1971).
- (c) Pooled sample of 300 observations on seventy countries (I.B.R.D.).
- (d) Median values of coefficients in separate equations for sixteen Latin American countries (Chenery and Eckstein, 1970).

The most important of these findings is the negative association between the level of savings (*S*) and the resource inflow (*F*). As

[1] See Landau (1971), Chenery, Elkington and Sims (1970), Griffin and Enos (1970), Singh (1971), Chenery and Eckstein (1970), Weisskopf (1972), and Papanek (1972).

Papanek (1972) has pointed out, this result stems largely from the conventional definition of savings as investment minus the import surplus. It does not necessarily imply a change in the marginal propensity to save, defined as the partial derivative of savings with respect to income. However, it does imply that – contrary to the national accounting assumption – an increment in external resources is typically divided between investment and consumption.

These results suggest the following extension of the savings function. First, we assume that

$$C = c_0 + c_1 Y + c_2 F \tag{1}$$

where c_1 is the marginal propensity to consume out of G.N.P. and c_2 is the (policy determined) fraction of the resource inflow going to consumption.

Second, we allow for the well-established effect of the share of exports in G.N.P. on savings.[1] Combining the (positive) effects of increased exports and the (negative) effects of increased capital inflow gives the following equation for *potential* savings ($\bar{S}$):

$$\bar{S} = s_0 + \bar{s}_1 Y + \bar{s}_2 F + s_3 E \tag{2}$$

This relationship is assumed to hold *ex ante*[2] – i.e. unless other constraints intervene. Observed savings (S) will be lower when the trade gap is binding and potential savings cannot be realised.

There are two important modifications to be made in the *investment function* to reflect its interdependence with other elements of the model. It has been widely observed that more rapid growth leads to lower capital requirements per unit of output through economies of scale, fuller utilisation of capacity, and the smaller proportion of gross investment required for replacement and social overhead facilities.[3] Secondly, capital requirements are raised when import substitution is pushed too far, distorting the allocation of capital throughout the economy. These two elements are reflected in the following function for the investment required to sustain a given increase in G.N.P.:

$$I = b_1 Y + b_3 \Delta Y \tag{3}$$

where: b_3 is the marginal capital–output ratio applicable to increases in G.N.P. and b_1 is the share of G.N.P. required for replacement and social overhead investment. In a disaggregated analysis, it is useful to add a third term to reflect the additional capital cost

[1] See Vanek (1967), Maizels (1968), Chenery and Eckstein (1970), Weisskopf (1972). The present formulation follows the latter two.

[2] Potential savings and required imports are indicated by barred values.

[3] See Strout (1965), Leibenstein (1966), Vanek (1967), Chenery and Eckstein (1970).

incurred by excessive import substitution, which can be diagnosed in country studies.

The *import requirements function* can be made more accurate by specifying the import content of each of the major components of G.N.P. For our purposes it is more important to distinguish imports of capital goods than those required to maintain the existing level of output. This leads to the following *import requirements* function:

$$M = m_1 Y + m_3 I \tag{4}$$

Exports have been treated as exogenous in most planning models, on the grounds that income and price elasticities of demand for most primary products are low and hence the growth of export earnings is largely determined by external factors. However, the development of non-primary exports in a given country depends largely on government investment and trade policies. The latter can be more usefully considered as separate policy instruments in analysing development performance. This breakdown leads to the following formulation of the export function:

$$E_t = E_{p0}(1 + \epsilon_p)^t + E_{m0}(1 + \epsilon_m)^t \tag{5}$$

where E_p is primary exports, E_m is non-primary exports and the growth rate of the latter (ϵ_m) is taken as a policy variable.

The four structural equations comprising the aid–development relationship have been stated in a general form that can be modified to suit the needs of cross-section or time series estimation techniques or for purposes of policy simulation. The latter version is shown in Table 14.1, which can be considered as a generalisation of the Chenery–Bruno–Strout planning models. The extended version is useful for comparative statistical analysis and is also richer in policy implications.

Growth limits and statistical estimation

The Solow–Denison approach to growth accounting relies heavily on the existence of equilibrium, both in factor markets and in the demand and supply of individual commodities. Under these assumptions neither balance of payments adjustments nor other structural problems have any effect on the observed rate of growth, which is determined only by the supply of labour and capital and technological progress.[1] Furthermore, the assumption of equilibrium in factor markets is relied on to provide estimates of the relative weights to be used in determining the contribution of labour and investment

---

[1] Denison (1967) and Maddison (1972) introduce several structural corrections into this basic methodology – effects of the reallocation of labour, gains from trade, and economies of scale – on a fairly intuitive basis, without otherwise modifying the underlying assumptions.

to growth. Attempts to apply this methodology to developing countries have generally rejected the assumption of equilibrium in factor markets and given considerably greater weight to capital accumulation.[1]

Abandoning the assumption of general equilibrium greatly complicates the problem of modelling the dynamic behaviour of the system. When the Chenery–Strout type of model is used for planning purposes, the system can be closed either by assuming a level of capital inflow or a rate of growth of G.N.P. and assuming that other elements will adjust to it. The adjustment process is more complex in actual economies, and some additional assumptions must be made in order to estimate the structural relations from time series analysis.[2]

Two approaches have been followed in comparative analysis based on the two-gap model. In the first approach, alternative specifications are tested for each country and the set of estimates is retained that most nearly satisfies predetermined criteria.[3] Alternatively, additional information can be used to specify the adjustment mechanism for each country, thus determining which set of structural equations provides the effective limits to the growth over a given period.[4] Elements of both approaches will be used here.

II. DEVELOPMENT PERFORMANCE IN THE SIXTIES

We will now use this analytical framework to examine the performance of the principal developing countries in the past decade, focusing on the relations between the internal and external constraints to growth. We utilise for this purpose two sets of estimates: the projections of feasible growth and aid requirements compiled by Chenery and Strout for a sample of fifty countries for the period 1962–75, and estimates of the actual values of the parameters in this model for the period 1960–70, covering thirty-seven of the principal countries in this sample. Comparing the projections to the actual results provides a basis for interpreting differences in performance among countries as well as a test of the general methodology of disequilibrium analysis.[5]

[1] Williamson (1969), Bruno (1967), Robinson (1971). In inter-country regressions, the growth of the labour force adds little or nothing to explanations based on capital and foreign exchange availability, as shown by Chenery, Elkington and Sims (1970).

[2] The problem of identification involved in converting from a planning model to a behavioural analysis was first stressed by Fei and Ranis (1968).

[3] This procedure is particularly useful in studying single relations, such as the savings function, as shown by the work of Landau (1971) and Weisskopf (1972).

[4] This approach was followed by Chenery and Eckstein (1970) and Papanek (1972).

[5] For the latter purpose, we have also made time series estimates of the equations in the extended model, which are presented elsewhere.

While we cannot estimate the relations in the aid–development model with any accuracy because of the periodic existence of disequilibrium in most countries, there are several aspects of the Chenery–Strout analysis that can be evaluated:

(1) the extent to which growth has been accelerated, and the relative importance of internal and external factors in this result;

(2) the extent to which each economy has been able to absorb external resources for productive uses;

(3) the extent to which the inability to adjust the trade and savings limits has produced disequilibrium conditions;

(4) the extent to which the allocation of external capital has departed from the amounts needed to sustain minimum rates of growth and the differences in the distribution of benefits that have resulted.

III. OVERALL COMPARISONS

The projections

The Chenery–Strout Projections were made for the U.S. Agency for International Development (A.I.D.) to determine the needs of developing countries for external capital under various assumptions as to external trade and aid policies and internal resource mobilisation. Projections for each year (1962–75) were made for fifty countries, using the planning model summarised in Table 14.1. These projections were based on four analytical elements:

(i) past performance of each country, particularly in the preceding five-year period (1957–62);

(ii) development programmes of all countries for which they were available;

(iii) inter-country econometric studies of the principal parameters of the system (capital–output ratios, import ratios, savings parameters); and

(iv) independent estimates of export prospects for the principal commodities which were used to modify individual country forecasts.

The total supply of external capital was not constrained, but it was assumed that the terms of lending would harden as countries developed.

Since the primary objective was to determine aid requirements as a function of growth and domestic performance, alternative assumptions were made for each set of policy variables, reflecting a subjective judgement as to the likelihood of their achievement. We will use the central set of 'plan' targets and 'plan' performance as a basis for the present evaluation, since they were then considered to be the most probable outcome.[1]

In the present analysis, we omit three of the larger countries in which there were political disturbances that significantly disrupted development and ten of the fourteen countries with populations below five million.[2] Concentration on the sample of thirty-seven countries permits a more valid comparison of performance to plans, and does not significantly affect the conclusions reached.

G.N.P. growth rates

Almost all countries that had not already achieved growth rates of more than 5 per cent in the fifties planned for accelerated growth in the sixties. Even after the downward revisions by Chenery and Strout to make the plan targets more realistic, a significant acceleration in the rate of growth was projected for forty of the fifty countries; in thirty-five of these cases some acceleration was achieved. As shown in Table 14.3, the (unweighted) average for the thirty-seven countries in our sample was raised from historical rates of 4·4 per cent in 1957–62 to 5·25 per cent in 1960–70, about the same as the Chenery–Strout plan projections.[3]

Table 14.4 gives a comparison of actual, planned and historical growth rates for three categories of countries: high (over 6 per cent), normal (4·9 per cent to 5·9 per cent) and low (less than 4·8 per cent). In twenty-five of the cases, actual growth was within $\pm 1·2$ per cent of the plan rate, and they are classified as 'planned'. The other twelve countries are fairly evenly divided, with five growing significantly faster than projected and seven significantly slower.

We focus our attention first on the means by which high rates of growth have been achieved or maintained – i.e. on the thirteen countries in Group I of Table 14.4. This group includes the principal developing countries outside of Europe whose past growth has

---

[1] These estimates were adjusted from the original plans of the countries according to the authors' judgement to make them more 'realistic' – i.e. with a probability of achievment of ·5. Other projections based on historical performance and an 'upper limit' estimate – defined by a probability of ·2 – were also made, giving a total of eighteen projections for each country.

[2] The larger omissions are Algeria, South Vietnam and Rhodesia. The only other major omissions from the original sample were Afghanistan, Nepal, Yugoslavia and Zaire. Eleven countries of population between 5 and 10 million were also omitted, for lack of data. Eastern European countries, N. Korea, N. Vietnam and Cuba were omitted as non-recipients of western assistance. The small countries retained in the sample were Israel, Jordan, Jamaica and Costa Rica.

[3] The growth rates used here have been recently recomputed by the I.B.R.D. and are published in the *World Bank Atlas* (1972).

L*

TABLE 14.3

Summary Values of Growth Parameters

Distribution of Parameters, 37 Country Sample

	Upper quartile	Median	Mean	Lower quartile
A. *Chenery–Strout estimates (1962–70)*				
I.C.O.R.	3·770	3·270	3·340	2·720
Rate of growth of G.D.P. (%)	6·000	5·300	5·290	4·750
Marginal savings rate (*ex post*)	0·235	0·200	0·140	0·150
Marginal savings rate (*ex ante*)	0·235	0·200	0·196	0·150
Marginal import rate (*ex post*)	0·331	0·200	0·251	0·260
Marginal import rate (*ex ante*)	0·236	0·190	0·204	0·164
Rate of growth of exports (%)	7·120	4·450	5·080	3·160
Rate of growth of imports (%)	6·470	4·770	5·270	3·720
Rate of growth of population (%)	3·000	2·700	2·600	2·300
Capital inflow (excluding outflows) (%)			6·440	
B. *Actual values (1960–70)*				
Rate of growth of investment (%)	10·160	7·900	7·440	3·580
I.C.O.R.	3·800	3·000	3·250	2·450
Rate of growth of G.D.P. (%)	6·450	5·100	5·360	3·900
Marginal savings rate	0·245	0·212	0·180	0·100
Marginal import rate	0·332	0·228	0·214	0·078
Rate of growth of exports (%)	8·090	5·370	5·140	2·640
Rate of growth of population (%)	3·100	2·900	2·740	2·450
Rate of growth of imports (%)	8·910	6·030	5·820	3·100
Capital inflow (excluding outflows) (%)			5·890	

TABLE 14.4

Projections v. Results: Growth of G.N.P.

Country	Historical rate (1957–62)	Plan rate (1962–70)	Actual rate (1960–70)	Actual minus Historical	Actual minus Plan
I. *High growth* (actual greater than 6%)					
A. *Planned*					
1. Israel	9·0	9·0	7·9	−1·1	−1·1
2. Greece	6·0	6·5	7·3	1·3	0·8
3. Mexico	5·0	6·0	7·2	2·2	1·2
4. Costa Rica	5·5	6·0	6·5	1·0	0·5
5. Jordan	5·6	5·6	6·4	0·8	0·8
6. Turkey	5·3	6·0	6·4	1·1	0·4
7. Malaysia	4·0	5·0	6·2	2·2	1·2
8. Tanzania	4·2	5·0	6·1	1·9	1·1

TABLE 14.4   *Continued*

Country	Historical rate (1957–62)	Plan rate (1962–70)	Actual rate (1960–70)	Actual minus Historical	Actual minus Plan
B. *Accelerated* (actual minus plan 1·5%)					
9. Taiwan	6·0	7·0	10·0	4·0	3·0
10. Korea	4·3	5·0	9·4	5·1	4·4
11. Iran	4·4	5·5	8·3	3·9	2·8
12. Thailand	5·0	6·0	8·0	3·0	2·0
13. Kenya	1·7	3·5	6·7	5·0	3·2
II. *Normal growth* (actual 4·9% to 5·9%)					
A. *Planned*					
14. Philippines	5·0	5·5	5·9	0·9	0·4
15. Venezuela	4·5	6·0	5·8	1·3	−0·2
16. El Salvador	5·0	6·0	5·4	1·4	−0·6
17. Brazil	5·5	5·5	5·3	−0·2	−0·2
18. Ecuador	4·2	5·0	5·1	0·9	0·1
19. Guatemala	4·0	5·0	5·1	1·1	0·1
20. Jamaica	4·0	4·5	5·1	1·1	0·6
21. Pakistan	4·5	5·3	5·1	0·6	−0·2
22. Uganda	1·7	4·0	5·1	3·4	0·9
23. Ethiopa	4·5	4·5	5·0	0·5	0·5
24. Colombia	5·0	6·1	4·9	−0·1	−1·2
III. *Low growth* (less than 4·8%)					
A. *Planned*					
25. Peru	5·5	5·5	4·5	−1·0	−1·0
26. Argentina	3·1	4·3*	4·0	0·9	−0·3
27. Ceylon	4·2	5·0	3·9	−0·3	−1·1
28. Morocco	2·8	4·0	3·9	1·1	−0·1
29. Chile	3·5	5·0	3·9	0·4	−1·1
30. Indonesia	1·0	3·0	3·0	2·0	0·0
B. *Retarded* (actual minus plan 1·2%)					
31. Egypt	4·5	5·5	4·2	−0·3	−1·3
32. Sudan	5·1	5·5	3·9	−1·2	−1·6
33. India	4·3	5·3	3·5	−0·8	−1·8
34. Tunisia	4·1	5·0	3·5	−0·6	−1·5
35. Nigeria	4·0	4·5	3·0	−1·0	−1·5
36. Burma	3·2	4·0	2·7	−0·5	−1·3
37. Ghana	4·5	5·5	2·2	−2·3	−3·2
TOTAL SAMPLE		5·4	5·4		0·0

equalled or exceeded the 6 per cent rate that has been taken as the objective for all countries in the present decade.[1] We will also be concerned with the six countries – India, Ghana, Tunisia, Colombia, Ceylon and Chile – in which growth has fallen significantly below realistic objectives for reasons that are not primarily political.[2]

External aspects

The projections of G.N.P. growth and required capital inflow started from an analysis of export growth that was then taken as exogenously given for each country. The export forecast, which was made on a commodity basis for developing countries as a whole, accurately predicted the slow increase in primary non-fuel exports of about 3 per cent (Table 14.5). The main difference is in the growth of manufactured exports and services, which have grown at 15 per cent compared to the anticipated rate of 6 per cent.[3] Total exports for the sample group have therefore grown at 5·9 per cent compared to the projected rate of 5·1 per cent.

The more rapid growth of exports has been offset by a slower growth of external capital. Annual requirements for the thirty-seven countries were predicted to double with a total net capital inflow between 1962 and 1970 of $69 thousand million. The actual inflow shown in Table 14.8 is about 40 per cent less. Although the total flow of imports was approximately what was estimated to be necessary to support realistic plans of these developing countries, the aid component was financed on considerably harder terms than was anticipated, thus biasing the distribution in favour of countries able to borrow on such terms. India has been most seriously affected by this policy; it has received only 55 per cent of the volume of assistance that was estimated to be necessary to sustain a growth rate of 5·3 per cent.

Since the overall supply of foreign exchange, which constitutes the principal exogenous element in these projections, has been roughly as predicted, our analysis can concentrate on the factors affecting its distribution among countries. The higher growth of mineral and non-primary exports has been of considerable benefit to six of the countries in our sample; shortfalls in primary exports have hampered another six. The distribution of external capital is a more

---

[1] Small, high-growth countries omitted from the analysis are: Panama, Trinidad, Nicaragua, Ivory Coast, Iraq, Zambia, Singapore and Hong Kong. These are discussed in the comparison of development strategies by Chenery (1971).

[2] Without undertaking a detailed analysis, we have assumed that the shortfall in growth in Nigeria, Sudan, Burma and Egypt – as well as in a number of the countries omitted from the sample – is largely political in origin.

[3] The principal source was the export projections made for AID by Balassa (1964). Other forecasts at the time were equally pessimistic.

complex phenomenon than is examined in detail in Section IV below. In general, successful development has usually led to increased supplies – usually on harder terms – whereas unsuccessful development has usually led to a reduction in the aid supplied. Therefore, although the total supply of public funds for external assistance can be taken as given, its distribution depends both on donor policy and the performance of the recipients.[1]

Internal aspects

As shown in Tables 14.3 and 14.5, the savings and investment performance of the sample group was somewhat more favourable than the values projected. The mean value of the incremental capital–output ratio (I.C.O.R.) was about 3·3 in both cases, but the effect of accelerated growth in lowering this value in the Group I countries was underestimated.

Interpretation of the savings results is complicated by the existence of disequilibrium in the *ex ante* trade and savings gaps. The Chenery–Strout projections assumed a median value of the potential marginal propensity to save of 0·24, but the projections resulted in a median *realised* propensity to save of 0·15. The median actual propensity to save was 0·21, which is consistent with the somewhat less restrictive supply of foreign exchange noted above.

When we consider total savings and investment for the thirty-seven country sample, we find both appreciably above the predicted totals. In Group I the higher than predicted growth rates have led to substantially larger amounts of savings and investment even though marginal savings are not generally higher than predicted. In the Group III countries of retarded growth, on the other hand, there has been less of a shortfall in savings and investment than in growth of G.N.P. As shown below, poor savings performance does not seem to have been a major factor in the failure to meet plan objectives.

We have also computed an approximate rate of growth in the capital stock of each country (Table 14.6) assuming a depreciation rate of 5 per cent and an initial stock-flow relation to 1950. Although the median growth of the capital stock (3·5 per cent) is sensitive to these assumptions, there are a number of countries (Iran, Korea, Taiwan, Tanzania, Malaysia, Pakistan, Kenya) in which the rate of G.N.P. growth is substantially higher than the rate of capital growth. These cases suggest that fuller use is being made of the existing stock of capital to secure an acceleration of growth over a limited period. It is notable that where growth has been rapid for a longer period –

---

[1] The projection model was based on a donor policy of equitable allocation of public funds. It did not take account of variations in the way that individual countries would react to borrowing opportunities.

TABLE 14.5

Projection v. Results: External Aspects (1960–70)

	Base Year (1960)				Growth Rates							Capital Inflow (1970)		
	Primary export	Mfg export and services	Capital inflow	Import	G.D.P.	Primary export (actual)	Mfg export (actual)	Total export (forecast)	Total export (actual)	Import (forecast)	Import (actual)	(Forecast)	(Actual)	Actual minus forecast
I. High Growth														
A. Planned:														
1. Israel	60	184	215	459	7·9	15·30	17·80	14·68	15·43	8·91	12·45	350	1,124	+774
2. Greece	279	43	510	832	7·3	3·64	22·79	7·12	8·56	6·72	6·85	363	908	+644
3. Mexico	1,239	210	160	1,608	7·2	3·60	12·22	7·03	4·68	5·76	5·47	−15	274	+288
4. Costa Rica	88	4	20	112	6·5	−4·28	26·73	4·63	9·68	5·15	11·35	53	91	+38
5. Jordan	33	3	95	130	6·4	8·37	19·25	7·48	8·27	4·77	7·45	133	132	−1
6. Turkey	146	20	134	300	6·4	13·02	13·33	4·00	7·72	8·03	6·25	627	327	−300
7. Malaysia	878	60	−219	718	6·2	4·08	13·70	2·76	5·37	4·33	5·68	61	−132	−192
8. Tanzania	171	12	−13	170	6·1	3·38	4·14	4·36	5·62	4·64	6·37	47	72	+26
B. Accelerated:														
9. Taiwan	150	24	117	291	10·0	2·90	46·58	7·12	20·68	6·57	15·51	196	23	−173
10. Korea	73	13	239	325	9·4	11·21	53·29	7·56	27·10	6·37	17·80	379	611	+232
11. Iran	694	41	−16†	575	8·3	10·78	6·32	7·12	10·68	8·08	13·30	111	−357	−773
12. Thailand	330	92	36	459	8·0	9·13	0·42	6·05	7·91	5·01	9·88	−2	272	+275
13. Kenya	258ᵇ	49ᵇ	−38	269ᵇ	6·7	2·61	2·85	4·45	2·38	4·24	6·67	11	23	+10
TOTAL 1	4,399	755	1,525	6,248								2,330	3,857	1,527
II. Normal Growth														
A. Planned:														

20. Jamaica	185	25	2	212	5·1	5·06	6·10	4·45	5·37	2·95	6·57	11	122	111
21. Pakistan	293	167[a]	185	646[a]	5·1	-3·55	13·89	4·89	2·72	5·49	5·16	578	389	-190
22. Uganda	130	10[a]	-12	118[a]	5·1	4·55	6·28	3·56	4·50	3·96	6·03	44	-89	+44
23. Ethiopia	93	3[a]	13	109[a]	5·0	5·70	-6·92	7·12	5·62	4·64	6·49	14	26	12
24. Colombia	508	7	0	515	4·9	1·81	28·76	3·56	3·80	5·54	3·92	573	102	-471
TOTAL II	4,336	338	427	4,444								2,174	967	-1,207
III. Low Growth														
A. Planned:														
25. Peru	418	171	-66	524	4·5	2·30	3·10	6·85	2·20	7·35	1·57	122	-161	-283
26. Argentina	1,371	144	172	1,687	4·0	1·05	10·13	3·74	2·64	5·20	0·30	706	16	-690
27. Ceylon	389	5	39	433	3·9	-0·96	4·83	2·31	-0·72	3·47	0·74	96	46	-50
28. Morocco	402	111	-21	491	3·9	2·08	2·33	2·67	2·72	3·41	2·80	174	57	-117
29. Chile	354	39	84	477	3·9	6·73	-0·29	2·49	6·20	3·34	2·48	387	-24	-411
30. Indonesia	1,056	7	-61	1,002	3·0	-3·23	43·51	1·42	4·97	1·53	10·09	302	581	279
B. Retarded:														
31. Egypt	590	57	-5	642	4·2	-2·90	12·60	1·78	0·15	4·24	1·92	546	254	-292
32. Sudan	169[a]	0[a]	-7	163[a]	3·9	3·47	-4·62	8·01	2·64	6·83	3·39	23	-8	-31
33. India	1,031	800	1,081	2,912	3·5	0·15	3·89	2·67	1·97	5·43	-0·38	1,775	249	-1,525
34. Tunisia	93	47	43	182	3·5	6·25	3·00	4·45	5·48	2·59	3·39	116	58	-57
35. Nigeria	504	10	192	706	3·0	6·05	15·90	7·12	7·57	6·69	3·55	295	113	-180
36. Burma	223	10	12	245	2·7	-12·15	-3·00	10·23	-11·68	10·61	-7·63	-17	35	52
37. Ghana	251	18	55	324	2·2	-4·42	15·70	2·05	-1·33	3·42	-4·20	197	-18	-150
TOTAL III	684	1,419	1,678	9,786								4,736	1,408	-3,260
GRAND TOTAL	15,584	2,513	3,630	20,477								9,239	6,233	-2,940

* Negative values are not included in adding I, II, III groups, as well as in the total of all the countries.

[a] 1961.

[b] 1964.

Note: Totals may not add right because of rounding.

TABLE 14.6

Projections v. Results: Internal Aspects

(figures in $U.S. million)

Country	Savings 1960	Savings 1970 (projected)	Savings 1970 (actual)	Capital inflow 1960	Capital inflow 1970 (projected)	Capital inflow 1970 (actual)	Investment 1960	Investment 1970 (projected)	Investment 1970 (actual)	Marginal savings rate (predicted)	Marginal savings rate (actual)	I.C.O.R. (predicted)	I.C.O.R. (actual)	Growth of capital stocks	Growth of G.D.P.
I. High Growth:															
A. Planned:															
1. Israel	257	−41	271	215	350	1,124	471	1,134	882	0·281	−0·0049	3·00	3·0	7·50	7·9
2. Greece	403	925	1,115	510	363	908	912	1,288	1,906	0·230	0·2208	3·10	3·8	7·34	7·3
3. Mexico	2,077	3,431	4,704	160	−15	274	2,237	3,416	4,978	0·170	0·2238	2·52	2·5	5·14	7·2
4. Costa Rica	59	94	96	20	53	91	80	146	186	0·200	0·1457	3·27	3·3	6·38	6·5
5. Jordan	−48	−34	−28	95	133	132	47	99	162	0·200	0·00261	3·37	2·2	4·11	6·4
6. Turkey	775	1,065	1,654	134	627	327	909	1,693	1,981	0·256	0·2285	2·91	2·7	4·57	6·4
7. Malaysia	434	289	717	−219	61	−132	215	350	585	0·200	0·2165	2·50	2·1	3·85	6·2
8. Tanzania	102	83	160	−13	47	72	89	129	174	0·150	0·2156	2·93	2·4	1·70	6·1
B. Accelerated:															
9. Taiwan	197	373	975	117	196	23	314	569	997	0·210	0·3509	2·62	2·4	9·92	10·0
10. Korea	42	148	997	239	379	611	281	526	1,608	0·150	0·2862	3·27	2·1	6·07	9·4
11. Iran	798	1,024	2,016	−161	111	−357	638	1,440	1,660	0·150	0·3034	3·70	1·9	3·09	8·3
12. Thailand	346	691	881	36	−2	272	382	688	1,153	0·250	0·2437	2·50	2·8	8·04	8·0
13. Kenya	157	121	202	−38	11	23	120	132	220	0·150	0·1468	4·00	2·5	1·70	6·7
TOTAL I	5,599	8,167	13,759	1,525	2,330	3,857	6,694	11,609	16,492						
II. Normal Growth:															

	(1)	(2)	(3)	(4)	(5)	(6)	(7)	(8)	(9)	(10)	(11)	(12)	(13)	(14)	(15)
19. Guatemala	81	184	219	18	95	9	100	279	229	0.200	0.2460	3.50	2.4	2.02	5.1
20. Jamaica	126	154	186	2	11	122	128	165	234	0.180	0.2404	3.50	4.6	4.55	5.1
21. Pakistan	670	1,237	1,408	185	578	390	856	1,815	1,762	0.240	0.1351	3.00	2.7	1.30	5.1
22. Uganda	70	55	159	-12	44	-89	58	99	151	0.150	0.2238	4.00	2.3	3.31	5.1
23. Ethiopia	106	127	155	13	14	26	119	141	183	0.170	0.1336	2.50	2.6	0.06	5.0
24. Colombia	681	1,430	998	0	573	102	680	2,003	1,056	0.260	0.2107	4.80	4.0	3.26	4.9
TOTAL II	6,393	9,681	11,020	427	2,174	967	6,098	11,128	11,288						
III. Low Growth:															
A. Planned:															
25. Peru	602	897	664	-66	122	-161	537	1,019	503	0.285	0.0003	4.94	3.4	4.26	4.5
26. Argentina	3,055	3,178	4,443	172	706	16	3,227	3,883	4,459	0.220	0.2701	5.30	6.3	3.45	4.0
27. Ceylon	146	253	354	39	96	46	185	348	405	0.150	0.2168	3.24	3.1	2.60	3.9
28. Morocco	235	259	328	-21	174	57	213	433	364	0.150	0.2118	4.00	2.7	0.76	3.9
29. Chile	410	481	770	84	387	-24	495	869	682	0.160	0.2963	3.40	4.2	3.40	3.9
30. Indonesia	689	571	898	-61	302	581	628	872	1,479	0.100	0.0233	2.75	2.3	-1.18	3.0
B. Retarded:															
31. Egypt	396	289	294	-5	546	254	379	835	551	0.170	0.0119	2.68	3.8	3.36	4.2
32. Sudan	126	238	151	-7	23	-8	119	261	186	0.150	0.0034	2.50	3.7	2.97	3.9
33. India	4,697	7,765	6,426	1,081	1,775	249	5,778	9,540	6,662	0.210	0.1016	3.20	4.5	3.18	3.5
34. Tunisia	45	103	160	43	115	58	88	218	218	0.200	0.3833	4.00	4.9	6.62	3.5
35. Nigeria	192	1,257	556	192	295	113	384	540	607	0.110	0.3758	3.80	4.1	4.10	3.0
36. Burma	130	324	194	12	-17	35	142	308	229	0.180	0.1101	4.00	3.6	2.62	2.7
37. Ghana	182	250	192	55	197	-18	237	447	174	0.072	0.0908	3.50	5.6	3.79	2.2
TOTAL III	10,904	15,865	15,428	1,678	4,735	1,408	12,410	19,573	16,519						
GRAND TOTAL	22,900	33,714	40,206	3,630	9,239	6,232	25,202	42,310	44,298						

Note: Totals may not add up because of rounding.

as in Israel, Taiwan, Mexico, Greece, and Thailand – the capital stock has grown at about the same rate as the G.N.P.

IV. THE CONSTRAINTS TO GROWTH

The Chenery–Strout projections are derived from a simplified linear model which exaggerates the likelihood of disequilibrium between internal and external constraints to growth, since normally one or the other constitutes the dominant limit. Although we and others have tested various methods of determining the relative importance of these constraints in actual cases, we have found none that is entirely satisfactory. Despite these difficulties, we cannot fall back on the methodology of general equilibrium analysis, which assumes that capital and labour are fully utilised and gives no role to external factors. We will therefore utilise the evidence of several sets of econometric tests[1] in addition to the plan comparisons in Tables 14.5 and 14.6 to form an intuitive judgement of the importance of the several factors involved.

In the cases where a 'pure' savings or trade constraint can be identified, the analysis can be based entirely on the corresponding sub-model in Table 14.1 and is relatively straightforward. In the savings-limited case – a surplus labour economy with adequate foreign exchange supplies – variations in the rate of growth are explainable by changes in savings rates, capital inflow, the productivity of additional investment, and the efficiency of the use of existing capital. In the pure trade constrained case, growth is determined by the availablity of foreign exchange, from exports or capital inflow. The latter case does not usually persist over long periods without corrective measures being taken, however, so our main difficulty lies in interpreting the experience of countries that are partially trade constrained. In this brief survey, we will try to indicate the relative importance of these factors in the countries having large deviations from the original projections: the five cases of accelerated growth – Taiwan, Korea, Iran, Thailand, Kenya – and six cases of retarded growth – India, Colombia, Ghana, Tunisia, Ceylon, now Sri Lanka, and Chile.

Cases of accelerated growth

When there are multiple constraints on growth and limited opportunities for medium-term substitution, an accurate assessment of the sources of improved performance can in principle be determined only from a solution to the planning model with alternative sets of

---

[1] Details are given in a separate annex.

TABLE 14.7

Growth Performance: Selected Countries

Country	G.N.P. Growth			Export Growth			Import Growth			Marginal Savings Ratio			I.C.O.R.			Total Capital Inflow		
	Plan	Actual	Difference	Plan	Actual	Difference	Plan	Actual	Difference	Plan	Actual	Difference	Plan	Actual	Difference	Plan	Actual	Ratio
Accelerated growth cases																		
1. Taiwan	7·0	10·0	3·0	7·12	20·68	13·56	6·57	15·51	8·94	0·21	0·351	0·141	2·62	2·4	-0·22	1,435·1	411·0	0·29
2. Thailand	6·0	8·0	2·0	6·05	7·91	1·86	5·01	9·88	4·87	0·25	0·244	-0·006	2·50	2·8	0·30	191·6	1,024·0	5·34
3. Korea	5·0	9·4	4·4	7·56	27·10	19·54	6·37	17·80	11·43	0·15	0·286	0·136	3·27	2·1	-1·17	2,769·4	4,026·0	1·45
4. Iran	5·5	8·3	2·8	7·12	10·68	3·56	8·08	13·30	5·22	0·15	0·303	0·153	3·70	1·9	-1·80	-13·5	-3,039·6	—
5. Kenya	3·5	6·7	3·2	4·45	2·28	-2·17	4·24	6·67	2·43	0·15	0·147	-0·003	4·00	2·5	-1·50	110·4	74·6	0·68
Retarded growth cases																		
1. Tunisia	5·0	3·5	-1·5	4·45	5·48	1·03	6·59	3·39	-3·20	0·20	0·383	0·183	4·00	4·9	0·90	1,062·0	1,553·0	1·46
2. Chile	5·0	3·9	-1·1	2·49	8·04	5·55	3·34	2·48	-0·86	0·16	0·296	0·136	3·40	4·2	·080	2,864·1	-112·6	-0·04
3. Ceylon	5·0	3·9	-1·1	2·31	-0·72	-3·03	3·47	0·74	-2·73	0·15	0·217	0·067	3·24	3·1	-0·14	530·7	394·1	0·74
4. Ghana	5·5	2·2	-3·2	2·15	-1·30	-3·45	3·42	-4·20	-7·62	0·07	0·091	0·019	3·50	5·6	2·10	1,310·9	233·7	0·18
5. India	5·3	3·5	-1·8	2·67	1·97	-0·70	5·43	-0·38	-5·81	0·21	0·102	-0·108	3·20	4·5	1·30	11,457·2	6,312·5	0·55
6. Colombia	6·1	4·9	-1·2	3·56	3·80	0·24	5·54	3·92	-1·62	0·26	0·211	-0·049	4·80	4·0	-0·80	4,409·1	411·0	0·09

assumptions. However, when the deviations from the plan assumptions are concentrated in two or three parameters, we can give an approximate evaluation of their importance by less formal methods. The major factors are summarised in Table 14.7. We would assess their relative importance in the five cases of accelerated growth as follows:

	External (%)		Internal (%)	
	Exports	Capital inflow	Savings	Excess capacity
Taiwan	50	—	50	—
Thailand	50	50	—	—
Korea	40	20	20	20
Iran	20	—	40	40
Kenya	—	40	—	60

The most significant difference is between Taiwan and Thailand on the one hand – where rapid growth was established in the 1950s – and the other three, where there was substantial acceleration in the 1960s. Taiwan had a very large increase in both export growth and savings, permitting both an acceleration of growth and a reduction in capital inflow, whereas Thailand required large additions of external capital. In Korea the substantial increase in external capital made possible a fuller mobilisation of the economy's resources. The existence of excess capacity is indicated by the substantial fall in the capital–output ratio from its previous levels.

In Korea and Thailand it is impossible to separate the effects of the added growth of exports from the additional external resources, since both were substantial. In Kenya, the problem is simplified since neither savings nor exports were higher than projected; capital inflow and better internal management were the principal sources of improvements over the plan.[1]

Cases of retarded growth

Analysis of the causes of the serious shortfalls from planned performance is complicated by the extensive interaction between external and internal performance. The two-gap model predicts that when there is a shortage of foreign exchange relative to minimum import requirements, there will be a fall in the savings rate and – unless increased external capital is forthcoming – a reduction in growth and under-utilisation of capacity. As Table 14.7 shows, these symptoms

[1] In countries where the economy had previously been growing slowly, the I.C.O.R. based on this experience overstates the capital requirement. A fall in the I.C.O.R. reflects both use of excess capacity and other aspects of internal management.

are present to a greater or lesser degree in Ceylon, Ghana, India and Colombia.

Internal factors provide the primary explanation of slow growth in Tunisia and Chile. In Tunisia, both exports and aid are above plan levels. Tunisia has deliberately allocated a large share of investment to less immediately productive uses over much of the decade, which caused a slowdown in growth even though the plan level of investment was maintained. Chile also showed little evidence of a trade limit, due to favourable copper prices during most of the period. The capital–output ratio rose as a result of excessive import substitution, while the savings rate fell below the plan level as a result of failure to control inflation.

In Ceylon and Ghana, the retardation of growth can be largely attributed to market conditions for their major primary exports – tea and cocoa, respectively – which account for over 50 per cent of total exports in each country. In Ghana, the problem was compounded by misallocation of investment and the consequent reduction of the inflow of external capital. Failure to anticipate and adjust to the slow growth of their principal export commodity must be considered the primary cause of retardation in both countries.

In India and, to a lesser extent Colombia, the reduction in external assistance played a major role in retarding growth. In both cases the resulting shortage of imports was more serious than the shortage of finance for investment. The foreign trade bottleneck was made worse in both countries by trade policies that discriminate against exports of manufactured goods, which their degree of industrial development would otherwise have supported.

In retrospect, the plan growth rates for these six countries (which are a close reflection of their own plans) seem entirely reasonable. Among the several elements causing the shortfalls, a reduction in the expected capital inflow was a major element in India and to a lesser extent in Colombia, Chile and Ghana. Internally, failures of resource mobilisation played a smaller role than failures of allocation, with too much reliance put on import substitution and little attention to export promotion or diversification.

V. DISTRIBUTION AND EFFICIENCY IN AID POLICY

The allocation of external resources is the result of the set of policies followed by the recipients as well as the allocation criteria of the donors. In the aid planning of the sixties, the donors were primarily concerned with (i) the efficiency of use of capital, (ii) the risk of loss, and (iii) inter-country equity. In recent years a fourth criterion, the effect on income distribution within countries, has been increasingly stressed, although it has not yet had much effect on the results.

The Chenery–Strout projections provide the only known 'plan' for aid allocation among countries drawn up on a consistent set of criteria. These implicitly assumed that external resources would not be provided to support unreasonably high growth rates – above 7 per cent – except for Israel, which has separate sources of finance. They also revised the estimates in country plans to make the internal performance estimates comparable among countries. Comparing the actual growth projections and corresponding aid allocations to the projections, therefore reveals something about the working of the mechanism through which external resources are allocated.

VI. RECIPIENT POLICY

The choices facing recipients of external capital vary considerably according to their past success in development. Countries that are seen to be effective users of external resources are favoured by both private suppliers and aid donors. The most successful countries have therefore had the choice of (*a*) accelerating growth further on the basis of additional external capital; (*b*) reducing their capital inflow, as envisaged in the prototype of the two-gap sequence.

The successful countries (in Group I of Table 14.4) have responded differently to these alternatives: Greece, Korea, Iran, Mexico, Costa Rica, and Thailand have chosen to increase both G.N.P. growth and capital inflow, while Taiwan, Turkey and Malaysia have reduced their external capital requirements from the plan levels through improved export performance.

The less successful countries (Group III in Table 14.4) have a more limited choice. In several cases they have tried to increase the inflow of capital to offset slow export growth with only limited success. Of the thirteen countries in Group III, only Indonesia, Tunisia, Sudan and Burma received amounts of external capital as great as – or even close to – the projected decade totals. While the reduction was usually justified by poor internal performance of the recipient, this was not always the case.

VII. THE DISTRIBUTION OF BENEFITS

The dozen or so agencies that provide the bulk of official assistance operate on different sets of criteria and with differing geographical and political preferences. Although there are some common elements – such as favouring countries that make effective use of aid – it is impossible to construct a general rationale for donor policy over the past decade. We can, however, derive some conclusions as to the distribution of benefits by comparing the overall results to those projected. Elements of a benefit-cost analysis are given in Table 14.8.[1]

On the benefit side, the decade growth of G.N.P. for the group was from $153 thousand million to $244 thousand million, which – by coincidence – was identical to the prediction. On the external cost side, the shortfall in capital inflow (from $68 thousand million projected to $40 thousand million actual) can be allocated in part (perhaps 30 per cent) to the substitution of manufactured and service exports for aid in countries such as Brazil, Taiwan and Turkey. A large part of the remainder is the result of a shift away from the less successful countries as measured by their growth performance.

The relation of growth and aid to the initial level of per capita income is shown in Table 14.8, in which countries are ordered by income level. The principal distributional effect can be brought out more clearly by treating India separately. On this basis, the projected and actual distribution of growth and aid for the three groups is as follows:

	Popu-lation (m.)	Total G.N.P. (U.S. $ billions)			G.N.P. growth (%)		Capital Inflow (U.S. $ billions)	
		1960	(Proj.)	(Act.)	Proj.	Act.	Proj.	Act.
A. 16 countries over $190 p.c.	321	74	120	126	5·0	5·5	30	13
B. 20 countries under $190 p.c.	606	44	67	70	4·3	4·8	24	20
C. India	538	35	56	48	4·8	3·2	12	6
	·1,465	153	244	244			66	40

On this basis, the shift in distribution is striking. The first two groups achieved growth rates 10 per cent higher than projected, and the lower income group received 80 per cent of the capital inflow estimated to be needed. India, in contrast, received only 55 per cent of the estimated need, and this shortfall was probably the main single factor in her inability to grow more rapidly. In this case there is a clear failure of the system of international distribution of assistance, which is heavily biased toward smaller countries.

VIII. EFFICIENCY OF THE AID PROCESS

The negative association between capital inflow and savings has led some authors such as Griffin and Enos (1970) to question the

---

[1] In subsequent work we will use the grant equivalent of the capital inflow rather than the total.

TABLE 14.8

Distribution of External Capital and Growth
(figures in U.S. $ million)

Country	Per capita G.N.P. (1960)	Population 1970 (000's)	G.N.P.	G.N.P. 1970 (projected)	G.N.P. 1970 (actual)	Growth of G.N.P. per capita (projected)	Growth of G.N.P. percapita (actual)	Total Capital Inflow 1962-70 (projected)	Total Capital Inflow 1962-70 (actual)	Ratio actual-projected
A. G.N.P. per capita (1960) > $190										
1. Israel	843	2,910	1,781.5	4,198.3	3,772.1ᵃ	5.5	4.7	3,656.8	4,487.7	1.23
2. Venezuela	752	10,399	5,003.0	9,150.3	9,087.0	2.6	2.3	-6,111.4	-3,007.3	—
3. Argentina	681	23,212	14,208.6	17,038.1	19,512.3	2.6	2.5	4,565.3	-1,196.7	-0.26
4. Greece	417	8,892	3,475.5	6,389.9	6,286.8ᵃ	5.6	6.6	2,635.0	5,218.1	1.98
5. Jamaica	388	1,888	580.9	1,048.1	866.6	3.2	3.5	197.2	224.7	1.14
6. Chile	371	9,780	2,848.4	5,109.0	4,135.2ᵃ	2.7	1.6	2,884.1	-112.6	-0.04
7. Mexico	352	50,670	13,197.7	22,592.8	26,105.5	2.9	3.7	670.1	423.5	0.63
8. Costa Rica	340	1,727	416.4	744.3	778.8	2.1	3.2	361.5	343.2	0.95
9. Guatemala	253	5,190	967.0	1,591.2	1,594.5	2.0	2.0	836.1	184.5	0.22
10. Peru	247	13,586	2,482.4	3,750.8	3,975.5	3.2	1.4	1,015.1	-167.0	-0.16
11. Colombia	221	21,632	3,310.7	6,839.6	5,056.3ᵃ	3.2	1.7	4,409.1	411.0	0.09
12. Turkey	217	35,230	6,014.9	9,693.8	10,691.5	3.1	3.9	3,587.1	1,820.3	0.51
13. El Salvador	210	3,534	516.6	840.0	846.4ᵃ	3.3	1.7	185.0	157.3	0.85
14. Malaysia	208	10,945	1,683.3	2,801.3	3,273.1	1.8	3.1	-112.1	-920.7ᵃ	—
15. Brazil	193	92,764	14,091.1	21,566.9	21,953.9ᵃ	2.4	2.4	4,936.3	-113.9	-0.02
	192	28,662	2,802.4	7,074.9	7,961.7ᵃ	3.0	5.4	-13.5	-3,069.6	—

#	Country										
18.	Morocco	167	15,495	1,941·7	2,705·7	2,876·4[a]	1·3	1·0	1,421·9	265·1	0·19
19.	Jordan	160	2,317	271·3	524·2	540·6[a]	2·9	2·9	1,041·2	1,076·4	1·03
20.	Ghana	158	8,640	1,047·5	2,322·0	1,379·4	3·0	-0·4	1,310·9	233·7	0·17
21.	Tunisia	156	5,075	606·5	1,091·8	980·8	2·9	0·5	1,062·0	1,553·0	1·46
22.	Philippines	149	36,850	3,715·6	5,814·9	6,297·4[a]	2·3	2·9	1,040·7	773·9	0·74
23.	China (Taiwan)	147	14,035	1,558·5	3,101·3	3,796·4	4·1	7·1	1,435·1	411·0	0·29
24.	Ceylon	131	12,514	1,309·4	2,148·2	2,086·6	2·2	1·5	530·7	394·1	0·74
25.	Egypt	129	33,329	3,138·4	5,666·1	4,740·9	3·0	1·7	3,539·3	1,697·4	0·48
26.	Thailand	111	36,218	2,427·9	-4,588·7	-5,116·9	2·9	4·9	191·6	1,024·0	5·34
27.	Korea	104	31,793	2,566·8	3,217·9	6,126·6	2·1	6·8	2,769·4	4,026·0	1·45
28.	Kenya	101	11,250	906·6[d]	-945·5	-1,264·1[a]	0·5	3·6	110·4	74·6	0·68
29.	Indonesia	89	115,567	7,976·1	10,575·0	11,261·0	0·7	1·0	2,507·9	3,430·7	1·37
30.	Uganda	89	9,814	566·3[b]	621·3	901·4[a]	1·5	2·4	362·2	208·7	0·58
31.	Sudan	88	15,695	997·9[b]	1,898·4	1,357·4[a]	2·7	1·0	254·8	244·5	0·96
32.	India	83	538,129	35,341·0	56,246·9	48,276·5[a]	2·9	1·2	11,457·2	6,312·5	0·55
33.	Pakistan	71	130,166	7,318·8	11,413·8	11,894·1[a]	2·7	2·4	3,997·8	3,478·4	0·87
34.	Nigeria	70	55,070	3,568·1	4,883·5	4,407·2[c]	2·5	0·1	2,210·1	854·4	0·39
35.	Tanzania	65	13,270	624·2	882·0	986·8[f]	3·0	4·1	402·4	-50·8	-0·13
36.	Burma	56	27,584	1,189·2	1,922·8	1,623·9	1·8	0·6	-116·2	88·9	—
37.	Ethiopia	45	24,625	984·7[b]	1,252·9	1,301·4[c]	3·1	2·8	217·6	208·0	0·96
	SUB-TOTAL (b)		1,143,529	78,847·2	123,089·1	118,421·6			36,255·9	*26,520·9	0·73
	TOTAL (a & b)		1,464,550	153,227·6	243,518·4	244,318·8			*66,194·6	*39,791·2	0·60

* Exclude negative numbers.

[a] 1969. [b] 1961. [c] 1967. [d] 1964. [e] 1966. [f] 1968. [g] 1964–70. [h] No data for 1964.

efficiency of the aid process.[1] The proper test of the effectiveness of aid, however, is its effect on growth or other social objectives rather than on savings as conventionally measured.[2] The two-gap model in its optimising version[3] demonstrates that with a trade constraint it is optimal policy to increase the capital inflow even though the effect will be to raise consumption as well as investment, and the productivity of external capital in this case is very high.

We have conducted several tests to try to determine whether most of the negative effect of capital inflow on savings can be explained as purely a two-gap phenomenon, as suggested by Landau (1971). In one set of tests, regressions run on the Chenery–Strout projections produced results qualitatively similar to those observed by Weiss-kopf (1972) and others. However, there are a few countries[4] in which a trade constraint can be ruled out; here the negative coefficients can be taken as indications of inefficiency in transforming the capital inflow into increased investment. However, the countries that have raised their savings rates as a result of the aid-supported growth process greatly outweigh the cases in which an unnecessary diversion to consumption can be demonstrated.

[1] See Table 14.2.
[2] Papanek has demonstrated that much of the apparent association is explainable on purely statistical grounds.
[3] E.g. Chenery and MacEwan (1966).
[4] Thailand, Venezuela and Jordan.

Discussion of the Paper by
Professor Chenery and Dr Carter

Professor Chenery (U.S.A.) introduced his own paper, which had not been available to participants in advance. He said that this material presented one of the rare opportunities to return to a set of original projections and to compare them with actual development. The basic analysis had been made in 1962 by the U.S. A.I.D. agency which then provided about 60 per cent of the total of public capital funds to the developing countries. The purpose of the projection was to provide a quantitative framework for allocation of those funds and also a basis for analysing the possibilities of accelerating growth through a capital inflow. It was of some interest in retrospect not only from the point of view of improving the model used but also as suggesting some conclusions about capital inflow to the developing countries from both East and West.

The model originally developed in 1962 assumed that in most cases labour was not scarce but that foreign exchange was scarce. So it was a two-factor model, and it was not assumed that there was immediate adjustment through substitution between capital and foreign exchange. Such substitution took time and did not always take place. It was a disequilibrium model which assumed that in the long run lack of foreign exchange slowed down development of a country.

What was instructive was not the accuracy of the model, which in fact was very crude, but how its variables had performed throughout. It was the performance of different groups of countries, not of one individual country, from which there was most to learn. If a country performed well and that was expected by the model, it merely verified our existing knowledge. But if a country performed better than was predicted it was much more interesting. It was the two-gap model, introducing two constraints in the form of both capital inflow and foreign trade (that is to say both internal and external factors of development rather than either of these separately) that proved to be most successful.

It was noteworthy that only in one case, namely Tunisia, could retarded growth be explained by inefficient management of the existing capital. In all other cases it had to be explained by external factors: either by less-than-predicted exports or by a combination of factors resulting in a narrowing of the country's ability to supply itself with necessary resources, which in turn called for restructuring of the economy in accordance with the demands of the external market.

Professor Machlup (U.S.A.) commented that in any projection the planned growth rate was not actually planned but was assumed as a given or exogenous variable for a plan. He thought that nothing should be described as 'planned' that would happen equally in the absence of a specified and deliberate decision or action. Growth could be predicted, projected or expected, but not planned.

The growth of the G.D.R. was a sustained increase over a long period, and as such could only to a negligible degree be accelerated by a deliberate action. It could be hampered or even prevented by exceedingly stupid policies. It could be promoted by certain policies. But it could not be turned up or turned down, as it would have to be to deserve the designation 'planned'.

Professor Chenery (U.S.A.) said that fifty countries in the sample accepted accelerated growth as their deliberate policy, and for every other country it was one of the objectives of their national policy to accelerate their growth. In thirty-five of these cases there was an actual acceleration of growth through the policies followed. He would say that acceleration of growth was 'planned' in these cases and the plan was successful in a great majority of them. The policies that achieved it were interactions between taxation, savings, exports and capital inflow, all of which were easily measurable.

Professor Fritsch (Switzerland) said that it had been estimated that for a group of twenty countries with national income under $190 per capita a capital inflow of a total of $24 thousand million would be necessary to sustain a 4·3 per cent rate of growth. The actual inflow totalled $20 thousand million, whereas the rate of growth was higher than that projected. Did that imply that Professor Chenery's projections were too pessimistic in respect of these twenty countries? *Professor Chenery* replied that the main difference between his projection and the actual results was that exports had grown more rapidly. They were not widely wrong about import requirements but they were wrong about the success of some of the developing countries in exporting. In some cases the actual inflow of capital exceeded that projected, but on average it was less, and the principal reason was not primary exports but manufactured exports; that had been the largest single factor.

Professor Robinson (U.K.) wanted to know whether the countries' own estimates of growth rates were worse than those of the U.S. A.I.D. projections. *Professor Chenery* said that most of the countries concerned had their own plans in this ten-year period, but they were shorter-term plans and on a different basis in each case, so that only in a few cases were such comparisons possible. For example, a Turkish plan which fell somewhere in the middle of the period studied – 1963–7 – had a 7 per cent growth target. They had used 7 per cent as an upper estimate with a probability of 0·2, and they had used 6 per cent as a median and most likely rate of growth. The actuality was 6·5 per cent. But such comparisons had been made for a few principal countries only.

Professor Bruno (Israel) asked whether allowances had been made for changes in the terms of trade and for the return from exports, especially in the case of primary products. *Professor Chenery* said that they had implicitly taken the actual value of exports, but they had not tried to isolate it as a single factor. Thus the original projection did not take account of the worsening of the terms of trade. It considered only the total value of exports without trying to explain the specific sources of the value. Export of primary products was no different, although bigger mistakes had arisen with respect to manufactured products. Some countries had, of course, benefited from the terms of trade.

Professor Marczewski (France) asked whether, in the appraisal of the results of the model, distinction had been made between the estimates of exogenous variables, based on some hypothesis, and estimates of endogenous variables which depended, first, on the estimates of the exogenous variables, and second, on the internal relations of the model. Such distinction seemed to be very important in evaluating the model.

Professor Chenery answered that the whole methodology was designed to do that. Instead of just looking at the general results, they had made such a distinction, with endogenous variables expressed by such parameters as the capital–output ratio, the marginal savings rate, or the marginal export rate, and with such exogenous parameters as capital inflow and export growth. They had also been interested in how the model worked structurally, and in the extent to which the two exogenous variables were substitutes for each other. Professor Chenery went on to comment more generally that there was a kind of technical debate in western journals on whether aid was entirely wasted or not. Checking of various functions such as exports – or savings – or capital-inflow-functions often resulted in negative coefficients for income, which was often interpreted as implying that increasing capital inflow ended by increasing consumption rather than in increasing investment. It was true that many cases seemed to prove it. On the other side, if one optimised subject to both constraints and exports flowed slowly, then you were led to increase the capital inflow and thus the optimising solution would produce the same result. In other words, if the trade gap were larger than the *a priori* or potential savings gap, and you were maximising either growth or consumption, you would be led to an increase of capital inflow beyond the amount that would be required to satisfy the savings constraint.

The problem was how to separate these two possible hypotheses. The first was that this was a natural result of optimisation policy and did not indicate that the capital was being wasted. The other held that this model did not prove anything. One way was to separate the countries which had serious trade limitations and to see whether this negative coefficient showed up, which by and large was the case. There are a few countries of which it was difficult to say whether they had any restrictions on growth and which still had negative coefficients. Here the conclusion would be that part of the capital inflow was not used to increase investment. Thus in general his conclusion was that a country perhaps benefited from capital inflow to a greater extent if the capital was used to increase exports than if it went to supplement savings.

15 Technological Forecasting

E. Mansfield

I. INTRODUCTION

The past decade has seen a spectacular increase in the amount of attention devoted to technological forecasting by social scientists, management scientists, and others involved in R & D planning, industrial management, defence problems, environmental protection, technology assessment, and a host of other areas. Books and articles in considerable number have appeared on the subject.[1] New journals devoted entirely to this subject have been born.[2] Firms and research organisations specialising in the subject have sprouted in various parts of the United States – and the world. Given the impressive amount of activity in this area, the time seems ripe to survey and appraise what has been going on. In particular, what is meant by 'technological forecasting'? What sorts of techniques and models have the technological forecasters developed? How accurate are these techniques and models? To what extent are they used? What are the problems and defects in existing techniques and models, and how can they be improved? My purpose in this paper is to answer these questions as best as I can within the space available.

It is customary in the literature on technological forecasting to distinguish between *exploratory technological forecasting* and *normative technological forecasting*. Exploratory technological forecasting attempts to predict the technological state-of-the-art that will be attained and used at future points in time if certain conditions – such as levels of research support – are met. On the other hand, normative technological forecasting attempts to specify a rational allocation of resources – research and development personnel, facilities, and so forth – among alternative uses in an attempt to influence the rate and direction of technological change within a firm, a government organisation, or the country as a whole. Needless to say, these two broad classes of technological forecasts are closely

---

[1] Among the most prominent texts on this spbject are E. Jantsch, *Technological Forecasting in Perspective* (O.E.C.D., 1967); J. Bright, *Technological Forecasting for Industry and Government* (Prentice–Hall, 1968); M. Cetron, *Technological Forecasting: A Practical Approach* (Gordon and Breach, 1969); and R. Ayres, *Technological Forecasting and Long-Range Planning* (McGraw–Hill, 1969).

[2] Examples are *Technological Forecasting and Social Change* and *Futures*. Also, articles on this subject are found in journals like *R and D Management*, *Research Policy*, *Technology Assessment*, and *Long Range Planning*.

related. However, in keeping with most discussions of this subject, I shall treat these two classes separately. Sections II–VI deal primarily with exploratory technological forecasting, Sections VII–X deal primarily with normative technological forecasting, and Section XI provides some concluding remarks concerning both types of technological forecasting.

II. INTUITIVE AND DELPHI METHODS

It is widely agreed that technology is a relatively difficult variable to forecast, because there is so much uncertainty concerning what will be produced by R & D efforts, and concerning what break-throughs will occur, and when. How do the people engaged in technological forecasting go about making their forecasts? According to various surveys, as well as the leading texts on technological forecasting, simple intuitive projections seem to play a very important role in exploratory technological forecasting.[1] For example, suppose that a firm or government agency wants to forecast the maximum speed of commercial aircraft in 1985. One way of obtaining such a forecast is simply to ask an expert, or group of experts, to guess as best they can what the maximum speed will be at that time. Certainly, this approach is straightforward enough and relatively cheap. But it runs into a number of difficulties. First, technologists are no more in agreement about the future than economists are, the result being that the answer is likely to vary, depending on the choice of expert. Second, even when based on the opinion of distinguished experts, such forecasts can contain large errors. For example, Vannevar Bush predicted in 1945 that a 3,000 mile rocket would 'be impossible for many years'.[2]

To cope with some of the problems involved in simply asking a group of experts for a consensus guess, Helmer and Gordon, while at the RAND Corporation formulated a technique, known as the Delphi method, which attempts to utilise expert opinion more effectively. For example, to forecast the maximum speed of commercial aircraft in 1985, users of the Delphi method would ask a number of experts to formulate separate and independent estimates. Then the median and inter-quartile range of the estimates would be communicated to each of the experts, and they would be asked to reconsider their previous answers and revise them if they wanted to.

[1] For some results of a survey of firms to determine the sorts of technological forecasting techniques in use, see M. Cetron and C. Ralph, *Industrial Applications of Technological Forecasting* (Wiley, 1971).

[2] For other examples see E. Mansfield, *The Economics of Technological Change* (Norton, 1968) pp. 38–40.

Then those people whose answers lie outside the inter-quartile range would be asked to state why they disagree to this extent from the other members of the group. Then their replies would be circulated among the group, and the members would be asked once again to make a forecast. This iterative process would continue until there was a reasonable convergence of the individual forecasts.

The Delphi method has been used in fields as diverse as defence, pharmaceuticals, political science, and educational technology. According to its developers, it is a useful tool for technological forecasting. However, it is important to recognise the obvious fact that the results of the Delphi method can be no better than the foresight of the individual experts. And as noted above, this foresight can be very imperfect. Moreover, by relying so heavily on a consensus, the Delphi method assumes that collective judgement is better than individual judgement. This is a dangerous assumption, as evidenced by the many important technological advances that have been made by individuals and groups that acted contrary to prevailing majority – and elite – opinion.[1]

III. TREND EXTRAPOLATION AND LEAD-LAG RELATIONSHIPS

Another technique that plays an important role in exploratory technological forecasting is simple trend extrapolation. For example, to forecast the maximum speed of commercial aircraft in 1985, one could obtain a time series of the maximum speed of such aircraft at various points in history, and project the historical trend into the future. In fact, this simple sort of extrapolation technique has been used in the U.S. Department of Defense, where much of the work on technological forecasting originated.[2] It has also been used in commercial work of various kinds. Of course, economists themselves

---

[1] See the articles by O. Helmer and T. Gordon in J. Bright, op. cit. Also, see T. Gordon and O. Helmer, *Report on a Long-Range Forecasting Study*, RAND Corporation Report P–2982 (Sep 1964).

Another well-known technique based on subjective estimates is the 'cross-impact method', also pioneered by Gordon and Helmer. According to this method, one estimates the effects of one event on the probability of occurrence of other events. Then one goes through a Monte Carlo process to estimate the unconditional probabilities of occurrence of various events. See T. Gordon and H. Becker, 'The Cross-Impact Approach to Technology Assessment', *Research Management* (July 1972); and N. Dalkey, 'An Elements Cross-Impact Model', *Technological Forecasting and Social Change* (1972).

[2] For example, see R. Lenz, 'Practical Application of Technical Trend Forecasting', in M. Cetron and J. Goldhar, *The Science of Managing Organized Technology* (Gordon and Breach, 1970), and R. Lenz 'Technological Forecasting Methodology', in Cetron and Ralph, op. cit.

have long used such techniques. For example, about twenty years ago, John Kendrick discussed the use of such crude techniques to forecast productivity change in the American economy.[1]

The problem with naïve extrapolation techniques of this sort is that, unless the fundamental factors determining the technological parameter in question operate much as they have in the past, previous trends will not necessarily be a good guide to the future. For example, a host of factors, including the allocation of R & D resources and the pressure of environmental concerns, may see to it that the maximum speed of commercial aircraft increases at quite a different rate than it has in the immediate past. Or take the case of productivity increase. There is considerable evidence that productivity increase has not occurred at a constant rate in the United States. The moral, well known to economists, is that a naïve projection of historical trends is a dangerous business, particularly when long-term forecasts are being made.

Besides trend extrapolation, the technological forecasters have adopted another old favourite of the economic forecasters – lead–lag relationships. For example, to forecast the maximum speed of commercial aircraft in 1985, one could plot the maximum speed of commercial aircraft against the maximum speed of military aircraft. Finding that commercial speeds have lagged military speeds, one might be able to use this relationship to make the desired forecast.[2] Of course, here too the problem is that the historical relationship may not continue into the future.

IV. THE USE OF INPUT–OUTPUT MODELS

The available evidence indicates that most exploratory technical forecasts, both in industry and in government, are based on the simple intuitive methods and extrapolation techniques described in the previous two sections. In addition, however, there has been some experimentation with at least three types of somewhat more sophisticated types of exploratory forecasting techniques: input–output models, production models containing R & D expenditures, and diffusion models. To begin with, let us consider the use of input–output models. There has been some experimentation with the projection of input–output structures into the future. In order to make such projections, one must forecast both the input requirements of future techniques and the rate of diffusion of future

---

[1] J. Kendrick, 'National Productivity and Its Long-Term Projection', in National Bureau of Economic Research, *Long-Range Economic Projection* (Princeton, 1954).
[2] For example, see Lenz, op. cit.

techniques, since the input–output coefficients will be a weighted average of existing and future techniques, the weights depending on the rate of diffusion.

In this section, we shall focus attention on the estimation of the input requirements for future techniques, since the estimation of the rate of diffusion is discussed in Section VI. One way that economists have tried to forecast input–output coefficients in a particular industry is to assume that new technologies have a weight proportional to investment in new capacity. By observing the changes in the industry's average input–output structure, and its expenditures on new plant and equipment, one can estimate what the input–output coefficients for the new 'layer' of capital must have been. Then, to make short-term projections, one can assume that the coefficients for the new 'layer' will remain constant, and increase the weight given to these coefficients (in proportion to expected invest-investment). This method, used by the Harvard Economic Research Project, is crude at best. All that its users claim is that it gives 'ball-park' estimates.[1]

Another way of projecting input–output structures is through the use of expert opinion. For example, Battelle Memorial Institute and Scientific American are sponsoring a study of this sort, the object being to estimate inter-industry purchases, including labour requirements, per dollar of output for a 'typical' new plant to go onstream in 1975.[2] About 100 industries are included in the study. As recognised by the study's authors, these projections are plagued by the same sorts of difficulties we cited in Section II. Moreover, there are other problems as well. For one thing, the industrial classification employed in the input–output model is broader than the product categories that the technologists making the forecasts are used to dealing with. For another thing, it is difficult to include qualitative changes, like new products, within the input–output framework. At present, the use of input–output analysis in connection with technological forecasting is still in its infancy. All that can be said is that it represents a promising area for future research.

V. PRODUCTION MODELS CONTAINING R & D EXPENDITURES

Next, let's consider the use of production models containing R & D expenditures. In recent years, a number of economists, including

---

[1] A. Carter, 'Technological Forecasting and Input–Output Analysis', *Technological Forecasting and Social Change* (1970) pp. 331–45.
[2] Ibid.

Solow,[1] Denison,[2] Griliches[3] and myself,[4] have attempted to formulate econometric models of production in which research and development plays a role. These models are over-simplified and incomplete in many respects. Yet they provide reasonably persuasive evidence that R & D has a significant effect on the rate of productivity increase in the industries and time periods that have been studied. For example, in his study of agriculture, Griliches investigated the relationship in various years between output per farm in a given state and the amounts of land, labour, fertiliser, and machinery per farm, as well as average education and expenditures on research and extension in a given state. The results indicate that, holding other inputs constant, output was related in a statistically significant way to the amount spent on research and extension. Turning to manufacturing, a study of my own, based on data regarding ten large chemical and petroleum firms and ten manufacturing industries, indicated that the measured rate of productivity change was related in a statistically significant way to the rate of growth of cumulated R & D expenditures made by the firm or industry.

These models can be used for technological forecasting. In particular, they can be used to forecast the effects on productivity or output of a certain investment in research and development at various points in time.[5] Moreover, they can be used to forecast future requirements for labour and other inputs.[6] Of course, they cannot be used to forecast the precise nature of the technology that will result from an investment in R & D. But they can provide some idea of the input–output relationships that this technology will permit – and for many purposes these relationships are what really count. For example, if we can be reasonably sure that a given investment in R & D will result in a certain reduction in cost (or in the use of certain crucial inputs), this may be all that is really relevant in making

[1] R. Solow, 'Technical Change and the Aggregate Production Function', *Review of Economics and Statistics* (Aug 1957).

[2] E. Denison, *The Sources of Growth in the United States*, Committee for Economic Development (1962).

[3] Z. Griliches, 'Research Expenditures, Education, and the Aggregate Agricultural Production Function', *American Economic Review* (Dec 1964).

[4] E. Mansfield, *Industrial Research and Technological Innovation* (W. W. Norton for the Cowles Foundation for Research in Economics at Yale University, 1968).

[5] Somewhat similar models have been used in defence. For example, see C. Trozzo, 'Productivity of Defense R D T and E', Institute for Defense Analysis, Paper P–825 (Oct 1971). Also see R. Isenson, 'Technological Forecasting Lessons from Project Hindsight', in Bright, op. cit.

[6] For example see E. Mansfield, 'Innovation and Technical Change in the Railroad Industry', in National Bureau of Economic Research, *Transportation Economics* (Columbia University Press, 1965).

certain decisions. The precise nature of the new technology may not matter much.

It might be noted that some of our government agencies have become interested in these models in recent years. Specifically, these models suggest that the marginal rate of return from certain types of civilian R & D is very high, and that we may be under-investing in such R & D. It is difficult, of course, to tell how much influence these models had on the recent decisions by the American government to experiment with various devices to encourage additional R & D in various civilian areas. But I know that they were one of the influences at work. However, lest anyone gets the impression that these models are sufficiently dependable to play a dominant role in influencing such decisions, let me add that they are extremely crude and subject to considerable error. In a recent paper, I set forth a rather detailed evaluation of these models and a list of relevant areas and topics that, in my opinion, are in need of further research.[1] Much more work needs to be done.

VI. DIFFUSION MODELS

Finally, let's consider the use of diffusion models. In the past fifteen years, a number of studies have been made of the diffusion of innovations. The results suggest that it is possible, on the basis of fairly simple econometric models, to explain fairly well the differences among industrial innovations in their rate of diffusion. In 1961, I presented a simple model – based on variables like the profitability of the innovation, the size of the investment required to adopt the innovation, and the organisation of the industry of potential users – to explain differences in the rate at which innovations spread.[2] This model explained the rates of diffusion of a dozen major innovations in the United States very well. Moreover, subsequent work has shown that it is also useful in explaining the rates of diffusion of other innovations – and in other countries.[3]

[1] See E. Mansfield, 'Contribution of Research and Development to Economic Growth in the United States', *Science*, 8 Feb 1972. Also see the papers by Griliches, Minasian, Terleckij, Fellner and Nelson cited there.

[2] E. Mansfield, 'Technical Change and the Rate of Imitation', *Econometrica* (Oct 1961). Also see Z. Griliches, 'Hybrid Corn: An Exploration in the Economics of Technological Change', *Econometrica* (Oct 1957), and E. Rogers, *Diffusion of Innovations* (the Free Press, 1962).

[3] See E. Mansfield, J. Rapoport, J. Schnee, S. Wagner and M. Hamburger, *Research and Innovation in the Modern Corporation* (Norton, 1971), R. Hsia, 'Technological Change in the Industrial Growth of Hong Kong', in B. R. Williams (ed.), *Science and Technology in Economic Growth* (Macmillan, London, 1973), and the unpublished doctoral dissertations of F. Husic and A. Romeo, both carried out at the University of Pennsylvania.

Models of this sort can be used for technological forecasting. For many purposes, it is extremely important to know how rapidly a new technique will displace an old one. Obviously, this is of crucial importance to the firm marketing the new technique. But it may be of great importance to other groups as well. For example, government agencies are sometimes concerned with the extent to which labour will be displaced and the way in which particular areas will be affected. Also, labour unions and competing firms have a great interest in this question. For many purposes, the important consideration is not when an entirely new process or product will be invented in the future. Instead, it is how rapidly one can expect the new processes and products that have already been invented to diffuse. Certainly, in view of the long time lags in many sectors of the economy, this often is all that matters in the short run – and the intermediate run as well.

Diffusion models have found a variety of uses in technological forecasting. My own model has been used to forecast the rate of diffusion of numerically controlled machine tools in the tool and die industry.[1] Subsequent events indicate that, so far at least, these forecasts, made for a government agency, have been quite accurate.[2] In addition, this model has been used by a number of firms in a variety of industries. For example, a leading chemical firm has been experimenting with the use of this model to forecast the market penetration of its new products. And a leading aircraft engine manufacturer has used this model in its internal planning.[3] Of course, the fact that this model has been used does not mean that it is other than a simple first approximation. We are continually refining it and testing it on a wider and wider variety of technological and product areas. We are still far from having a satisfactory understanding of the diffusion process.

VII. NORMATIVE TECHNOLOGICAL FORECASTING

As pointed out in Section II, normative technological forecasting attempts to specify a rational allocation of R & D resources. More specifically, most of the literature on normative technological fore-

---

[1] It might also be noted that the 'substitution model' used by some technological forecasters is similar to models developed by economists. Apparently, some technological forecasters, unaware of the economics literature, do not realise that the parameters of their models can be explained by economic models.

[2] E. Mansfield, 'Determinants of the Speed of Application of New Technology', in B. R. Williams, op. cit.

[3] A. Wade Blackman, 'The Rate of Innovation in the Commercial Aircraft Jet Engine Market', *Technological Forecasting and Social Change* (1971).

casting is concerned with the choice of R & D projects. A variety of models have been developed to help solve this problem. These models vary enormously in sophistication, some relying on the crudest sorts of ranking procedures, some employing fairly straight-forward adaptations of capital budgeting techniques, some using linear programming, some using dynamic programming, and some using Bayesian decision theory. Among the best known of these techniques are PROFILE (Programmed Functional Indices for Laboratory Evaluation) and QUEST (Quantitative Utility Estimates for Science and Technology), both of which were developed for the U.S. Navy, and PATTERN (Planning Assistance Through Technical Evaluation of Relevance Numbers), developed by Honeywell.[1]

For present purposes, it is sufficient to present a relatively simple programming model to illustrate the nature of normative techno-logical forecasting. Suppose that a firm has a list of n possible R & D projects that it might carry out and that the ith project would cost C_i dollars to carry out. Moreover, the ith project is estimated to have a probability of success of P_i, and if successful, it will result in a profit (gross of R & D costs) of π_i. Then, if the firm can spend no more than C dollars on R & D, its problem can be represented as follows:

Maximise
$$\sum_{i=1}^{n} X_i(P_i\pi_i - C_i),$$

where
$$\sum_{i=1}^{n} X_iC_i \leqslant C$$

and
$$X_i = 0, 1.$$

In other words, the firm's problem is to choose the X_i – where $X_i = 1$ if the ith project is accepted and 0 if it is rejected – in such a way that the expected value of profit is maximised, subject to the con-straint that the total amount spent on R & D be no more than C. This, of course, is an integer programming problem.[1]

Of course, this is a relatively simple model. It is possible to make this model more realistic by recognising that the firm may be inter-ested in parameters of the probability distribution of profit other

[1] See M. Cetron, R. Isenson, J. Johnson, A. Nutt and H. Wells, *Technical Resource Management Quantitative Methods* (M.I.T., 1969), as well as the works cited in n. 1, p. 334 and n. 1, p. 335 above.

[1] This model is somewhat similar to one proposed by R. Freeman, 'A Stochastic Model for Determining the Size and Allocation of the Research **Budget**', *IEEE Transactions on Engineering Management* (Mar 1960).

than the expected value. It is possible to recognise that, in most cases, there are a variety of expenditure levels at which a project can be carried out. It is possible to recognise that the impact of one project may depend on the outcome of another project. If one is willing to cope with the complexities and data requirements that result, it is possible to extend this model in many directions. But for present purposes, this simple model is a suitable illustration.[1]

VIII. THE APPLICATION OF NORMATIVE TECHNOLOGICAL FORECASTING

It is difficult to measure with accuracy the extent to which normative technological forecasting is being used in the United States. Our own surveys indicate that a large proportion of the laboratories – particularly the larger laboratories – in the chemical, drug, and electronics industries are using some form of quantitative project selection technique. But it is difficult to tell how significant such techniques are in the decision-making process. In some laboratories, they are taken much more seriously than in others. Indeed, one suspects strongly that in some laboratories these techniques are little more than window dressing, the real determinants of project selection – professional hunch, intra-firm politics, as well as a host of other factors – being at work behind the facade.[2]

However, one thing appears to be clear: the more sophisticated types of normative technological forecasting models are not being used very extensively. For example, Cetron and Ralph report that only 20 per cent of the firms responding to their survey had tested or used linear programming models and that only about 10 per cent had tested or used more complicated techniques like PROFILE, QUEST or PATTERN.[3] And for a variety of reasons, I suspect that these figures are over-estimates for American industry as a whole. In the American government, there has been considerable attention devoted to normative technological forecasting, particularly in the Department of Defense. But it is difficult to tell with any certainty the extent to which these models have actually been applied.

There are a number of reasons why the more sophisticated normative technological forecasting models have not found extensive use. First, even the more sophisticated models are often over-

---

[1] For more complex models, see the references in n. 1, p. 334 above.

[2] Mansfield, Rapoport, Schnee, Wagner and Hamburger, op. cit.

[3] Cetron and Ralph, op. cit. Also see N. Baker and W. Pound, 'R and D Project Selection: Where We Stand', *IEEE Transactions on Engineering Management* (June 1964).

simplified in important respects. For example, many models fail to recognise that R & D is a process of buying information, that 'unsuccessful' projects can provide much valuable information, and that the problem is one of sequential decision-making under uncertainty. Thus, they fall into the sorts of traps that the RAND studies of military R & D describe so well.[1] Second, application of the more sophisticated normative technological forecasting is not cheap. For example, Jantsch has estimated that the cost of setting up a PATTERN model is about $250,000 and that the cost of 'maintaining' the model is about $50,000 per year. Needless to say, many techniques do not cost nearly this much, but they are far from costless. Third, and perhaps most important, these models are based on estimates that are extremely unreliable, as we shall see in the following section.[2]

IX. ACCURACY OF ESTIMATES

Practically any normative technological forecasting model requires estimates of the cost of carrying out a prospective R & D project, the time that it will take, the probability that it will achieve certain results, and the value of these results, if achieved. Unfortunately, these estimates tend to be quite inaccurate. In the military field, it is well known that there tend to be large over-runs in R & D costs and lesser over-runs in R & D time. For example, Peck and Scherer found that for a sample of twelve airplane and missile development projects, the average ratio of actual to estimated cost was 3.2, and the average ratio of actual to estimated time was 1·4.[3] In civilian fields, there seems to be more optimism concerning the accuracy of these estimates, with a surprising number of R & D managers regarding such estimates as good or excellent. However, the available evidence indicates that these estimates are almost as bad for civilian as for military work when reasonably large technical advances are attempted.

Even when firms doing commercial work attempt relatively minor advances, these estimates tend to be considerably wide of the mark.

[1] T. Marschak, T. Glennan and R. Summers, *Strategy for R and D* (Springer Verlag, 1967).

[2] For a hard-hitting critique of the technological forecasting methods proposed in the works cited in n. 1, p. 334, n. 1, p. 335 and n. 1, p. 342, see E. Roberts, 'Exploratory and Normative Technological Forecasting: A Critical Appraisal', paper presented at the NATO Defence Research Group's Seminar on Technological Forecasting, 12–14 Nov 1968. Roberts describes some of the principal reasons why these methods have not found extensive use.

[3] M. Peck and F. Scherer, *The Weapons Acquisition Process* (Harvard University Press, 1962).

For example, in a proprietary drug firm we studied, the average ratio of actual to estimated development cost was 2.1, and the average ratio of actual to estimated development time was 2.9. Moreover, the standard deviation of the cost ratio was 3.2, and the standard deviation of the time ratio was 1.6. Clearly, these estimates of development cost and time were very inaccurate. Studies of the accuracy of estimates of the probability of technical success indicate that they too are not very trustworthy. For example, in the proprietary drug firm cited above, although the estimated probabilities of technical completion are of some use in predicting which projects will be completed and which will not, they are not of much use. Indeed, they do not do much better than one would expect by chance. To top it all off, it is generally agreed that the value of the R & D results, if achieved, is even harder to predict than the other things noted above. For example, the extent and duration of the market for a new product is very difficult to forecast.[1]

Given the large biases and errors in the estimates that are used in normative technological forecasting models, it is no wonder that managers have not been quick to adopt them. Indeed, as noted above, there is some evidence that managers may be more optimistic than they have a right to be about the accuracy of some of these estimates. If they had a better idea of how bad these estimates tended to be, they might be even more reluctant to place any dependence on them. With regard to these errors and biases, it should be noted that, to a considerable extent, they are not merely a product of uncertainty. It would be naïve to close one's eyes to the fact that these estimates are used to allocate the firm's or agency's resources. Consciously or unconsciously, cost and time estimates may be biased downward – and estimates of the value of research results may be biased upward – to 'sell' projects to management. This factor, as well as the uncertainties inherent in research and development, is responsible for the large errors in these estimates.

X. EXPERIMENTS TO IMPROVE THE ESTIMATES AND TO EXTEND THE MODELS

How can these estimates be improved? To try to find out, my co-workers and I have carried out several studies of the development and innovative process, particularly in the pharmaceutical and chemical industries, to see the extent to which econometric models

---

[1] For the results underlying this paragraph of the text, see Mansfield, Rapoport, Schnee, Wagner and Hamburger, op. cit. Also see D. Meadows, 'Estimate Accuracy and Project Selection Models in Industrial Research', *Industrial Management Review* (Spring 1968).

M*

can be used to forecast development cost. Needless to say, development cost is only one of many things that one would like to forecast, but it seemed to be a reasonable place to begin. The results have proved encouraging to date. For example, an attempt was made to explain a new drug's development cost by the nature of the new drug (product category, type and number of dosage forms, and spectrum of activity), the extent of the technological advance, the use of parallel development efforts, the priority attached to the project, and a trend term. When the accuracy of this model's forecasts was compared with the accuracy of the estimates made at the outset of each project by the firm, we found that, for most types of projects, the model-generated forecasts were more accurate than the firm's forecasts.[1]

In addition, econometric studies have been carried out to determine how long it takes to develop various types of products and to determine the extent of the non-R & D costs that are involved in successful product innovation in various industries. For example, models have been constructed to explain the percentage of the total costs of a product innovation that is incurred in the following stages of the innovation process: (1) applied research, (2) specification of product specifications, (3) prototype or pilot-plant design, construction and testing, (4) production planning, tooling, and construction and installation of manufacturing facilities, (5) manufacturing start-up, and (6) marketing start-up. These models may be of use in providing certain kinds of estimates needed in normative technological forecasting. They may also be of use in exploratory technological forecasting. For one thing, they demonstrate the important fact that major innovations generally take quite a long time to go from conceptualisation to commercial introduction. For example, the average time interval between the discovery of a new drug and its first commercial introduction in the United States seems to have been about five years – and this lag appears to be shorter than the lag in other industries.[2]

Despite the fact that research is going on to improve existing

---

[1] Most of the results in this section of the paper are described in more detail in ibid.

[2] Also see F. Lynn, 'An Investigation of the Rate of Development and Diffusion of Technology in Our Modern Industrial Society', *Report of the National Commission on Technology, Automation, and Economic Progress* (Washington, D.C., 1966), and C. Freeman, 'Research and Development in Electronic Capital Goods', *National Institute Economic Review* (Nov 1965).

These relatively long lags are also important in connection with technological assessment. For example see National Academy of Sciences, *Technology: Processes of Assessment and Choice*, Committee on Science and Astronautics, U.S. House of Representatives (July 1969), and National Academy of Engineering, *A Study of Technology Assessment*, Committee on Science and Astronautics, U.S. House of Representatives (July 1969).

estimates, it seems doubtful that we will ever be able to forecast the relevant variables very accurately. Thus, more emphasis should be placed on various kinds of sensitivity analysis to show the effects on the results of errors in the estimates. For example, returning to the model in Section VII, one could obtain data concerning the frequency distributions of the errors in C_i, P_i and π_i in the past. Then one could use these frequency distributions to generate a set of 'errors' that could be used to modify the estimates of C_i, P_i and π_i for each of the projects under consideration. Then one could solve the model a number of times, each solution corresponding to a random drawing of 'errors' from the historical frequency distributions. Finally, one could compute for each project the proportion of the cases where it was included in the optimal solution. A comparison among projects of the resulting proportions would indicate how sure one could be that various projects should be carried out.

XI. TECHNOLOGICAL FORECASTING: A BRIEF APPRAISAL

In conclusion, it seems fair to characterise the present state-of-the-art in technological forecasting as follows: First, most of the techniques commonly used for exploratory forecasting seem crude, even by the standards of the social and management sciences. In view of this crudeness, it seems unlikely that the results can be at all accurate. But as matters stand, one cannot even be sure of this, since there have been no studies measuring the track record of various kinds of technological forecasting techniques. Such studies seem to be called for. It would be useful to have some idea of how well these techniques have performed under various circumstances, and of which sorts of techniques seem to do better under particular kinds of circumstances. Without such information, it is hard for anyone to make decisions concerning the types of exploratory forecasting activities that are worth carrying out.

Second, although the crudeness of most existing techniques may be lamentable, there is no doubt that technological forecasting is a necessary part of the decision-making process in firms and government agencies. Just as there is no way to avoid forecasting the economic future – explicitly or implicitly – so there is no way to avoid forecasting the technological future. But this does not mean that it is necessarily worthwhile for a firm or government agency to support any formal work in technological forecasting. Whether or not it is worthwhile to support such work depends on whether – under the particular set of circumstances facing the firm or agency – the potential gains seem to outweigh the costs.[1] And given the lack of reliable data regarding the likely gains from various kinds of technological forecasting, this is not an easy comparison to make.

Third, there is a great need for studies leading toward a better understanding of the process of technological change. Until the fundamental processes are somewhat better understood, it seems unlikely that much improvement will occur in exploratory forecasting techniques. The area that is perhaps best understood at present is the diffusion process – and this is the area where forecasting currently seems most effective. Needless to say, I am not suggesting that a moratorium be declared on technological forecasting until we understand the basic processes more thoroughly. What I am suggesting is that more emphasis be placed by researchers and practitioners on the accumulation of the basic knowledge that is required if this field is to become more of a science and less of an art.

Fourth, if normative technological forecasting is to become of widespread use, it is important that better methods be developed to estimate development cost, time, the probability of success, and the value of the outcome if achieved. At present, such estimates tend to be so biased and error-ridden that it is difficult to place much dependence on the results. There is some evidence that econometric models of the development process may result in improved estimates, but it will be some time before we will have any real idea of how far we can go along this route. In view of the inaccuracy of these estimates, organisations that use normative technological forecasting techniques would be well advised to carry out sensitivity analyses to see the effect of such errors on the results. And they would be well advised to see how big the errors in these estimates have been in the recent past – since there seems to be some tendency to underestimate their size.

Fifth, despite the problems in normative technological forecasting, it may be worthwhile for an organisation to devote some effort to such forecasting. After all, if the model is roughly correct – which admittedly is a big 'if', judging from some of the models that have been proposed – the model focuses attention on the relevant variables and forces people to think about them. Even if it is very difficult to come up with accurate estimates of these variables, an exercise of this sort can be worthwhile. (It is easy to underestimate the usefulness of such exercises, unless you have seen the way that some organisations actually work.) However, if such exercises are

[1] Thus, Quinn is, of course, quite correct in stressing that technological forecasts need not be completely, or even very accurate to be useful. The correct test is whether their value exceeds their cost. See J. Quinn, 'Technological Forecasting', *Harvard Business Review* (Mar 1967).

to have any real impact, the work of the technological forecasters must be integrated properly with the decisions of the planners and the managers. Too often, the work of the technological forecasters is largely ignored in the decision-making process. If this work is worth doing at all, it should be related and coupled with long-range planning and decision-making.[1]

Finally, it is important to recognise that technological forecasting, if done right, involves much more than just science and engineering. One cannot estimate the probability that a particular technology will come into being on the basis of technological considerations alone. Economic, social, and political considerations often play an equally important role. Moreover, one cannot decide how an organisation's technological resources should be allocated and utilised on the basis of technological considerations alone. Clearly, economic, social, political, and other considerations are involved here as well. Thus, regardless of what sort of mechanism a firm or agency uses to supply its technological forecasts – whether that mechanism be a formal group or an informal one, and whether it uses intuitive or more objective techniques – it is important that the mechanism be properly tuned in to the economic, social, and political environment, as well as to the relevant science and technology.

---

[1] See P. Thurston, 'Make TF Serve Corporate Planning', *Harvard Business Review* (Sep 1971), J. Dory and R. Lord, 'Does TF Really Work?', *Harvard Business Review* (Nov 1970), and Quinn, op. cit.

16 Problems Created by the Increasing Pace of Technical Progress

H. Aujac

I. THE PROBLEMS

Technical progress has accelerated, sometimes spontaneously, some-times through stimulus by the public authorities. It has brought with it a new set of problems. This note examines certain aspects of two of them. The first problem is that of the possible dangers for general economic development arising when official policy aims to raise the technical level of the production system generally by foster-ing the development of high technology industries. The second problem is that of the conflicts implicit in the rules for managing the human capital represented by the technical knowledge and know-how of the economically active population. In some respects these rules are economically irrational and socially unacceptable.

II. DANGERS FROM HIGH TECHNOLOGY INDUSTRIES

It has recently been shown that unco-ordinated acceleration of technical progress can weaken an economy, and in extreme cases dislocate it entirely. It is noteworthy that the absence of co-ordina-tion as such has been discovered only after the event. Initially, it was aimed to achieve it and the official authorities sponsoring the technical progress were seeking the opposite result, a strengthened structure of the production system.

Many countries have followed the American example in recent years, and have created 'new' or 'advanced' industries. We shall refer to them as 'high technology' industries. Examples are civil and military atomic energy, electronic computer manufacture, the aero-space industries. Their original purpose was to serve the needs of national defence, economic independence or prestige, but the powers-that-be tend to justify the massive outlays incurred by another argument, with which this paper is concerned. It is that the high technology sector will necessarily speed the rate of technical progress of the economy at large, through the introduction of new techniques, the development of new products, and in particular, technological 'fall-out'.

The hope, in other words, has been that the initial, deliberately engendered, unbalance between the various sectors of the economy would act as a driving force raising the technical level of all of them. It has turned out to be largely illusory in many countries, even the United States. Only in a few rare instances (the computer is one) has the purposely caused disequilibrium done what was expected of it. More usually, it has remained 'unco-ordinated' with, if anything, a detrimental effect on the economy.

It is worth trying to see why these bright hopes have so often been disappointed. No one explanation can fit all countries; there are too many differences in the nature of the central authorities, the type of technical progress they have encouraged, the forms of incentive provided, and the political context. Nevertheless, as a working hypothesis, there may be a sufficiently general explanation available to account for the fact that in certain circumstances technical advance can take place in some sectors to the benefit of all, whereas in others its effects are ultimately harmful.

The following picture must naturally be drawn with broad strokes. The main way in which a high technology industry differs from a traditional one lies in its requirement for highly qualified men capable of designing and using advanced techniques, products and equipment.[1] It will pay a high price for its inputs of brainpower, equipment and techniques, for its promoter – the official sector – is willing to pay heavily. Conversely, the traditional industries are content to have men, products, equipment and techniques of more limited potential, and as far as possible will buy them cheaply. Their customer is the public, and the movement of their costs is the determinant factor in their further growth.

When the first high technology industries were built up, only weak links existed between them and the traditional sector. Several types of development were then possible. Two of them will be described schematically: one, achievement of the public sector's original goal, integration of the technical advances into the economy generally, and the other, the failure of this policy, with technical acceleration emerging as an 'unco-ordinated' element of economic activity.

In the first case, if the firms forming the high technology industry expand fast enough (i.e. if the official authorities provide a large, secure and dynamic market for their output), the cost of their men, products and techniques will tend to decline, and other industries can afford to use the personnel they have trained, the products they market, and the techniques they have developed. They will have

---

[1] Clearly a high share, or even a very high share, of the outlays in creating a 'new' industry is devoted to traditional facilities: plant, offices, machine tools, etc. Here, however, we are abstracting, to focus on the aspects that are specific to a high technology activity.

acted as a powerful, dynamic technical training institution at the service of industries generally. In a second stage, the traditional industries will, with the passage of time, become more and more demanding in their technical requirements, and so more closely concerned with further improvements in results, i.e. the two groups' best interests are mutually supporting, but this will only happen in practice when the high technology industries' costs fall to a level at which the traditional industries find the partnership an economic proposition. The process will culminate in full symbiosis, at which point it can validly be stated that the high technology industries of today have played a decisive role in general economic development.

However, things can go sour. As was noted, success in this area is determined by the correspondence of two rates, one the rate of expansion of the technical requirements of the traditional industries, the other a decline in the relative cost of the men, equipment and techniques available in and through the new industries. Anything that fosters a more rapid increase in the two rates makes the optimistic outcome more plausible. Any check to either tilts the balance in the direction of failure of the integration process.

If the gap between the technical requirements of the high technology and traditional industries widens, the potential wealth embodied in the teams of scientists, engineers and architects, created to implement the public sector's programme, is irremediably sterilised, as is the contribution of the equipment they design and develop. The full burden of the substantial effort is borne by the economy, and must be charged to the needs of defence or prestige. In this particular case, either is in contradiction to a policy of higher welfare or even true strengthening of power.[1]

These, then, are some of the risks to the economy inherent in excessively divergent and therefore unco-ordinated trends in the rate of technical advance of two groups of industries. However, the example is only partial and needs to be generalised. Even in a rudimentary analysis of the modern economy, at least five types of activity must be distinguished for an adequate description of economic and social development. These are research and development (R & D); high technology industries; raw materials and semi-finished products; manufacturing proper (with its two sub-groups, consumption and production goods manufacture); and services. All five must be brought under review simultaneously to avoid unco-ordinated technical acceleration of any one of them, and, more importantly, to secure harmonious, integrated technical advance.

---

[1] A high technology policy can indeed damage not only the economy at large, but also the defence effort. See 'Military Efficiency and Economic Social and Political Structures' [in French], *Revue Economique* (July 1971).

They are so interdependent that a policy of technological development that closes its eyes to them or merely makes insufficient allowance for them, is liable to yield exactly the opposite results to those originally intended.

III. WASTAGE OF INTELLECTUAL CAPITAL

Wastage of intellectual capital is another danger to which unco-ordinated technical acceleration may give rise. This danger is of course not unconnected with the problems discussed above.

A characteristic of technical progress is that it renders products, productive facilities, firms, and industrial structures obsolete. In so doing, it also renders obsolete skills and qualifications, and therefore men themselves as regards an essential component of their personal make-up. This is normal and desirable. It is a condition of all economic and social progress, and may even be one of the most powerful factors making for enrichment of the human personality.

Nevertheless, there are limits to everything. It is easy to perceive that over-rapid obsolescence of existing know-how, skills and qualifications may entail a waste of intellectual capital that is detrimental to society as a whole.

It is to be feared that high-level technical personnel[1] may in future be the main victims of this phenomenon of technological obsolescence, and their position will therefore be taken as an illustration of the point to be made here. Although considerably more thorough analysis is required for formal proof, there is a growing body of evidence to suggest that, astonishingly, technical progress is changing the status of technical executives in exactly the opposite direction to the trends observed in the case of the unskilled labour force.

There is no need to restate the extent to which industrial mechanisation has transformed the structure of the work force. Highly specialised skilled labour has gradually been replaced by unskilled manpower, easily trained and easily interchangeable. This has important implications for employment policy. When use of skilled labour predominated, balance between the demand and supply of jobs was sought in the individual labour markets relating to specific qualifications and skills. This was always a difficult problem, and up to the French Revolution the corporative system was the solution implemented, at a price in foregone technical progress. The change-over to use of unskilled labour facilitated matters in as much as

---

[1] *Ingénieurs* in French. This term has no direct equivalent in English. It refers to persons with advanced training, usually at university graduate level, in their particular speciality, which may range from civil engineering to agriculture or even marketing.

technical progress has increased occupational mobility. All that is needed today for a full employment policy is to balance overall supply and demand. There is no need to look for equilibrium in individual markets.

The question is whether technical progress may not engender exactly the opposite trend for high-level technical personnel. Until recently, demand greatly outran supply, and these employees could easily adapt to different activities, since specialisation essentially meant entering a branch directly related to a common trunk of scientific and technical knowledge at the disposal of all. There was no problem about finding jobs or securing a satisfactory career. Today, however, the faster pace of scientific discovery and technical progress and, most important, the need for specialised awareness in an ever more diversified and divorced range of fields, has splintered the common trunk in favour of specialised educational streams. Technologically specialised staff have become less and less adaptable to activities outside their speciality. The usefulness of their knowledge is brought into question more and more frequently at the same time as their transfer elsewhere is increasingly hampered by the speed at which technical progress is taking place.

The problem of the social cost of the obsolescence of diplomas, degrees and skills, may be one of the most intractable difficulties harassing economic and social development over the next few decades. Comparison of two rates is again decisive in helping to understand the origin and nature of this situation. On the one hand, there is the rate of renewal of technical knowledge of a given type necessary to maintain technical progress; on the other, the rate at which it is possible to retrain displaced personnel for activities in high technology industries.

Until recently, the second of these two rates was higher, and the existence of the problem was hidden. At best, there may have been some regret that technical progress was occurring too slowly to draw in enough people, with mild depreciation of the corresponding failure to achieve full personality enrichment.

In the opposite situation, with technical progress now calling for a renewal of knowledge much more quickly than individuals can meet the demands on them, there may be wastage. At the overall level, new techniques may contribute less than the cost of premature withdrawal of men and machines. On the human side, the people affected feel beyond their depth, whatever their efforts or their capacity. This is a massacre of intellectual and technical knowledge, one of the fundamental components of personality.

An intermediate position would no doubt be an economic and social optimum, namely evolution of techniques and human capacity at a comparable pace. Economic and social development would remain in balance from the twin points of view of the economy as such and the quality of life. Many would be called on, but no one for more than he can offer.

If this is right, any policy aiming at matching the two rates we have been discussing is good for the economy and its members. Any other policy which hinders or delays the process will lead to economic and human waste. The maximum tolerable rate depends in the final analysis on the practical possibility of retraining personnel to endow them with the fresh technical qualifications necessary.[1]

This indicates that if the optimum just defined is to be attained, light must be thrown on the factors governing the two rates which we now know to be the master force. This is an enormous, and enormously difficult subject, on which the following comments can nevertheless be offered.

The rules of the economic mechanism set an 'economic' limit to the rate at which investments can be renewed. The textbooks use an admittedly over-simplified but helpful example: under sound economic management, equipment in service should only be scrapped when prime costs per unit of output (i.e. variable costs excluding overheads) are greater than market prices.

This management rule efficiently protects existing investment from the competition of alternatives, whose cost structure is loaded by the need to take account of overheads in determining economic rates of return. Its effect is to determine the most profitable rate at which an enterprise should renew its facilities. Any deviation from this rate reduces actual earnings below their potential level, whether due to economically unjustified technical innovation or, in the opposite direction, technical over-conservatism.[2]

Curiously, there is no similar rule to regulate the rate of human renewal, i.e. renewal of the intellectual capital formed by know-how, skills, training and knowledge.

---

[1] This being so, wastage of this kind should not be imputed to unco-ordinated technical acceleration except to the extent that individual retraining is being undertaken at the highest feasible rate, i.e. to the extent it is really in the power of individuals to make full use of their personal scope for drawing full advantage from the retraining facilities at their disposal.

[2] The rule is often infringed in public sector investment programmes, because of the methods used to finance R & D investment, and occasionally productive investment proper. While there must be some suspicion of unco-ordinated economic advance through technical progress, this is not invariably true. 'Structurally-related' outlays that modify the economic and social environment in which they will be used, should probably not be subjected to these rules. This is not the place, however, to go into this difficult problem.

It is easy to see why, in present circumstances, enterprises cannot carry out this regulatory function. The comparison between human and physical capital[1] immediately discloses that a firm wishing to replace a member of its technical staff by another can ignore the costs of technical training, because under the current ground rules of the economic process it will never have to pay them. They are borne first by parents and then by the educational system. Of course, the picture would change if the firm had to 'purchase' its training, for example, by refunding the corresponding training costs on each new hiring to the educational system.[2] This would obviously cause firms to draw as fully as possible on the retraining potential of their existing personnel, and the resultant turnover rate of high level technical staff would be no more – and no less – economically justified than that governing the rate of renewal of investments which is judged optimum from the standpoint of profitability.

It follows that the system chosen for imputing the costs of human training determines the speed at which firms will turn their personnel over. It is surprising to find that the problem of the 'best' system of imputation has apparently not been formulated clearly. Yet it is decisive for the future of the economy and society.

IV. SOME CONCLUSIONS

The sole purpose of the discussion above has been to draw attention to some of the dangers with which an economy may be beset by unco-ordinated acceleration of development.

Up to now, it does not seem that the main responsibility for unco-ordinated technical progress lies with the major corporations, which have sought security through forced demand growth and control of the economic and political environment, but have not been dynamic propagators of technological innovation. The finger must be pointed squarely at the central authorities. The power to solve the problem is also in the hands of the central authorities – although they may not yet have all the requisite knowledge.

As the economy functions at present, conflicts will inevitably emerge between the needs of overall development on the one hand

[1] The writer is full aware that this approach to the problem may appear to fall far short of the respect due to human integrity, and that it may shock the reader. It is intended only as a preliminary approach. For an overall, humanist discussion of the issue – and none other is acceptable – see for example François Perroux on 'les coûts de l'homme' [the cost of man].

[2] Of course these are difficult and complex problems. To avoid all ambiguity as regards the scope of the comments made, it should be repeated that the only purpose of the study is to raise these problems, not to express an opinion as to the propriety of various possible solutions.

(which is desired and in part engendered by the public authorities who are usually acknowledged to act in the general interest), and on the other the respect of personal interests as currently defined, especially in the framework of the existing rules for distributing income and costs. These latent conflicts will become visible once awareness develops of the complementarity (indeed, the solidarity) under conditions of rapid economic growth between, on the one hand, the technical and economic stagnation of certain sectors, which is felt by those concerned in the form of loss of capital, unduly low earnings and even unemployment, and, on the other hand, the rapid growth of other sectors which yields those participating in it massive uncovenanted capital gains or an unwarrantedly high level of income.

The enrichment of some and the impoverishment of others have up to now been considered as independent phenomena, the results of the encounter of chance and individual effort. This view can no longer be defended. It is abnormal and immoral to consider that some must be kept in poverty and misfortune in order to nourish overall growth and augment the wealth and happiness of others. New rules for the distribution of incomes and costs will have to be written, translating the solidarity which binds men working in different sectors of the economy. Those whose specific welfare has been raised by development will have to bear the costs of reorienting the less fortunately placed, or, more radically, to finance a suitable quality and standard of living for those on whom the costs of supporting development have fallen. Contrast this with the position today, in which the whole burden of the cost of development falls on the income and assets of those who can least afford it.

Discussion of the Papers by
Professor Mansfield and M. Aujac

Professor Sedov (U.S.S.R.) in opening the discussion of these two papers said that Professor Mansfield dealt with the extremely important subject of a comparison of different methods of technological forecasting in the U.S.A. The goals and possibilities of technological forecasting were examined from the economist's point of view, and the methods discussed included heuristic and Delphi methods, extrapolation, inter-sector balance, production functions and models of diffusion of new technology. It was to be noticed that none of these methods took adequate account of technological progress and that the estimation of prospective coefficients of material and labour inputs for inter-sector balances greatly depended on the estimator's ability to forecast technological changes.

It could be added that the most important and challenging task for technological forecasting was to blend different methods into a coherent methodology and to design a system of models which would make it possible to dovetail forecasting and modelling at plant, sector and economy levels. By combining a balancing technique, methods of production forecasting, models of diffusion of new technology, and future resource allocation, it should be possible to turn technological forecasting into the major instrument of long-term planning and economic policy making.

Professor Mansfield had examined the problem of accuracy of forecasts with regard to initial information by the use of normal statistical methods of error evaluation and had made certain recommendations. While agreeing with Professor Mansfield's general criticisms of the state of technological forecasting, he would like to emphasise that turning technological forecasting into a science was wholly dependent on the solution of three interrelated problems: first, improvement of one's powers of analysis of the various objectives of technological progress and the relationships between them; second, the creation of an information and statistical basis for forecasting and for developing a system of indicators, both of them employing methods of data collection on some international standard; third, a considerable further improvement of mathematical apparatus and forecasting models, and their co-ordination into a single coherent system that would permit transitions from micro- to macro-level and *vice versa*. For the moment major progress had been achieved in modelling while there was still a lag in respect of qualitative analysis and information and of the statistical background. Technological forecasting was so remarkably short of statistics that every forecast demanded enormous effort to collect and process the required information. That was why technological forecasting was extremely expensive and came up against the passive reluctance of planners to its acceptance. The U.S.S.R. experience had shown that all the three tasks had to be solved simultaneously to make it possible to introduce technological forecasting into the practice of planning.

M. Aujac had sought to answer two questions in his paper. First, he had examined the economic and socio-economic consequences of the state policy

for encouraging technological progress. In his opinion, the uneven technological development of different sectors of the economy as the result of
government action had led to negative or disappointing results. His hypothesis
was that under certain conditions priority given to certain industries could
cause unfavourable effects on the rest of the economy.

This was to be explained by the fact that labour and material resources
switched from traditional to new industries increased costs in the new
industries and decreased efficiency in the old industries. The total efficiency
of technological progress depended on balance between the rates of technological advance in the old industries and the rates of decrease of the unit manpower and resources costs that were necessary for the economy and were
produced by it. A gap between those two rates resulted in new industries
being financed at the expense of the old ones. Such financing was usually a
consequence of defence or national prestige considerations and was contrary
to the welfare and real development of the nation.

A logical conclusion was the necessity for a complex approach to the
problem of the technological advance of the national economy. One could
only agree with this conclusion, as well as with M. Aujac's emphasis on the
interdependence and interrelationship of all branches of an economy. It was
equally true that a system approach should underlie the technological policy
of the state. This was a justifiable conclusion; but in his opinion, it should
not be made obligatory.

Under conditions in which available resources were limited, a national
technological policy could not be anything but the priorities given to industries
that were essential for the future development of national economy. Equal
development of all branches of an economy was impossible even with
international economic aid, and technological modernisation of different
sectors could be done only by degrees. Thus, a complex approach had to be
regarded as necessary to maintain some dynamic balance in the development
of old and new industries. To illustrate his hypothesis, M. Aujac had drawn
attention to the damaging consequences for the economy as a whole from the
development of the nuclear, computer and aero-space industries. This example
seemed to Professor Sedov rather to illustrate the effects of military expenditures upon the economy.

Secondly, M. Aujac had argued that uneven and unco-ordinated growth
tended to result in the loss of 'intellectual capital', that was to say, in non-
rational use of manpower and skills. Technological progress caused changes
in the social status of highly skilled manpower and in its composition, led to
greater specialisation and to earlier and premature obsolescence of professional skills, degrees and diplomas. The social costs of these consequences
were very substantial and would affect the economy for decades to come.
The effect of introducing new technology could be nullified by under-use and
intellectual obsolescence of more highly skilled people as a result of too rapid
technological progress. Of very great importance in this context was the
relationship between the rates of modernisation of technical know-how and
the rates of retraining of manpower in the use of the new technology. The
latter had until recently far exceeded the former and the problem had not then
emerged.

In his opinion, the main reasons for this danger were to be found not in technological policy itself but in the absence of co-ordination between technological and social policies. It was vitally important that technological policy should be based on a system of professional and advanced retraining which would make possible a redistribution of labour resources under the conditions of more rapid technological progress. The experience of the socialist countries, all of which had systems of higher and special education and advanced training and retraining, showed that social policy could thus make it possible to avoid any damaging social consequences that might arise from technological progress.

M. Aujac had concluded by putting the blame for the damaging social consequences upon the government. Professor Sedov thought that it would be improper, under conditions of private property, to put the whole blame solely upon the government. The government's technological policy was under permanent pressure from large-scale private industry and its interests. Moreover, the technological policy of large corporations was in itself a major independent factor which helped to shape the structure of the national economy, in the U.S.A. as in some European countries.

Nor did he think that one could and should count on everybody realising the necessity for a general approach to these problems and acting correspondingly. Being a Marxist, he believed that the damaging social consequences of technological progress were caused by a particular social system rather than by technology itself. In short, he fully agreed that the problem needed to be tackled, but did not agree as to the nature of the problem and the ways to cure it.

He would like to know M. Aujac's views on the possibility of estimating the efficiency of an economic system under the conditions of technological progress, or at least, on the methods that should be used for quantitative estimation of the losses caused by uneven growth of different sectors of a national economy and by imbalance between technological progress and manpower training.

Professor Khachaturov (U.S.S.R.) thought that technological forecasting, and especially a long-term forecast, was an extremely difficult task, because many scientific discoveries simply could not be foreseen, whereas they were capable of changing substantially the course of technological progress. He agreed that all the methods suggested by Professor Mansfield should be employed. At the same time there was still another method being used in the U.S.S.R. to throw light on the basic trends of technological progress. It was what he would call collective discussion of the possibilities of certain developments in science and technology not by individual experts and not on specific objects, but by research institutions in regard to certain fields of science and of the national economy. He had in mind the discussions of intended developments of organic chemistry, of new transportation systems, and so on, that represented a kind of collective investigation of the field, its prospects and its possibilities, which had been organised jointly by the Academy of Sciences and its research institutions, by industrial research centres, and by planning organisations.

He agreed with M. Aujac that balanced introduction of new technology was of considerable economic importance, but he did not think that one should be afraid of identifying the mainstreams of technological progress on which there should be concentration. Historical experience showed that this had been and still was the path of technological discovery. Unquestionably it resulted in unbalanced development, yet these disproportions were advantageous rather than disadvantageous. For example, the advance in the space programme had required substantial improvements in the general technology of computers, of construction materials, of energy sources and other things and had provided an important stimulus to the development of many sectors of the economy.

Rapid progress in certain spearhead directions, requiring substantial capital investment, was the characteristic of modern technology and stimulated economic growth in many other directions. He did not think one ought to be afraid of these disproportions. It was very important in this context that long-term planning should provide for greater co-ordination in the growth of all sectors of the economy. It was in this sense that the analysis of economic efficiency was of crucial importance in making it possible to distinguish between different trends of development.

Dr Grove (U.S.A.) said that it was interesting to have in mind what some of the major corporations were doing about these things. As regards their role in general technological advancement, he thought one should make a clear distinction between invention and innovation. There had been a number of studies in the U.S.A. on the question whether corporations were the main source of invention. Whatever the answer to that, it would be difficult to dispute that they had been the major source of innovation or application of inventions. Corporations had a big incentive to make inventions useful in the market. As to Professor Sedov's comments, as one who worked for a large corporation, he would be very shocked if that corporation were to try to decide what the market ought to need rather than try to respond to what the customers wanted. The way they typically approached the problem of innovation was to try to anticipate what the needs of the market would be. This was done by elaborate survey of how customers' costs could be reduced, and then the technical people were told to find ways in which they could meet the needs of the customer. If a corporation was in the position to take some responsibility for technological progress that would be completely independent of the market needs, that would indicate first, that it had a great deal of monopoly power, second, he would think, that it would not retain that power for very many years, because other competitors, more responsive to the market, would increase their share. It was his belief that the wisdom of the corporation people was sufficient for them not to attempt to decide what should be best for the country as a whole.

He thought that dependence of technological advancement on military expenditures was greatly exaggerated. First, if one looked at defence companies in the U.S., most of them had not been outstandingly successful from the shareholders' standpoint. Heavy dependence on defence orders did not seem to be at all a good indicator of financial success of a corporation. Moreover, when he looked at the innovations which had contributed most to the technological advancement of the U.S., it was difficult to find many which would be connected with their military sales. Contrary to what most people thought, most of the improvement in computer capabilities had been designed in response to the commercial market needs. Some products such as military and space computers were so highly specialised that they could hardly be attributed to computer industries at all, and at least from the standpoint of his own corporation, military business was not considered highly profitable. A number of major innovations, such as copying machines, had no relation to military needs whatsoever. There were, of course, certain industries – for example, the aircraft industry – where the opposite was true. But they accounted for a rather small part of the whole economy. He thought that there was some general misunderstandings of the role of the military.

Professor Robinson (U.K.) was worried that we were promising more in the way of forecasting than it was at all possible to achieve. Could one forecast the rates technological progress in specific fields and in relation to specific inventions? He had himself spent several years on what was then called the Council of the Department of Scientific and Industrial Research, which allocated the greater part of the government contributions to research in the United Kingdom. He remembered very clearly that of all the research they were financing, only a small proportion ever came to birth at all. He would have found it very difficult to estimate in advance which of the projects they supported would finally produce some practical results. First, there was a time interval between the original idea and the initiation of the research project, and this interval varied enormously. Secondly, there was the problem of moving on from the laboratory result of the project, when and if it was successfully achieved, to some designed hardware that was saleable. Third, there were the problems of diffusion of the new technology and finding a market. No doubt one could break technological progress into sectors and industries and attempt to build up a general picture in this way; but he believed that technological progress was more predictable in overall terms than in terms of specific forms and industries. In this latter case, when Delphi methods were used for technological forecasting, did one get a convergence on what really proved to be the truth, or did one get convergence on what the most obstinate and dogmatic members of the committee insisted on arguing to be the truth?

Professor Machlup (U.S.A.) completely shared Professor Robinson's pessimism concerning forecasts of technological progress. He believed that in this case doubts were much better justified than optimism would be, and he would like to call attention to a *type* of invention and innovation which had not been mentioned. Very often chemical researchers came up with a new material without knowing in advance what it might be good for, and then they set about trying to find some application for whatever they had discovered. In other words, this was the type of advance which was certainly not determined by demand. There was no way of forecasting development of new things when one did not even know what they could be used for.

Professor Vinogradov (U.S.S.R.) felt that in response to Dr Grove he would like to quote the example of the Polaroid Corporation. When the Polaroid camera was invented, it was rejected by all the big corporations, and a special company had to be established to start manufacturing cameras which had now a world-wide reputation. He thought this was an illustration of the fact that it was not always the large corporation that was at the head of technological progress, even if the opposite way was also often true.

Dr Grove replied that suppose someone had come to a planning authority in the U.S.S.R. and suggested a method of photography which would involve a larger camera, a more sophisticated and much less convenient developing process and poorer quality of pictures than were already available, he felt very sure that the decision of the Soviet planning authorities would have been the same as that of the large American corporation. But the inventor had been a very persistent man, and he discovered that people attached great import-ance to getting an instant picture, no matter what the quality of the picture or the inconvenience of the process might be. So he achieved success. The point was that everyone could make mistakes, and this was an understandable mistake. A similar but less understandable mistake had been made by the I.B.M. Corporation, when it was offered the invention of the copying machine. One could find many mistakes of this type, but he was not at all sure that state planning authorities would take different decisions in similar cases. It was very difficult to estimate the demand for new products, and they in the I.B.M. Corporation believed that the permissible margin of error for forecasting the demand for basically new products could vary from about 25 per cent to something like 400 per cent in a fairly good prediction made at the time when it was decided to go ahead and have a product (they called that time the 'go/no-go' point. He might add that they used the Delphi method, calling in not only the experts of the Corporation but outside scientists as well, and they arrived at convergence of mediocrity rather than at new insights into the future of the field.

Professor Porwit (Poland) agreed with M. Aujac that the problem of balance or imbalance in static or of dynamic terms should not be worked out precisely but be considered in a preliminary way from the point of view of changes of relative costs, prices and efficiency for the prospective buyer. In regard to the human capital becoming obsolete, they were facing a situation in which young people entering industry got salaries that were far from commensurate with their knowledge and abilities, while older people received salaries that were disproportionately high in comparison with their industrial contribution. There could be two approaches to that problem. One was to try to change in some way the relative costs of hiring such people – that is, to make new entrants rather more costly. Another and more promising way was to make the values of the groups more proportionate to their present salaries. This meant a much greater stress on retraining schemes not only inside firms but also as a function of the educational system as a whole.

Professor Bénard (France) said that M. Aujac had made a very interesting distinction between the new and the old industries, the former having a special kind of spearheading technological effect on other industries. It was also suggested that making enterprises pay the costs of investment in human capital would be a strong incentive for them not to waste this capital. This was an interesting and important suggestion, but it created two problems at least. One was whether a labour market was in fact competitive. If it was, the cost of labour, including, of course, salaries of management and technical staff would be close to marginal cost, and thus the enterprise would pay that cost. But was that marginal cost a private cost or a social cost? In countries like France there was a big difference between private and social cost because higher education was practically free, and the conditions of the labour market could lead to inequality between the labour cost (or salary cost) and private marginal cost, and thus this market equilibrium was not an optimal allocation of resources. The difference between social and private education costs could be corrected through the budgetary and taxation system. If free higher education had to be paid back at a later stage when people started working, then the burden could be switched from the individuals and the labour market to firms. But if the market was competitive, this would occur through adjustment of salaries. But if the whole of taxation were regressive, especially that providing for education, the burden of taxation would be less than the benefits from education for the upper middle classes, while there was a category of people who were not taxed for education but on the other hand did not provide a substantial share of students. In the circumstances it would be anomalous to require enterprises, and not the beneficiaries, to pay the cost of education; he thought that would simply result in price increases which would shift the burden to the population in general.

Professor Denison (U.S.A.) thought that in one sense the notion of obsolescence of human skills could easily be over-rated. The usage of the term in the paper had been rather broad, and he thought it should be put in a somewhat different context. It should be remembered that in the U.S.A., and to a lesser extent in other countries, many of those who were formally qualified as highly skilled manpower, were in practice engaged in quite ordinary operations, and equivalence of training and work was far from perfect. As to the equity problem raised by M. Aujac, he thought it was to some extent a question of generation-wise inequity which was due to practically free higher education and the tremendous post-education opportunities now enjoyed by younger people, but which people of the older generations had never had. The equity problem itself did not appear to be clear.

Professor Topala (Roumania) thought that technological forecasting should be taken into account from the very first stage of long-term social and economic forecasting. There were two aspects of technological forecasting that needed consideration: the possibilities of technological progress and its probable trends, and the probable emergence of products that would be wholly new or would be substitutes for products of which there was a shortage. Technological forecasting could also solve certain problems raised by socio-economic forecasting. Of course it could not provide all the answers, but it could provide indications as to how such problems should be tackled, and what results might be expected.

One could argue that it was impossible to make technological forecasts for a small country with a limited range of resources both because of its limited research facilities and because of shortage of skilled manpower, and that for such a country it was more sensible to acquire licences, or in other words, to buy science from abroad. This had, however, both its advantages and its disadvantages, the latter being the technological and scientific backwardness that would result. No firm would sell a licence for the most advanced technology it possessed. Nor did the acquisition of a foreign licence guarantee the high quality and competitiveness of the product. It was usually necessary to adapt the foreign technology to the means and resources of the country that acquired it. One interesting form of technological progress took the form of the transplantation of methods used by certain industries to other products and other industries. Standardisation which had begun in engineering had now been transplanted to construction; industrial methods of production were being introduced into agriculture, and so on.

Professor Marczewski (France) wished first to comment on the role of the enterprise in the spread of innovations. He thought one should not try to draw a border-line between the roles of a big corporation and of a small firm or enterprise. Many examples of both the types mentioned by Dr Grove and Professor Vinogradov could be quoted, but he himself believed that the main border-line lay between what he would call a free market enterprise and an enterprise in an administrative economy. To avoid misunderstanding, he wanted to emphasise that this distinction was *not* identical to that between a socialist and a capitalist economy, because one could find many examples of administratively managed enterprises in a capitalist economy (for instance in their nationalised sectors), and equally there were market-operating enterprises in a socialist economy. The difference between these two types of enterprises in the application of innovations was simply that a free market enterprise had to maximise its profits just to survive. Such an enterprise had much more incentive to look for innovations and new products. It was also true because labour unions were more powerful in free market conditions, so that often wages might be increasing faster than productivity. As a result, an enterprise operating under free market conditions was absolutely obliged to look for innovations to preserve its share in the market and thus to survive in the face of competition and wage increases. On the other hand, under the conditions of the administrative economy an enterprise often regarded an innovation as a kind of nuisance which intruded into its smooth routine operation, and made it more difficult to execute its quantitative plan targets. As a result such an enterprise was not particularly willing to introduce innovations unless it was absolutely necessary.

His second comment concerned the balance between professional training and the needs of the economy. He did not see any ready solution to this problem which had already become important and would be of increasing importance in the future. One possible future solution might be greater international mobility of specialist labour. This could be very valuable within the E.E.C. as well as for smaller countries. Another solution was, of course, reform of the planning of education, with emphasis on less specialised education. Yet another solution might be more specialisation of smaller countries – and he included even France in this category – on a limited range of industries. The need for such specialisation was obvious, though the choice was not going to be easy and the responsibility of planners would be extremely heavy, especially if they were to avoid hasty decisions while keeping open broad contacts with foreign markets. It would be additionally necessary to be cautious over government-supported industries, because the need for support itself indicated that the industry was of doubtful viability.

Professor Kantorovitch (U.S.S.R.) said that he wanted to emphasise that the problems of estimating the economic effects of technological innovation were fundamentally different from the usual problems of estimating the economic effectiveness of capital investments, and thus demanded a wholly different approach and method. The difficulties involved in such estimates stemmed from the fact that precise figures covering an extremely long period were wanted, that great uncertainty was involved as to the very existence of the thing forecast and as to the capital investments necessary, and that the economic results of the technological advance were to be shown not in specific profits but rather in a general contribution to the national growth resulting, the last of which was specially important for a socialist economy. This presented various problems.

First, the development and implementation of new ideas ought to be treated not as a sum of certain costs but as a kind of special capital investment which involved a temporary loss of industrial output, long-term expenditures, a greater capital stock in a particular enterprise and finally its increased efficiency. All these should be – but often were not – taken into account.

Next there was the overall economic effect which was very different from the profits received. Considerations of what might be a reasonable and competitive price often made it impossible for the industry concerned to secure the equivalent of the whole benefit in the form of a price imposed upon the consumer, and thus the industry producing the innovation did not receive the full revenue which was theoretically proper.

There was also the value of the side-effects of an innovation on related industries. It had already been mentioned that space research, for example, without producing direct results, had contributed to the development of a whole variety of industries. Innovations which produced this kind of result should be sought out and developed on a long-term basis, even though they could not be expected to produce any immediate results in terms of economic gains.

In this context he wanted also to mention the inevitable economic and technological risk involved, since arrangements for economic compensation for that risk were still not quite clear. In some industries such risks had become inevitable. It was expected, for example, that of ten holes drilled in searching for oil, nine would be barren. By analogy, he would regard it as sensible for a firm to undertake work on several innovations while expecting only one of them to pay off. And in the same way, competition between different designs for a single similar innovation could be very advisable in a socialist economy.

He wanted to emphasise again the difficulties involved in estimation of the economic effects of innovations. He thought that mathematical models might be used here, in a somewhat more sophisticated way than had been suggested by Professor Mansfield, to identify and take account of different factors involved. In this sense estimating the effects of innovation was no less important than designing the innovation itself, and one was completely impossible without the other.

M. Aujac (France), in winding up the discussion, said that in France they had made no quantitative inquiry into the problems raised in his paper, basically because of the expense such an inquiry would involve. Thus he would have to be very cautious so far as any recommendations for labour training policy were concerned. What needed to be taken into account were the different competing alternatives, as well as the different rates of growth of various industries and the relative efficiency of skilled labour used in these industries. There was no set of rules for choice between various solutions.

In his paper he had attempted to discuss the difficulties that a medium-sized country like France met in trying to plan technological progress. The difficulties involved primarily the desire to maximise the satisfaction of a demand while at the same time trying to determine what that demand was. One could, of course, re-plan the development of the national education system. But if one aimed at greater and narrower specialisation, then there was the problem of how to predict what specialised fields would be needed and in what quantities. The overall planning of education had its own difficulties stemming from the necessity to aggregate various separate forecasts.

In general, he was convinced that analysis of these difficulties, as well as analysis of the experience and errors of planning, was essential for improvement of the methods of planning and forecasting. It could make a valuable subject for another conference.

17 Long-term Projections of Consumer Demand in the United Kingdom: the Cambridge Growth Model

A. S. Deaton

I. CURRENT METHODOLOGY

The projections of consumer demand which are described in this paper are undertaken as part of a large disaggregated model of the United Kingdom. This model, which has been constructed over a number of years by Professor Richard Stone and his colleagues in Cambridge [4], contains some 1,000 equations as well as distinguishing thirty-five industries and more than forty commodities. Within such a system the accurate projection of consumer demand is a matter of considerable importance. Forecasts of industrial structure and of employment patterns are perhaps most immediately affected, but since the model is closed, these in turn reflect back via the distribution of income and relative prices to consumer demand itself. In the present discussion this simultaneity is ignored and we present only the consumption sector itself. More precisely, we describe how total consumers' expenditure on non-durable goods is allocated between the different commodities in the budget. The total itself is determined as a function of disposable income using a model of the type described by Stone [9].

The model of demand which underlies our projections is the *linear expenditure system,* first applied to British data by Stone nearly twenty years ago [8]. The basic equation may be written

$$p_i q_i = p_i c_i + b_i(\mu - \sum_k p_k c_k) + v_i \qquad (1)$$

$$\sum b_i = 1,$$

where, apart from the stochastic term v_i, p_i is the price of good i, q_i is the quantity of it purchased, μ is total money expenditure (income for short), and b_i and c_i are parameters. The index i runs from 1 to n, the number of goods. This system has a simple interpretation; the c_i's are committed expenditures which are purchased first, leaving residual income to be spent in the fixed proportions, b_i, on each of the commodities. Once the parameters are estimated, the model's linearity in prices and income renders it very convenient computationally within the main model and its compatability with consumer demand theory ensures that it is unlikely to generate absurd or implausible forecasts.[1] However, the model is not entirely satisfactory in this basic form. Linearity of the Engel curves, implying as it does that all income elasticities tend to unity, is not borne out by the data. The simplest way of dealing with this is to allow linear time trends in the b coefficients;[2] the model is now written

$$p_i q_i = p_i c_i + (b_i^0 + b_i^1 \theta)(\mu - \sum_k p_k c_k) + v_i \qquad (2)$$

$$\sum b_i^0 = 1, \sum b_i^1 = 0,$$

where θ is time. Even so, for a model containing forty commodities, estimation to a satisfactory degree of convergence becomes highly problematic. The model is non-linear in 120 parameters, not to speak of the 820 distinct elements of the variance–covariance matrix of the residuals. To avoid the impasse which would be created by having to face this as a routine exercise we have adopted an hierarchic estimation and forecasting procedure. Since the system can be derived from the maximisation of an additively separable homogeneous utility function, we know from the work of Gorman [6] that expenditures on groups of goods may be predicted using total income and group price indexes while the group expenditures may themselves be used, in conjunction with the individual prices to yield expenditures on the individual commodities. If we denote the groups by capital letters, and if good i belongs to group G, we may sum equation (2) over the group to give expenditure on the group, denoted μ_G, by

$$\mu_G = \sum_{k \varepsilon G} p_k c_k + (b_G^0 + b_G^1 \theta)(\mu - \sum_G \sum_{k \varepsilon G} p_k c_k) + v_G, \qquad (3.1)$$

where $b_G^0 = \sum_G b_i^0$, $b_G^1 = \sum_G b_i^1$ and $v_G = \sum_G v_i$.

This may be approximated by

$$\mu_G = \pi_G c_G + (b_G^0 + b_G^1 \theta)(\mu - \sum_G \pi_G c_G) + v_G, \qquad (3.2)$$

where π_G is the Paasche price index for the group derived by dividing current price by constant price expenditures, thus

$$\pi_G^\theta = \sum_G p^\theta q^\theta / \sum_G p^0 q^\theta \text{ so that } c_G \approx \sum_G p^0 c / \pi^\theta \approx \sum_G p^0 c. \qquad (4)$$

[1] For a fuller discussion of this and other points see the survey article [3], especially Sections I and IV.3.

[2] Time trends may also be added to the c's; these add less to the performance of the model.

N

Using the expression for group expenditure from (3.1) we may re-write the individual commodity equations as

$$p_i q_i = p_i c_i + (\beta_i^0 + \beta_i^1 \theta)(\mu_G - \sum_G p_k c_k) + v_i^*, \tag{5}$$

provided only that b_G^1 is small relative to b_G^0. The β parameters are given by

$$\beta_i^0 = b_i^0/b_G^0; \; \beta_i^1 = b_i^0/b_G^0 \{(b_i^1/b_i^0) - (b_G^1/b_G^0)\}.$$

Clearly the β_i^0 parameters sum to unity and the β_i^1 parameters to zero, a property shared by b_G^0 and b_G^1. Thus equations (3.2) and (5) are mathematically identical to the original equation (2) and may be estimated by identical techniques. In this way it is possible to deal with a large number of commodities while only having to estimate relatively small systems. In the hierarchy we have used, there are nine broad subgroups; namely, food, footwear and clothing, housing, fuel and light, drink and tobacco, travel and communication, entertainment, other goods, and other services. Excepting the last two, each of these is disaggregated further into between two and ten more detailed commodities. The selection of which goods go into which groups is governed by two criteria. First, the approximation which allows equation (5) to take the same form as equation (2) must hold. Thus groups must be chosen so as to have as small time trends as possible; in no case must the total marginal budget share approach zero. If this last occurs, the hierarchic process breaks down and the model is liable to give absurd projections. Second, if hierarchic estimation is to cost relatively little in terms of lost likelihood, groups must be selected in accordance with the structure of the variance–covariance matrix of the stochastic disturbances. In a model such as the linear expenditure system, where specific substitution and complementarity relationships are explicitly excluded, any which exist in reality will appear as strong correlations between the disturbances of individual equations. In a hierarchic model such correlations are ignored between goods in different groups, and so the classification must be chosen so that goods which stand in some special relation one to another are always put together. Fortunately, this criterion will usually be satisfied by grouping commodities according to some broad unity of purpose, e.g. food, clothing, etc., very much as is normal.

The maximum likelihood estimators for each sub-system may be described as follows; we discuss the case without time trends as here there is no difference of principle. For the errors of each level of estimation it is supposed that only contemporaneous correlations are non-zero, i.e.

$$\varepsilon(v_{it}, v_{jt'}) = \delta_{tt'}\,\omega_{ij}, \text{ for all } t, t', i, j. \tag{6}$$

There is a minor difficulty in that the matrix Ω (whose i, jth element is ω_{ij}) is singular; this follows from the fact that the right hand side of equation (2) adds up without error to income, thus

$$\sum_j \omega_{ij} = \sum_j \varepsilon(v_{it}, v_{jt}) = \varepsilon(v_{it}, \sum_j v_{jt}) = \varepsilon(v_{it}, 0) = 0. \tag{7}$$

This is dealt with, following Barten [2], by use of the generalised inverse of Ω. Assuming normality he has shown that for n commodities, with a sample of T observations, the likelihood is given by

$$L = n^{\frac{1}{2}T}(2\pi)^{-\frac{1}{2}T(n-1)}(\det V)^{\frac{1}{2}T} \exp\left\{-\tfrac{1}{2}\sum_t v_t'\,V^{-1}v_t\right\}$$

where $V = \Omega + (1/n)\,ii'$ and i is the vector of units. The next step is to take logarithms and maximise the log likelihood function with respect to the elements of Ω such that the singularity constraint (7) is satisfied. This gives a maximum likelihood estimator of,

$$\tilde{\Omega} = \frac{1}{T}\sum_t \tilde{v}_t \tilde{v}_t', \tag{8}$$

where $\tilde{v}_t$ is the estimate of v_t corresponding to given values of b and c, and a concentrated log likelihood function

$$\log L^* = \tfrac{1}{2}T\left\{\log n - (n-1)(1 + \log 2\pi)\right\} - \tfrac{1}{2}T \log \det \tilde{V}. \tag{9}$$

Since $\tilde{v}_t$ is a function only of the parameters b and c, so is (9), and MLE's are given directly by the maximisation of this function. The first-order conditions are

$$\frac{\partial \log L^*}{\partial b} = \sum_t (\mu_t - p_t'c)\,\tilde{V}^{-1}\{\hat{p}_t q_t - \hat{p}_t c - b(\mu_t - p_t'c)\} = 0 \tag{10.1}$$

$$\frac{\partial \log L^*}{\partial c} = \sum_t (\hat{p}_t - p_t b')\,\tilde{V}^{-1}\{\hat{p}_t q_t - \hat{p}_t c - b(\mu_t - p_t'c)\} = 0 \tag{10.2}$$

This set of equations is non-linear in the parameters and the system is solved by using a Taylor linearisation of the expression in braces in terms of δb and δc. A linear step, hopefully towards the maximum, can then be calculated for any given values of the b's and c's. In practice, the constraint on the b's must also be taken into account, and tendencies for the process to diverge must be countered.

By and large, both the estimation procedure and the hierarchic disaggregation of the system have given satisfactory results. Over the data period 1900–70[1] the broad groups are explained to a high degree of precision by total income and the price indexes, while the individual commodities seem to be equally well described in terms of group expenditures and the individual prices. This is true not only for expenditures but also for the constant price quantities, an achievement which has been found much more difficult in the past. And this hierarchic model has important advantages in addition to its ease of computation. The high degree of independence between groups renders it extremely flexible. For example, from the estimation point of view, the structure of a sub-group can be altered without having to re-estimate the whole of the rest of the model, and in forecasting exercises, unless *all* expenditures are required, there is no need to evaluate all the branches of the model. This flexibility is of course purchased by having a lower total likelihood for the system than could be achieved if simultaneous estimation were feasible. But in most cases it is not, and it is possible to go further and to argue that, *a priori*, the form of the error matrix *should* be restricted so as only to permit the full range of interaction between commodities in the same group.

II. DEVELOPMENTS: ALTERNATIVE COMPUTATIONAL METHODS

In spite of the strong arguments in favour of the hierarchic approach, it is always wise to be aware of alternatives, and in the face of a number of minor difficulties with the present method we have been led to consider a number of these. For example, the approximation linking c_G with the sum of the individual c's over the group is often much less exact than might be expected given the collinearity of many of the prices. Again, experiments with a further aggregation of the main groups indicate that, in some cases at least, the estimate of the sum of the b's differs by more than is perhaps desirable from the sum of the detailed estimates. These difficulties indicate only that the assumptions needed for aggregation are not costless. To take an example, if the errors in equation (2) were not correlated between equations, there would be nothing to choose between alternative aggregations. Since it is possible that this cost is large enough even to outweigh the advantages of the hierarchy in other respects, it is wise to examine ways whereby simultaneous maximum likelihood estimates for the whole system might conceivably be found. Normally this would be impractical for a system of this size, but there are two possibilities in this case which hinge upon the peculiar structure of the first order conditions (10).

[1] Excluding 1914–22 and 1939–54.

Note that in the first of these (10.1) the matrix $\tilde{V}^{-1}$ can be cancelled out since the quantity $(\mu_t - p_t'c)$ is a scalar; this leaves an equation which for any given c is linear in b, i.e.

$$\tilde{b} = \left\{ \sum_t (\mu_t - p_t'c)\hat{p}_t(q_t - c_t) \right\} \Big/ \sum_t (\mu_t - p_t'c)^2. \tag{11}$$

It is thus possible to use the solution of (11) to substitute for b in the second first-order condition (10.2); maximisation can then be carried out in terms of a much smaller number of parameters, n instead of $3n$ if time trends are used. This, though more complex algebraically, is likely to save considerably on computation time; repeated inversion is conceivable for a matrix 40×40 but not for one 120×120. It is hoped to try this technique in the near future if a convergent programme can be constructed.

The second possibility is a variant of Stone's original iterative procedure: this makes use of the fact that for ordinary least squares estimation not only are the b's linearly estimable if the c's are known, but *vice versa*. Note that this is not true for M.L.E.; the second first-order condition contains both b and c non-linearly in $\tilde{V}$. However the condition (11) does give a linear estimator for b and furthermore it is identical to the O.L.S. estimator given c: from this several propositions may be deduced. First, and most obviously, any O.L.S. estimators of b and c satisfy the condition $\partial \log L^*/\partial b = 0$; this in itself is not necessarily important since the second condition is not satisfied. However the evaluation of the Hessian of the likelihood function shows that the second derivatives with respect to the b's are much greater than those with respect to the c's. The likelihood function may thus be pictured as a ridge running parallel to the c–directions with a sharply determined peak in the b–directions. Consequently, any estimates satisfying the condition $\partial \log L^*/\partial b = 0$, though not maximum likelihood even asymptotically,[1] will tend to have two important properties. One, the b's should be close to the M.L.E.'s, and two, the value of the likelihood function should not be too far from the true maximum. An efficient procedure might then be as follows. First, find some reasonable estimates the c's (perhaps by taking the first few iterations of the method outlined above); then calculate b's directly from equation (11). For many purposes these may turn out to be highly satisfactory estimates; they are certainly relatively easy to compute.[2]

---

[1] The M.L.E.'s of b and c can be shown to be not asymptotically independent; if they were, any consistent estimators of c would give estimates of b with all the asymptotic properties of M.L.E.'s.

[2] Note however that further iteration between the b's and the c's à la Stone is not likely to be productive; the c's evaluated at these b's by his formula, based on O.L.S. estimation, though decreasing the residual sum of squares, would not necessarily increase the likelihood.

III. DEVELOPMENTS: ALTERNATIVE MODELS
OF DEMAND

A considerable amount of work has already taken place in this second area and firmer conclusions can be given than in Section I. The full experiments and results are reported elsewhere [5] and only a summary of the relevant parts is given here. The study was confined to the nine broad groups described above over the 1900–70 period, and it considered a number of demand systems; apart from the linear expenditure system, several variants of the Theil–Barten Rotterdam model [10] [1] [2] were considered, as well as the direct addilog system [1] and a model which excluded the substitution effects of prices explaining changes in consumers' expenditure solely in terms of changes in real income. Each of these models was reduced to a common algebraic format and estimated subject to a common stochastic specification by maximum likelihood; they were then compared in terms of the likelihood values generated. The linear expenditure system performed worse than its most direct competitor, the direct addilog model, though this was probably due to an over-rigid specification of the Engel curves, an aspect with which the study was not primarily concerned. In any case this is almost certainly remedied by the introduction of time trends in the models discussed above. Perhaps more importantly, the study showed that the modelling of price behaviour implied by the use of an additive utility function – and the L.E.S. embodies this – is not in accordance with the evidence. The trouble lies in the fact that, for additive systems we may write

$$s_{ij} \propto \frac{\partial q_i}{\partial \mu} \cdot \frac{\partial q_j}{\partial \mu}, \quad (i \neq j), \tag{12}$$

where s_{ij} is the compensated derivative of q_i with respect to p_j. This effectively rules out specific interactions (i.e. complementarity or close substitutability) between goods, and it is interesting that (12) appears to be generally untrue even for broad categories of goods. Clearly, then, a further important area of further research will be to modify the system so as to include wider substitution possibilities. It is beyond the scope of this paper even to outline the possibilities; several which have been suggested are examined in Section IV.3 of the survey [3]. So far we have only completed the initial stage, that leading to the recognition that such a modification is indeed necessary.

REFERENCES

[1] A. P. Barten, 'Evidence on the Slutsky Conditions for Demand Equations', *Review of Economics and Statistics*, vol. 49 (1967).

[2] A. P. Barten, 'Maximum Likelihood Estimation of a Complete System of Demand Equations', *European Economic Review*, vol. 1 (1969).

[3] J. A. C. Brown and A. S. Deaton, 'Surveys in Applied Economics: Models of Consumer Behaviour', *Economic Journal*, vol. 82 (1972).

[4] Cambridge, Department of Applied Economics, *A Programme for Growth*, vols 1–11 (London: Chapman and Hall, 1962–71).

[5] A. S. Deaton, 'The Analysis of Consumer Demand in the United Kingdom, 1900–1970', *Econometrica*, vol. 42 (1974).

[6] W. M. Gorman, 'Separable Utility and Aggregation', *Econometrica*, vol. 27 (1959).

[7] H. S. Houthakker, 'Additive Preferences', *Econometrica*, vol. 28 (1960).

[8] J. R. N. Stone, 'Linear Expenditure Systems and Demand Analysis', *Economic Journal*, vol. 64 (1954).

[9] J. R. N. Stone, 'Spending and Saving in Relation to Income and Wealth', *L'industria*, no. 4 (1966).

[10] H. Theil, 'The Information Approach to Demand Analysis', *Econometrica*, vol. 33 (1965).

Discussion of the Paper by
Dr Deaton

Professor Volkonski (U.S.S.R.), opening the discussion, said that the aim of this paper was to present a long-term model of consumer demand which formed part of a general economic model being developed in the United Kingdom. Dr Deaton dealt mostly with a linear model of consumer demand in which consumer expenditures were a linear function of the corresponding incomes. Prices influenced consumption only in a sense that, with given expenditures, consumption of products varied in accordance with their relative prices. He thought this was a very useful and elegant way of determining parameters for such a model by use of optimal and maximum likelihood procedures.

He thought it was very important, both practically and theoretically, that when modelling consumer demand a hierarchical model should be built which should include, first, a model of expenditures for large categories of goods and services, and secondly, sub-divisions within each category, using as indicators the general volume of spending for the whole of the category and the corresponding price index. In short, all the parameters relating to a given category should be used to build a detailed model describing expenditures on specific types of services or commodities. No quantitative results were here presented but references to publications containing such results were given.

At the end of the paper it was mentioned that the research described in the paper threw a certain amount of doubt on the additive utility method. He understood this in the sense that Dr Deaton based his research on the assumption of full complementarity of commodities as contrasted with the assumption of the relatively broad substitutability of commodities implied by the additive utility hypothesis. Professor Volkonsky thought that to compare these two types of models it would be valuable to compare some quantitative results. It was quite possible that both types were capable of producing satisfactory results within permissible error margins.

What were the reasons for using the linear-type models apart from simplicity of computation? He thought it would be equally possible to use a model that was linear in respect to the logarithms of variables, and this would not make computation much more difficult, while the results obtained on such models in the U.S.S.R. seemed to show that linear-logarithmic models were easier to reconcile with the statistics.

He wanted to ask what was Dr Deaton's view about the combination of family budget information and information from time series? It seemed to him that the introduction of the time factor into the model could be correctly made only if the relationship between consumption and income were studied on the basis of family budget information while different parameters emerged for different time periods.

Unfortunately, nothing was said in the paper as to the periods for which these types of linear models could be regarded as reliable. He himself found it difficult to see how satisfactory corrections of these models for a time factor were to be made. Time and income parameters were highly intercorrelated and it must be statistically very difficult to separate their effects. Yet a model could not be sufficiently trustworthy for a comparatively long period without such corrections.

Finally, if long-term planning were being considered, he thought that one could hardly restrict oneself exclusively to income and prices as initial parameters, and that exogenous parameters should be introduced; this was actually being done in the computations. He would think that one had to begin with a more complete model with more parameters, including exogenous parameters, and then try to simplify it in order to incorporate this model into a more general model of the national economy.

Professor Khachaturov (U.S.S.R.) said that Dr Deaton had dealt with the methodological problems of forecasting consumer demand, and he appreciated that it was not his intention to go beyond that. None the less there were two aspects of this that interested him, and about which he would like to ask. First, on what statistical information was this model based? It seemed that this information might be the results of interviews, questionnaires and the like. What were likely to be the major requirements for such materials? Secondly, what practical results had been obtained and what conclusions had been drawn from the computations? How were they used practically? In other words, did the model described have some implications *per se*, and not only as a part of a larger national economy model?

Professor Marczewski (France) asked whether Dr Deaton thought that the Stone model was applicable to long-term forecasts? Were there no explanatory variables in addition to prices and incomes that needed to be introduced when one was dealing with periods as long as fifteen to twenty years?

Professor Vangrevelinghe (France) asked whether Dr Deaton could comment on how to separate shorter-term effects from medium-term effects in his model? What were the relationships between short-term and medium-term income-elasticities and price-elasticities?

Professor Malinvaud (France) said that some similar work was being done in France by M. Nasse. They were working with data which were not as good as the data existing for Great Britain; the periods covered were much shorter and covered only post-war data, while in Great Britain they covered the period 1900–70. Precisely the same type of model was used, but other generalisations had been attempted in addition to those of the basic Stone linear expenditure model. It had also been attempted to find a formulation in which the nature of substitution would be more general than that found in linear and general system approaches.

That work had led M. Nasse to think that when the core of consumption was analysed there was very little advantage for the time being to be gained from a more elaborate formulation than that which Dr Deaton had been using, because the nature of the substitution and complementarities was not such as to make an elaborate model completely applicable.

Professor Malinvaud's second comment concerned the numerical expression of the estimates. The estimation procedure raised no difficulties except that serial correlations were not explained. But how was one to compute efficiently an estimate with the suggested model which was rather large and difficult to solve, as well as non-linear? Essentially the methods used were the same as those adopted by Stone, although they were, of course, more elaborate.

The only criterion in respect to numerical estimation was that of experience – there was no theory here – and that showed that Stone's method of separate consideration of each parameter was not efficient for numerical computation. Although there were cases in which each parameter was linear if taken separately, if one took them together the model became non-linear.

Mr Hjerppe (Finland) suggested that there was the so-called Törnquist function of demand, which as compared with the Stone system, showed that there was a certain core of expenditures, with the remaining income spread evenly over other groups of commodities. The Törnquist idea was to divide commodities into three groups which were regarded as necessities, relative luxuries, and luxuries, each of the two latter groups not being purchased until a given income level was reached. This type of approach might be of interest for long-term planning.

Professor Ultanbaev (U.S.S.R.) said that this suggested hierarchial principle was very similar to methods that were being developed in the U.S.S.R. and were known among the Soviet economists as a 'chain reaction method'. The idea of that method was that computation proceeded from the more general to the more specific. That method had proved useful. It had been found that larger commodity groups enjoyed more stable demands than smaller ones, that is that macro-demand was more stable than micro-demand. His question was how the commodities had been grouped. They had sometimes reached a result that total calculated demand was exceeding total income. How was this problem of balancing solved in Dr Deaton's model? And did Dr Deaton believe that a function based on one parameter (income) was sufficient for long-term planning? They in the U.S.S.R. believed that long-term demand was affected not only by prices and incomes, but also by the proportions of rural and urban population, its age and sex composition, and other factors. This was particularly important in respect of some specific groups of commodities.

Dr Deaton (U.K.), replying, said that this work had been continuing since the paper was written, and some new results were now available. Professor Volkonski was quite right that they had rejected additive utility functions. There was some difficulty in using the terms 'complementarity' and 'substitutability', but if one assumed an additive utility function from which the linear expenditure system could be derived, then what occurred was that essentially one could deal only with substitutes; it was not possible to deal with complementarity relationships between various goods, and there were also very great difficulties about dealing with inferior goods. If one had relatively fine disaggregation of commodities, then one had to deal with inferior goods which tended to be replaced by others.

It was very difficult to produce numerical results for the two models. There were different ways of obtaining them, and it depended on the purpose for which the demand model was to be used. The way he had done it in the paper was to reduce each of the different models to the point where they depended on exactly the same related variable. Each model was then predicting exactly the same quantity so that the models could be compared quite directly. He then calculated the value likelihood when the latter was maximised under the assumptions of each of those models, and then compared the likelihood. This seemed the simplest way to have one single criterion for judging between those models.

But if, on the other hand, one was particularly interested in some specific commodity, then one model could be better than the other for that particular commodity, and quite a different criterion might be chosen. There was no simple answer to that question.

Professor Volkonski had said that in the U.S.S.R. experience with log-linear models seem to be more consistent with the data than the simple linear models. This was generally true, but there were difficulties with the log-linear models. One of them was that it was impossible to have log-linear models which balanced total expenditure, and the prediction of a log-linear model had to be scaled or modified in order to get balance with the index of total monetary expenditure. This was not in itself impossible, but he thought that one's belief in a model which did not satisfy the most elementary constraints that one would expect it to satisfy must be to some extent diminished, while there was no problem of balancing within a linear expenditure system.

Combining time series and budget data seemed to be a very important area for further research. Many budget studies existed and many time series studies existed, but there was very little data which was consistent between both time series and budget data, for instance longitudinal studies of individual families. So it was very difficult to know whether the income elasticities that one observed from budget data were indeed of any use whatsoever in time series analysis. He supposed the only way to do this would be to derive some budget elasticities and then, by using a likelihood test, to try to see whether they were consistent with time series elasticities. He had not attempted this.

The question which had come up most often was the question of other factors in demand besides incomes and prices. He certainly accepted that these other factors were very important, but the methodological context within which he had been working was directed to seeing how the income and price factors could be modelled. In their model in Cambridge they had a very large number of sectors, and the government was assumed to control the economy partly by changing the relative prices for commodities in the different sectors. Thus it was important to have a model which would allow for full generality of the price structure effects. It became very difficult to build a model which would do this *and* include other factors as well. If the other factors were also built into the model, it was very difficult to find the price effects. That was why they did not use a dynamic model. One might hope that if one estimated a dynamic model in a non-dynamic way then the parameter estimates would be right in the long term. These parameters would certainly not be sensitive enough to pick up the cycle, but one was in any case not interested in cycles in the long term.

As to the influence of income distribution and urbanisation, they tended to change very slowly in the United Kingdom, and they were probably sufficiently taken into account from the practical point of view, although theoretically it was certainly unsatisfactory. Nevertheless, in a single country and with seventy years of data it was really difficult to consider a number of these other factors, though they might be important in the long run. This obviously varied from country to country. In a country like the U.S.S.R. with a large rural population and changes in organisation this factor would be really important. Perhaps some progress here might be achieved by studying cross-sections of family budget expenditures in different countries, which might yield results that would be more significant than those of a time series analysis in a single country.

Much of the early data on which their model had been based had been generated by Professor Stone in his study of the national income statistics for the United Kingdom. But the principle of it was the one on which their Central Statistical Office generated time series data in the United Kingdom, which was a mixture of budget surveys with evidence from manufacturers. The price series was generated by dividing the current price system by a constant price system, and so it was really a price index for whatever might be the conglomeration of goods.

As to the conclusions drawn from the model, what had really turned out was that, in spite of all, a hierarchical model was not satisfactory; neither was it solving the problem. He was not quite sure why it should be true, but if one wanted a good estimate of all the parameters, it did seem to be necessary to estimate all the demand functions simultaneously, and that was a very difficult task. Probably the hierarchical system was inefficient because of erroneous classification of goods into groups, but this again was a very difficult problem.

He was not sure whether the Stone model was any better for long-term forecasting than any other model. There were difficulties about substitution effects, but it did have certain good properties. Notably, it did satisfy the balancing equation; it was homogeneous in the sense that if prices and incomes were doubled, the total volume of purchased goods remained the same. The log-linear model did not produce such a result.

He did not quite agree that increasing substitutability and complementarity within groups was of no particular use. This was a rather technical point, but M. Nasse's generalisation, though quite general in theory, when applied seemed to suffer from certain restrictions mainly because of the short time span of his data, which Dr Deaton thought created problems for his results. In particular, M. Nasse had assumed that the specific substitutional matrix should be block diagonal, thus allowing increased substitution and complementarity within groups but not between groups, whereas the latter seemed to be necessary to achieve the results. It might well be that the use of M. Nasse's model with different assumptions about the structure of the substitution matrix might solve a number of problems about substitutability in their model.

He had taken no account whatsoever of serial correlation. The apparent serial correlation of the residuals was much improved by the time change in the parameters. This was not in itself a very satisfactory result, but one which might indicate the allowance for serial correlation. On the other hand, the problem of allowing for serial correlation in a non-linear model was not an easy one.

As for the Törnquist functions, he thought they were mainly used for budget studies rather than for time series analysis, given that they were mainly concerned with the specification of the Engel curve rather than with the specification of the price response. There were other difficulties with these functions. The three distinct function forms, which their model had, made the model very flexible, but on the other hand for any single commodity they presented one with the difficulty of having to switch from one functional form to another. It seemed to him that perhaps the Törnquist functions might be replaced by work on the log-normal Engel curves which allowed a rather wide range of income elasticity for the same good without the problem of changing the functional form, because in practice goods began as luxuries, then became semi-luxuries, and not long after became conventional necessities.

The grouping principle was also a very difficult one. One could specify a matrix of the residuals of demand in a way which reflected the grouping of the commodities. Given that, one could estimate the whole system of forty commodities or so in the way he had described; one could compute a maximum likelihood estimate of the matrix of the system; and one could examine it for any information it might contain on which goods should go into which groups. This could be done by some sort of factor or cluster analysis, and this sort of analysis he was attempting to use.

18 Long-term Projections of Household Consumption in France

G. Vangrevelinghe

Without consumption, which exists to meet the needs, the convenience, the pleasures and the aims of mankind, would production represent wealth? François Quesnay, 1758

I. THE IMPORTANCE OF DEMAND PROJECTIONS

It has long been trite to emphasise the importance of consumption in economic development. Consumption has been continually growing for more than twenty years under the influence of important needs that have not been met. The pressure of the resulting aggregate demand has been an essential condition for the continuing growth of production and for changes in the productive system.

The growth of consumption, determining as it largely does the growth of economic activity in the country, represents one of the best indicators, partial though it certainly is, of the change in the way of life of the French people and in the relative importance of their different needs as their standard of living rises.

Within the range of all the research being carried out in France to provide a model description of the economy as a whole, the construction of models to describe the way in which consumption expenditure is distributed in relation to the growth of family income and to the relative prices of consumption goods has occupied an important place. The analysis and estimation of complete systems of demand functions are, in France just as elsewhere, good examples of the possibilities provided by a good combination of economic analysis and empirical estimation on the basis of adequate data derived from past experience.

Economic analysis in this field is sufficiently refined, without being too restrictive, to lead to theoretical models that are both logically sound and realistic; progress achieved in the techniques of econometric estimation, as in methods of calculation, now makes possible a satisfactory solution of problems posed by the numerical values of the parameters of the model and the verification of the adequacy of the observed data.

II. THE MODELS USED HITHERTO

Both in their logic and in their statistical framework, all models of overall demand have great similarities, which are found notably in the linear system of expenditures proposed more than twenty years ago by Richard Stone, a system which has occupied a central place among all expenditure models.

There is to be found in that system a breakdown of the behaviour of consumption into a regular or 'minimal' part, usually corresponding to the medium-term growth of the whole structure of expenditure, and an 'excess' part, more fluctuating, measured by the difference from the former and which therefore usually reflects more short-term forces.

Generally speaking, the deviations that may appear in each of the components distinguished in the total of consumption in relation to their theoretical specifications are of a significant covariance; moreover, the matrix formed by these covariances has the peculiarity of being singular.

III. THE NEED FOR A NEW APPROACH

In France, in the form of complete systems of demand equations, various pieces of work have been carried out in order to explore the different theoretically possible specifications, and at the same time to apply them to the observed data of our country ([1], [2], [3], and [3a]).

The first results of this work have been used to show, in the comprehensive model of the French economy used to make the projections required for the Sixth Plan for Economic and Social Development, how the structure of consumption may be expected to emerge by 1975 on the basis of given hypotheses for total consumption and the structure of prices.

If in this perspective the approach adopted has shown itself to be satisfactory, it has also become clear that a complete model of the distribution of expenditure within the household consumption budget is insufficient to handle the problems that confront a planner in respect of the long-term growth of consumption. Let us be quite clear about the meaning of the expression 'long-term'.

'Medium-term' forecasts of consumption usually attempt to describe the growth of the principal components, measured by the proportion that they form of the total consumption budget. This growth results from the interactions of economic and demographic variables, in a given social environment and institutional framework.

On the other hand, it may be assumed that 'long-term' projections attempt by definition to escape from present circumstances, from the limits imposed by psychological attitudes and institutional frameworks. Such an approach, which requires some sort of 'visionary' or 'prophetic' imagination, is in practice entirely beyond the grasp of the 'expert'.

In fact, the experience of preparing the Fifth and Sixth Plans in France ([4], [5]) has shown that, in the long-term projections of consumption, attention was drawn to long-term trends that were already discernible to an attentive eye in existing developments. These long-term trends are not in most cases likely to affect substantially the result of an extrapolation, with a limited medium-term time-horizon, of the structure of expenditure on the basis of the expected growth of incomes and variations of prices, and reflecting the statistical parameters established for the past. Yet because of the continuing consequences that may derive from them, they may force themselves upon the attention of planners and influence their immediate decision-making.

This consideration results in consumption-projection models of the 'complete system of demand functions'-type being given a predominant place only in the working out of medium term perspectives, and in their being given only a secondary role in any long-term study.

Certainly in the latter case the effect on the structure of consumption implied by a continuation of the recent trends of the behaviour of households is one of the factors that first deserves attention.

Nevertheless, in any analysis of this behaviour, the relative shortness of the statistical series available (since 1950), their uneven quality, and at the same time the large number of cyclical fluctuations in the course of the period covered, have led us to specify dynamic models of demand, distinguishing short-term effects but permitting also the introduction of the hypothesis of an influence exercised by past events (habits of consumption or the effects of 'stocks') on the behaviour observed at a given moment ([6], [7], [8]). Conversely, the usual specification of complete models of demand is generally non-temporal, in the sense that it makes implicitly the assumption of the instantaneous adaptation of consumption to the variables – incomes or prices – that determine it.

It was certainly to be hoped that the advantages of each of these methods might be combined into one single specification. But the difficulties raised by econometric studies, together with those imposed by the inadequacies of the available data, have made such an objective unattainable.

Thus for each of the components of consumption regarded

separately, we have confined ourselves to a specification of the demand function, showing how the volume of consumption of the goods or service concerned in the course of each period represents a function:

(i) of current variables: the purchasing power of income; the relative price of the goods or service concerned as compared with the generality of prices in consumption;

(ii) of a variable of conditions which in any period involved is represented by the effect on present consumption of the consumption of past periods.

This variable of conditions is represented, in the case of durable goods, by the value of the holding or fixed capital resulting from the purchases of past periods. In the case of perishable goods or of services, this same variable is designed to represent the 'habit' of consumption induced by the behaviour of previous periods.

This approach is in fact that which had previously been adopted by Stone and Rowe and Houthakker and Taylor ([7], [8]). It is, moreover, easy to show that these two specifications, if slightly different on the theoretical level, lead to an identical equation defining the consumption of each period in terms of directly observable variables. It may also be shown that this last equation is equally compatible with a specification directly inspired by the work of Friedman [9], introducing a division of consumption into two components, 'permanent' and 'transitory'.

In other words, the different theoretical models of consumer behaviour which have been proposed do not appear, as regards the equation that forms the basis of estimation, to be distinguishable.

That apart, the econometric properties of the equation to be estimated (with auto-regressive errors) make non-convergent estimates inevitable and may show a substantial bias, if the method of least squares is used. The three-pass technique, ('three pass least squares') equally leads to biased estimates. It seemed to us that under the circumstances the instrumental variable technique was more appropriate.

The method employed seems for the present to be that which is best adapted to reproduce the characteristics of the dynamic evolution of consumption, and at the same time to identify the fluctuations connected with the conjunctural cycle of long-term development. In this sense, it is well adapted to our purpose.

If the specification adopted has the property of making it possible to reproduce effectively the dynamic characteristics of the growth of the various components of consumption, it has on the other hand, the inconvenience of not expressing directly the interactions (in the form of substitution or complementarity) which operate between different forms of consumption, otherwise than by effects on the total of consumption.

IV. THE NEED TO INTRODUCE FACTORS OTHER THAN INCOMES AND RELATIVE PRICES

Thus, when it became apparent that these other factors were of importance, we were driven to make them directly explicit.

As regards final results, the detailed approach to which we have shifted has enabled us to attempt to derive a new 'typology' of consumption, based on the observed characteristics of the different laws of behaviour. Indeed, if the usual functional approach, used especially in overall systems of demand functions, is imposed upon the analyst from the start, it appears to be inadequate to synthesise all the information on long-term trends in the structure of consumption. The new approach brings to bear all the analogous research which has been made with the same perspective in the form of the analysis of consumer behaviour through enquiries of the 'family budget'-type ([10], [11]).

The introduction of a variable of conditions into the demand equation allows us to have a model specification that introduces both a demand for consumption and a demand for 'assets': stocks of durable goods, consumption habits. In a long-term analysis, the latter is particularly useful when long-term consumption is liable to undergo a change of trend, whether because the holding of durable goods reaches a level of equilibrium or because consumption of perishable goods or services is reaching a state of saturation.

We have just seen that, in any long-term analysis of consumption, it is essential to go beyond the analysis of the effects of incomes and of relative prices on consumption as seen in its traditional structure: other ways of sub-dividing consumption may be pertinent, and the effects of variables other than incomes and prices may be important.

Besides the variables represented by the holdings or stocks of durable goods, or consumption habits, other variables must unquestionably be taken into account. Thus in the field of transport demand, all the expenditure that one sees is essentially a dependent variable of the growth of the automobile population, and of the structure of transport demand in its various different components: journeys between place of residence and place of work, journeys for leisure purposes, journeys on holiday. In the field of food expenditures, nutritional requirements and fashions in food play a fundamental role in the changes of the pattern of demand.

The interconnections between the flows of demand and the levels of stocks, which have been seen in the case of transport demand and the automobile, sometimes go beyond any strict definition of consumption expenditure.

Thus, a study of consumption expenditures for household purposes cannot, in a long-term perspective, be conducted independently of the analysis of behaviour concerned with the acquisition of housing. And in addition to the flow of investment, to the cost of acquiring property, and to the repayment of loans, changes of conditions regarding inheritance have also to be considered, and such factors as patterns of real assets and medium or long-term indebtedness. Indeed, rising rents, as an example, only represent the changes of values, real or imputed, of the use of the national inheritance of living accommodation.

It is necessary, therefore, to go beyond a narrow definition of consumption expenditure. To pursue this point, one final comment must be added. In practice, it has hitherto been assumed that the behaviour of households can be analysed as a whole. But, in a long-term perspective, it must be remembered that any total behaviour results from numerous individual forms of behaviour which, as all investigations show, have considerable disparities.

Now it is quite possible that the composition of the population and the resources and living conditions of different types of households, will change considerably in the future in ways which do not represent a continuation of the trends recorded in the past. In particular, it may be expected that a significant change of income distribution, or of the age structure of the population, or of the extent of urbanisation, may occur. All these are phenomena likely to have effects on the pattern of the average consumption of all households that will prove important in proportion to the extent of the disparities in behaviour that have been observed.

V. NON-MONETISED CONSUMPTION

Nor can there be any question of confining ourselves simply to the monetary expenditures of households. Thus, in the field of leisure activities (whether at home or away from home), of holidays, and of consumption outside the home, the dividing line between monetary and non-monetary expenditures is not significant; for it is only the result of its influence by more fundamental factors, such as the use of time.

If systematic collection of statistical information, usually by means of sample enquiries, regarding these non-monetary aspects of French behaviour – leisure or holiday behaviour, time and motion studies –

is a fairly old method, it is only since 1966 that a systematic effort has begun to be made in this direction.

These enquiries have made it possible for certain forms of consumption behaviour to be better understood and their growth to be more satisfactorily predicted. At a higher level, they have made it possible to see more clearly the choice to be made between more rapid growth of private consumption, more rapid growth of public revenue and expenditure, and an increase of leisure. It was in this way that the desire for a lengthening of annual holidays first became evident in France (the annual holidays now last four weeks or more); for four or five years there has been a desire for a significant reduction in the length of the working week that has been stronger, but without any willingness to curtail the rapid growth of the real purchasing power of money incomes.

It is essential that, in a medium-term perspective, this sort of choice should be made clear.

A further important dimension in our analysis must be this. To start with, we were concerned essentially with the pattern of household consumption expenditure, as affected both by its total level and by the structure of relative prices. Implicitly, there has been assumed a stability in the field represented by private consumption satisfied by marketed goods. But, here and now, an important part of the field is satisfied outside the market – the consumption connected with health, education or leisure activities.

Even if it is regarded as unlikely within a medium-term horizon that the institutional framework will be substantially changed, it must not be forgotten that in a longer term very considerable changes may take place. Certain expenditures may become chargeable to the community. On the other hand, other forms of consumption, hitherto provided freely by the community, may come to be paid for (for example, driving or parking on certain public thoroughfares).

It is, however, far from certain that the method of covering expenses always affects the rate of growth of consumption. Thus, international comparisons seem to show that the rapid growth of expenditure on health is little affected by the very different systems of financing health services that exist in one country and another.

It is advisable, moreover, in any study of collective consumption, to distinguish carefully between three types:

(i) that which is consequent on the community taking responsibility for the expenditure relating to the satisfaction of individual needs;

(ii) that which relates to communal equipment necessary to satisfy individual needs (facilities on roads or in towns);

(iii) that which relates more precisely to collective functions, of common interest, of which the essential characteristic is that it is not possible to identify the individual beneficiary.

Systematic efforts to calculate collective demand have been continuing for some years. It is at least as much a matter of finding a measure of the relevant phenomena and their magnitudes, as of understanding the behaviour of the economic factors of which they are the expression.

The measurement is difficult. Indeed, a market price does not usually exist, and expenditure can only be derived with a good deal of difficulty from the costs of the factors employed. Thus, it often proves necessary to associate with these expenditures quantitative indicators or non-monetary variables – the amount of use of the collective property, for example. As between these quantitative indicators one must be careful to distinguish those which refer to resources (the number of beds and hospitals, for example) from those which represent objective tests (for example, the amount of ill-health).

VI. SOME FINAL COMMENTS

At the moment important conceptual and statistical work is being undertaken in France to collect the necessary information, to analyse and interpret the behaviour, and to clarify the decision-making problems of the planners.

In summing up this brief review of what is being done in France to study some of the problems posed by the long-term growth of household consumption, it may be said that the projection of the pattern of consumption expenditure is certainly one of the important features of the study of long-term forecasting, but that, from the evidence, it used not to be regarded as one of the essential aspects.

The French experience leads one to realise more generally the wide range of problems of every kind that the long-term growth of household consumption presents for the planner. This realisation makes one reconsider the whole traditional framework of analysis. It leads to a redefinition of what must be the new requirements for the improvement of the statistics and for economic and social research, if all the elements necessary for action are to be brought together.

REFERENCES

[1] C. Fourgeaud and A. Nataf, 'Consommation en prix et revenu réels et théorie des choix', *Econométrica*, vol. 27, no. 3 (1959).
[2] Ph. Nasse, 'Analyse des effets de substitution dans un système complet de fonctions de demande', *Annales de l'I.N.S.E.E.* no. 5 (1971).
[3] Ph. Nasse, *Système intégré de fonctions de consommation* (1971).

[3a] Ph. Nasse, *Estimations économétriques sous contraintes*, Colloque Franco Sovietique en Informatique (1972).

[4] *Reflexions pour 1985* (la Documentation Française, 1964).

[5] *Rapport du groupe de prospective 'Consommation, modes de vie'* (Commissariat Général au Plan, 1971).

[6] G. Vangrevelinghe, 'Modèles et projections de la Consommation', *Economie et Statistique 1970*, no. 5.

[7] R. Stone, Brown and Rowe, 'Demand Analysis and Projections for Britain: a Study in Method' (North Holland, 1964).

[8] H. Houthakker and L. D. Taylor, *Consumer Demand in the United States* (1929–1960–1970).

[9] M. Friedman, *A Theory of the Consumption Function* (1957).

[10] Ph. L'Hardy and A. Villeneuve, 'Le Comportement des Consommateurs d'après l'enquête budget de famille de 1963', *Etudes et Conjoncture* (Nov 1968).

[11] N. Tabard, 'Structures de Consommation', *CREDOC* (1968–9).

[12] J. Desce and A. Foulon, la 'Consommation élargie', *Consommation*, no. 3 (1971).

[13] *Le modèle physico financier dans la préparation du VI° Plan* (Commissariat Général au Plan, 1971).

Discussion of the Paper by
M. Vangrevelinghe

Professor Marczewski (France), introducing the discussion, said that M. Vangrevelinghe had described the history of consumer demand forecasts in France, which had been in existence for at least twenty years, but the techniques and theories of complete systems of demand functions had been applied only recently to the preparation of the sixth French plan for 1970–5. The procedure consisted in deriving the breakdown of consumer expenditure in main categories as a function of incomes and prices. This had led to a variant of the type of complete demand model initiated by Richard Stone in 1954. Recent studies in France as well as other countries had established the common logic of these models. Several methods were available which enabled them to calculate parameters of such models in a way that was both satisfactory statistically and manageable in terms of computations.

This created a possibility of medium-term forecasts in which it was implicitly assumed that the interplay of the economic and socio-demographic variables· remained within an established institutional framework. But this assumption could not be maintained in a long-term study for three reasons. First, long-term planning of consumption could not be limited to mere consideration of consumers' expenditures. Other aspects of consumer behaviour had to be taken into account. Second, some explanatory variables other than incomes and prices might have a significant role in the long-term study. Third, the institutional framework might undergo substantial change as a result either of a deliberate plan or simply by its own evolution.

In spite of all these restrictions, the work on the long-term projections, as it was being done in France, started always with a detailed forecast of consumption as a function of incomes and prices, in order to obtain a first approximation of the structure of consumption expenditures, as usually described. In France, this forecast had been established by using the Taylor method rather than the Stone method, because the former permitted separate analysis of each component of total consumption. Of course, they were aware that this method involved neglect of the links between different items of consumption, but it enabled them to take into account in a precise way the dynamic trends of each item. This last factor was very important in distinguishing between long-term plans and cyclical ones.

Whatever might be the method used for forecasting the composition of consumer demand as a function of income and prices, the results obtained did not fully meet the requirements of those working on the long-term plans. Those planners were interested in specifically long-range developments for which these aspects of consumption expenditure might not be of great importance. To meet the special requirements of planners working on long-term projections, it was necessary to enlarge the scope of the analysis and even to modify substantially the information system currently used. The extension of the analysis had been achieved on various lines. First, certain consumption expenditures had to be considered in relation to certain other items of household account. This was typically the case with housing services which could not be analysed independently of the corresponding capital expenditure. Second, certain items of consumption could not be regarded as determined solely by incomes and prices. It was necessary to introduce other variables, such as copying the habits of other consumers and other such things. For instance, the expenditures on motor cars depended not only on incomes and prices but also on the ownership behaviour of other consumers and on the long-term growth of new transportation requirements, which could be influenced by a wide variety of factors. In the same way, food expenditures were influenced not only by nutrition factors but also by consumer habits. In the long run all these factors were capable of being substantially changed and thus had to be considered independently of prices and incomes. Third, the total amount of consumption itself could not be considered independently of the demand for leisure. The relation between public and private consumption had also to be considered, especially as it could be changed in the long run. Even within public consumption it was necessary to distinguish individual benefits provided by collective services, representing the financing by public authorities of individual needs, from the collective needs of the community such as general administration, defence, security, and the like, which benefit the population as a whole.

As to the information system, the changes concerned the functional analysis of public expenditure, the setting up of so-called social indicators, and the extension of the field covered by surveys of household behaviour. The functional analysis of public expenditure could be illustrated by an example of what was being done in the matter of health. In parallel with the classical approach to budget expenditures by administrative units, an attempt had been made to distinguish and assemble all expenditures related to health in the form of a system of social indicators, some of them showing the results to be achieved, others defining the means to be employed even if these could not be expressed in monetary form.

The surveys of household behaviour which until recently had been limited to family budget-type analysis were now extended to other aspects, such as asset–debt management, time budget analysis, leisure time activities, and so on.

The first question Professor Marczewski wished to ask was whether it was possible to outline the general theory underlying the author's empirical statements regarding the inadequacies of demand models based on incomes and prices for long-term forecasts. It was not that he disputed the necessity of introducing other variables; but he wondered if there was no possibility of doing that in a more systematic way on the basis of some general theory. What seemed to him striking was that in his very interesting and no doubt still somewhat provisional paper Dr Deaton had commented that the Stone model was not yet fully satisfactory, so why should it be different in France? There was, of course, a difference in the statistical data available, which in itself might be an important reason. Perhaps the other reason was that the British economy was less dynamic and had witnessed fewer changes in the post-war period than had the economy of France. It would none the less be very interesting to know if there was any theoretical reason for this marked difference.

Mr John (Hungary) agreed that in planning consumption one could not operate with a single model, however perfect it might be, and several methods had to be used, including not only incomes and prices but other parameters also. In his view (and in those of a number of Hungarian planning authorities and economic organisations also) consumption should include not only material but also non-material elements, and in their planning they took account of that additional consumption. This was a very broad concept which covered not only material consumption but also the capital investment needed to provide for consumption. They in Hungary believed that this concept should also be reflected in the organisation for the planning of con-consumption. The interests of various social groups should be taken into account, and planning should be done jointly by planning organisations and other social institutions, such as the consultative planning commissions which existed in Hungary and which included not only representatives of state planning organisations but also trade unionists, medical doctors, sociologists, university professors, and the like. They firmly believed that long-term planning should be made on the basis of broader participation than was usual for medium-term or short-term planning.

Dr Deaton (U.K.) said that he wished to comment on something that Professor Marczewski had said in opening the discussion. The Taylor method, although it did take account of cycles, made use of variables which depended on the lags of the model's equations. He wondered what technique M. Vangrevelinghe could visualise to avoid inevitable accumulations of rather substantial errors. If he might turn to prices, these could be approached in two ways. One was that changes in prices were a headache in every model. Another was that prices were not likely to change substantially within a certain period, and some results could be expected. For example, when forecasting imports in the U.K. prior to the devaluation of the pound sterling in 1967, economists had found themselves in the very difficult situation of having forecasted that devaluation would have no effect on imports, which was very far from true. The significance of this seemed rather obvious: the economic theory of price behaviour should be taken into account in order to consider substitutability in the demand models. He would like to point out that there were models which reflected both these attitudes.

Professor Bénard (France) said that the two papers by M. Vangrevelinghe and Dr Deaton were both contrasting and supplementary to each other. The French forecast used the Stone-type system, and he wondered whether the choice between various types of demand functions was made in the French case mainly for practical statistical and econometric reasons, as a result of the poverty of the French statistics, or mainly for theoretical reasons, and if the latter, what the theoretical reasons were. The conference realised that the authors felt that the linear demand system was consistent with the classical, supposedly rational behaviour of a consumer maximising his utility functions subject to his budget restraints. Were the demand functions suggested by M. Vangrevelinghe really consistent with this rational behaviour? Or would they become consistent only if some additional hypotheses or assumptions were introduced, such as the state variable assumptions? The integration of the state variable might have two different implications. In the case of material goods, one might wish to express the fact that for these goods only services were obtained apart from them. Or the state variables might be introduced for some theoretical reason. As regards the distinction between public and private consumption, was it hoped to construct some demand function not only with prices and incomes but with other variables also? And in that case, with what variables?

Professor Nick (G.D.R.) wished to know what role such models had in relation to other models, and who was to draw conclusions not only for the theoretical study of consumption trends, but also for the purpose of influencing them. If he might speak of this problem as it presented itself in the G.D.R., he had to confess that, until recently, consumption and the planning of consumption were not considered in long-term planning. This had been changed in the recent five-year plan and in planning in general from a principal concern with planning the allocation of resources to concern with the planning of consumption as well. This reflected, of course, not only changes in economic thinking but to an even greater degree changes in objective economic conditions. They were now trying to make the increase of living standards the starting point for the whole planning, and this turned out to be rather difficult. It involved not only the development of consumption but also the development of needs, which was by no means the same thing, and it involved also co-ordination between resource allocation and the emergence of new forms of demand. Perhaps they could have some comment on this problem.

Mr Hjerppe (Finland) agreed with what Mr John had said about the forecasting of future demand. He did not think it was impossible to forecast a significant part of prospective demand. If one looked at the development of economies one could see that they had passed through three stages. The first was dominated by primary production of food and shelter. The second was dominated by production and consumption of manufactured goods. The third stage could be called the service stage. He thought that in future one would have to pay much more attention to collective consumption which had to be planned and not just forecasted on the basis of common sense and the supposed rational choice of an individual.

M. Vangrevelinghe (France), replying to the discussion, said that he felt that, in the field of the long-term planning of consumption, the forecasting of consumers' expenditures should be the first step. At present he did not have a complete theory of long-run consumer behaviour, but he was sure that just to take into account consumer expenditures and to assume that the consumer was maximising his satisfactions within his given environment was not enough, because essential elements of this environment might change and the definition of consumption expenditure might itself change.

He did not think that a general theory, taking into account the allocation of the budget, of time, and so on. would solve the problem, because it would be too general to be of any practical use. But in any case, he thought that such a theory had to be formulated, and he had attempted to suggest certain empirical ways of thinking about the problem. Teams in France were beginning research into the general theory of consumer behaviour, going far beyond consumer expenditures. His own concern was merely for the purpose of empirical application of statistical apparatus.

They had been reluctant to use the results of the Stone model for long-term forecasting merely because at the time they had to tackle it they had been very sceptical about the value of price elasticities. They had the full matrix of price elasticities but were very sceptical about their empirical value. Moreover, they found it difficult to forecast the trends of prices for a period as distant as one ending in 1980 or 1985.

They knew, of course, that if they turned to the Taylor model they would have other kinds of difficulties. First, they did calculate the price elasticities for a number of items, and these elasticities were quite believable. Second, he did not think that state variables represented anything more than a description of the interplay of long-term and short-term effects of prices and incomes. They had felt it necessary to try to distinguish between short-term and long-term elasticities, and they were well aware that they could run into the difficulty of accumulating errors.

To sum up, he did not necessarily advocate what was done in France, but he thought it was a sound empirical approach, particularly because French planners were not interested in having detailed descriptions of consumer expenditures down to 1990. Their main interest was in what might be the consumption trends in the near future rather than in the 1990s.

As to the long-term planning of consumption in France, it had to be remembered that this was of a purely consultative character in that country. The teams that worked on the problem included people from the government planning offices, the trade unions, the manufacturers' associations, as well as economists with certain ideas about growth.

As to quantitative information, they had a sample survey concerned with traffic congestion first made in 1959 and since then repeated several times, so that they knew the number of cars, the effects of urbanisation on the use of alternative competing forms of transportation. They had been trying to estimate the total effect of urbanisation and had managed to find out how many people refused to have a car because there were too many cars owned by others. Thus, they were trying to quantify and assess different factors of long-run and medium-run significance by means of a structural analysis. Similar work had been done with respect to leisure, where they now had to face the pressure for transition from the traditionally longer working weeks and longer vacations to what seemed to be a desire for shorter weeks. This choice was unquestionably of long-term importance, and they were currently at the stage of asking questions and trying to obtain quantitative data. They hoped that a theoretical analysis might give them more insight into how these problems might be tackled.

In France they started by trying to estimate the future needs of the consumer, though the trends of consumers' needs were not to be taken for granted. They were attempting to influence consumers' needs by acting on prices and on the general environment. They had a model to demonstrate the interplay of consumption and living standards with the allocation of resources and production, but this was mainly for the medium term. As part of this work, they had published projections for 1975 which were made with a reduction of this full-scale model. His own view was that they should improve those projections to form a general framework rather than engage in more specific forecasting.

19 Long-term Global Optimisation in Educational Planning

C. C. von Weizsäcker

I. INTRODUCTION

Long-term planning of the public sector has become increasingly important in most industralised countries. The methods which are used so far are different from the sophisticated mathematical optimisation techniques which have been developed in the different disciplines of operations research. While the application of cost–benefit analysis (which is also an optimisation technique) for problems of a more local character has quite frequently been a success, more global tasks, such as planning for an entire national educational system, have not yet effectively been assisted by optimisation techniques.

I have been involved in recent years in research related to educational planning in Germany. A team, of which I am a member, has developed a planning model and has provided data for it, so that we were able to make projections for the period from 1970 to the year 2000.[1] This work was closely related to work on an official general plan for the educational system of West Germany and thus we were not free to choose our model. The model does not imply any optimisation of an objective function and in many instances it introduces as fixed parameters what in optimisation models would become a variable. It restricts itself to parameters and variables which are easily measurable. It is thus heavily input oriented, since the true outputs of educational processes are difficult to measure.

In what follows I want to propose an approach to the problems of measurement of variables and parameters which are important but difficult to measure. This approach involves in an essential way the use of optimisation techniques for educational planning. I believe that the principle of the approach is quite general, but I do not want at the present moment to talk too much about generalities. I rather prefer to present a simple example which is of special interest to me because it is a first attempt (so far not a practical one) to overcome the deficiencies of educational planning models which I have men-

[1] C. C. von Weizsäcker, W. Konrad, H. Kurth, K. Uh Oh, W. Sutter and H. Vollet, *Simulationsmodell für Bildungssysteme* (Weinheim, Germany, 1972).

tioned above. But the generality of the principle underlying the simple example is mentioned as a justification for its presentation at this conference.

II. THE MODEL

To make things abundantly clear we have chosen a rather simple model. It has four main parts:

- (1) the population and students model;
- (2) the teacher supply model;
- (3) the educational production model;
- (4) the objective function.

(1) *The population and students model*

Let $n(j,t)$ be the number of persons of age j at time t in the society under consideration. It may be useful to explain $n(j,t)$ by means of the following equation:

$$n(j,t) = p(j,t)n(0,t-j)$$

$n(0,t-j)$ is of course the birth rate at time $t-j$.

Let $x(j,t)$ be the average amount of time used for learning of a person of age j at time t. We assume $n(j,t)$ or $n(0,t)$ and $p(j,t)$ to be exogenously given. But $x(j,t)$ is one of the important variables of the model. In this simple model, time expenditure for learning is not divided up according to different fields or institutions of learning. The index j runs from 0 to J.

(2) *The teacher supply model*

Let $J0$ be the age at which teachers normally enter the teaching profession. $J0$ is exogenously given. Let $K0$ (also exogenously given) be the normal length of time it takes to be trained as a teacher. Let $Z(t)$ be the number of teachers leaving teaching training colleges and entering the teaching profession in period t.

To have a realistic model of teacher supply we must take into account that the tendency to leave or to re-enter the teaching profession is strongly age dependent. It is therefore appropriate to differentiate teachers by age. Now, for empirical and computational reasons it is perhaps sensible to distinguish only a few age groups each of which comprises several unit period age cohorts of teachers. Let k be the index of the teacher age groups, k goes from l to m. Let $L(k,t)$ be the number of teachers in age group k in period t. We then introduce the following system of equations

$$L(1, t+1) = Z(t) + [1 - \lambda - \lambda(1) - \lambda(1,2)]L(1, t)$$

$$L(2, t+1) = \lambda(1,2)L(1, t) + [1 - \lambda - \lambda(2) - \lambda(2,3)]L(2, t)$$

$$L(k, t+1) = \lambda(k-1, k)L(k-1, t) + [1 - \lambda - \lambda(k) - \lambda(k, k+1)]L(k, t)$$

$$\text{for} \quad k = 2, 3, \ldots m-1$$

$$L(m, t+1) = \lambda(m-1, m)L(m-1, t) + [1 - \lambda - \lambda(m)]L(m, t)$$

The $\lambda(k, k+1)$ are the transition proportions between the different age groups. Naturally they are inversely related to the number of unit period age cohorts contained in age group k. $\lambda + \lambda(k)$ is the proportion of net flows from teachers of group k into the outside world. It consists of the constant $\lambda(k)$ and of a variable part λ whose determinants will be discussed below. It is an interesting question: how to construct age groups optimally, if we want a model in which each age group is to be considered homogeneous in the way we have done above.

Let us now consider the influences on the teacher flows. Let $w(t)$ be the wage rate of teachers at time t as a proportion of the average wage rate in the economy. Let $d(t)$ be the teaching load of a teacher at t. Let $\hat{w}(t)$ be an exponentially weighted average of past values of w, so that

$$\hat{w}(t) = \gamma w(t) + (1 - \gamma)\hat{w}(t-1)$$

Similarly $\hat{d}(t)$ is defined by

$$\hat{d}(t) = \gamma d(t) + (1 - \gamma)\hat{d}(t-1)$$

We now assume that λ is a function of $\hat{w}$ and $\hat{d}$

$$\lambda = \lambda(\hat{d}, \hat{w})$$

Also $Z(t)$ is supposed to depend on the working conditions of teachers. Remember that $K0$ is the time it takes to train a teacher. We then assume

$$Z(t) = q(t)n(J0 - K0, t - K0)$$

where $q(t) = q(\hat{w}(t), \hat{d}(t))$

The proportion of an age group who want to become teachers, q, depends on the working conditions of teachers. The variables $w(t)$ and $d(t)$ are control parameters of the planners. Many reasons point to the assumption that the rates of change of w and d cannot be too large, hence we introduce the restriction

$$|\Delta w(t)| = |w(t) - w(t-1)| \leqslant \Delta_1$$
$$|\Delta d(t)| = |d(t) - d(t-1)| \leqslant \Delta_2$$

where $\Delta 1$ and $\Delta 2$ are constants.

(3) *The educational production model*

This model defines the 'production functions' of the educational process. The total supply of teacher inputs, measured in efficiency units, $A(t)$, is determined by the total number of active teachers

$$L(t) = \sum_k L(k, t)$$

and the average teaching load $d(t)$. We assume

$$A(t) = L(t)g(d(t))$$

Effective teacher input is proportional to the number of teachers and a function g of the teaching load. For sufficiently large values of d a law of diminishing (at least, perhaps even negative) marginal efficiency of the teaching load operates. We thus may assume $g''(d) < 0$ for sufficiently large d and $g'(d) > 0$ for sufficiently small d.

Let $1(j, t)$ be the teacher intensity of the education of age group j. The total teacher input requirement at time t is therefore

$$\sum_{j=0}^{j} n(j, t)x(j, t)1(j, t)$$

It cannot be larger than $A(t)$.

Let $B(j, t)$ be the level of education already attained by group j at time t. Here, we shall not discuss how to measure $B(j, t)$. More will be said on this point later in Secion II. Let $D(j, t)$ be a measure of what has been learned by age group j during period t. We then assume

$$B(j+1, t+1) = (1-h)B(j, t) + D(j, t), 0 < h < 1$$

This means: the level of knowledge of the group born in period $t-j$ in period $t+1$ is explained by the level of knowledge of that group in period t and the amount which has been learnt during period t. Because of subjective processes of forgetting and objective processes of obsolescence there arises a phenomenon of 'depreciation' of knowledge which is represented in the equation above by the rate of obsolescence h.

The output of the learning process of age group j, $D(j, t)$, is now linked to the inputs into that learning process by means of an 'educational production function'

$$D(j,t) = \alpha\psi(j, x(j,t))\varphi(j, \beta(j,t))$$

where $\beta(j,t)$ represents the teacher inputs and physical inputs (teaching material, equipment, buildings, etc.) per unit of time used by age group j for learning purposes. In general, we can assume that φ and ψ are functions exhibiting diminishing marginal returns, at least for sufficiently large values of their augments. The number α is basically a parameter for the relative importance attached to learning by society. The variable $\beta(j,t)$ is defined by means of a linear homogeneous production function whose inputs are $l(j,t)$, the teacher input intensity and $s(j,t)$, the physical input intensity.

$$\beta(j,t) = F(j, s(j,t), 1(j,t))$$

where F is homogeneous of degree one in $s(j,t)$ and $1(j,t)$. This assumption is less restrictive than one may perhaps suppose. Basically it means that the set of indifference curves for a given educational output and given other inputs on the $s(j,t)$, $1(j,t)$ diagram is homothetic. If that is the case, a linear homogeneous function exists which can be taken as a representation of joint teacher and physical inputs such that it reflects accurately the effect of these two inputs on the output.

I may refer the reader to the theory of 'true' indexes, such as the true cost of living index or a 'true' index of real income. Any non-proportionality between inputs and output can be captured by the properties to be assumed about $\varphi(j, \beta(j,t))$.

(4) *The objective function*

We want to maximise the value of the function

$$V = \sum_{t=t0}^{\infty} R^{t-t0}\left[\sum_{j=0}^{j}(B(j,t) - x(j,t)s(j,t) - v(j)x(j,t)n(j,t))\right]$$
$$- \sum_{t=t0}^{\infty} R^{t-t0}w(t)L(t)$$

The number R is a discount factor which we introduce here as an exogenous parameter. It would be of particular interest to observe the sensitivity of the optimal solution to changes in R. As the last term of the objective function indicates, we are measuring all values in units which are equivalent to the average wage rate in the economy, since $w(t)$ was defined in these units. If the average wage rate rises through time, the discount factor R is different from what it would be if we had chosen money units to measure the values. Indeed, if the rate of growth of the average wage rate is equal to the rate of interest (a situation not very far off from reality in many western countries), the discount factor would be equal to unity. The first term in square brackets, $\sum_t \sum_j B(j, t)$, represents the output of the educational system in terms of the achievements in training of the population. The second term, $-\sum_t R^{t-t0} \sum_j x(j, t)s(j, t)n(j, t)$, represents the costs of physical inputs into the educational system; the third term, $-\sum_t \sum x(j, t)v(j)n(j, t)$, represents the opportunity costs of the time spent by pupils in the educational process. We assume here that the opportunity costs per unit of time, $v(j)$, only depend on j and not on t. The fourth term, $-\sum_t R^{t-t0} w(t)L(t)$, represents the costs of teachers.

III. STEADY STATE ANALYSIS

Our main purpose in the present paper is the development of a method which allows us to obtain reasonable data for long-term optimisation models such as the example discussed here. The method is quite general and it can be used for other planning problems, too. In particular, it can be used to obtain approximate data for variables measuring the global benefit of activities such as education, health services, traffic, etc., where conventional methods of measurement are difficult to apply. On the other hand, I must warn the reader not to expect revolutionary advances from this method. On the contrary, in a way it is anti-revolutionary, because it starts with the assumption that there are good reasons for the real world processes, corresponding to our model processes, to take on the values of the variables they are observed to take on. It does not mean that these processes develop optimally, but it means that realistically we should not strive for more than gradual and piecemeal improvements.[1]

Our method proceeds as follows. There are quite a few functional relations whose parameters are not known to us. Now we look at stationary (steady state) optimal solutions of our model, which have rather convenient mathematical properties. It is fairly easy to compute optimal steady state solutions for given parameter values of the functional relations. We thus can study the implications of different sets of parameters on the optimal values of control and state variables of the system without having to solve a rather complex dynamic programme. The control variables and state variables (such

---

[1] Cf. Popper's concept of piecemeal engineering in K. Popper, *The Open Society and its Enemies* (Princeton, 1950), or Braybrooke's and Lindblom's concept of disjointed incrementalism in D. Braybrooke and Ch. Lindblom, *A Strategy of Decision* (Glencoe, Ill. – London 1963).

as teachers' salaries, teaching loads, teacher inputs, physical inputs, time expenditure for education, etc.) frequently have real world counterparts for which statistical data are available or can with some reasonable effort be made available. We thus can ask the question: which sets of (not directly measurable) parameters of the model are consistent with optimal values of control and state variables corresponding to real world values. Assuming that the real world values are not very far from a steady state optimum we get hints at the values of the parameters of the functional relations in the model. Not all parameters can be estimated in this way. The steady state analysis leaves us with a few degrees of freedom with respect to parameter values consistent with the steady state optimality hypothesis of observed data. Indeed, these degrees of freedom are crucial to make the whole analysis worthwhile, since it is our hypothesis that the properties of non-steady state optimal paths are quite sensitive to assumptions made which allow us to get rid of the indeterminacy of the parameter values.

It is then our final purpose to study the implications of the choice of the remaining free parameters on the optimal path. Here, we no longer assume that the real world development of the past has been optimal, since, of course, this real world did not solve a complicated dynamic programme before starting on its course. The computational simplicity of policy decisions in the real world probably makes our approach justifiable: the attempts to optimise, which implicitly are made by policy-makers, are of a computational nature similar to the analysis of steady states. For instance we may refer to discussions of whether it is worthwhile to reduce pupil–teacher ratios, to raise the school leaving age, to expand the university systems. Thus we may think of observed variables to be the result of an 'as-if-steady-state optimisation'. On the other hand, experience shows that the intricacies of the dynamics of an educational system have been beyond the computational capabilities of policy-makers and public opinion. As an example, we may point to the world-wide phenomenon of over-reacting with respect to shortages of qualified manpower causing the surpluses or tendencies towards surplus observed in almost all industrialised western countries. Thus the real path will not be optimal dynamically, and it is here that models of the type proposed in this paper could help.

In our steady state analysis we put $R = 1$ and we assume a stationary population. There arises the difficulty that the objective function may diverge in this case. We therefore do not work with the function V but rather with the function $\overline{V}$ giving the average value of the components whose sum (over t) is equal to V. Since we look at steady states, the values of the variables do not change with t and we may thus write (dropping the index t)

$$\overline{V} = \sum_{j=0}^{J} n(j)[B(j) - x(j)s(j) - x(j)v(j)] - wL$$

It is reasonable to assume $B(0) = 0$. We then can write, using the equation of the educational production model,

$$B(j) = \sum_{i=0}^{j-1} (1-h)^{j-i-1} D(i)$$

Also

$$A = Lg(d) = \sum_{j} n(j)x(j)1(j)$$

implies

$$\frac{\partial L}{\partial 1(j)} = \frac{n(j)x(j)}{g(d)}$$

We have to recognise that there exists a functional relationship between the stationary values of w and d and the stationary value of L. We can write $L = L(w, d)$ and we assume

$$\frac{\delta L}{\delta w} > 0, \frac{\delta L}{\delta d} < 0.$$

To incorporate the restriction concerning teacher input into our analysis we form the Lagrange expression

$$Lg \, \overline{V} = \sum_{j} n(j)B(j) - wL(w, d) - \sum_{j} n(j)x(j)(s(j) + v(j))$$

$$+ \mu\left(L(w, d)g(d) - \sum_{j} n(j)x(j)1(j)\right)$$

We differentiate with respect to w and d and put the derivation equal to zero,

$$\frac{\delta Lg \, \overline{V}}{\delta w} = -L(w, d) - \frac{\delta L}{\delta w} w + \mu g(d)\frac{\delta L}{\delta w} = 0$$

$$\frac{\delta Lg \, \overline{V}}{\delta d} = -w\frac{\delta L}{\delta d} + \mu g(d)\frac{\delta L}{\delta d} + \mu L(w, d)g'(d) = 0$$

Let us now assume that we know the elasticities

$$\varepsilon(w) = \frac{\delta L}{\delta w} \cdot \frac{w}{L} \quad \text{and} \quad \varepsilon(d) = \frac{\delta L}{\delta d} \cdot \frac{d}{L}$$

describing the long-run (i.e. steady state) supply behaviour of teachers. The first equation can be written

$$1 + \frac{\delta L}{\delta w}\frac{w}{L} = 1 + \varepsilon(w) = \frac{\delta L}{\delta w}\frac{\mu g}{L} = \frac{\mu g}{w}\varepsilon(w)$$

or

$$\frac{g(d)\mu}{w} = \frac{1 + \varepsilon(w)}{\varepsilon(w)}$$

μ is the shadow price of an efficiency unit of teacher input; thus, $\mu g(d)$ is the shadow price of a teacher. The ratio of shadow price and market price of a teacher is determined by the wage elasticity of supply of teachers. It is, of course, the Cournot point of the monopsonist 'educational system' on the teacher market. Let us now look at the second equation where we replace $g\mu$ by $w[1 + \varepsilon(w)/\varepsilon(w)]$. After dividing by wL and multiplying with d we have

$$-\frac{d}{L}\frac{\delta L}{\delta d} + \frac{1 + \varepsilon(w)}{\varepsilon(w)}\frac{d}{L}\frac{\delta L}{\delta d} + \frac{1 + \varepsilon(w)}{\varepsilon(w)}\frac{dg'(d)}{g(d)} = 0$$

$$-\varepsilon(d) + \frac{1 + \varepsilon(w)}{\varepsilon(w)}\varepsilon(d) + \frac{1 + \varepsilon(w)}{\varepsilon(w)}\frac{dg'(d)}{d} = 0$$

$$\frac{\varepsilon(d)}{\varepsilon(w)} + \frac{1 + \varepsilon(w)}{\varepsilon(w)}\frac{dg'(d)}{g(d)} = 0$$

$$\frac{dg'(d)}{g(d)} = -\frac{\varepsilon(d)}{1 + \varepsilon(w)} = \frac{|\varepsilon(d)|}{1 + \varepsilon(w)}, \text{ since } \varepsilon(d) < 0$$

The elasticity of teacher input with respect to teaching load in the optimum is proportional to the absolute value of the long-run teacher supply elasticity with respect to the teaching load. These formulas are of some interest. Assuming that they are approximately fulfilled in the real world they allow us to compute certain parameters, if others are known. If, for example, we have estimates for $w, d, \varepsilon(w), \varepsilon(d)$, we can compute $dg'(d)/g(d)$ and $\mu g(d)$, magnitudes indicating something about the effects of teaching and variations of teaching loads on the output of the educational system (as seen by decision-makers).

The effect of w and d on the long-run value of L is intermediated by the dependence of q and λ on w and d. We shall not discuss the steady state properties of this functional relationship. Let us just say that this analysis gives us insights about the parameters of the functions $\lambda(\hat{w}, \hat{d})$ and $q(\hat{w}, \hat{d})$ which are important for a dynamic analysis.

We now turn to a discussion of the 'production function'. For this purpose we differentiate and put the derivative equal to zero:

$$\frac{\delta Lg \ \bar{V}}{\delta l(i)} = \sum_j n(j)\frac{\delta B(j)}{\delta l(i)} - \mu n(i)x(1) = 0$$

or, remembering the formula for $B(j)$,

$$\frac{\delta D(i)}{\delta l(i)}\left[\sum_{j=i+1}^{J} n(j)(1-h)^{j-i-1}\right] - \mu n(i)x(i) = 0$$

We define
$$H(i) = \sum_{j=i+1}^{J} n(j)(1-h)^{j-i-1}$$

and obtain, remembering the structure of $D(i)$,

$$H(i)\alpha\psi(i, x(i))\varphi'(i, \beta(i))\frac{\delta F(i)}{\delta l(i)} - \mu n(i)x(i) = 0$$

where
$$\varphi'(i, \beta(i)) = \frac{\delta\varphi(i, \beta(i))}{\delta\beta(i)}$$

Similarly optimisation with respect to $s(i)$ yields

$$H(i)\alpha\varphi(i, x(i))\varphi'(i, \beta(i))\frac{\delta F(i)}{\delta s(i)} - n(i)x(i) = 0$$

These two equations imply

$$\frac{\delta F(i)}{\delta l(i)} = \mu\frac{\delta F(i)}{\delta s(i)}$$

But this is the condition for maximisation of $F(i)$ under the constraint of given 'costs' of inputs

$$C(i) = s(i) + \mu l(i)$$

where teacher inputs are weighted with their shadow price μ. Hence, the problem of choosing the right point on the isoquant corresponding to the function $F(i)$ can be solved whenever μ is known and without regard to similar problems for other age groups j. This property should facilitate the computation of a dynamic optimal programme. Given μ we can now consider $F(i)$ as a function of the 'costs' $c(i)$ and hence also $\varphi(i)$ can be interpreted as a function of costs: $\varphi(i) = \varphi(i, c(i), \mu)$. There remains the problem of optimisation with respect to $x(i)$. We differentiate and put the derivative equal to zero

$$\frac{\delta Lg \ \bar{V}}{\delta x(i)} = \sum_i n(j)\frac{\delta B(j)}{\delta x(i)} - v(i)n(i) - s(i)n(i) - \mu n(i)1(i) = 0$$

or

$$H(i)\alpha\psi'(i, x(i))\varphi(i) = n(i)[v(i) + s(i) + \mu l(i)]$$

where

$$\psi'(i, x(i)) = \frac{d\psi(i, x(i))}{dx(i)}$$

Obviously we have

$$\frac{\delta\varphi(i, c(i), \mu)}{\delta c(i)} = \varphi'(i)\frac{\delta F(i)}{\delta s(i)} = \frac{1}{\mu}\varphi'(i)\frac{\delta F(i)}{\delta l(i)}$$

and hence the optimisation conditions with respect to $s(i)$ or $l(i)$ yield

$$H(i)\alpha\varphi(i)\frac{\delta\varphi(i)}{\delta c(i)} = n(i)x(i)$$

Rewriting this equation and the optimisation condition with respect to $x(i)$, we obtain

$$\frac{\psi'(i)x(i)}{\psi(i)} = n(i)x(i)\frac{v(i) + c(i)}{H(i)\alpha\varphi(i)\psi(i)}$$

$$\frac{\delta\varphi(i)c(i)}{\delta c(i)\varphi(i)} = n(i)x(i)\frac{c(i)}{H(i)\alpha\varphi(i)\psi(i)}$$

This implies

$$\frac{\delta\varphi(i)}{\delta c(i)}\frac{c(i)}{\varphi(i)} = \frac{c(i)}{c(i) + v(i)}\frac{\psi'(i)x(i)}{\psi(i)}$$

This is an interesting equation since it yields a simple relation between the elasticity of educational output with respect to direct costs of education (teachers and physical inputs) on the one side, and the elasticity of educational output with respect to pupils' time expenditure on the other. The values of $c(i)$ and $v(i)$ are not difficult to measure or estimate in principle. It is then possible to get estimates for these elasticities of educational output from the last three equations, if we assume that real world variables are similar to steady state optimal conditions. In preparing a numerical treatment of the problem we would choose functions φ and ψ which are characterised by a small number of parameters and then use the derivation above to get some indication about the numerical values of the parameters. I have made some investigations in this direction. I shall not describe them here, in order to avoid having to write a rather lengthy paper.

There is one additional interesting problem which so far has not been discussed. It is the extent to which it is possible to substitute physical inputs for teacher inputs or vice versa. To treat this problem it is best if we assume that the functions $F(j)$ are of the C.E.S.-type

$$F(j) = [\delta(j)1(j)^{-\rho} + (1 - \delta(j)s(j)^{-\rho})]^{-1/\rho}$$

where $\sigma = 1/1 + \rho$ is the elasticity of substitution.

Steady state analysis does not allow us to obtain indications about the value σ. Unless there are other indications about the elasticity of substitution we shall have to try out how sensitive the optimal dynamic programme reacts on changes in σ. For any given σ we are able to find indications about $\delta(j)$; we are able to derive in a straightforward fashion the following relation between $c(j)$ and $s(j)$

$$c(i) = \left[\mu^{1-\sigma} \left(\frac{\delta(j)}{1 - \delta(j)} \right)^{\sigma} + 1 \right] s(j)$$

Since we have estimates for $s(j)$, $c(j)$ and μ, this equation and the choice of the parameter σ determine the parameter $\delta(j)$.

These are a few examples for finding empirically reasonable values of the parameters of the model by means of steady state analysis.

IV. COMMENTS ON THE DYNAMIC ANALYSIS

I shall not discuss here the technical and mathematical problems of setting up a dynamic programme to solve the optimisation problems. I only want to make a few remarks concerning the purpose of this exercise. Since it will take some effort to carry this optimisation through, it is worthwhile to speculate about possible results. I shall give an example: the problem of forecasting teacher requirements.

In the sixties and seventies quite substantial quantitative and qualitative changes in the educational systems of most countries took place and will yet take place. They are thus far from a steady state. In their plans for the educational system planners and governments have tried to forecast the teacher requirements over a period of ten to twenty years into the future. Their method has been to lay down teacher–pupil ratios and then to forecast the number of pupils. In the language of our model, the $1(j)$ and the $x(j)$ have been fixed exogenously, and then the teacher requirements have been computed. Is this a good method to plan the educational system? We want to study the dynamics of our model, among other things, in order to answer this question.

The following two hypotheses draw on the intuition of the economist. The hypotheses, if warranted by a more thorough investigation, would be a negative answer to this question. The two hypotheses apply to two different parameter constellations, which we call the high elasticity and the low elasticity case. The high elasticity case is characterised by a high elasticity of substitution σ in the production function and a high sensitivity of the optimal cost level $c(j)$ with respect to changes of parameters, say, α. In the low elasticity case the opposite is true. Our hypotheses are:

(1) In the high elasticity case a substantial change in, say, α will induce substantial changes in the input mix between physical inputs and teachers in the direction of higher physical inputs. Costs $c(j)$ per unit of pupil time will rise substantially, basically by raising $s(j)$ and μ, not so much by raising $1(j)$. The relative wage rate of teachers will rise. The additional supply of teachers effected thereby will mainly be used for raising education time of pupils $(x(j))$, not so much for raising $1(j)$, which may actually fall. The optimal value of $1(j)$ is mainly affected by the teacher supply conditions and by the size of the system $(x(j))$. It is thus not reasonable to introduce $1(j)$ as a parameter which is independent of the teacher wage rate, the teacher supply rate, and the size of the system (number and time expenditure of pupils).

(2) In the low elasticity case the $1(j)$ are rather insensitive to changes of parameters like α. Their introduction as parameters in a conventional planning model is therefore not a severe mistake. But the low elasticity case also implies that $1(j)$ should remain rather stable over time, which it usually does not in conventional planning models. Also, the rate of expansion of the system (rate of change of $x(j)$) should not be introduced as an independent parameter. Rather, the optimal development of $x(j)$ depends very much on the supply conditions of teachers and the parameters $1(j)$.

Thus, in both cases the traditional planning approach is not justified, if our hypotheses are validated, by the computation of optimal programmes.

Discussion of the Paper by
Professor von Weizsäcker

Professor Yershov (U.S.S.R.), in opening the discussion, said that Professor von Weizsäcker's purpose was to construct a relatively simple model or logical scheme of a process that needed to be planned. It did not represent planning so much as a preliminary analysis designed to focus the problems to be faced when one came to actual planning of this complex process. It raised three issues. What problems needed to be examined for the purpose of forecasting or planning the needs of education? What economic parameters and phenomena needed to be considered and included in a model? What should be the structure of the model itself?

The model proposed could be discussed in terms of the particular functions introduced and the constraints on them, in terms of the exact meanings of some of the functions, or from the point of view of the actual calculation of the quantitative parameters. Professor von Weizsäcker had been principally concerned with the first, and to some extent the second of these issues. The construction of a model of this kind involved a number of difficulties, since not all the relevant variables and conditions could be quantified.

The purpose of the model was to find the optimum solution with a set of variables representing the process of educating an exogenously given population, distributed in age groups, without taking account of the different types of education and with cost–effectiveness as the criterion of optimisation. A fundamental issue was the question of the measurability of the effectiveness of education, particularly from a long-term point of view. It was not at all clear how we could measure the actual level of education.

The process of education involved on the one side the time devoted to it by the student, and on the other side the time spent by the teachers and the material expenditures involved. The model implied certain relationships between social resources made available at different periods and educational standards reached by populations in different age groups. It also implied that people were attracted to teaching jobs to an extent determined by the average teacher's wage and by teaching loads – two variables which actually introduced a dynamic factor into the model.

A more sophisticated element in the model established relationships between the number of teachers and the volume of allocated resources on the one hand and variations in the educational standards of the population on the other hand, involving some 'depreciation' of knowledge. Thus the parameters of that section of the model were teachers' wages, a variable representing the professional qualifications of teachers, and the size of the population groups requiring education. A dynamic analysis with such a model would be extremely difficult since not all of its elements were capable of being precisely defined or measured. Thus the model could be solved only for a static case.

Professor Yershov found it very difficult to discuss the applicability of an axiomatic model of this kind because of the many allowances that had to be made if one was to remain within an axiomatic framework rather than an empirical framework. One advantage of axiomatic models was that they set planners free from the dilemma that the more one knew about a model, the greater the difficulty of solving it. But two comments about this model were legitimate. First, the model did not take into consideration the demand for education. In other words the model assumed that its parameters could be manipulated purely on the basis of certain global criteria of optimisation without taking anywhere into account whether people did or did not want to have a higher standard of education. A second point was that the effectiveness of education was discussed completely in isolation from other parameters influencing economic growth. He thought that it would be valuable to extend this pioneering work to include a study of the value of education not merely for itself but also as part of a process of social development.

Professor Bruno (Israel) wished to ask how such models could be made more realistic, which he felt sure was possible. For example, the model dealt only with a single generalised kind of education. One could clearly apply the same system to different kinds of education and make it more sophisticated in a variety of ways.

Professor von Weizsäcker's paper attached chief importance to the initial methodology. If one had a dynamic model covering a series of time periods, one could look at the steady state for each of these moments and discover how the model might operate beyond the steady state. His first question was whether Professor Weizsäcker believed that a study of steady states could provide good indicators of what might happen beyond the individual steady state; whether his view was based on personal empirical observation or whether it was a general case. Was it not the case that most of the problems of planning were problems of adjustment, perhaps from one steady state to another, in non-steady state situations? The question was how much we could learn about such situations.

He believed that there were planning situations in which a steady state did not exist, but the planning problem might be capable of solution. In a specific field of education this model might not be able to take account of certain changes likely to occur in the future, such as technical progress and new educational techniques. In some cases we did not even know the direction in which change might take place over time. The same was true on the demand side. The value to be attached to training, and particularly to specific types of training, might be unknown for remote periods in the future. The demand for education was a derived demand from the growth of the economy, with a great deal of uncertainty involved. The question was whether this could be taken into account by the methods proposed. More generally, in such an educational model as this, how could one take account of the need for revision as new knowledge came in? How could the educational system be made flexible enough to make it possible to improvise when necessary?

Professor Khachaturov (U.S.S.R.) said that the problem raised by Professor von Weizsäcker was one of great interest to the U.S.S.R. It would be interesting to apply his techniques to the ten-year secondary education of the U.S.S.R. and to use it to estimate the total cost that might be involved in a compulsory ten-year programme. He thought it was more difficult to apply it to education as a whole. The amount of compulsory education was determined by the decision to have it. In the case of higher education there was the problem of its economic effectiveness from a national point of view. It was, of course, possible to calculate how many posts in the national economy ought to be filled by university graduates, but it was not clear whether these posts could be filled by persons with practical experience, particularly if one took into account the cost of higher education. He thought this presented a vast field for research by economists both in the East and the West and should be developed to cover the contribution of education to the acceleration of economic growth and the requirements for education seen from the point of view of the national economy.

Professor Bénard (France) was feeling somewhat confused about the real meaning of some of the coefficients, the objective function, and the so-called shadow prices. In this objective function the social value of knowledge, the monetary values of inputs, and the opportunity cost of education were all taken as given, after appropriate discounting, of course. But how did one evaluate the coefficients for the future if one was dealing not with a supposed steady state but attempting to work out a truly optimal solution with a truly dynamic model? Was it not necessary to seek the solution in a general optimisation model both for the economy and for education in which the shadow prices would be dual variables? If so, the shadow prices could become part of the objective function of the general optimisation model. Otherwise what one was comparing were one's own shadow prices for, for example, teaching input with market prices for that input, which, he felt, were two different things. It had not been shown that the market prices were close to the optimum. The whole procedure would be clearer if the stability of only small deviations from the market level had been demonstrated.

Professor Fritsch (Switzerland) said that the assumptions underlying Professor von Weizsäcker's four models included certain variables that were assumed to be exogenously determined. If the supply of teachers was a function of economic development which in turn was a result of improvement of education, then the resulting feedback became of practical importance. In Switzerland they had an intensive and specialised system of education. So far as this education system created job opportunities, economic development had the effect of attracting away teachers to other sectors, so that teacher supply was becoming a function of economic development.

Professor von Weizsäcker (F.R.G.), replying to the discussion, said that the central purpose of his paper had got somewhat lost in the discussion of the formulae. His purpose was to show how one could in practice obtain quantitative estimates of something that was implicitly quantified in their administrative decisions but which was very difficult to estimate econometrically. There was an analogy in physics. There was a principle in optics which laid down that the path of light from one point to another was the path which minimised the time of passage from the source to the end point. This principle made it possible to compute the speed of light both in the medium of air and in the medium of water, which was very difficult to measure directly. This was very much what he had been trying to do in a very complicated social context. The essential analogy was that it was very difficult to agree on the value of education and to measure the real output of education. Planning implied that some decision had to be made involving these issues. Whatever the methods of analysis of the problem, a decision had to be reached, and this decision reflected the valuation that the society concerned gave to education.

The trouble was that educational planners were not trained to handle complicated dynamic problems. Thus, the decisions that they reached in terms of the student–teacher ratio were reached in terms of a model that was much simpler than a proper dynamic model. They made the implicit assumption of a steady state situation since there was no time to develop a more complicated model. Thus the decision implicitly represented the choice of the optimum of a number of steady states. He had assumed that the decision could be interpreted as reflecting some implicit model of optimisation. Thus, adopting the principle of the analogy that he had quoted, one could infer the parameters representing the valuation of educational output accepted by the administrators. It was possible, for instance, to assume that the teaching load could increase along some curve up to a certain point, giving a corresponding increase of educational output. Above a certain level a further increase of teaching load would not produce similar educational output and might even reduce total output, since there were diminishing returns.

Thus he had been able to calculate a relationship between teaching load and educational output which one could not measure directly as well as other parameters which were more capable of estimation, such as the elasticity of supply of teachers in response to teachers' salaries, by making the assumption that an implicit optimisation was taking place. But if he had already assumed this process of optimisation, why should he add a second optimisation model? He was assuming that administrators did not have the leisure and ability to conduct a dynamic analysis, but that they did implicitly achieve a steady state optimisation.

It was then possible to introduce other important parameters, such as the elasticity of substitution between teacher inputs and material inputs, which was important in educational planning. Alternative assumptions and calculations could be made in terms of these parameters, making it possible to solve the dynamic problem.

In West Germany until lately a comparatively small share of the national income had been devoted to education, and the increase implied that the value attached to education had risen greatly. In terms of his model some of the parameters had changed substantially. That meant that the system was disturbed from the steady state in which it had previously been. The administrators were now having to cope with the dynamic problems of the system, with long-term results. They would make many mistakes because they did not understand the dynamic behaviour of the complicated system. It had been his purpose to help them.

Part Five

Planning in a Market-economy Corporation

20 Business Planning and Forecasting in the United States from a Business Economist's Viewpoint[1]

D. L. Grove

I. INTRODUCTION

At least three approaches to the subject of 'corporate planning' come to mind. One approach, a very narrow one, is to treat corporate planning as a mechanism for bringing some overall organisation and co-ordination to a dispersed decision-making apparatus – a framework for providing a needed degree of integration and co-ordination of actions which have been taken, or are to be taken, by what often are a large number of geographic and functional parts of the firm. This approach to planning usually focuses on the details of the apparatus. It is what economists would call an 'institutional' approach.

Another, and extremely broad approach is to consider corporate planning as embracing the *entire* decision-making process of the firm – the unstructured as well as the structured, the qualitative as well as the quantitative, the purely intuitive as well as the carefully reasoned and tested elements that, added together, comprise the total system. Using this all-encompassing approach would require going far beyond the content and procedures of what is called 'the planning process' in most large American corporations.

In actual practice, many of the most critical and pervasive decisions in the life of a corporation are made by the chief executive largely on an intuitive basis, after receiving advice and counsel from some of the other senior officers of the firm, but with little or no use of any formal planning apparatus the firm may have, and often with little statistical data or quantitative analysis of the long-range benefits and costs of alternative courses of action. This tends to be especially true of decisions determining the long-term direction in which the firm wishes to move.

This is not too surprising, because often it is impossible to foresee the long-range implications of such basic decisions very clearly. Certainly it is impossible to quantify them with enough accuracy to warrant the effort. Often all the chief executive can do is to *rank* the major long-range options open to him, by making a forecast of the

---

[1] The views expressed herein are solely those of the author and should not be identified with his business affiliation.

probable *relative order* of benefits and of the long-term costs to the firm of adopting or not adopting certain courses of action. Sometimes the differences among options seem to be sufficiently overpowering as to make detailed quantitative analysis and forecasts unnecessary in any event.

I.B.M., for example, decided to go into the computer business not because of the findings of any rigorous analytical forecasting process but rather because the corporation's top management felt very strongly that computers were the machines that would dominate the future and that I.B.M. simply had to enter into the computer business vigorously if it was to prosper. This conviction was not the product of thorough quantitative forecasting; it was a product of deep personal conviction and insight.

Very often, therefore, the content of the formal planning process *takes off* from critical predetermined starting points arrived at in this largely informal and intuitive fashion. This should be borne in mind in reading this paper, because it will not be raised explicitly in the ensuing sections.

In this paper, I shall shun the narrow institutional approach, because I think it has relatively little interest to most economists. Neither shall I endeavour to undertake the overly ambitious task of discussing the many-faceted aspects of the complete decision-making process. Instead, I have chosen to limit the paper to an analysis of those planning activities which normally are labelled as such and which usually produce a Plan document (or documents) as a regular part of the activity (although the planning process comprises considerably more than is finally reported in the Plan document).

The definition of planning which I shall use follows. Note that the definition can be interpreted as being broader than my proposed treatment of the subject. Therefore, the constraints I have chosen to impose should be kept in mind.

Planning fundamentally consists of identifying and reviewing alternative, presumably realisable, goals and alternative courses of action, and selecting the ones to be adopted and carried out. This requires analyses and decisions to be made concerning anticipated relationships between *actions* at specified times, with respect both to resources and other variables within the control of the firm, and desired or expected *results* from those actions, and the timing of those results.

The *actions* contemplated in the planning process generally refer to actions that will be taken (though not necessarily be completed) *in the short-term*. If some *results* are expected to flow from those actions *in the short run*, the related decisions and actions are considered to be part of the Short-term Plan. If results are expected to appear only *beyond* the period covered by the Short-term Plan, then the decisions and actions are considered to be part of the Long-term Plan. The distinction between long-term planning and short-term planning, therefore, refers to the timing of the expected *results*, not the timing of the contemplated actions. In either case, contemplated actions are limited to those which the firm will begin to take in the year or two immediately ahead. The reasons for this are straightforward. It would be meaningless to plan for future results without simultaneously planning for the actions that the attainment of those results would require. Similarly, it would be valueless to make decisions now about actions which need not, and will not, be *begun* to be taken until some period quite some time from now, because any decision is more likely to be a correct decision if it is made no farther in advance than is necessary in order to affect the results.

The independent component of the relationship between actions and results can be either the results side of the relationship or the resources side. In other words, planning can set out to achieve certain desired or expected results and address itself mainly to what volumes and deployments of resources are needed to achieve those results. In this case, the dependent variables are the resource variables. Or, alternatively, planning can begin with certain assumptions about resource constraints and then endeavour to determine the optimum results that can be obtained from those resources.

In practice, business planning involves a mixture of these two approaches, because there usually are some resource constraints, especially in the short run. One of the principal differences between short-term and long-term business planning, apart from the timing of the expected results, is that constraints that may be governing over the short run can be relaxed the longer the period addressed. The number of alternative feasible strategies open to the firm will be greater, which is another way of saying that it will have a larger range of options open to it.

The relationships between decisions about resources and the expected results are dynamic relationships – there are critical time dimensions both for the actions and for the results. Moreover, the decisions about resource needs and resource employments have to be made *in advance* of the results. *The expected results, therefore, are always forecasts.* The forecasts may be quantitative or non-quantitative. They may be very general or very detailed. They may be explicitly stated or merely implied. But in essence they always are forecasts.

In a very fundamental sense, therefore, the keystone of organised planning is forecasting. This is as true for government planning as for business planning, and it is true both for short-term and for long-term planning.

The more explicit and formal the forecasting methods and predictions, the more useful the organised planning process is likely to be, in two senses. First, in terms of predictive accuracy, and, second, in terms of providing a supportive background for the largely intuitive decision-making that goes on outside of the formal planning process.

What I shall present in this paper is perhaps a somewhat idealised description of the extent to which certain rationales and concepts actually are accepted and employed in the formal corporate planning process of large American firms. However, the description does generally fit what I have observed from personal observation and discussion with others, though much of what is said in this paper unavoidably requires subjective interpretations by the author. I shall make little or no distinction between short-term and long-term planning, because nearly all of what I have to say applies to both.

II. WHAT SHOULD BE FORECASTED?

If the keystone of organised planning is forecasting, the next question that needs to be addressed is what variables should be forecasted. In a business firm, the most important dependent variables typically are measures of business volumes, because potential business volumes will be critical determinants of resource needs and of revenues. But business volumes will be critically dependent on decisions about such matters as pricing and product introductions, and these in turn will be strongly influenced by forecasts of costs and of competitors' prices and market behaviour in other respects. Moreover, as has been mentioned, many of the forecasts have to operate within a number of other parameters imposed on the firm, all of which have a cost. Examples would be its access to capital funds, the time needed to expand production and sales facilities, and standards imposed by law (e.g. safety requirements).

What emerges, therefore, is that, in an ideal form, planning can be regarded as a system of equations, with some parameters subject entirely to external forces, which must be solved simultaneously. This ideal form is never achieved in practice, but an aim of the formal planning process should be to move it in that direction – away from non-specification of relationships and away from 'partial equilibrium' approaches and toward fuller specification and a 'general equilibrium' approach.

In order to proceed in this manner, a firm must try to determine what variables must be forecasted in order to optimise the volume and time pattern of the firm's profits. It must determine when a fixed condition or predetermined values of certain variables no longer will be unalterable. It also must try to discover the degree of accuracy with which the forecasted variables can be predicted, the rate of fall-off in accuracy as the length of the time period is extended, the cost to the firm of forecast errors in those variables, and the shape of the cost-of-forecast error function.

More will be said about forecast accuracy and cost of forecast errors, and their relationship to planning, in later sections of this paper. The principal point which is being made in this section is that the choice of variables to be employed in any firm's planning process should be directly linked to the relevance of those variables to the decisions that have to be made in order to produce the desired end results of the process. The dominant end result ordinarily is the firm's profit flow. Unless the relationship between a plan variable and the desired end result is predictable within significant limits, the place of that variable in a firm's formal predictive process is open to serious question, at least from an analytical (as contrasted with an accounting) point of view.

III. WHO SHOULD DO THE FORECASTING AND HOW?

Once it has been decided what the critical variables should be in a firm's formal planning process, the next step is to decide who should do the forecasting and what methods should be employed.

These last two considerations are closely intertwined, and a number of issues arise. For example, should the forecasting of attainable results be done by those at the divisional level who are expected to attain the planned results, or should the forecasting be done by those who are less directly involved? In any case, there must, of course, be close interaction between those who set the expected performance and those who must produce that performance. The expected results specified must be both challenging and attainable if the goals are to be realistic and are to carry with them a sense of commitment by those at the operational level.

While these precepts may seem obvious, the best way of implementing them within any given firm may not be easy to determine. An acceptable balance usually is attained only after considerable experimentation.

Another way of looking at this problem is to query whether the planning process should be mainly a 'top downward' process or a 'bottom upward' process. Or should both approaches be followed, and one used as a test of the reasonableness of the other?

Basically, under the 'bottom upward' approach, the planning process begins at a greatly disaggregated level, and essentially consists of a micro-economic partial equilibrium approach. It probably involves forecasts by local and regional sales forces about prospective levels of demand for each customer set, often down to the local level, and by individual product. These forecasts then are summed, probably after some adjustments. The resource needs and deployments similarly are derived mainly by a process of aggregation.

The other approach, the 'top downward' one, is to forecast large aggregates, such as total sales, and then distribute these by customer industry, by sales region, and by individual product, and then derive the resource needs from the business volume data.

In practice, most large U.S. corporations use both methods, though in varying degrees, and have some institutional mechanism for resolving major differences in predicted results and resource needs.

The approach most congenial to economists is the 'top downward' one, largely because it is best adapted to the types of data and tools of analysis at their disposal, whereas the 'bottom upward' approach is preferred by most executives in the operating divisions because they believe it permits a much larger number of market and resource considerations to be taken into account, and it relates forecasting to the variables which they encounter in their daily activities. In addition, it is difficult to inspire any sense of commitment by the operating divisions to produce the planned results if those results are not compatible with what their 'bottom upward' approach indicates can be achieved.

The 'top downward' approach is more suitable for long-term forecasting than is the 'bottom upward' approach. The latter by its very nature tends to focus more on contemporary phenomena; it is likely to underestimate long-term potentials and therefore the importance of new product introductions, or new lines of business, to achieve those potentials.

There is an advantage in employing both methods independently, up to the final planning stage, in order to be able to develop an historical record of the forecasting performance of each approach and to have a basis for later comparison of the forecast strengths and weaknesses of each. While the final planning decisions in any firm usually represent a compromise between the forecasts derived by both methods, subsequent reviews of outcomes versus the values predicted by the two approaches can be enlightening if the planning framework is set up with this purpose in mind.

Since this paper is supposed to deal primarily with the role of economics in business planning, most of the rest of the paper will discuss how economists can contribute to business planning, and little more will be said about the 'bottom upward' approach.

Essentially the contribution of economists consists of: (1) forecasting the international, national, and industry economic environment in which the firm will be operating during the period for which planning is being undertaken, (2) determining what business volume goals would appear to be attainable in that environment if management responds effectively to the opportunities the environment will offer, and (3) testing the strategies and other components of planning for consistency with that environment and the potentials it offers.

Frequently this work will involve making independent forecasts using variables which economic theory teaches are influential in determining demand and supply conditions. It should be borne in mind, however, that this approach usually involves working with rather large aggregates, and relationships among aggregates, and does not provide the detailed disaggregation which must be provided at some stage in the planning process. This is less of a handicap in long-term planning than in short-run planning.

IV. FORECASTS BY ECONOMISTS FOR USE IN PLANNING

The inputs of economists in the planning process of a firm usually start with a forecast of general business activity, as measured by the G.N.P. and national income accounts. From this starting point, the economist proceeds to develop forecasts of attainable business volumes of the firm. In I.B.M., for example, not only are the national income and product accounts forecasted, for a period seven years ahead, but so is gross product originating in seventy-six industry categories, using an input–output model.

In I.B.M. the economists' approach to forecasting the firm's business volumes involve three types of models: growth models, behavioural models, and tracking models.

V. GROWTH MODELS

At the outset of the planning process for any given period, and especially in connection with the preparation of the firm's long-term or 'strategic' plan, it is useful for the firm to develop some notion as to what *targets* or *goals* it should consider setting for its business volumes. First, because in order to plan effectively the firm has to have some conception as to how well it should be *able* to do. Second, because the setting of goals provides a means of measuring the gap between whatever is the level of business volumes that probably *ought* to be attainable and the volumes which current programmes, and especially currently planned product introductions, are *expected* to produce. *The size of the gap, or shortfall, is a measure of the challenge to management to develop the needed new programmes and products.*

In searching for the appropriate target levels, the first step is to determine the historical trend of the business volumes. A second step is to incorporate any aggregate economic variable or variables which have had a significant, stable, and hence reliable relationship to business volume performance in the past, provided that the relationship (a) satisfies the test of reasonableness in terms of economic theory, (b) appears, in the light of all other information, likely to hold in the future, and (c) involves an economic variable which can be predicted satisfactorily in the economic forecast. Regression techniques are employed to estimate the function.

In effect, what a 'growth' model does is to decompose the business volume history of the firm into two components: (a) the part induced by the growth of the economy, and (b) an average rate of growth resulting from the *combined* effect of factors internal to the firm (or perhaps the industry), such as the development of new products and sales efforts. The specific behavioural variables which produced the second component, however, are not specified.

Projections made with these models can be described as follows: given the economic conditions that prevailed over the historical period for which the equation was fitted, the firm (or division of the firm) was able to produce a certain average rate of growth in its volume of business during that period. On the assumption that the firm should, in the absence of any convincing evidence to the contrary, be able to develop programmes, introduce new products, and take other strategic actions for the future which will be at least as productive as those of the past, the firm should be able to achieve a growth rate equal to that of the past *after that rate has been adjusted for the anticipated difference in external economic conditions in the two periods.*

It should be emphasised that what comes out of these models really is not a forecast of expected actual performance of the firm. Rather, it is a useful input for the setting of preliminary targets in the planning process and for assessing the challenge the firm faces. Equally, it can be used as a yardstick for measuring the reasonableness of preliminary goals established by other methodologies and techniques.

The advantage of this approach is that, by making a clear distinction between targets and forecasts, and between what the new plans should try to achieve and what the current programmes expect to achieve, management then can focus on developing and evaluating conditional action programmes that might achieve these preliminary targets. In the process of conducting this exercise, management may very well conclude that the preliminary targets should be revised; perhaps they are too challenging, and hence are unlikely really to be attainable, or perhaps they are not challenging enough.

This approach helps the firm to distinguish between those aspects of the environment which the firm cannot control and those aspects over which it may have some degree of control. Another advantage is that this approach provides a *reproducible* method for the initial stab at the business volume figures to be set by the planning process, and this makes it possible to assure consistency in initial goal-setting in successive planning cycles. Finally, this method utilises past performance in a disciplined way to provide a rough guide for top management as to what it should be able to reasonably expect from the organisation, barring convincing evidence to the contrary.

VI. BEHAVIOURAL MODELS

Once the *goals* have been set, the next stage in the planning process is to develop actual *forecasts* which incorporate whatever strategic decisions management has elected to adopt. So-called 'behavioural forecasting models' often are used for this purpose. The key element in such models is that they imply a considerable amount of understanding of the forces which influence the variable or variables being forecasted. In this sense, they differ importantly from the simple 'growth models' used to provide a first approximation to what the firm's *goals* should be. Those models, it will be recalled, do not attempt to sort out the individual effects of the key policy variables the firm can influence. Rather, they measure the *combined average historical effect* of those variables.

Behavioural models should be specified to include several theoretically important variables, such as, on the demand side, income effects, relative price effects, substitutes, complements, and short-run and long-run adjustments. On the supply side, explanatory variables which reflect the structure of the marketplace and technological change should be incorporated.

Here, as in all econometric model-building, the raw materials are essentially a body of economic theory and some observed data – in this case, data concerning the economy, the firm and/or perhaps the industry. Economic theory is employed to specify a structure that then is tested and revised by fitting data to that structure. The model is not considered complete unless it has met certain criteria. Most important among these criteria are predictive reliablity (as determined by *ex post* forecasting over some historical periods not covered by the period of estimation of the model), and signs and sizes of coefficients in the model which are consistent with the theoretical specifications.

Of course, often some initial variables for which the model-builder had high hopes have to be excluded from the final model because they prove to be statistically insignificant in their effects or because the coefficients are unstable, so they turn out to be unreliable as predictors. Often other variables which would seem to be promising from a theoretical viewpoint, cannot even be tested because of non-availability of data in satisfactory form. To the extent that such data limitations are subject to correction by actions within the power of the firm, however, the economist can render a service to management by pointing out the potential value of such data for planning and decision-making purposes. Hopefully, this will lead to the necessary effort to collect that data in the future.

VII. THE ROLE OF BEHAVIOURAL MODELS IN THE PLANNING PROCESS

What emerges from behavioural models should be regarded as *conditional* forecasts – conditional on the correctness both of the assumptions about the *external environment* (especially the assumptions about government policy and, in some firms, major labour union negotiations) and of the assumptions about *actions which the firm contemplates taking*. These assumptions are embodied in what are called the 'exogenous' variables of the model.

The forecasts derived from behavioural models provide a valuable independent check on the business volume forecasts built from 'the bottom up' in great detail by the market-research and other staffs. The employment of behavioural models has the merit of helping to focus the planning process dialogue on: (*a*) what effect government economic policy will have on the firm's prospects; (*b*) how general and specific market conditions are expected to differ from those which have prevailed in the recent past; (*c*) what effect these differences will have on the firm's performance and why; and (*d*) whether the proposed actions of the firm over the variables it controls or influences appear to be the appropriate actions.

Under certain circumstances which will be discussed in the next section, one of the most valuable uses of behavioural models is to make *alternative* forecasts based on different sets of assumptions about key variables. Their employment in this fashion can help management formulate its strategies; in addition, it can help to alert management to the nature and extent of some of the exposures to which the firm's plans will be subject as a consequence of whatever assumptions are chosen for those plans. By engaging in this sort of exercise, management is less likely to be taken by complete surprise by ensuing developments and, thus, ordinarily should be able to respond to them more promptly and effectively.

It is worth repeating that the use of behavioural models implies some understanding of the forces that influence the dependent variable or variables being forecasted – an understanding not only of what the forces are but also of their weights, and, above all, an ability to be specific about them. Any forecast derived from such a model, therefore, should be considered as the product of a hypothesis, or a set of hypotheses, about the forces which determine the value of the forecasted variables under specified conditions. *A test of the validity and completeness of the hypotheses will be the subsequent degree of accuracy of the forecast.*

VIII. IMPLICATIONS OF FORECAST ERRORS WITH A BEHAVIOURAL MODEL

The magnitude of a subsequently revealed forecast error made by a behavioural model can serve as a rough measure of the degree of ignorance about the operation of the forces which determine the forecasted variable.

If a model does poorly in actual forecasting not because of structural defects but because the forecaster has assigned erroneous values to the exogenous variables, then one has a situation which can be especially frustrating. The importance of correct values for the exogenous variables in most business forecasting models explains why most business economists in the United States spend much of their time analysing developments in government economic policy and the likely outcome of major labour negotiations.

If a model forecasts well when it is fed the correct values for the exogenous variables beyond the period of estimation of the model, then, as was mentioned in the preceding section of this paper, there are a number of benefits to be derived from making alternative forecasts employing various sets of plausible assigned values for the exogenous variables. On the other hand, if a model provides quite unreliable results *ex post*, then the range of forecasts which would fall within the error band with any *given* set of assumptions may be as large as, or even larger than, the range of *most probable* forecast values derived from *alternative* sets of assumptions about the exogenous variables. In this situation, it is questionable whether much is contributed to the planning process by preparing alternative forecasts. This is a consideration which is relevant to the question of how far out the planning period should extend.

IX. HOW TO LIVE WITH FORECAST ERROR

One of the few things that one can say with certainty about planning is that there will be errors, and the part of planning that relies on econometric models will be no exception. Even if a model has done very well in *ex post* forecasting, this is no guarantee that it will continue to do well in the future. If a model should begin to forecast poorly in actual use, after previous good performance, the most disturbing aspect may not be the immediate consequences of the forecast error. Instead, it may be a threat that the firm may not be able to plan effectively henceforth unless it can develop and verify a new set of hypotheses which appears adequately to explain the recent past and offers acceptable promise of relevancy for the future. This threat is reduced if the firm has other forecasting methods, perhaps of a 'bottom upward' sort, provided they usually produce reasonably satisfactory results. This is another reason why a firm is wise not to put all its forecasting eggs in one basket.

Given this constant exposure to forecast errors, no matter how the forecasts are derived, how can the planning system best adapt to it? Basically, there are two ways. The first is to try to develop methods for early recognition of forecast errors. The second is for the firm to develop capability to respond quickly to errors, once recognised, so that the ultimate cost of errors can be minimised.

Beyond a certain point, it will become much more productive to use additional analytical resources to attain earlier recognition of initial forecast error than to use further resources to attempt to improve the quality of the *initial* forecasts underlying the planning decisions. Both approaches are needed to progress toward the real goal, however, which is to reduce the *cost* of forecast error. The cost of forecast error, of course, is the amount of profits the firm foregoes as a result of not having made correct initial forecasts of its resource needs and sales potentials when it made its plans.

It might seem that early recognition of forecast error is primarily relevant to short-run planning and is of much less importance for long-term planning. By and large, this is true, but not entirely so. Sometimes a difference of a few weeks or months in discovering that forecasted business volumes are going off the track may be of great value by forcing a review of investment decisions, and perhaps some other kinds of decisions, that have long-term implications but which still are not so far advanced as to be incapable of being postponed or modified.

The really difficult problem is to determine how much of an error in the forecasts has to occur before a firm is convinced that something needs to be done. How does one separate the always-present static from the true signal? If performance is falling short of the forecast, most business planners have an understandable tendency to hope that the shortfall soon will be offset by an error in the opposite direction, and that the firm's goals, especially the longer-term ones, still can be realised. Similarly, if performance is coming in well above what was planned, there is a tendency to delay revising planned volumes upward, and acquiring the additional resources that would be required, until it is very clear that the initially planned volumes really are much too low in relation to potential.

XI. TRACKING MODELS

Sometimes a simple auto-regressive model can be helpful in separating the short-run static from true signals where business volumes are concerned. By drawing on past experience to give some notion of the significance of the size of the error, and whether the firm's plans should, in the absence of other more precise information, be modified, such a model can contribute to earlier recognition and reduced cost of initial error.

These auto-regressive models have been given several names in the literature: 'adaptive models', 'error-learning models', and 'tracking models'.[1] They imply no understanding of motivation or causality. None the less, they have their merits in some situations. They can take advantage (*a*) of situations in which business volume behaviour in a given month or quarter has a significant relationship to what happened in the preceding months or quarters, and (*b*) of the fact that business volume forecasts in most firms are made for spans of *fixed* twelve-month periods (rather than '*rolling*' twelve-month periods).

In addition to lagged variables measuring the behaviour of business volume, these models can incorporate one or more current economic variables. As a consequence, should the forecast of the economic variable or variables be revised *before* data on actual business volume behaviour have become available, the significance of this revision for the forecast of business volume can be assessed.

Similarly, should the economic and business volume outcomes of a quarter, once the data become available, reveal that there was an error in both the economic and the business volume forecasts, then an estimate can be made of the component of the business volume

[1] See *Economic Forecasts and Expectations*, Studies in Business Cycles, no. 19, National Bureau of Economic Research, ed. by Jacob Mincer, chap. 3 by Jacob Mincer and references therein.

forecast error that should be attributed to the economic forecast error. If the business volume results for the year-to-date cannot be fully explained by the error in the economic forecast, which usually is the case, the residual is attributable to other factors. The size of the residual error is helpful in ascertaining whether some action by management to correct the situation is called for, and whether the initial forecast needs to be revised beyond any revision that might be appropriate merely because of alteration of the *economic* forecast.

One of the undesirable characteristics of these auto-regressive models is that they have systematic error build-up in the forecast errors of the following periods; that is to say, a component of the error term of a given future quarter's forecast is the sum of the forecast errors of the earlier forecasted quarters of the planning period. However, if the coefficient of the lagged forecasted variable is greater than zero and less than unity (which is a required condition if the model is to have any usefulness for forecasting), then the actual errors made by the model as the planning year progresses are transmitted in a diminishing distribution over the balance of the planning period. As a consequence of this characteristic, a substantially more than proportionate part of the total error for the year ordinarily will be recognised early in the year if the model has good forecasting properties and if the forecast is revised periodically as actual data become available.

Related to their usefulness for early recognition of error is the value of these error-learning models in providing a systematic method for evaluating actual results against expectations. In addition, they provide a mechanism both for revising the forecast when error begins to become evident and for making constructive use of the size of the previous forecast error in the process of the revision.

These models, it should be emphasised, are not a substitute for detailed analysis of the causes of forecast error; neither are they a substitute for other forecasting models. They are not likely to yield good results for more than several quarters ahead, in most cases. They should be regarded as more useful in providing a reasonably narrow estimated *range* of probable outcomes than in providing a *point* estimate. Their greatest value is that they help the planner to determine whether, on the basis of past experience, an initial error is likely to persist, and, if so, to what extent – not precisely, but within an acceptable range. Inasmuch as most long-term plans of firms take off from a starting point determined by the short-range plan, a revision of the short-term plan may have significance for the firm's long-term plan as well. Certainly the question of relevance to the long-term plan should be raised when the planned business volume measure gets off its near-term track.

XII. RESOURCE-MANAGEMENT RESPONSE TO ERROR

One of the most important aspects of business management concerns the capability of the firm to respond effectively to revealed errors in its plans. In considerable measure, the form in which a firm organises itself should reflect the firm's capability to forecast the relationship between planned actions and planned results.

For example, if a firm consistently can forecast quite accurately, it probably can minimise its long-term average unit costs and maximise its sales by incurring certain fixed costs which it would not be wise to incur if its forecasts typically are subject to huge errors. In the latter case, long-run average costs may be minimised, and long-term profits maximised, by willingness to pay an 'insurance premium' for greater resource flexibility. The 'insurance premium' may be regarded as the difference between average unit costs in the actual world of uncertainty and what the firm's unit costs would be in a world in which business volumes could be forecast with complete accuracy.

XIII. APPROPRIATE DETAIL AND TIME SPAN OF PLANNING

It is clear from the foregoing that the character of a firm's planning activities to a considerable degree should be influenced by the degree of accuracy with which the firm can forecast the outcome of planned actions. The greater the forecast capability, the longer the period over which planning is worthwhile, and, generally speaking, the greater the amount of detail which can meaningfully be put into the planning process.

In this connection, it is interesting to speculate about why the most successful entrepreneurs in some industries appear to be men who have no confidence in rigorous analysis or in detailed planning. They prefer to operate from week to week and month to month. Yet they are very successful. Why?

I would venture the guess that the reasons for their success are:
(1) they are very sensitive, in an intuitive way, to current developments;
(2) they have organised their businesses so that they can react to changing circumstances very quickly and efficiently;
(3) the nature of their industry is such that none of their competitors can forecast with much accuracy.

The importance of this third point is central, of course; if the competitors could forecast with considerable accuracy, they would have an advantage in the form of lower costs, since flexibility almost always has to be bought at a price. It probably also would enable the competitors to cover a larger marketing area.

The corollary of the foregoing is that over-planning can produce expensive rigidities in a firm's cost structure and retard its capability to respond effectively to change. By over-planning I mean planning in excessive detail and for too long a time period.

If it is accepted that the character and time span of a firm's formal planning should be influenced by its ability to forecast accurately, then it follows that it is valuable to develop an historical record of planned versus actual results and to make a careful study of what can be learned from the record, both about the adequacy of the forecasting techniques and about the content and direction of the planning process itself.

XIV. SHAPE OF THE COST OF FORECAST ERROR

In addition to the need for methods which will yield accurate forecasts, effective business planning requires an understanding of the shape of the cost of forecast errors. Actually, a firm is not so much interested in reducing *average forecast errors* to a minimum as it is in reducing the *cost* of forecast error to a minimum. As mentioned earlier, the cost to the firm of a forecast error is the amount of profit the firm forgoes as a result of not having made a correct initial forecast of its resource needs and sales potentials. In practice, the cost of forecast error frequently is difficult to determine precisely, but in most firms a good approximation should be possible.

The cost of forecast error may not be symmetrical. In fact, often it is not. Thus, the cost of an overestimate of business volumes by, say, 10 per cent may be quite different from the cost of an underestimate of the same magnitude. In some industries, if a firm plans too high it may incur much greater-than-planned average unit costs. In such circumstances, effective planning might call for planning goals somewhat below those with maximum probability of attainment. For example, such an approach might call for frequent reliance on overtime work, or external sourcing, to meet levels of demand in excess of the planned volumes. Or it might even involve some forgoing of potential sales. On the other hand, in some other industries, long-term maintenance and growth of market share may be dependent upon planning for business volumes somewhat in excess of the most probable forecasts, and it may be profitable to do so.

XV. 'CONSISTENCY CHECKS' OR 'TESTS OF ECONOMIC REASONABLENESS'

From time to time in the planning process there are certain items, or relationships among items, apart from those embodied in models, which can be tested for economic reasonableness even though the numerical values cannot actually be *forecasted* with accuracy by the economist. It is important that such testing be done wherever possible.

The development of specific tests of economic reasonableness may involve substantial or little employment of econometric and statistical techniques, depending on the item being tested. The nature of this part of the planning process, especially with respect to the economist's role in it, may perhaps be presented adequately merely by giving some typical illustrations:

(a) Are the planned rates of increase in employee compensation consistent with the macro-economic forecast of behaviour of average hourly earnings in the economy?

(b) If substantial changes are to be made in the prices of certain specific products of the firm, are the sales forecasts for those individual products consistent not only with the macro-forecasts of incomes and prices, but also with whatever can be determined about the price elasticity of demand for the products?

(c) Is the part of total sales which is expected to be made to state and local governments consistent with the macro-economic forecast of total purchases of goods and services by those levels of government?

(d) Are the forecasted increases in total number of employees, or in certain categories of employees, consistent with the planned increases in output and sales, when specific consideration is given to the historical behaviour of labour productivity in the firm in comparable periods?

(e) Is the expected behaviour of interest rates adequately reflected in those planning decisions for which this variable is relevant? It would be relevant, for example, if the firm plans to raise additional capital in the marketplace. For a company which both sells and leases its products, it would be relevant to the predicted ratio of rentals to outright sales.

XVI. CONCLUSIONS

The central theme of this paper is that the keystone of planning really is forecasting – forecasting the results which are expected to follow from a set of management decisions and actions. The accuracy with which the forecasts of results can be made, and the shape of the cost-of-forecast-error functions, will have important bearings on a large number of management decisions.

This approach to business planning can be greatly advanced by use of properly constructed econometric forecasting models. If these forecasting models are to be used effectively, however, they must meet certain critical standards.

First, they should be reproducible by others; inputs of subjective judgement should be readily identifiable. Otherwise, the decision-makers will be unable to understand the nature of any differences between the econometricians' forecasts and those coming to them from other parts of the organisation. Without such understanding they will be unable to make the final decisions intelligently.

Second, models should be rigorously tested for correspondence between the propositions stated by the models and observable facts. After all, a model embodies a set of propositions about certain determinations and relationships. The validity of these propositions should be tested. In order that this be possible, however, the model itself must be properly specified, estimated and validated. The stability of the estimated coefficients should be determined. Simulation of the model, both within and beyond the sample period used in fitting the model, should be undertaken to determine the extent to which the model's predictive ability is independent of the particular goodness of estimation of the equations in the sample period.

Finally, in any business environment, *competing* propositions about what influences the firm's results are likely to be held by individual members of the firm's top management. It is important to try to devise competing formal models which specify these competing propositions, to do so in a rigorous, reproducible fashion, and then to *test* the propositions.

The quantitative approach to formal business forecasting and planning outlined in this paper, which in general terms increasingly is being adopted by large American corporations and is extensively used in the I.B.M. Corporation, would be practically impossible without the use of computers. With their ready availability to business firms and with increasing skill in their use, computers are coming to play a rapidly growing role in management decision-making and planning in the United States.

21 The Long-range Corporate Plan of a Private Business Enterprise in Japan

M. Horimoto

I. FOREWORD

Under the system of a free market economy, private business enterprises are always faced with the problem of how to adjust themselves to given conditions which are beyond their control. If they are able to forecast correctly such uncontrollable conditions and consequently adapt themselves to them properly, the companies will possibly gain profits as expected; but if they fail they may suffer losses and, in the worst case, they may lose even the foundations of their businesses.

Japan is a country where the allocation of resources is carried out basically through the price mechanism in the markets. Even though Japan thus maintains a free economy, depending on necessity, long range national economic plans are issued by the government: for example, the Income Doubling Plan of 1960, the Medium Range Economic Plan of 1965 and the Socio-economic Development Plan of 1967. These are, however, neither central planning of the nation nor binding on private enterprises in their business activities. They are little more than the forecasts on which the government is going to administer their national economic policies. Accordingly, they are treated as 'guide-lines' by the private industries for their future business activities.

These guide-lines are of course macro-economic and not tailored to the individual companies for their planning use. Thus, each enterprise has to prepare the basis of its planning by its own method and judgement, evaluating the competitiveness of its own products and forecasting their life cycles and other elements such as possible technical developments, availability of raw materials and labour. After such evaluation and forecast, the company plans production, sales, capital investment, cash flow, personnel requirements, and the rest, and incorporates all of these in the projected profit and loss statement, balance sheet, and other forms of statement that the company needs, and thereafter the management guides the operations to reach the goals of the plan in accordance with its specific corporate management procedures.

But, no matter how beautifully prepared our long-range plan may

TABLE 21.1

SUMITOMO CHEMICAL AND ITS ORGANISATION

(a) Establishment: June 1925

(b) Type of business and line of product:

general chemical producer and seller (industrial chemicals, chemical fertilisers, plastics, light metals, dyestuffs and other fine chemicals, pesticides and pharmaceuticals)

(c) Corporate data ($1 = ¥ 308):

   (i) Capital stock outstanding   ¥ 44,800 million ($145 million) as of 31 December 1971

   (ii) Total assets   ¥ 328,800 million ($1,068 million) as of 31 December 1971

   (iii) Sales   ¥ 241,900 million ($785 million) in 1971

   (iv) Number of employees   14,526 as of 31 December 1971

(d) Characteristics of production:

The company handles a very large number of mass produced products.

(e) Operational management: divisional systems

(f) Place of business:

Head Office   Osaka

Branches   Tokyo and Wellington (New Zealand)

Sales offices   Nagoya and Fukuoka

Manufacturing plants   Niihama, Ohe, Kikumoto, Nagoya, Toyama, Osaka, Ohita and Chiba (Sumitomo Chiba Chemical Co., Ltd., the company's 100 per cent-owned subsidiary)

Research laboratories   Central Research Laboratory (Takatsuki), Takarazuka Research Laboratory

(g) Organisation Chart

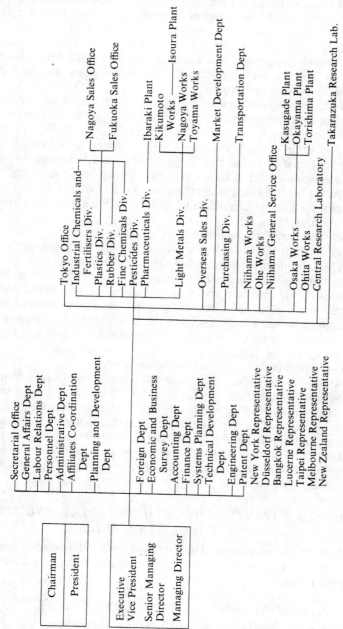

be, it must be recognised that such a long-range plan of today stands on a very unstable foundation because the market is very competitive; the technological innovation is quite rapid; and other business environments are always changing at a very high rate. Under such circumstances, it would be almost impossible to prepare a plan effective for a period as long as five years with a high probability of its realisation.

If the company is an electric power company or a steel manufacturer, however, forecasting will be much easier than in other types of industries, even though some of their business conditions are still beyond their control, because a power company is freed from competition owing to its legally approved regional monopoly while the steel manufacturers have a relatively simple line of products.

On the other hand, a company like ours has extreme difficulty in making long-range forecasts. Such difficulty comes from the following circumstances.

(a) The line of products is much diversified.

(b) Most products are 'market-oriented' (not 'made-to-order').

(c) Technological innovation is very rapid and dramatic.

In the case of a company with many operating divisions like ourselves, the optimisation of one division, that is called 'sub-optimisation', does not necessarily guarantee the total optimisation. Therefore, a simple aggregation of the forecasting and planning of each division cannot be employed as a method for preparing a long-range corporate plan. A different approach for seeking a total optimisation must be selected by the company.

Another thing I must mention about a 'long range-plan' is that it should not be too rigid; it should be flexible in its implementation as the environment changes. In the case of our company, a long-range plan is a kind of forecast embodying our ideal state of operations some years ahead, but it is an important means through which the management as well as the ordinary employees can clearly understand the corporate objectives, future directions, and methods for achieving the objectives.

II. THE JAPANESE CHEMICAL INDUSTRY AND ITS LONG RANGE STRATEGIES

The business of the chemical industry has certain characteristics, and our long-range plans and strategies are prepared with due consideration for them:

(1) *Technical characteristics*

  (a) *Scale competition.* Generally speaking, the chemical industry is highly capital-intensive. The larger the size of the plant, the less will be the percentage of fixed cost in the total cost of the product when the plant is operated nearly at its full capacity. Therefore, the management is always tempted to expand the plant size, harnessing the economies of scale.

(b) *Diversification.* The chemical industry is one of the typical process industries which inevitably yields by-products and co-products. Therefore, the product line is destined to be diversified and the industry is self-expanding by its nature. When a new investment is in plan, it is necessary to examine also the marketability or usability of such by-products and co-products. In the long-range planning, the first thing is to determine the production capacity of the main product; the second is to set the policies on its by-products and co-products.

(c) *Technological innovation.* In the chemical industry, especially in the petro-chemical industry, the technology advances at a rapid pace. To the management, this implies a fearful possibility that a product and its equipment may become obsolete all of a sudden. The life cycle of a product is becoming shorter and shorter. On the other hand, the technological innovation opens up the door to the so-called pioneer's profit which is often larger than was expected. In other industries, new investments are often made because of the demand growth of existing products. But the relatively young chemical industry has witnessed that technological innovation gives birth to new products, inducing new investments. The result has been the rapid entry of many companies with new technologies into the market, keeping the structure of the industry always fluid. The difficulty of forecasting the outcomes of R. & D. activities is a decisive problem in preparing long-range plans. At most, a perspective of industrial and social needs will hint at the direction towards which the R. & D. should respond.

(2) *Characteristics of the market*

(a) *Uniformity of products.* As most of the chemical products are basic materials and intermediaries for other industries, they can hardly be differentiated in quality. The competition tends to be based on the selling price rather than the quality, brand name or service. Together with the rush towards larger-scale production, the competition based on price is likely to keep bringing down the selling price. This makes difficult the correct price estimation in the long-range planning.

(b) *Created demand.* In most cases, the chemical industry has grown by replacing natural products or creating markets for new products. If other industries grow mainly in correspondence with the increase of existing demands, the chemical industry expands by creating new demands. The market size for a product of this nature is more affected by the price than by the income level of the consumers. A sudden leap in demand to be brought by a price cut is sometimes left out from the forecast based on a simple extrapolation method. In Japan, in many cases the forecast was smaller than the actual, and the chemical plants were expanded little by little like a patchwork. Probably wrong methods of demand forecast were selected without clear understanding of the price–demand characteristics of the chemical products.

(3) *Managerial characteristics*

(a) *Decentralised structure of the industry.* The growth of the Japanese chemical industry owes much to the purchase of foreign technologies. Thus, even companies with little technical capability have had access to new products, and consequently the industry has been flooded with many companies each having a relatively small production unit. In addition, the industry has been protected from foreign competitors by governmental measures; that is to say, the industry has grown without undergoing elimination and reorganisation through free competition.

(b) *Financial weakness.* In order to purchase new technologies and keep investing in new plant and equipment, the Japanese chemical industry has had to depend for its financing on outside sources. The keen competition has prevented the chemical companies from keeping a proper level of profits for themselves and has made it practically impossible to invest sufficiently in R. & D. The tendency has been to pursue the pioneer's profit by introducing foreign technologies with relatively little attention to the financial conditions.

(c) *Petro-chemical complex.* In the petro-chemical industry, the necessity of a large amount of investment and of a strong sales force has led to joint operations of various companies in petro-chemical complexes, thus enabling each participating company to enjoy the economies of scale and the wider product line. In the near future, however, the Japanese market will be opened to the free entry of foreign firms and the Japanese chemical market will see much keener competition. Already there is a sign that the Japanese companies are trying to meet this challenge by forming a so-called 'combined complex' and by encouraging more joint investments in huge projects. Our long-range strategy, therefore, must be determined with due attention to probable reshuffles among the Japanese chemical companies.

III. SUMITOMO'S CORPORATE PLANS AND THEIR ADMINISTRATION

It is not my intention to discuss here the scientific method for preparing a long-range plan in a general way. Instead, I would like to describe how it is related to our management systems and functions in our corporate operations.

We have three kinds of plans: long-range (for a period of five years), medium-range (three years), and short-range (one-half year). The following is a rough outline of our planning and administration systems.

(1) *The short-range plan*

The major purpose of this plan is budget control and cost control. This is compiled on a semi-annual basis. Before compilation, guidelines (after approval or confirmation by the management) are shown to each department. Such guidelines are given in a manner compatible with the long-range and medium-range plans, detailing economic situations, trends of customer industries, financial possibilities, etc. for the coming six-month period, so that each operating unit can work out the plan in line with the shown targets and the expected business environment. Guidelines are sometimes growth-oriented and sometimes based on risk-minimising principles. Each operating division drafts its sales, production, expenses, capital investment and R. & D. for the next six-month period and submits such a draft proposal to the Administrative Department at the Head Office according to a certain time table. The Administrative Department collects all those proposals including those of staff departments and compiles a comprehensive corporate budget through various negotiations from the corporate standpoint. The comprehensive corporate budget thus drafted is reported to the board of directors for its approval. The costs used in the plan are the standard costs effective during the period through which the cost control and budget control are exercised by comparing 'actual' with 'plan' on a monthly basis. Thus, the short-range plan is, in its real sense, a 'working' plan according to which daily operations are practised.

(2) *The medium-range plan*

This covers a period of three years and deals with fairly concrete capital investment plans which are more certain to materialise than those in a long range plan. Incidentally, the medium-range plan is not a procedure to approve each capital expenditure. We have a separate procedure for that. A three-year range is sufficiently long to have a fairly clear prospect. Particularly from the viewpoint of capital investment, 'three years' is meaningful: that is to say, a plant construction takes about two years from design to completion (except the cases of large-scale projects including purchase of plant site), and in the third year the plant starts to contribute to profit-making. The method for working out a medium-range plan is similar to that for a short-range plan.

(3) The long-range plan

This covers a period of five years. Details will be given later. The 'nature' of the long-range plan is much discussed even in our company. Some say it reflects an 'ideal' of the company while others say it is a kind of 'expectation' based on the trend. From a practical point of view, it is a 'guide-line' based on which the management determines allocation of corporate resources (personnel, money and materials) in the most efficient way from the long-range point of view.

IV. OUTLINE OF SUMITOMO'S LONG-RANGE PLAN

(1) Purpose and function of a long-range plan

For a business enterprise, it is vitally important to forecast the trend of the economy and society which surround it and to react to the changing social needs with high flexibility. It is necessary for us to assess as far as possible the influences which the forecasted changes would give to the organisation. On the other hand, we have to examine the competitiveness of our company five years ahead and the consistency in capacities between production, sales, investment, finance, personnel, etc. during the five-year period. All of these are carried out in our long-range planning systems. As the final form, long-range management goals are explained and the strategies toward such goals are determined. The purpose of laying out such a long-range plan is not to examine each project, but to examine competitiveness and life cycle of major products and forecast future possibilities and finally determine the strategic policies.

(2) Goals

　(a) *General.* Goals are not single and they are certainly not rigid. They are pluralistic and flexible in the long run. They vary depending upon different historical phases. It is only a little over ten years since our company began to employ the long-range planning system as a corporate practice. It is a responsibility of the management of a business corporation to visualise the desirable long-term goals of the corporation and to run the business so as to bring it closer to these goals, even if no formal long-range planning is practised.

A goal of our company in the past was to change from a mere fertiliser manufacturer to a modernised and diversified chemical company, because the fertiliser business showed no favourable sign, and our strategy for it was to reduce gradually the weight of fertilisers and to increase the weights of petro-chemicals and fine chemicals.

Another goal was to strengthen our overall competitiveness. Originally, our plants were located only in the western part of Japan and we experienced marketing disadvantages in the eastern part of Japan, particularly in Tokyo area. To improve this situation, we employed a strategy that was to build big manufacturing plants near Tokyo. Sumitomo Chemical is now the largest chemical company in Japan on a non-consolidated basis, with a diversified product line and several manufacturing plants disseminated all over Japan.

(b) *Goal of the long-range plans in the 1960s: a billion dollar company.* The Japanese economy in the 1960s experienced a rapid economic growth without historical precedent. In fact, the unexpectedly high growth always surpassed such forecasts by the government as the Income Doubling Plan of 1960, the Medium Range Economic Plan of 1965, and the Socio-economic Development Plan of 1967. Thus, the growth of the Japanese economy was constantly underestimated. Such conditions of the national economy were well reflected in the strategies and behaviours of Japanese companies in the 1960s. In Japan, the competition within the industry is extremely keen, and this keenness is a driving force for the development and the growth of the industry. Under such circumstances, the long-range plans of our company in the 1960s were basically 'growth-oriented'. For example, the gist of the most recent five-year plan of our company, which was drawn up in 1968, was to increase the sales by an average of 21 per cent every year from 1969 through 1973. The sales goal in the final year was the annual sales of ¥360 thousand million (U.S. $1 thousand million at the old exchange rate).

We called this plan 'the-way-to-a-billion-dollar-company plan' and made efforts every year to reach this goal. The basis for creating a thousand million dollar company as a goal was as follows.

(i) It was attainable judging from the actual growth rate observed until 1968 as well as the upper feasible limit of future plant and equipment investments.

(ii) Since the annual sales of an average international chemical firm in the United States and Western Europe was around $1 thousand million at that time, we treated sales of this amount as a qualification for an international corporation.

Table 21.2 shows the sales of each product category in 1968, when

TABLE 21.2

Sumitomo's Share in National Sales of Various Chemical Products

	1963		1968		1973		
	National ¥ 000 million	Sumitomo ¥ 000 million (%)	National ¥ 000 million	Sumitomo ¥ 000 million (%)	National ¥ 000 million	Sumitomo ¥ 000 million (%)	Average increase rate (%)
Fertilisers	165	10 (6)	213	13 (6)	259	19 (7)	8
Industrial chemicals	338	11 (3)	665	38 (6)	1,289	81 (6)	16
Plastics	168	12 (7)	459	29 (6)	864	75 (9)	21
Synthetic rubber	19		73		131	20 (15)	
Fine chemicals	51	11 (22)	82	21 (26)	140	63 (45)	25
Gunpowder	13		17		19		
Tar products	15		20		26		
Photo sensitive materials	32		61		111		
Paint and printing ink	128		231		395		
Pesticides	39	3 (8)	75	8 (11)	130	21 (16)	21
Pharmaceuticals	341	4 (1)	612	9 (1)	1,102	36 (3)	33
Aluminium	47	13 (28)	100	29 (29)	212	65 (31)	18
Oil and fats	92		156		248		
Total	1,448	65 (4)	2,764	149 (5)	4,922	380 (8)	21

this five-year plan started. For comparison the sales in 1963 and the target sales in 1973 are shown. The prices of chemical products go down every year because of market competition and technical innovation. A 3 per cent price fall annually is assumed in setting the sales goal in this long-range plan. The sales of our company accounted for 5 per cent of the total output of the Japanese chemical industry in 1968. The corresponding ratio is estimated to be 8 per cent in 1973.

(c) *Future prospects.* The basic structure of the Japanese economy has changed drastically with the current economic slowdown beginning in 1970 and the international monetary realignment made in 1971. There are many serious problems facing us in the national and international fields. During the period of high economic growth which we in Japan enjoyed in the 1960s, the major cities became overcrowded, the natural environment, including air and water, seriously deteriorated to the extent of becoming a menace to social life. Japan's continuing positive international balance of payments, resulting from the mounting exports to foreign markets, became exposed to the policies of foreign countries. At this stage, Japan was urged to shift its priority from a growth-oriented policy to a social welfare or balanced growth policy.

With the slowing down of the economy, the business environment has changed substantially. In particular, the gap between production capacity and effective demand has widened. This is especially true for such basic industries as steel and petro-chemicals.

Let me explain in detail, taking the petro-chemical industry as an example. The development of the petro-chemical industry during the past fourteen years has formed a succession of cycles of growth of output, summarised as follows: Scale-up of plant capacity employing newly developed process technology→reduction of manufacturing cost→reduction of market price→formation of mass consumption market→scale-up of plant capacity→.

Certainly in recent years, this cycle has ensured the growth of any petro-chemical company. In practice since 1960 the average reduction of the manufacturing cost of chemicals has been 6·9 per cent a year per unit of product while that of the market price has been 5·2 per cent a year.

In the 1970s, however, the circumstances surrounding the industry have thus far been showing a complete change. Each company has expanded its production capacity enormously in recent years. But demand is estimated to be growing at a lower rate in the 1970s. Hence, supply is exceeding demand substantially and the market prices of a number of major products are being lowered even below their manufacturing costs. The Japanese petro-chemical industry is regarded as having arrived at the stage of maturity, and profit is no longer expected simply from quantitative growth.

Since the environment has changed, our management policy must be changed by placing more emphasis on 'quality' than 'quantity'. In other words, the management policy must be to emphasise the development and improvement of products having high value added to increase the total profitability of the company, while strengthening the financial foundations so that they can be well maintained even if the growth is slowed down.

There are certain other factors to be taken into account in long-range planning: for example, environmental problems and the consumers' movement. Support and acceptance by the public are now indispensable to the operations of a company. Thus, the social responsibility which a company must accept is becoming greater and greater. When the business environment changes, we have to modify our long-range plan.[1]

In this new, changing world, what goals should we have in our long-range plan? Frankly speaking, we are still thinking. But in general terms, what we must do is to identify the social needs quickly, develop new products meeting such needs as they arise, place more emphasis on R. & D., and guide our operations so as to satisfy other requirements of society. To do this, we will have to make our

[1] Incidentally the achievement of a thousand million dollar company (the sales goal of our long-range plan) seems to be merely a matter of time, particularly because the yen was revalued last year. So this is losing its importance in any practical sense.

management systems more flexible and, in addition, create a new corporate outlook in which social contributions are positively valued in management decisions.

Our traditional goal of 'an international chemical company' will be carried forward into the future long-range plans. This goal is particularly important because international co-operation is now badly needed in those sectors of the economy in which the participation of private companies is essential. Our strategy in this area will be to set up business operating units in various parts of the world and to manage all operations in an international framework.

As I mentioned earlier, the goals of a long-range plan are not single, and furthermore, they should not necessarily be quantifiable goals. We are anxious to establish our long-range goals after examining the problems from various angles and taking all the above-mentioned conditions into account.

(3) *The procedures for long-range planning*

(a) *An outline.* Long-range planning starts with a survey of the environment. Business prospects for the coming several years, especially those of each specific field of the chemical industry and related industries, are surveyed by several forecasting methods, utilising various available sources of information including the long-range economic prospects published by the government agency. The major purpose of this survey is to know which fields or divisions will have improved profit opportunities in future. Based on the survey results, the present organisation and product lines are examined. Among the questions raised are these: Which fields should be strengthened or what type of product should be added? How should we expand R. & D. activities to meet such demands? How should we proceed with capital investment to support corporate operations?

Answers are given by the respective divisions as well as by the corporate staff and analysed by the Administrative Department at the Head Office. The results, which are those of still hypothetical ideas, are shown in quantified statements. If there is any discrepancy between such results and those which the management desire, modifications are made in the hypothesis. Such modifications are repeated until satisfactory results are obtained. This operation is done by our computerised corporate simulation model.

Empirical data such as output (production)–input (investment) ratio, variable cost ratio, personnel increase rate, labour cost increase rate, etc. are already set in the model. Then, policy variables, which are input data, are put in the model. The model simulates such a case and produces output data such as the capital investment, the cost variance, the financial results. The results are reviewed by those responsible and modifications are made, if necessary, in the input data. Then, the calculation is repeated until the results show a satisfactory set of outputs. In the process of review, management problems are clarified and working targets or tactics are listed.

(b) *Forecast of the industry and the environment*. The chemical industry is always moving, driven by incessant technological innovation. Thus, no long-range forecast can be made without a technology forecast, which is, however, very difficult. As a first approximation, we forecast the future technology more or less in a qualitative manner. With regard to future demands, first, each division makes a forecast and the Administrative Department aggregates them all and

TABLE 21.3

Estimate of Shipments of Chemical Products by Sumitomo in 1975

	Index (1960 = 100)		Annual increase rate (%)	
	1966	1975	1960–6	1966–75
All products	232·1	585	15·0	10·9
Fertilisers	140·6	225	5·8	5·4
Soda chemicals	141·9	261	6·0	7·0
Inorganic chemicals	257·8	717	17·2	12·0
Explosives	139·8	172	5·7	2·3
Tar products	161·6	332	8·3	8·3
Intermediates, synthetic dyes	163·0	363	8·5	9·3
Organic chemicals	297·5	845	19·7	12·2
Synthetic resins (non-petro-chemical)	296·8	1,024	19·6	14·4
Petro-chemicals	1,014·8	4,384	47·0	17·6
Photo-sensitive materials	191·2	494	11·5	11·1
Oil and fat products	134·2	176	5·0	3·1
Paints, printing ink	209·0	476	13·2	9·6
Animal oils and fats, vegetable oils and fats	141·4	206	6·0	4·3
Pharmaceuticals	220·7	505	14·1	9·6
	(1,000 t)	(1,000 t)		
Aluminium ingot	358·2	1,163	18·5	14·0

The demands for major products will be as follows (10,000 tons):

Ammonia	470–90
Ethylene	440–70
High-density polyethylene	120–40
Vinyl chloride	170–90
Synthetic dyes	6–7
Aluminium metals	110–20

then checks the results against those obtained from macro-economic statistical models, i.e. correlation equations covering indexes of national product, consumption, house construction, capital investment, and other related indexes.

I cannot describe in detail all the statistical methods, but I will show the results of our forecast with regard to the shipment value of chemical products, classified by major category, obtained in our latest long-range planning. These are a part of the basis for our demand forecast. The end-year is 1975. The growth rate during the period 1966–75 was estimated to be lower than that of the previous five-year period. The total shipment in 1975 will be ¥5,200 thousand million (about $18 thousand million) in Japan, which is about 2·3 times as much as that of 1966.

(c) *The computerised corporate model.* For the purpose of preparing a long-range plan, we have designed a computerised corporate simulation model which is already in use. This model handles the interrelations among sales, costs, profit, assets, debts, labour, etc. of the company for from five to ten years ahead. The basic idea of this model is that we first estimate the total domestic demand for products, their prices, raw material costs, wages, and other parameters related to our business and then determine the policy variables (such as capital investment, additional employment, and the like) and use those data in the computerised model. The model simulates the business operations under such assumptions and gives us the results.

We review the computer outputs, particularly sales, profit, financial soundness and some other major management objectives. If all the items satisfy the wishes of the management, the assumption will be accepted as a plan. But if not, we first identify the items which failed and suggest another set of inputs. Then, we run the simulation model again. In our model, very complicated relations are omitted, but it is very useful when we try to find what is critical for our attaining the growth or stability of the company. By testing this simulation, we are able to know the total amounts of required funds, personnel, and other inputs which will in turn become constraints to the operations and investment plans at the division level.

(d) *Drafting a long-range plan at the division level.* Overall business prospects of the chemical industry and its related industries are reported to each division, and at the same time the corporate objectives and policies are explained to the division. Based on these, each division drafts its own divisional long-range plan. First of all, the division analyses the current position and identifies the problems. Then it establishes its own objectives and strategies compatible with, and supporting, the corporate policies and goals. Objectives may vary from division to division, but in most cases, they are increased sales and profits. The main strategies for these are usually as follows:

(i) diversification of the product line and development of new products;

(ii) consolidation of the sales network;

(iii) counter-measures against competitors;

(iv) promotion of vertical integration.

In order to give effect to the above strategies, various projects are programmed for reinforcement of R. & D., equipment investment, acquisition of other companies, and the like. A feasibility report is prepared in the form of a profit and loss statement on each project. However, in the case of a long-range plan, unlike a short-range plan, such a divisional plan is not a 'working' programme, but a kind of reference for compiling a long-range corporate plan. The purpose of the planning system is to determine the future priorities between operating divisions and examine the consistency between production, sales, profit, finance and other important corporate activities when such operations are carried out with given limited funds, technologies, and R. & D. capabilities, as described in the long-range plan. The contents of the plan serve, of course, to indicate the desirable state of our company in the future, and in the process of compilation the division manager himself is made to face our problems and his responsibilities.

(e) *Relations between the long-range plan and specific projects.* The long-range plans I have referred to are all quantified plans, which are presented to the management in the form of various tables such as P/L statements and B/S. At the same time, there are various projects to be implemented during the five-year period, or some longer period. Some of these projects may be entirely new. They may be handled by new divisions which do not now exist, while the rest will be handled by existing divisions. The quantifiable estimates for such projects are, of course, included in the long-range plan. Long-range profits are calculated on a marginal cost and revenue basis by starting from the current figures. Timing of any new stock issue is determined in the course of examining the long-range cash flow.

(f) *Quantified plan.* Sales plans drafted by respective operating divisions and those of new projects drafted by the Corporate New Projects Department are aggregated by the Administrative Department. Production, investment, labour, finance and other elements are first reviewed by the Administrative Department. Strategic considerations are taken into account in the plan; some arise from the beginning while others appear in the course of compilation of the plan. A profit disposition plan is obtained more or less as a by-product of major statements except for the dividend rate which is determined as one of the policy variables.

The long-range plan, when quantified, consists of the following tables:

(1) annual sales classified by product group;

(2) annual profit and loss classified by division;

(3) annual exports and their ratio to total sales, classified by division;

(4) change in product mix and market share;

(5) the annual capital expenditure schedule;

(6) the annual cash flow;

(7) a balance sheet at the end of the final year.

(g) *Projects.* Each division suggests and proposes several projects, including those requiring capital expenditures, which must be compatible with, and contribute to, the corporate strategies. The proposed projects are first screened by the Administrative Department in terms of the company's investment evaluation standards. Thus, we have a special procedure for selecting projects. Those which have already been selected are, of course, included in the long-range plan. The projects which are included in the long-range plan are, however, not necessarily approved at the time of compilation of the plan, particularly those projects which will appear in the fourth or fifth year of the plan. The figures for those not yet approved are merely estimates for the purpose of the long-range plan. Some projects may be entirely outside the experience of the company and may require a new site, a new organisation, a longer development time, and so on. Parts of these projects may not be quantified, but the quantifiable portion, if any, must, of course, be included in the long-range plan. Incidentally, if such a new project is very huge in scale, a project team or some other separate organisation will be formed to deal with it exclusively. But if not, the Corporate New Projects Department acts as the project promoter.

(h) *Principles of new investment evaluation* (*general*). Capital investment is indispensable to the growth of a chemical company, and its success or failure influences the fate of the company. Thus, the selection of projects is one of the most important decisions to be made by the management. It is certainly a key issue in corporate strategies. The total investments of the company are usually determined on the basis of the overall corporate policy with regard to equity–debt ratios, dividend rates, and other criteria.

During the high growth period, a relatively low equity–debt ratio was permitted, and consequently a larger investment was allowed. As a matter of fact in Japan, which enjoyed a continuous high growth, most companies depended heavily on borrowed money for their finance. Even our company, which is said to maintain a relatively sound financial standing among chemical companies, has an equity – debt ratio as low as 24 per cent.

Since the beginning of 1970, Japan's economic structure has changed, and such a high growth as we experienced in the past is no longer expected. Under a lower growth economy, the company should have a higher equity – debt ratio. Selection of investment must therefore be made to satisfy such a condition. More specifically, if a project can apparently contribute to the improvement of the equity – debt ratio, it will have a higher priority than otherwise; but if not, possibility of approval will be very slim. For this selection, cash inflow of the project and possible need for a new capital issue will be taken into account.

(i) *Principles of project selection.* Our company has several divisions classified by product group. As mentioned earlier, we first determine the priorities on a divisional basis and then, within the division, decide the order of importance of the proposed projects. Criteria include profitability, the strategic nature of the product, competitiveness, social impact, and similar considerations. The most important of all is profitability. If the life cycle of a given product or its capacity is comparatively short, a profit higher than 30 per cent per annum on the investment is required (the investment should be recovered within three to four years). Generally, if the investment carries a profit which enables us to maintain a reasonable dividend rate, it will be accepted. With regard to the strategic investments, however, different standards are applied. In this case, short-range profit is not so important.

Discussion of the Papers by Dr Grove and Mr Horimoto

Professor Krasovski (U.S.S.R.), introducing the two papers, said that they shared a common subject matter but were substantially different both in structure and in approaches. Dr Grove's paper was more concerned with methodology, suggested many generalisations, and put its emphasis on comparison of the roles of quantitative and qualitative factors in planning, on intuitive forecasting, and on the consequences of errors in forecasting; Mr Horimoto reviewed the practice of planning as conducted by a large Japanese corporation in the chemical industry within the context of the Japanese economy today, with particular attention to the operational information, the managerial structure, and the probable developments of the corporation.

Dr Grove dealt with planning as it was typically, in his opinion, in most U.S. companies. That implied that decisions essential to the activities of the corporation were generally taken by its central management and were usually based on intuition and informal analysis, backed by the opinions of consultants, almost without any form of quantitative analysis. Thus, formalised planning began only after the essential framework had been chosen by such intuitive and informal analysis.

Dr Grove defined planning in a corporation as consisting of the establishment of alternative goals, alternative forms of activities, and choice between them of those actually to be followed. Actions were considered as part of the process of planning within a one-year or five-year time-horizon. Thus, actions with their expected outcomes within this time-horizon were considered as composing a short-term plan, while actions the outcomes of which extended beyond that time horizon fell into the category of long-term planning.

Dr Grove considered two possible forms of planning which were usually combined in the planning within a corporation. The first was the determination of final goals and expected results, with the appropriate allocation of resources to achieve them. The second arose when a plan was restricted by the availability of resources and was aimed at the optimal achievement of the set goals with the available resources.

The expected results always represented a forecast, which could be either quantitative or qualitative in character and was a key element in planning. The parameters to be forecasted included the volume of business activities, the basic capital stock and time required to achieve the set goals, and so on. 'From the top' and 'from below' approaches were possible, and both were actually combined in planning; the first was more appropriate to economic analysis, while the second was preferable when considering the needs and requirements of the various branches or divisions of a corporation.

Dr Grove had dealt principally with the 'from the top' approach which involved, first, forecasting the international, national and sector levels of business activities for the planned period; second, the establishment of targets and volumes of output achievable in the expected situation; and third, the planning of the business strategy in accordance with the expected conditions.

Three methods were used in economic forecasting: models of growth, behavioural models, and methods to discover and correct errors in planning and forecasting. Models of growth were used to analyse the impact of endogenous or intra-corporate factors on the general trends of economic growth and the average rates of growth. It was emphasised that these models did not enable one to forecast the actual growth but simply to compare the targets with existing historical trends in order to adjust the targets. Models of growth were also of help in identifying the factors that lay outside the scope of corporation control. When the targets had been chosen, the next step was to obtain forecasts relevant to the strategic decisions to be taken by the management. Behavioural models were necessary for understanding the forces that influenced the forecasted variables, and they produced forecasts that include such factors as government policy, external conditions, the market situation, labour policy, as well as any action which could be taken by the company itself.

Even a good model could produce erroneous results. There were two ways of tackling this problem: either to develop techniques for early discovery of errors or to develop the company's ability to respond quickly to discovered errors. If, upon the receipt of quarterly information, it was discovered that errors had been made in the economic forecast, it was possible, with some approximation, to determine what part of them were to be explained by errors in the general economic forecast, and what part by various other factors.

Professor Krasovski thought that the section of the paper that dealt with the problem of the allocation of resources and its dependence on the source and magnitude of errors was of extreme interest for the making of a realistic forecast. If the errors were insignificant, the company could maximise its profits by maintaining fixed prices and minimising the long-term average costs of production; this was not true if the errors were more significant. Moreover, the planned horizon and the detailed sub-plans could be somewhat extended if the forecast was subsequently expected to be subject to minor errors.

Those who initiated the activities of the firm often made decisions without formal analysis, first because they were capable of doing so, second because the company was thus able to respond quickly to a changing situation, and third because the nature of industry was such that very precise forecasts were unattainable. One section of the paper dealt with the various sorts of errors encountered in forecasting and planning. The questions he wished to put to Dr Grove were these. How did Dr Grove think that the investment policy of a corporation should be shaped to take advantage of his suggested system of planning? What was the body of information used in forecasting, particularly with regard to the progress of technology in engineering? He would also appreciate a little more information on the methods used in corporation planning and forecasting, which Dr Grove had only outlined in rather general terms.

By contrast to the first paper, Mr Horimoto provided a great deal of practical and analytical information about company planning and specific cases which had arisen in the Japanese chemical industry. The paper began with a brief review of government economic forecasts which were too macroscopic and were used by private companies only as general rather than specific guidelines. The characteristics of the particular company in relation to the rest of the Japanese chemical industry were brought out and also the managerial structure of the company. It was to be noticed that, because of the large size of the enterprises, their rapid technological advance and the great diversity of their products, forecasting had become more difficult. More attention had now to be paid to prices and sales volumes and to the quality of products. At the same time, efforts were being made to stimulate greater demand for the products of the chemical industry.

Mr Horimoto distinguished three types of corporate plans: long-term plans covering a period of up to five years; medium-term plans, up to three years; and short-term plans, within a half-year period. The last were concerned chiefly with costs and budget control, while the medium-term plans related to investment policy. Two concepts or approaches could be adopted in framing a long-term plan: it could either be a projection of a possible optimum state of the corporation or industry or it could be a probabilistic picture of expected outcomes. Examples of goals are given, with illustrations of how these goals had changed in different periods in relation to changes in the general economic situation.

A corporation model was considered which made possible the estimation of capital stock, manpower and other resources needed to achieve the task of increasing output by 2·3 times by 1975 as compared with 1966. Different forms of plan were given, together with a special examination of certain large-scale projects with emphasis on the appropriate long-term investment decisions. The questions that Professor Krasovski wished to put to Mr Horimoto were these. Could he give them some more information about corporate investment prognosis, with reference to geographical redeployment of its business activity and the structural and technological changes expected during the 1970s? What was the role of the corporation's own research facilities in corporate forecasting? How did they relate to the forecasts of government and foreign research centres?

Professor Marczewski (France) wanted to ask, in respect of both these papers, what was the link between the macro-economic and the micro-economic variables in the company planning? By macro-economic variables he had in mind those determined at the official level, either by a president or by a government, or by governmental organisations. Were there any macro-variables determined by the companies themselves, and if so what was the relation between them and those determined by the government? He wanted to ask, secondly, how far a multi-national corporation would make use of the macro-economic variables of all the different countries in which it operated? Finally, which macro-economic variables did they consider the most relevant – gross national product, gross industrial output, national income, and so on? And which micro-economic variables of the corporation – sales volume, gross profit, and so on – were similarly important?

Dr Fels (F.R.G.) asked how a large corporation could plan without knowing what other competing corporations were planning? In his opinion such autonomous planning became possible only if the corporation held a strong monopolistic market position. But if there was competition in the market, the behaviour of competing companies was inevitably an important parameter of forecasting and planning. And, for these reasons, what could be said about the secrecy of forecasts made by competing companies?

Professor Oelssner (G.D.R.) said that if he had understood Mr Horimoto's paper correctly, a corporate plan was compiled as a means to competition. That meant that plans of different companies were not integrated into a single plan but rather were in opposition to each other. Mr Horimoto had drawn attention to the necessity for compiling a single national economic plan. But he had indicated that this would not be a directive plan; it would not restrict private companies in their business activities, and it was not intended to be used in corporate planning. If this was indeed so, then what was the purpose of making a government plan? What influence did it have upon either the national economy as a whole or upon the actions of specific corporations? Secondly, what means did the Japanese government possess to influence foreign trade and the overseas operations of private business, apart, of course, from financial and credit policy? Finally, how far was the price of land purchased by a private enterprise subsequently included in prices of the products manufactured by the company?

Professor Topala (Roumania) was anxious to know what was the role, in each of these cases, of the technological forecast in the general framework of the long-term economic forecast? He had in mind both the scope of any technological improvements that might be made by the firm itself and those which were expected in the world outside.

Professor Augustinovics (Hungary) wanted to know more about the sources of information used in the input–output model mentioned in Dr Grove's paper. Was this model for seventy-six branches run entirely by the corporation's experts, or was some external data bank or some project like that of Maryland University used? And in that model, did they use constant input coefficients over time, or were there changing input coefficients? If the latter were true, then how were forecasts for seventy-six branches based on changing coefficients? He would also appreciate more general information on the kinds of data that were used in forecasting macro-economic variables.

Professor Khachaturov (U.S.S.R.) said that in the socialist countries they knew relatively little about exactly how planning and forecasting was being done in large western corporations, and for this reason the two papers were of very great interest to them. In his view, labour requirements were currently changing very rapidly in response to changes in science and technology. How was this kind of change reflected in corporate plans? How did the corporations plan to attract more highly trained manpower to meet ghe opportunities they faced? What were the sources of supply of manpower to the corporations?

Professor Bruno (Israel) reminded the conference that if one looked at the size of the two companies discussed in the papers, the volume of their business activity was about equal to the G.N.P. of a moderate-sized economy. The Sumitomo Company had a target equivalent to the G.N.P. of Israel, and the I.B.M. target was probably twenty times that size already. His questions were: What mechanisms did they use within such large corporations for the allocation of resources between different departments? What was the degree of decentralisation? For such a mechanism had potentially a strong tendency towards great centralisation.

Professor Bénard (France) was puzzled as to how, since the computer industry was a very rapidly developing one, their forecast of technological progress was to be integrated into a general economic forecast? How did one tackle all the problems of uncertainty involved in the costs of returns, new products, new technologies and so on?

Professor Porwit (Poland) was not clear in what sense the 'from top to below' and 'from below' approaches to planning differed in practice, and what elements in each were later selected to form a compromise. He had understood from an earlier discussion that there was a preference for not making a decision too early, so as to secure fuller knowledge. On the other hand, there were obviously decisions concerning the early stages of some new development that had to be taken early. Could Dr Grove say a word on these problems?

Professor Machlup (U.S.A.) wondered whether the conference was being overly impressed with the novelty of long-term planning by firms. He believed that investment decisions had always been planned, in the last century just as much as now. The only difference was that one was now dealing with a more sophisticated use of data, and that one was faced with larger corporations. He doubted whether anything but the technology of data processing had changed since the late nineteenth century. He suggested that the major difference lay in the terminologies that they were now using and in the sophisticated data processing that was now possible.

Dr Grove (U.S.A.), replying to the discussion and the various questions addressed to him, said that he did not himself make any clear distinction between long-range and short-term planning because he thought it was dangerous to emphasise the distinction, for many of the problems were very similar. In the I.B.M. Corporation the aim of long-term planning was to determine the goals. They used the phrase 'challenging but attainable'. That was the reasonable goal or target to be set for the firm, with reasonable chances of it being achieved.

His next point had also been made by Professor Augustinovics. This was that long-range planning was by nature an iterative procedure between goals and growth paths. They also stressed this very much. They paid similar attention to planning being done both in constant and in current prices. Much of their forecasting was done in terms of business volumes, and then they tried to determine what prices could be attached to these volumes. At the same time, emphasis was put on alternatives, and they had a similar problem of finding an adequate number of alternatives.

One of the purposes for setting goals and one of the purposes of their growth model was to determine how far it would be possible for the corporation to reach the point it wanted to reach in future years on the basis of the existing products, and the existing programmes for them. The difference was known as a wedge, or a gap between what was presently planned to be produced, and the new products and programmes to be developed if the corporation was to achieve the growth targets it had decided were reasonable. These were the technical instructions to the planners, who either could or could not fill the gap between what was desirable and what was reasonably achievable.

A long-term plan had three components: programmes that could be identified sufficiently from the point of their revenue; new products which could be calculated in terms of economics; new products which could be envisaged technologically but the economic aspects of which could not be estimated. After the goals had been set, the next stage was the interaction between the operational divisions and the management of the company and its corporate staff, engaged in the process that was called 'constructive abrasion', which meant that it was the duty of the corporate staff to test the plans for reasonableness so as to ensure that they were both sufficiently realistic and sufficiently challenging. This was a very serious business because of the need for commitment of divisions to achieving the goals decided. Within that general programme for the division, the allocation of resources was determined by the division manager, who was given a specific task and specific financial resources but was not told what means to use to fulfil the task.

Each division had its own planning staff, which did not make much use of models – although there were some models in use. They acted primarily through business decisions and allocation of resources. At the corporate level they did not get into the detail of division management operations, but were interested in the programme as a whole and its expected results.

This was what he meant by 'bottom up' and 'top down' planning. When the divisions prepared their plans they did it on the basis of a tremendous amount of detail, and it was an aggregated process. The 'top downward' process was to check these aggregates for reasonableness, and to check the detail as much as possible. But there was not much checking of the details for two reasons. One was that no one but the division manager himself had access to all the detail. The second was that it was really the division responsibility.

The plan was constructed after the preliminary process of goal-setting and after there had been agreement of what would represent a reasonable general goal. When there was agreement about goals they started to put flesh on bones, and if in doing this they found that the goal appeared to be unreasonable or not sufficiently challenging, then there was further negotiation until the target was finally set. From this point on there was detailed planning. When the detailed plan was ready, it came to the corporate staff to be tested.

There was no direct connection between the corporate plan and government research. The research community in the United States was kept as fully informed about what was going on as was possible, both in the government and in industry, but there was no formal linkage.

One example of a strategic decision related to a forecast was when a given generation of computers seemed likely to run out of demand and a new generation was needed. This was a constant problem. The technical people would like to delay introduction of new generations because of pressure on production facilities and other considerations. The marketing people would want a new and better machine right now. They had tried to forecast the likely demand for the existing and new machines. This involved consideration of what competitors were going to do, and in many cases they projected the total market first. The demand in general depended not on the price of a particular machine, but on the price of the type of material it produced and on its quality. It also depended on the prices of I.B.M. compared with competitors' prices and on the productivity of the various machines.

As to the relationship between the macro-economic and micro-economic parameters of the firm and those of the government, the I.B.M. Corporation made its own estimates of national income and G.N.P. of the United States. This was done for a variety of reasons. First, the official forecasts represented policy goals. They were not really forecasts exclusively but a combination of forecasts and political goals. Another reason was that the Corporation needed a forecast at the time that they made their plans, and the timing of official and other forecasts did not always coincide with the timing they needed. Yet another reason was that they needed conditional forecasts, showing to what extent changes in the economic policy might affect their production and the economic parameters that they used.

There was essentially one most important micro-economic variable for the firm, that was the performance characteristics of new products, relative to the present ways of doing things, and relative to the present products produced by themselves and their competitors. It was the price–performance ratio, or the cost of one minute of computer time relative to the number of operations that could be done in a minute.

Technological changes were taken into account in this way: they had research laboratories that were working on pure research, not on something that could be used in any specific application; when they got a product or a process to the point where it could be developed for a market use, it then moved to the research and development division; the division tried to find products which could employ these new processes. Before they could introduce a product into their plan, they had to have at least some target performance measures which they felt the product would meet. They then tried to estimate the possible effect of the new product or new process on data processing in terms of what the saving would mean to the customer. There was a problem, of course, of taking account of technological progress which no one could see at the moment, but that did not go into their plans. He wanted to emphasise that the plan was action-oriented, and one could not plan one's actions on the basis of something that one could not foresee.

Index

Entries in **bold** type under the names of participants in the conference indicate their papers or discussions of them. Entries in *italic* indicate contributions by participants in the discussions.